PAUL D. SANSONE, O.F.M.

AN EXODUS SCROLL FROM QUMRAN

HARVARD SEMITIC STUDIES

HARVARD SEMITIC MUSEUM

Frank Moore Cross, Editor

AN EXODUS SCROLL
FROM QUMRAN
4QpaleoExod[m]
and the Samaritan Tradition

Judith E. Sanderson

Scholars Press
Atlanta, Georgia

AN EXODUS SCROLL FROM QUMRAN
4QpaleoExod^m
and the Samaritan Tradition

Library of Congress Cataloging in Publication Data

Sanderson, Judith E.
  An Exodus scroll from Qumran.

  (Harvard Semitic studies ; 30)
  Bibliography: p.
  1. Bible. O.T. Exodus. Hebrew. Dead Sea
scrolls. 4QpaleoExodM. 2. Bible. O.T. Exodus—
Criticism, Textual. 3. Bible. O.T. Exodus—
Manuscripts, Hebrew. I. Title. II. Series:
Harvard Semitic studies ; no. 30.
BS1245.2.S25 1986   222'.12044   86-15421
ISBN 1-55540-036-1 (alk. paper)

Printed in the United States of America
on acid-free paper

To my parents

with love and gratitude

CONTENTS

PREFACE

This work is a virtually unrevised form of my dissertation, which was completed in May 1985. My decision not to make any substantive revisions was based on the urgency of the task of bringing the Dead Sea Scrolls to publication. It has seemed best to issue this text-critical analysis of 4QpaleoExod^m in its present form so that the findings can be more quickly made available to a broader audience. The time that would be required to refine the analysis of one scroll will be more wisely spent in working on the edition of several further scrolls.

From 1982 to 1985 I conducted the research and wrote the dissertation at the University of Notre Dame with the guidance of Eugene Ulrich. During the same period he and I were collaborating on the edition of 4QpaleoExod^m, to be published by Oxford Press in the series *Discoveries in the Judaean Desert (DJD)*. Before his death in 1980 Professor Patrick W. Skehan had worked several years preparing a draft of this edition, which served as the basis for our work (see below, p. 14). The current volume reflects the status of our work on the edition as of April 1985. Since then we have completed the transcription of the entire scroll from the infrared photographs, but the task of checking our work against the actual leather fragments in Jerusalem still remains. Meanwhile we have also been collaborating on 4QpaleoExod^l, and hope soon to begin work on the other scrolls from Cave 4 in the Palaeo-Hebrew script, so that they can all be published as soon as possible.

When the *DJD* volume appears, the transcriptions in the analysis can be compared with those of the official edition. Presumably the status of a few letters will have changed, and probably the existence of three or four variants will have been affected. Given the present total of 174 variants, the loss or gain of three or four will be a minor matter. It is virtually certain that the major variants, those typological of the $\mathfrak{Q}^{\mathfrak{a}}\mathfrak{m}$ tradition, will not be affected.

Three significant publications have come to my attention too late to be used in this work. In any future study of 4QpaleoExod^m and/or of the Samaritan tradition, it will be important to take these into account. They are:

Freedman, D. N., and Mathews, K. A. *The Paleo-Hebrew Leviticus Scroll (11QpaleoLev)*. With contributions by R. S. Hanson. Winona Lake, IN: Eisenbrauns, 1985.

Tov, Emanuel. "The Nature and Background of Harmonizations in Biblical Manuscripts." *Journal for the Study of the Old Testament* 31 (1985) 3-29.

Weiss, Raphael. "Synonymous Variants in Divergences Between the Samaritan and Massoretic Texts of the Pentateuch." *Studies in the Text and Language of the Bible*. Jerusalem: Magnes Press, 1981. pp. 63-189. [Hebrew]

One point should be noted especially regarding the dating of Exod^m. As stated in Chapter I.B., in 1964 R. S. Hanson suggested 225 – 175 B.C.E. for the copying of the scroll, and in 1982 M. D. McLean suggested 100 – 25 B.C.E. Hanson's article in the Freedman-Mathews volume of 1985 shows that he has changed his earlier opinion and now dates the scroll around 100 B.C.E. (see especially p. 23 of their volume).

I look forward to the day when the text of 4QpaleoExod^m can be compared with the fourteen other scrolls of Exodus found at Qumran as well as with 4QNum^b, which shares some major expansions with the Samaritan tradition. My contribution will be collaboration on the sixteen Palaeo-Hebrew scrolls and the edition of seven of the scrolls of Exodus in the square script. When they are all published in *DJD* they should be compared with this analysis of Exod^m, and some of the judgments here may need revision or at least refinement.

My fascination with the Scrolls dates back at least to 1965, when I waited in a very long queue at the British Museum to see the special exhibition, *The Dead Sea Scrolls of Jordan*, arranged by the Smithsonian Institution in cooperation with the Government of the Hashemite Kingdom of Jordan and the Palestine Archaeological Museum. I even mailed a copy of the 36-page exhibition guide to my parents, with the result that in 1982, when I began my dissertation, we both were able independently to discover that I had already seen "my scroll" in 1965.

I well remember my first trip to Qumran in 1977, when my teacher, James M. Monson, ended our tour with this admonition: "If you forget every archaeological detail that you are seeing today, do remember the one most significant contribution of the discovery of this community and its library: the evidence it provides of the diversity within 'Judaism' at the turn of the era." A few months later, however, when I watched the Samaritan celebration of Passover I could not yet appreciate that the diversity I had glimpsed at Qumran could bear any relationship to my experience on Mount Gerizim. That understanding would await my work on Exod^m.

It is an honor and a pleasure to express my thanks to those who have contributed in many ways to the publication of this volume.

Professor Eugene Ulrich taught and guided me at each step of the way, from the mysteries of palaeography through the art of evaluating readings to the imaginative reconstruction of the history of the text. It has been a privilege to work with someone so consistently patient, generous, and encouraging.

Professor Kevin G. O'Connell, S.J., of John Carroll University very kindly agreed to serve as reader for the dissertation. I am grateful for his helpful suggestions at the planning stages and for his meticulous reading and expert attention especially to text-critical and stylistic matters.

It is a pleasure to express my gratitude to Professors Joseph Blenkinsopp and Roger Brooks of the University of Notre Dame for their careful reading of various drafts and their questions and suggestions designed to help me speak to those in the broader field of biblical scholarship.

Professor John Wm Wevers of the University of Toronto very kindly provided me with a pre-published form of his critical text of the Göttingen Septuagint of Exodus. I am grateful for his careful reading of my work and his valuable suggestions.

I wish to thank the University of Notre Dame and the American Association of University Women Educational Foundation for dissertation fellowships granted me for the years 1983-84 and 1984-85 respectively.

I am grateful to Professor Frank Moore Cross for his support of the project as editor of the series and to Princeton Theological Seminary for its contribution to the publication.

This volume is dedicated to my parents, whose generous gifts over the years have run the gamut from a love of the Bible to a word processor that can speak three languages.

I am especially grateful to my housemate, Gina, who has supported and encouraged me at each stage of the work.

Princeton Theological Seminary
31 July 1986

SIGLA AND ABBREVIATIONS

Following are the sigla and abbreviations used in the text and footnotes of the volume. Complete bibliographical information is given in the bibliography.

TEXTS AND VERSIONS

A   Codex Alexandrinus

A⁺ (etc.) Alexandrinus (etc.) plus other witnesses

B   Codex Vaticanus

BHS   *Biblia Hebraica Stuttgartensia*

Boh   Bohairic text

G   Old Greek text, to the extent that it can be reconstructed. Authorities: Wevers, Brooke-McLean, Rahlfs

vG   von Gall's edition of the Samaritan Pentateuch

L   Old Latin text

𝕸   Massoretic Text. Authority: *Biblia Hebraica Stuttgartensia*

𝕸ᵃᵖ   A reading collated in the apparatus of *BHS*

Qᵃ   4QpaleoExodᵐ. Authority: *Discoveries in the Judaean Desert,* to be published

R   Rahlfs' edition of **G**

Rᵉᵈ   The reading in the critical text of **G** established by Rahlfs

S   Peshitta

Syh   Syro-hexapla

𝔐   Samaritan Pentateuch. Authority: von Gall's edition

𝔐ᵉᵈ   The reading in the critical text of the Samaritan Pentateuch
             established by von Gall

𝔐ᵃᵖ   A reading collated in the apparatus of von Gall's edition of the
             Samaritan Pentateuch

T   Targum

V   Vulgate text

REFERENCE WORKS

BDB   Brown-Driver-Briggs

Bl-D   Blass-DeBrunner

HR   Hatch-Redpath

M   Mandelkern

SYMBOLS

𝟙   Palaeo-Hebrew *waw*. The scribe of **Qᵃ** placed a large Palaeo-
             Hebrew *waw* alone in an interval in the line to signal a
             paragraph division; the rest of the word followed on the
             next line.

ד,ג,ב,א   Designate the number of the variant within one verse; e.g., **7:15ב**
             is the second variant in that verse.

ᵃ or ᵇ   Follows the verse number to designate a major expansion where
             Qᵃ = 𝔐, following vG's usage; e.g. **9:5ᵇ** falls between 9:5
             and 9:6 of 𝔐.

☐**Qᵃ**   The passage is no longer extant in **Qᵃ**.

Symbols Used to Classify Variants:

+   Expansion, defined as a minor or moderate addition to the original.

++   Major Expansion, defined as a more extensive and deliberate expansion to the original text. All but one occur only in the textual tradition to which $\mathbf{Q^a}$ and Ⱶ belong.

−   Omission, defined as an unintentional omission from the original text.

2V   Secondary Variant, defined as a qualitatively different reading which is considered to be secondary.

~   Transposition.

X   Error, defined as a reading which is not only secondary but actually grammatically or contextually wrong.

≅   Synonymous Variant, defined as two or more readings, either or all of which could have been original, which are parallel, and which have similar claim on originality. They are two or more good ways of expressing the same thing.

Symbols Used in Text-Affiliation Formulae:

G   Full agreement

(G)   Probably favors, but not certain

(G?)   Possibly favors

; **G?**   The Hebrew *Vorlage* of this Greek reading cannot be determined.

/G/   Material agreement which, however, does not indicate affiliation; i.e., the Greek does on the surface appear to agree with one Hebrew text, but there is no necessary dependence.

_____   Underlined text(s) is considered to preserve the preferable reading

ABBREVIATIONS OF JOURNALS AND SERIES

BA	*Biblical Archaeologist*
BASOR	*Bulletin of the American Schools of Oriental Research*
BIOSCS	*Bulletin of the International Organization for Septuagint and Cognate Studies*
CBQ	*Catholic Biblical Quarterly*
DJD	*Discoveries in the Judaean Wilderness*
HSM	Harvard Semitic Monographs
HTR	*Harvard Theological Review*
HUCA	*Hebrew Union College Annual*
IDB	*Interpreter's Dictionary of the Bible*
IDBS	*Interpreter's Dictionary of the Bible. Supplementary Volume*
IEJ	*Israel Exploration Journal*
JAOS	*Journal of the American Oriental Society*
JBL	*Journal of Biblical Literature*
JJS	*Journal of Jewish Studies*
JNES	*Journal of Near Eastern Studies*
JSJ	*Journal for the Study of Judaism in the Persian, Hellenistic and Roman Period*
JSOT	*Journal for the Study of the Old Testament*
JSS	*Journal of Semitic Studies*
JTS	*Journal of Theological Studies*
NT	*Novum Testamentum*
NTS	*New Testament Studies*
RB	*Revue biblique*
RevQ	*Revue de Qumran*
SNTSMS	Society for New Testament Studies Monograph Series

VT	*Vetus Testamentum*
VTSup	Vetus Testamentum, Supplements
ZAW	*Zeitschrift für die alttestamentliche Wissenchaft*

CHAPTER I

STATE OF THE QUESTION

INTRODUCTION

Before 1952 little attention was paid to the text of the book of Exodus. Since there seemed to be few problems with the Massoretic Text in that book, there was little incentive to devote a great deal of effort to the text or the history of the text. There had been general studies of the Samaritan Pentateuch[1] as well as general studies of the Septuagint,[2] but little time had been expended specifically on Exodus, since it offered no special challenges and therefore seems to have sparked little interest.

In 1952 4QpaleoExod^m was found, as well as at least fourteen other scrolls of Exodus.[3] Thus far none of these fifteen has been published, and only scattered references and reports touching difficult passages have appeared.[4] No account of the text of Exodus in general as it is represented in the Dead Sea Scrolls has appeared.

This study seeks to remedy that lack in a preliminary way, by analyzing one scroll, the most extensive, the most unusual, and the most significant of the fifteen: 4QpaleoExod^m. The focus will not be on passages

_____

[1]The standard work on the Samaritan Pentateuch is that of Guilielmus Gesenius, *De Pentateuchi Samaritani origine, indole et auctoritate: commentatio philologico-critica* (Halle, 1815). See also Shemaryahu Talmon, "The Samaritan Pentateuch," *JJS,* 2 (1951), 146-150, for an article published just prior to the discovery of 4QpaleoExod^m.

[2]E.g., Henry Barclay Swete, *An Introduction to the Old Testament in Greek,* 2d ed. (Cambridge: Cambridge University Press, 1902).

[3]Geza Vermes reports a total of fifteen scrolls of Exodus in *The Dead Sea Scrolls: Qumran in Perspective,* 2d ed., (Philadelphia: Fortress Press, 1981), p. 201 (hereafter cited as: Vermes, *Perspective).* Judging from the fact that the sigla range from 4QExod^a to 4QpaleoExod^m, thirteen were found in Cave 4.

[4]For instance, Frank Moore Cross devoted a two-page footnote to Exod 1:1-5 in 4QExod^a in *The Ancient Library of Qumran and Modern Biblical Studies,* rev. ed. (Garden City, NY: Doubleday, 1961), pp. 184-185 n. 31. Hereafter cited as: Cross, *Library.*

which are problematic in the Massoretic Text or which are difficult to understand, but rather on the general questions: What can we learn about the text of the entire book of Exodus? How does this new discovery, a scroll that has lain hidden for two thousand years, relate to the three traditions[5] of Exodus that have been known to us heretofore, the Massoretic Text, the Samaritan Pentateuch, and the Septuagint? When there are discrepancies among them, can one reading be determined to be preferable? How often does 4QpaleoExod^m agree with each of those three traditions? How often do they agree among each other? How often does the scroll preserve a reading that none of the three traditions has passed down to us? How different is a scroll that has lain untouched and unread for two millennia from texts that have been copied and recopied by a host of scribes and used by a community down through the ages?

Briefly, the method will be as follows. In every place where 4QpaleoExod^m ($\mathbf{Q^m}$) is extant, it will be compared with each of the other three witnesses: the Massoretic Text ($\mathfrak{M}$), the Samaritan Pentateuch ($\mathfrak{m}$), and the Septuagint ($\mathbf{G}$). Whenever there is disagreement among any of the four, that reading will be considered a "variant." All of the variants are listed in chapter-verse order in Appendix 2 for convenient reference.

The first question will be: Can we decide that one of these readings is the preferable text? If so, this variant will appear in Chapter II along with the other readings where we can make a choice with some degree of probability. If not, this reading will be classified as a synonymous variant, i.e., one where it is impossible to decide among the two or three different readings, and it will appear in Chapter III, along with the other synonymous variants.

Having determined preferable readings where possible, the next question will be: How do these four witnesses to the text of Exodus relate to each other? Do any of them give evidence of being related, of having shared a common history at some period? Chapter IV will present the evidence for textual affiliation.

After answering the question of relationship among the four witnesses, the next task will be to describe each of those four witnesses on its own in Chapter V. First of all, what can we now say about $\mathbf{Q^m}$? Second, what new light has the discovery of $\mathbf{Q^m}$ shed on the nature of each of the

---

[5]See below, Chapter I.C., for a discussion of this terminology and the problems involved.

three textual traditions, 𝔐, 𝔐, and 𝔊? And third, what new insight have we gained into the history of the text of Exodus?

In Chapter VI we will leave the matter of the four witnesses and pose new questions to the variants. What kinds of variant readings have we found? How did they arise? What can these variants tell us about the methods and the attitudes of scribes during the late Second Temple period?

Chapter VII will bring together the conclusions from the investigation regarding broader issues ranging from the history of the text of Exodus to the origins of Samaritanism.

But before we can approach the text of Exodus, we must set the stage in Chapter I by reviewing developments since the discoveries starting in 1947 of the Dead Sea Scrolls. Much has been written in the last thirty-five years that must be briefly considered here, especially concerning textual criticism and the history of the Second Temple period.

A. MODERN STUDY OF THE TEXT OF EXODUS

As stated above, little work has been published so far regarding the text of the book of Exodus. Whereas the text of Daniel, for example, was thoroughly treated by Montgomery in the International Critical Commentary,[6] the Exodus volume in that series was never completed, and the volumes on the other books of the Pentateuch pay scant attention to textual history and textual criticism.

Neither of the two major commentaries on Exodus which are in current use deal with text-critical matters systematically. Noth's commentary[7] virtually ignores textual questions. Childs's commentary[8] does have a section entitled "Textual and Philological Notes" for each pericope, but it generally confines itself to discussing only those passages where 𝔐 is problematic and where the meaning is affected, and to

---

[6]James A. Montgomery, *A Critical and Exegetical Commentary on the Book of Daniel,* The International Critical Commentary (Edinburgh: T. & T. Clark, 1927).

[7]Martin Noth, *Exodus: A Commentary,* The Old Testament Library (Philadelphia: Westminster Press, 1962).

[8]Brevard S. Childs, *The Book of Exodus: A Critical, Theological Commentary,* The Old Testament Library (Philadelphia: Westminster Press, 1974). Hereafter cited as: Childs, *Exodus.*

approving or rejecting emendations according to the sense. There is no comprehensive treatment of the text nor is there any attention to the history of the text.[9] This may well be an adequate method for a commentary for general use, particularly given the present state of research on the text of Exodus. On the other hand, it is to be hoped that analyses such as the present study, which attempts to shed light on the question of what was happening with the text of Exodus during the later Second Temple period,[10] will eventually affect our understanding of the text and contribute to the writing of commentaries in the future.

Gooding published a monograph on the one major textual problem that has been generally recognized in Exodus: the two-fold account of the tabernacle.[11] Though his work appeared in 1959, he took no notice of the

---

[9]The same is true, at least so far, for the first three fascicles which have appeared of Werner H. Schmidt, *Exodus*, Biblischer Kommentar -- Altes Testament, ed. Siegfried Herrmann and Hans Walter Wolff, II:1-3 (Neukurchen-Vluyn, Neukirchener Verlag, 1974-1983).

[10]As will become evident below, the exact limits of the period under discussion cannot be known on the basis of our present evidence. Dates suggested for the copying of Q^m, for instance, vary from 225 to 25 B.C.E. (see section B). The date most often proposed for the presumed authoritative redaction of the Samaritan Pentateuch is ca. 100 B.C.E. (see section D). On the basis of the relative uniformity of the biblical scrolls found from the time of the Second Revolt at Masada and Wadi Murabba'at, "the propagation of one, universally recognised text form" for Jews, i.e., the "Proto-Massoretic" text, is dated to the years between the two revolts, 70-130 C.E. (see, e.g., Shemaryahu Talmon, "The Old Testament Text," *The Cambridge History of the Bible*, 1, *From the Beginnings to Jerome*, ed. P. R. Ackroyd and C. F. Evans [Cambridge: Cambridge University Press, 1970], pp. 159-199; the quotation is from p. 11; cf. also p. 25 [hereafter cited as: Talmon, "Text"]). The translation of the Pentateuch into Greek is generally dated in the third century B.C.E. (this view has been held by people in the past such as Thackeray [cf. Sidney Jellicoe, *The Septuagint and Modern Study* (Oxford: Clarendon Press, 1968), p. 67], and it remains generally held today [see, e.g., Ernst Würthwein, *The Text of the Old Testament: An Introduction to the Biblia Hebraica*, tr. E. F. Rhodes (Grand Rapids: Eerdmans, 1979), p. 51]. Even when there are extant documents to be dated, as in the case of Q^m and Proto-Massoretic texts from Qumran and Masada, the question remains: When did the distinctive traits of this text arise?

[11]D. W. Gooding, *The Account of the Tabernacle: Translation and Textual Problems of the Greek Exodus*, Texts and Studies, N.S. VI, ed. C. H. Dodd (Cambridge: Cambridge University, 1959).

Qumran finds, probably because his purpose was to focus on the Septuagint and its special problems. For both reasons his work is of limited use for this study. Nelson[12] has recently been working on both the Hebrew and the Greek versions of the tabernacle account. Future studies of that problem will have to take the theories of both Gooding and Nelson into account. Both are rather too specific in their orientation to have been of much value in the present investigation, because relatively few of the variants involved in the extant parts of Q^n occur in either tabernacle account.

Another very specific aspect of Septuagintal studies, the Theodotionic revision of the Greek translation, has been investigated by O'Connell.[13] The contribution of his work is in providing a general orientation to questions of textual criticism of Exodus and in providing a high standard in methodology. But his results do not directly bear on the specific subject of this dissertation, since the Greek text used for comparison here is that of the Old Greek, or G, rather than Theodotion.

The work of Wevers, on the other hand, relates immediately to this analysis. He is producing the edition of Exodus for the Göttingen edition of the Septuagint, i.e., that text which represents the closest we can come to the Old Greek, or the original translation from Hebrew. Professor Wevers has very kindly made his edition available to me in pre-published form, so that the variants discussed in this dissertation could be determined on the basis of his work.[14]

B. Q^n: 4QpaleoExod^m

About one hundred biblical scrolls were found in Cave 4 at Qumran in 1952. Half of these were entrusted for publication to Patrick W. Skehan of the Catholic University of America and half to Frank Moore Cross of Harvard University. Several of the scrolls were written in the Palaeo-Hebrew

---

[12]I wish to thank Russell Nelson for private communication concerning his dissertation at Harvard University on the Greek text of the tabernacle account.

[13]Kevin G. O'Connell, *The Theodotionic Revision of the Book of Exodus,* HSM 3 (Cambridge, MA: Harvard University Press, 1972).

[14]His edition will appear as the *Exodus* volume in the series Septuaginta: Vetus Testamentum Graecum Auctoritate Academiae Scientiarum Gottingensis (Göttingen: Vandenhoeck & Ruprecht).

script, i.e., in characters resembling the old Canaanite script which the Israelites had used during the monarchy.[15] These were among the fifty-three entrusted to Skehan.

A word is in order about the use of this "Palaeo-Hebrew" script. The vast majority of all the scrolls in the Qumran caves were written in the Aramaic or square script which had come into popular use also for Hebrew during the Second Temple period. The discovery that some scrolls, however,

---

[15]Compare, e.g., the Lachish ostraca and the jar handles from Gibeon, of the sixth century; Solomon Birnbaum, *Hebrew Scripts*, II (London: Palaeographia, 1954-1957), numbers 23-26; James B. Pritchard, *Hebrew Inscriptions from Gibeon* (Philadelphia: University of Pennsylvania, 1959); Frank Moore Cross, "Epigraphical Notes on Hebrew Documents of the Eighth--Sixth Centuries B.C.: III, The Inscribed Jar Handles from Gibeon," *BASOR* 168 (1962), 18-23.

were written in a script resembling the ancient script[16] at first suggested
to scholars that this "Palaeo-Hebrew" script represents a revival of a style

---

[16]Thirteen biblical scrolls, one non-biblical, and two still
unidentified scrolls have been isolated in the Palaeo-Hebrew script. In
1965 Skehan gave a catalog which was complete at that time and listed 10
in Palaeo-Hebrew script, 9 from the Torah and 1 of Job (Patrick W. Skehan,
"The Biblical Scrolls from Qumran and the Text of the Old Testament," *BA*
28 [1965], 88; hereafter cited as: Skehan, "Text").

In 1982 McLean listed and analyzed the script of the following:
1QpaleoLev, Num?, and Lev[b]; 2QpaleoLev; 4QpaleoGen, Exod[m,n], Deut[B], Job[x],
Sn44[a,b], 4Q186; 6QpaleoGen, Lev; and 11QpaleoLev (Mark David McLean,
"The Use and Development of Palaeo-Hebrew in the Hellenistic and Roman
Periods," Unpublished doctoral dissertation, Department of Near Eastern
Languages and Civilizations, Harvard University, 1982, pp. 41-47 [hereafter
cited as: McLean, "Palaeo-Hebrew"]). The four from Caves 2, 6, and 11 are
listed with the same sigla in Joseph A. Fitzmyer, *The Dead Sea Scrolls:
Major Publications and Tools for Study,* Society of Biblical Literature,
Sources for Biblical Study 8, ed. Wayne A. Meeks (Missoula, MT: Scholars
Press, 1977), pp. 18, 20, 35.

The sigla now used for the biblical scrolls from Cave 4 are:
4QpaleoGen[l], Exod[l,m], Deut[r,s], and Job[c]. It should be noted that McLean's
"Exod[m]" has retained its designation since McLean wrote; it is his "Exod[n]"
that has become "Exod[l]."

4QSn44[a,b] are so far unidentified. McLean describes 44[a] as "a variant
text of Joshua 21 or a non-biblical text drawing heavily upon the language
of this chapter" and 44[b] as "non-biblical" (*Ibid,* p. 44). It is possible that
further study will change that. In 1982 Ulrich was able to identify
fragments in his allotment that had been classified as "non-biblical Greek"
as biblical (Eugene Ulrich, "The Greek Manuscripts of the Pentateuch from
Qumrân, Including Newly-Identified Fragments of Deuteronomy [4QLXXDeut],"
*De Septuaginta: Studies in Honour of John William Wevers on his Sixty-Fifth
Birthday,* ed. Albert Pietersma and Claude Cox; Mississauga, Ontario:
Benben, 1984, pp. 71-82).

A brief note in Skehan's papers indicates that a third previously
unidentified fragment has been transferred to J. T. Milik, which would seem
to indicate that it was identified as a non-biblical scroll that belonged
more properly with the group of scrolls that Milik is publishing. Hence my
total of 13 biblical, 1 non-biblical, and 2 still unidentified scrolls in the
Palaeo-Hebrew script.

According to Vermes (*Perspective,* p. 201), a total of 175 biblical
scrolls have been found in the eleven caves. 70 are from the Torah: 15 each
of Genesis and Exodus; 9 of Leviticus; 6 of Numbers; and 25 of Deuteronomy.
Thus 13 out of a total of 175 "biblical scrolls" according to our canon, or 12
out of a total of 70 Torah scrolls, are in the Palaeo-Hebrew script.

which had been virtually unused for centuries, a revival motivated by a desire on the part of some Second Temple Israelites to return to their "roots." According to this theory only a few scribes had perpetuated the memory of this script through the centuries, so that when an occasion arose for emphasizing traditional values, for returning to ancient Israelite roots, for expressing a special reverence, the script -- and scribal facility in that script -- lay ready to be put to use.[17]

This theory is supported by the nature of the texts which have been discovered in this script. First, the sixteen scrolls in Palaeo-Hebrew script include twelve of Pentateuchal books[18] and one of Job. Second, in some biblical scrolls written in the square script the tetragrammaton alone, plus sometimes other designations for God, are consistently written in the Palaeo-Hebrew.[19] Third, the coins of the Hasmonaean era and of the First and Second Jewish Revolts (66-74 C.E. and 132-135 C.E.) were minted using Palaeo-Hebrew script. Hence this is considered by many to have been a deliberately archaizing script, used for texts when the writer wished to accentuate the antiquity or the sacredness of his subject or nationalistic sentiments. It is argued that as the scrolls of the Torah were considered to

---

[17]Cf., e.g., Frank Moore Cross: "The Palaeo-Hebrew script of Qumran is properly described as an archaistic survival from the book hand of Israelite times. It shows little development in the interval between the epigraphs of the seventh-fifth centuries B.C. and manuscripts of Maccabaean or Hasmonaean date. Evidently the script was taken up anew in the era of nationalistic revival of the second century B.C., to judge from its use as a monumental script by the Hasmonaeans on their coinage, as well as its resurgence as a Biblical hand. ... Moreover, in the second century B.C., Palaeo-Hebrew forms, dormant for some four centuries, begin afresh to evolve at a fairly steady pace. ... On the other hand, the earliest exemplars of the Palaeo-Hebrew hand at Qumran exhibit a remarkable fidelity of form and stance, when compared with archaic scripts, and were penned with fluid grace and speed. One can best explain these characteristics of the Qumran Palaeo-Hebrew hand by assuming that though relatively static, the old script was preserved alive in some narrow circle, presumably by a coterie of erudite scribes, as a Biblical book hand." ("The Development of the Jewish Scripts," *The Bible and the Ancient Near East: Essays in Honor of William Foxwell Albright,* ed. G. Ernest Wright [Garden City, NY: Doubleday, 1961], p. 189 n. 4; hereafter cited as: Cross, "Scripts.")

[18]Two are of Genesis, two of Exodus (4QpaleoExod[l] and [m]), five of Leviticus, one of Numbers (questionably), and two of Deuteronomy.

[19]McLean ("Palaeo-Hebrew," pp. 41-47) deals with fourteen such scrolls.

be the most central of the Bible, so the book of Job partook of an especially sacred nature because it seemed to come from patriarchal times.[20]

Even on the basis of the above-mentioned evidence, of course, there was another possibility: that the use of this script had not been restricted to a small group of learned biblical scribes, but that it had continued to be used throughout the centuries, either exclusively or alongside the newer script, by other groups as well. And indeed, this is the theory which has been suggested more recently, in the light of further discoveries.[21] McLean has analyzed the script of materials spanning the Persian, Hellenistic, Hasmonaean, and Herodian periods and concluded that:

> ...the limited evidence available today allows us to make some revision of the minimalistic views of the use of Palaeo-Hebrew. While it is clear that the Palaeo-Hebrew script was continually being pushed aside by the overall daily use of the Jewish script, Palaeo-Hebrew was used and had some special meaning for all the major religious parties of our period: the "normative" community under the Hasmonaeans and the rulers of the First and Second Jewish Wars; the Essene community centered in Qumran but with adherents settled throughout the land; and the Samaritan communities with their center in Shechem.[22]

> From Persian times until the end of the Second Jewish War, every time it was politically feasible Palaeo-Hebrew appeared as the "official" or "national" script on the durable coins and stamps which have survived.[23]

Skehan chose to work on the Palaeo-Hebrew scrolls found in Cave 4. Of these, by far the most extensively preserved was one of the two of Exodus, 4QpaleoExod^m. Fragments from forty-four of the original columns had been found, ranging from Exod 6:25 to 37:16. Appendix 1 gives the complete list of the contents of each column. As the appendix indicates, several of the columns, particularly i, xvii, xviii, and xxxviii, are quite full,

---

[20]Skehan, for example, ventured the suggestion: "Because of the association of the person of Job with patriarchal times, and the speculation which placed the composition of the Book of Job in proximity to that of the Pentateuch?" ("Exodus in the Samaritan Recension from Qumran," *JBL* 74 [1955], p. 183 n. 2.)

[21]Due to the nature of Palestinian archaeology, of course, even the evidence which has become available is still quite limited.

[22]McLean, "Palaeo-Hebrew," p. 20.

[23] *Ibid*, p. 228.

so that Exodus 7, 17, 18, and 32 are quite well represented. Other columns, however, for example, vi, xiii, xvi, xxxix, and xlii-xliv, are represented by only one or two tiny scraps each; and of "col. xiv" no leather remains at all, that designation reflecting merely the results of Skehan's careful reconstruction of the entire scroll.

Since nothing has been preserved before Exod 6:25, nothing, of course, remains of the narratives of Moses' childhood and call. The narratives of the plagues (ch. 7-12), of the battle with the Amalekites (17:8-16), of Jethro's visit (ch. 18), of the Sinai theophany (ch. 19, 24), and of the golden calf (ch. 32) are, however, fairly well represented. Nothing at all remains of the Song in Exodus 15 or of the Decalogue (20:2-17). On the other hand, small but significant portions of the Book of the Covenant (20:21-23:33) have been preserved. The first half of the tabernacle account, that giving the instructions (25:1-31:11), is represented by a number of small fragments, but the second half, that reporting the construction of the tabernacle (ch. 35-40), is virtually lost. From Exodus 35 to the end of the book there is only one connected passage, presenting parts of eight verses, plus isolated words or letters from six other random verses.

The complete list of all variants, as defined above (see the Introduction to Chapter I) is given in chapter-verse order in Appendix 2. The interpretation of Appendix 2, the list of variants, will be aided by reference to Appendix 1, the list of all the extant passages. Why are there, for example, so many variants in chapter 18? A glance at Appendix 1 will show that Exodus 18 is especially well preserved. When more text is preserved there is proportionately more opportunity for variants.

The orthography of 4QpaleoExod^m is very full, i.e., many *matres lectionis* were employed to indicate vocalization. This trait, however, is typical of many of the scrolls that have been discovered from Qumran.

When Skehan began reconstructing and deciphering this scroll, the most fully preserved of the fifty-three scrolls in his care, he soon discovered that it was also the most unusual and the most significant.

What was much more surprising than either the script or the orthography of the scroll was the text itself. As he was deciphering the top of one of the best-preserved columns, xxxviii, he found in the midst of Exod 32:10 a sentence which did not belong anywhere in Exodus. Instead, it was from Deuteronomy, specifically Deut 9:20. Thus the passage presumably read as follows before the scroll deteriorated (the underlined words are from Deuteronomy):

"Now therefore let me alone, that my wrath may burn hot against them and I may consume them; but of you I will make a great nation. <u>And Yahweh was so angry with Aaron that he was ready to destroy him; but Moses prayed for Aaron</u>. But Moses besought Yahweh his God, and said, "O Yahweh, why does your wrath burn hot against your people ... ?"

Skehan's further investigation showed that the entire scroll was significantly different from the Massoretic Text. For one thing, there were lengthy repetitions, especially in the plague narratives, where an entire paragraph of instruction to Moses would be repeated word for word with slight changes to indicate that Moses had indeed carried out Yahweh's instructions to the letter. For another, the ten verses giving instructions for the incense altar were not in chapter 30, as in 𝔐, but in chapter 26. Third, other passages from Deuteronomy like that in Exod 32:10 appeared in the text of Exodus. That they were indeed being quoted in Exodus was clear from the fact that the handwriting, the leather, the juxtaposition of words, and the placement of the passages required that they were an integral part of this scroll.

The solution to the puzzle posed by this scroll lay in the Samaritan Pentateuch. Each of these three characteristics is also true of 𝔐. This Dead Sea Scroll, Skehan surmised, must be a copy of the Samaritan Pentateuch! The Essenes, that most hostile of religious sects, those "Sons of Light" who condemned all others as "Sons of Darkness," used and treasured a copy of Exodus similar to the one used by the Samaritans who were ostracized by other Israelites because they worshiped at Mount Gerizim.

In fact, Skehan was so excited that he published that telltale column, xxxviii, containing Exodus 32, very quickly indeed -- in 1955, under the title "Exodus in the Samaritan Recension from Qumran."[24] He reported that the

---

[24] *JBL* 74 (1955), 182-187. A plate of col. xxxviii was published with the article. It still gives a very good impression of this column, one of the most easily legible, although a few more tiny fragments have since been found which also belong on this column. It is important to note that this scroll was originally designated 4QEx$^{\alpha}$; Greek characters were chosen to denote scrolls in Palaeo-Hebrew script. Unfortunately this feature was not clear enough to many readers, with the result that the scroll has been frequently referred to as 4QEx^a, i.e., using the Latin character. The latter designation actually refers to another scroll in the square script, one that shares none of the unusual characteristics of the scroll being analyzed here. At least by 1965 this scroll had received its permanent designation, 4QpaleoExod^m.

scroll had "all the essential characteristics" of the Samaritan Pentateuch as far as the text was concerned.[25]   The script was not Samaritan, however, but "the fullest example we have, and a very fine one, of a quite regular Paleo-Hebrew bookhand."[26]   The orthography of the scroll was neither Samaritan nor Massoretic, but a "mild form of that fuller orthography" already known from Cave 1.

Although he announced the scroll as belonging to the Samaritan recension, Skehan did give the following caution:

> Whether from a strictly sectarian point of view there is anything specifically Samaritan about this MS, the writer is at present not in a position to say. Conclusive evidence either way could come only from extremely restricted portions of the text;   and since such evidence has thus far not been forthcoming, a suspended judgment seems called for.[27]

The "extremely restricted portions" that would provide the answer that Skehan was referring to were only two: Exod 20:17 and 24.   After 20:17 the Samaritan Pentateuch inserts a lengthy passage composed from Deut 11:29-30 and 27:2-7, commanding the Israelites to build an altar on Mount Gerizim, and in 20:24 it reads "in the place where I have caused my name to be remembered," as opposed to "in every place where I will cause my name to be remembered," as in 𝕸.   The effect of these two features is to raise the command to worship at Gerizim to the level of the ten commandments -- in fact to make it the tenth commandment -- and to allow for only one sanctuary in the land of Israel.   These are the only two phenomena in Exodus of 𝕸 that could be called "sectarian."   Their counterpart in Deuteronomy is the addition of the same "tenth commandment" in Deuteronomy 5 and the perfective reading ("that I have chosen") in 21 passages as opposed to the imperfective ("that I will choose") in 𝕸, referring to the place of worship, i.e., referring to Gerizim rather than allowing for a later choice of Jerusalem.   Unfortunately so little has been preserved of Exodus 20 that Skehan was unable to determine in 1955 whether or not either of these features was present.

Skehan further registered his surprise that as far as the text was concerned,

---

25 *Ibid.,* p. 182.
26 *Ibid.*
27 *Ibid.,* p. 183.

the Samaritan recension as it exists in, for example, A. von
Gall's edition, is shown by this scroll to have been preserved
with a measure of fidelity, from a time somewhere near the
origin of the recension, that compares not unfavorably with the
fidelity of transmission of MT itself ...[28]

This judgment regarding the fidelity of transmission of 𝔐 is worthy of note
and should be remembered in this study. The conception of 𝔐 as a
"recension," however, has been modified since 1955, as will be seen below.

In 1955 Skehan concluded that while the evidence of the scroll
demonstrated the antiquity and the constancy of transmission of the
Samaritan recension, it did not alter the judgment that much of what was
characteristic of 𝔐 was secondary, whereas the Massoretic Text preserved
the preferable form of the text.[29]

Skehan did not speculate on the reasons for the presence of a
Samaritan scroll at the Qumran community. But as he continued working on
the reconstruction of the scroll he was able to establish that there was not
in fact space for the lengthy "sectarian" expansion, the new "tenth
commandment," following Exod 20:17.

Thus in 1959 he published a qualification of his earlier article, giving
the details of his reconstruction.[30] He reiterated that the major expansion
following Exod 20:19 was present, and argued that its presence called for
the corresponding expansion following 20:21. The first is from Deut 5:24-
27 and the second is from Deut 5:28-31 and 18:18-22. Together they
supplement the Sinai narrative in Exodus with the fuller version in
Deuteronomy about Moses' acting as mediator; the second incorporates the
promise of a prophet like Moses in the future. Referring to them as
companion pieces, Skehan pointed out that a text would hardly have one
without the other. If both were indeed present there would be no room for
the earlier expansion after 20:17 about the altar on Gerizim.

The conclusion is that the paleohebrew Exodus is not a
Samaritan sectarian document, though it does offer the type of
text the Samaritans have preserved as their own.[31]

---

[28] *Ibid.*

[29] *Ibid.,* p. 187.

[30]Patrick W. Skehan, "Qumran and the Present State of Old Testament
Text Studies: The Masoretic Text," *JBL* 78 (1959), 21-25. Hereafter cited
as: "Present State."

[31] *Ibid.,* p. 23.

Skehan had finished his work on the edition of this scroll for the series *Discoveries in the Judaean Desert* by 1975, but publication of the volume had to await the completion of all fifty-three scrolls. After his death in 1980, and in accordance with his wishes, his scrolls were transferred to Eugene Ulrich of the University of Notre Dame for completion of the task. Due to the special significance of this one scroll, Ulrich and I are engaged in checking the decipherment and in writing much more extensive notes as well as a general introduction to it. The present study is not an edition, but rather an analysis, of the scroll.

Meanwhile others have studied the palaeography of this scroll along with other scrolls and coins in Palaeo-Hebrew script in an effort to date the various scrolls. Cross set the stage by dividing all the scrolls into three chronological groups, based on palaeographical analysis of scrolls in the square or Aramaic script:[32] Archaic or Pre-Hasmonaean, 250-150 B.C.E., the smallest group, including what he suggests to be the earliest scroll found at Qumran, 4QExod[f],[33] as well as 4QSam[b] and 4QJer[a]; Hasmonaean, 150-30 B.C.E., a larger group including 1QIsa[a] and 4QSam[a]; and Herodian, 30 B.C.E.-70 A.D., the largest group, including 1QIsa[b] and 4QNum[b].

In 1964 Hanson, on the basis of comparison with Hasmonaean coins dated from ca. 115-37 B.C.E. and four other Qumran scrolls, dated 4QpaleoExod[m] to the period 225-175 B.C.E., well before the first of the coins.[34] According to Hanson, the script of the scroll

> retains many lapidary or formal features and is under no circumstances a later stage of the cursive scripts we see in the late seventh-early sixth centuries B.C. ...this script was more likely a predecessor to rather than a contemporary of the scripts of even the earliest coins. It is clearly the beginning stages of a cursive script whose antecedent was a slowly developing formal hand.[35]

---

[32]See, e.g., Cross, "Scripts," pp. 133-139.

[33] *Ibid*, pp. 153-158; 166. In 1975 Cross dated 4QExod[f] and 4QSam[b] to 250 B.C.E. at the latest, and 4QJer[a] to about 200 B.C.E. ("The Evolution of a Theory of Local Texts," *Qumran and the History of the Biblical Text*, ed. Frank Moore Cross and Shemaryahu Talmon [Cambridge, MA: Harvard University Press, 1975], p. 316 n.8; hereafter cited as: Cross, "Evolution").

[34]Richard S. Hanson, "Paleo-Hebrew Scripts in the Hasmonean Age," *BASOR* 175 (1964), 26-42, esp. 34-37. But see now my Preface for Hanson's more recent opinion, published in 1985.

[35] *Ibid*, pp. 34 and 36.

Hanson's dating, 225-175 B.C.E., would place 4QpaleoExod^m in the Pre-Hasmonaean period, with the oldest scrolls, 4QExod^f, 4QSam^b, and 4QJer^a. Incidentally, Hanson dated the other four Palaeo-Hebrew scrolls of his study later than 4QpaleoExod^m. In 1965 Skehan himself placed the scroll between 200-175 B.C.E.[36]

More recently, however, McLean has studied the Palaeo-Hebrew script much more extensively and has dated 4QpaleoExod^m much later: in the first century B.C.E. He treats the three MSS, 4QpaleoExod^{l,m} together with the unidentified 4QpaleoSn44^b as one group,[37] which he places in the period from 100 to 50 or 25 B.C.E., with Exod^m as the latest of the three.

> Of these three contemporary manuscripts, I believe 4QpaleoExod^m to display the latest features and the greatest number of novel features which will see subsequent development. However, it is not possible to place any exact date on the manuscripts other than to say they belong within the first half to three quarters of the first century BCE.[38]

McLean's view, 100-25 B.C.E., would place Exod^m in the latter part of the Hasmonaean period or possibly at the very beginning of the Herodian.

We will return later (see Chapter V.A.5) to the significance of the question of the dating. For now, note that Hanson's dating would mean that the scroll had been copied well before the community at Qumran came into existence. According to the usual reconstruction of Qumran's history, the community was established around 150-140 B.C.E. and continued, perhaps with a short break in the last third of the first century B.C.E., until 68 C.E.[39] If Q^m had been copied between 225 and 175 B.C.E., its scribe must have lived

---

[36]See Skehan's note to Plate 9 (which pictures columns i and ii of 4QpaleoExod^m) in *Scrolls from the Wilderness of the Dead Sea: A Guide to the Exhibition, The Dead Sea Scrolls of Jordan,* Arranged by the Smithsonian Institution in Cooperation with the Government of the Hashemite Kingdom of Jordan and the Palestine Archaeological Museum (London: Trustees of the British Museum, 1965), p. 26.

[37]McLean, "Palaeo-Hebrew," pp. 66-78. See above, note 16, for explanation of these sigla. What McLean labeled as Exod^n is now designated Exod^l.

[38] *Ibid,* p. 78.

[39]See the earlier discussions such as Cross, *Library,* pp. 57-64; and more recently, R. de Vaux, "Archéologie," *Qumrân Grotte 4,* II, by R. de Vaux and J. T. Milik, DJD VI (Oxford: Clarendon Press, 1977), p. 21; Vermes, *Perspective,* pp. 32-35; and Philip R. Davies, *Qumran,* Cities of the Biblical Word (Grand Rapids, MI: Eerdmans, 1983), pp. 40-62.

elsewhere and someone must have brought it to Qumran when he visited or joined the community.

McLean's dating to 100-25 B.C.E., on the other hand, would make it quite possible that the scroll was actually copied at Qumran. This possibility may be supported by the similarities in preparation of the leather and other scribal activities between this scroll and the others found in the eleven caves.[40] It would be immensely helpful if we could know what biblical scrolls looked like in other communities at this time. Was there one standard method of preparing and inscribing scrolls, or was there variation from place to place? Were all or most of the scrolls found at Qumran actually copied there? Because we do not (yet?) have answers to these questions we must leave this issue.

Summary: A preliminary publication of **Qᵃ** in 1955 described it as a copy of the Samaritan recension. Further work showed that that was an overstatement, so that a second report in 1959 stated more precisely that it presents "the type of text that the Samaritans have preserved as their own."[41] As will become clear in the next section regarding "text-types," Skehan was thereby saying that 4QpaleoExodᵐ pre-dated the Samaritan Pentateuch and that the Samaritan Pentateuch is a development of this text-type.

No further details have been published about this scroll, except for two conflicting claims as to its date: 225-175 or 100-25 B.C.E. As will be seen in the following discussions, theories and counter-theories regarding text-critical matters such as text-types and regarding historical matters such as the origins of Samaritanism have been based on this scroll. But no further comparison of its text with that of the Samaritan Pentateuch has been published, nor any comparison with the Massoretic Text or the Septuagint.

Although expansionist tendencies in orthography and in text as well as the use of Palaeo-Hebrew script are not peculiar to this scroll, appearing individually in some other Qumran scrolls as well, 4QpaleoExodᵐ is the only scroll found at Qumran that combines all three features: Palaeo-Hebrew script, full orthography, and Samaritanlike text.

---

[40]E.g., ruling of lines and columns; for details, see the edition of **Qᵃ** in *DJD*.

[41]Skehan, "Present State," p. 23.

C. CURRENT DISCUSSION OF THE EXISTENCE AND NUMBER OF TEXT-TYPES IN THE SECOND TEMPLE PERIOD

As has already become clear, the biblical scrolls found in the caves at Qumran do not constitute a homogeneous group. Most are written in square script,[42] thirteen in Palaeo-Hebrew,[43] a few are Aramaic targumim,[44] and six are in Greek.[45] Of those in Hebrew, the orthography varies from very defective, i.e., with few or no *matres lectionis* to indicate vocalization, to extremely full, or *plene.*[46] Corresponding to the diversity in language, script, and orthography is a great diversity in text. While some have preserved a short text, others exhibit varying degrees of expansionism, and comparison of different scrolls of the same book shows that they preserve very different readings at many points. There was certainly nothing near a consensus about the text of Scripture among the Qumran community. Quite obviously, at least for their group, no standardization of the text had taken place.

Various theories have been suggested to account for these variations among the scrolls. One of those which has attracted the most attention is Frank Moore Cross's theory of three local text types. Cross was, however,

---

[42]Including, apparently, 14 of Exodus; see Skehan, "Text," p. 88, for a complete catalog as of 1965. He mentions 15 Hebrew scrolls of Exodus plus one included with Genesis, apparently making 16, of which 2 are in the Palaeo-Hebrew script.

[43]Including 2 of Exodus: 4QpaleoExod[l and m].

[44]I do not know of any targumim of Exodus at Qumran. In 1965 Skehan listed targumim of Leviticus and Job only ("Text," p. 88).

[45]Skehan listed four in 1965; by 1984 Ulrich had identified a fifth; (a sixth Septuagintal MS is of EpJer). These include one of Exodus: 7Q1 (Skehan, "Text," p. 88), which is now designated as pap7QLXXExod (Ulrich, "Greek Manuscripts," p. 71 n. 1).

[46]David Noel Freedman ("The Massoretic Text and the Qumran Scrolls: A Study in Orthography" [*Textus* 2 (1962) 87-102]) showed that the orthography of 4QSam[b], for instance, was more defective than that of 𝕸. As Skehan described the general picture at Qumran, "The spelling, however, in either script, may be a notably sparse one, with the weaker letters *w, h, y,* and *aleph* (ꞌ) used to a very limited extent to represent vowels. It may, on the other hand, in either script be an expanded orthography in which, as in Syriac, every *o* or *u* vowel, however slight, is represented by a *w* in the consonantal text." (Skehan, "Texts and Versions," *Jerome Biblical Commentary* (1968), p. 564).

not the first to make such a suggestion after the Qumran discoveries. In 1955 Albright had written a brief article describing various recensions of several biblical books. While he did not elaborate a theory of three local recensions, as a matter of fact he discussed three and only three recensions, assigning them with some supporting data to Babylon ("correct vocalizations of Assyro-Babylonian words and names" in 1QIsa[a]),[47] Egypt ("much evidence of pre-Septuagintal Egyptian influence on the text of several books,"[48] i.e., alterations of a Hebrew text in Egypt before it was translated, due to knowledge of Egyptian language and history), and Palestine (no textual evidence was given).[49]

One year later Greenberg published his own reconstruction of the history of the biblical text during the Second Temple period.[50] According to his theory the three recensions can be distinguished chronologically. The Samaritan Pentateuch is an early text type which originated probably in the fourth century and reflects the expansionism and harmonization of popular texts. The Septuagint, a new translation made in the mid-second century, was based on "the best Hebrew text of the time," which was much less full, reflecting considerable scribal editing and pruning.[51] The difference between those two texts was probably wrought by the *soferim* working in

---

[47]W. F. Albright, "New Light on Early Recensions of the Hebrew Bible," *BASOR* 140 (1955), 142-143. Hereafter cited as: Albright, "New Light."

[48] *Ibid*, pp. 143-145. For a criticism of Albright's suggestions about Egyptian influence, see Dominique Barthélemy, "A Reexamination of the Textual Problems in 2 Sam 11:2 - 1 Kings 2:11 in the Light of Certain Criticisms of *Les Devanciers d'Aquila," 1972 Proceedings: IOSCS and Pseudepigrapha,* ed. Robert A. Kraft (Missoula, MT: Scholars Press, 1972), pp. 56 ff.; and *Études d'histoire du texte de l'AT,* Orbis biblicus et orientalis 21 (Fribourg-Göttingen, 1978), pp. 238-241, 290-292. Cross responded in "Evolution," pp. 316-317. See also Emanuel Tov, *The Text-Critical Use of the Septuagint in Biblical Research,* Jerusalem Biblical Studies, ed. Ora Lipschitz and Alexander Rofé, 3 (Jerusalem: Simor, 1981), pp. 253-260 (hereafter cited as: "Tov, *Septuagint"*).

[49]In a footnote Albright referred to the Samaritan text and proto-Samaritan script of 4QpaleoExod[m], describing it as follows: "The recension differs only slightly from MT, and it obviously springs from the proto-Massoretic of Qumran" (Albright, "New Light," p. 33 n. 29).

[50]Moshe Greenberg, "The Stabilization of the Text of the Hebrew Bible, Reviewed in the Light of the Biblical Materials from the Judean Desert," *JAOS* 76 (1956), 157-167.

[51] *Ibid,* pp. 162-163.

the temple in Jerusalem, who labored consistently from the Ptolemaic
period until the first century C.E. on one recension, based on those MSS
which most nearly reflected the oldest traditions. Thus the Massoretic Text
in its final form is a still later recension, the ultimate result of three
centuries of careful editing by learned scribes in the temple, whose concern
was the repristination and stabilization of the text, the deletion of popular
expansions and harmonizations.

        Greenberg explained the many varieties of texts found at Qumran as
reflecting varying degrees of popular expansionism and of disciplined
editing and pruning toward the evolving Jerusalem standard, which was not
acknowledged as normative by all Jews until after 70 C.E. -- and certainly
would not have been recognized by the Sons of Light. The three recensions,
then, are the result of chronological developments and of the tension
between popular expansionism in orthography and text and the gradual
official production of a standard text.

        According to this reconstruction the Samaritan Pentateuch apparently
did not develop any further after the Samaritans "broke away from the Jews
during the 5th-4th centuries B.C., before the change from paleo-Hebrew to
the square character was made,"[52] since it thereby "broke away from the
line of further evolution at this time."[53] Greenberg, incidentally, was well
aware of the characteristics of 4QpaleoExod[m], but because of the
uncertainty about its date, drew no "far-reaching conclusions" from it other
than that it supported the antiquity of 𝍫.[54]

        Cross's view, published several times in the years following 1956,
represents a refinement of Albright's earlier suggestions.[55] He rejected the
concept of deliberate *textual recensions*, stressing that the *text-types*
were the result of natural developments -- but natural developments which
had only arisen during centuries of isolation from each other: hence his
suggestion of three widely separated localities in which the text-types
developed. He further rejected as anachronistic the idea of popular vs.
official texts, affirming that there was no official standard until after 70

---

        [52] *Ibid.*, p. 162.
        [53] *Ibid.*, p. 166.
        [54] *Ibid.*, pp. 163, 165.
        [55]Cross, *Library*, pp. 188-194; "The History of the Biblical Text in
the Light of Discoveries in the Judaean Desrt," *HTR* 57 (1964), 281-299;
"The Contribution of the Qumran Discoveries to the Study of the Biblical
Text," *IEJ* 16 (1966), 81-95; "Evolution," pp. 306-320.

C.E., when the rabbis of Yavneh promulgated, as he put it, the Massoretic Text.

Cross posited for the Torah and for the books of Samuel the existence of three local text-types, i.e., three clearly recognizably different text-types which must have arisen and developed in isolation from each other, one in Palestine, one in Egypt, and the third most logically in Babylon. In the Torah, the Babylonian text-type remained a short, pristine text, while the Egyptian was somewhat expansionist, and the Palestinian was the most expansionist both in text and in orthography and sometimes was written in Palaeo-Hebrew script. The Babylonian text-type was the forerunner of 𝔐, 𝔊 was translated from the Egyptian, and the Palestinian, which for Exodus is represented by 𝐐ᵐ, was the forerunner of 𝔚. By the time of the destruction of the Qumran community all three types were to be found in Qumran. The point is that they had by that time had several centuries to develop their special characteristics in geographical isolation from each other.

As evidence for the number of text-types Cross described extant MSS of the Torah and Samuel as representing three different types. In the Torah 𝔐 presents a pristine, short text with defective orthography; 𝔚, however, is quite expansionist in both text and orthography; and 𝔊 presents a moderately expansionist text. In Samuel 𝔐 is not only short but also haplographic; 4QSamᵃ,ᶜ are much fuller than 𝔐 in text and orthography; whereas 𝔊 is even fuller and different enough to represent a third distinct type. Other books are not so well represented, but there are two clearly divergent types for Jeremiah: one represented by 𝔐, which in this case is the fuller text-type; and the second by 4QJerᵇ and 𝔊, which is shorter than 𝔐 by one-seventh. Cross further argued that the history of the Greek texts provides a parallel to that of the Hebrew. Old Greek (𝔊) represents the Egyptian text-type; early revisions of the Greek were made according to Hebrew MSS of the Palestinian type; and still later revisions were made according to texts of the Proto-Massoretic, i.e., Babylonian, type.

As evidence for the three locations of their origin and early development, Cross pointed to the tradition of the Septuagint having been translated in Egypt (not, it should be noted, the tradition of its *Vorlage* having been brought from the temple especially for the purpose) and the similarity of 1 Chron 1–9 to 𝔚, suggesting that this text-type was the prevalent one in Palestine. Babylon was suggested as the third location apparently by process of elimination but also logically because of the possibility that the final redaction of the Torah was made there and because of the continuing presence of a large and literate Jewish community there.

Gooding[56] responded to Cross's theory by urging more precise use of terminology. For instance, Gooding wondered if perhaps Cross were

> using the term "Palestinian" in two senses: (1) "originating, or developed, in Palestine"; (2) "expansionistic". 4QSam[b], then, though not very expansionistic, as 4QSam[a and c] are, qualifies as Palestinian on the grounds that it originated in Palestine, while the Old Greek, though having close affinities with 4QSam[b], and that because it derived originally from a Palestinian text, cannot be called Palestinian, simply because it was developed in Egypt. ...if it were the fact that the Old Greek had been translated in Palestine instead of Alexandria, would its differences from 4QSam[b] be so much larger than those of 4QSam[a and c], that it would still have to 'be assigned to another Text-Type distinct from the Palestinian'?[57]

Though he phrased the question in terms of Samuel, this issue pertains also to the investigation of 4QpaleoExod[m] and its relationship to the Samaritan Pentateuch, both of which Cross has labeled "Palestinian."

While clearly stating that NT terminology is not directly applicable to OT textual criticism, Gooding appealed to Colwell's four criteria for determining the existence of a text-type in New Testament textual criticism. These criteria are: agreement in unique readings, i.e., readings peculiar to that text-type alone; agreement in a large majority of the total variants; families and text-types should be carefully distinguished, since a text-type, the largest of Colwell's New Testament MS groups, may be joined in many variants by another text-type against a third (whereas in the smallest grouping, a family, this would not be the case); and finally, agreement in secondary readings is more significant for determining the relationship of a group of MSS than agreement in original readings.[58]

---

[56] D. W. Gooding, "An Appeal for a Stricter Terminology in the Textual Criticism of the Old Testament," *JSS* 21 (1976), 15-25.

[57] *Ibid.,* pp. 20-21.

[58] *Ibid.,* pp. 21-22.

In 1970 Talmon[59] rejected significant aspects of the local text theory, notably the number three and what he referred to as Cross's implicit assumption of the existence of an *Urtext* from which the three local types represented deviation. Against the notion of an *Urtext* Talmon argued that:

> "the extant evidence imposes on us the conclusion that from the very first stage of its manuscript transmission, the Old Testament text was known in a variety of traditions which differed from each other to a greater or less degree."[60]

Against the notion of three types Talmon urged that there were far more than three different types, and that the reason only three types have survived until today is that each of the three was adopted and preserved by an integrated socio-religious community which managed to survive: the Samaritans (𝕸), the Jews (𝕸), and the Christians (𝕲). The existence of the *Gruppentext* and that of the *Gruppe* mutually reinforced and helped to perpetuate the other.

> A hallowed text-form adopted by a specific group has a decidedly integrating effect. A *Gruppentext* is as much a socializing agent as is a *Gruppensprache*.[61]

Talmon challenged textual critics both to attend more to "the social and societal aspects of the preservation of literature"[62] and to learn the lesson of the variety of texts found at Qumran. For scholars today to think in terms of three types of the Old Testament text is to continue to be influenced by accounts of the transmission of the New Testament[63] even

---

[59]Talmon, "Text," pp. 159-199, esp. pp. 193-199; and "The Textual Study of the Bible -- A New Outlook," *Qumran and the History of the Biblical Text,* ed. Frank Moore Cross and Shemaryahu Talmon (Cambridge, MA: Harvard University Press, 1975), pp. 321-400, esp. pp. 323-326 (hereafter cited as: Talmon, "Study").

[60]Talmon, "Text," p. 198. In his later article Talmon seems to have modified his view somewhat, since he conceded that "recent developments, on the whole, appear to weigh the scales in favour of a more consolidated concept of the early text of the Bible" ("Study," p. 324); yet he still seemed to favor the view that "primal traditions which varied among themselves to a limited degree progressively lost their lease on life and ultimately crystallized in a restricted number of *Gruppentexte*" (p. 327).

[61]Talmon, "Study," p. 325.

[62]*Ibid.*

[63]Talmon, "Text," p. 39. Tov would later refer to the analogy of the Septuagint as well as that of the New Testament; see *Septuagint,* p. 256.

after the discoveries of the Qumran scrolls should have taught us that there were, prior to 70 C.E., far more than three types of Old Testament texts.

In an excellent article in 1977 Albrektson amassed a devastating group of arguments, negative and positive, against "the current idea that the emergence of the standard text must have been the result of a conscious and deliberate text-critical activity with the purpose of creating a normative recension."[64] Negatively, he refuted four arguments: the usual analogy between the methods of the rabbis and those of Greek grammarians in Alexandria, the appeal to the exegetical methods attributed to Aqiva, the appeal to rabbinic statements about official texts kept and edited in the temple, and finally the adducing of the Murabba'at scrolls to demonstrate the date of the alleged standardization of the text.[65]

Positively, he argued that deficiencies of 𝕸 such as "inconsistencies of spelling and transpositions of letters, ... haplographies and dittographies, ... erroneous word-divisions and faulty joining of words" make it "virtually inconceivable that they could have been allowed to stand if the text had really been subjected to thorough and deliberate recensional activities."[66] Not only do they preclude text-critical activity on the part of the rabbis, but more, Albrektson claims, they also argue against "the concept of an official promulgation of a normative text." Regarding 𝕸 of Samuel he asked, "who would deliberately have preferred this inferior version to other and better manuscripts which were available?"[67]

Finally, Albrektson chided, it is anachronistic to suppose that variant readings would have been an embarrassment to rabbis. On the contrary, they delighted in variety and exploited it for their exegesis. "Such an attitude to variant readings would not seem to have been particularly fertile soil for tendencies towards a rigidly fixed recension."[68]

Albrektson concluded with his own suggestion about what happened: the text which was victorious "came to supplant other texts because the

---

[64]Bertil Albrektson, "Reflections on the Emergence of a Standard Text of the Hebrew Bible," VTSup 29 (1978), 50. Hereafter cited as: Albrektson, "Reflections."

[65] *Ibid.,* pp. 50–58.

[66] *Ibid.,* p. 59.

[67] *Ibid.,* p. 61.

[68] *Ibid.,* p. 62.

Pharisees supplanted other religious groups."[69] As he himself noted, Talmon had pointed in this same direction, while yet retaining the notion of a text-type. Albrektson's view would seem to unite the best of Talmon's emphasis on the socio-religious factors involved in the preservation of texts with a greater attention to historical factors and a more realistic appraisal of 𝔐:

> If the text which was to hold the field in the future was what Pharisaic scribes happened to have left after the defeats imposed by the Romans (to put it briefly and perhaps to oversimplify), this might explain both the merits of the text and its deficiencies. It had been handled in circles which devoted much care and attention to the word of Scripture, and so it is plausible that on the whole it should have an archaic and authentic character, lacking many of the defects which are typical of the so-called vulgar texts. But at the same time it is not the result of a thorough-going recension, it is based on manuscripts which happened to be preserved after the downfall, and its dominating position is not based on text-critical grounds -- and therefore in places it does display lacunae and errors which would not be found in a thoroughly revised text.[70]

Most recently Tov, while agreeing with Talmon that "the preservation of precisely these texts was coincidental from a *textual* point of view, although from a socio-religious point of view ... [it] is understandable,"[71] has gone much further in his rejection of Cross's theory by attacking the very notion of "text-type." This term carries with it two erroneous ideas. First, it "denotes an imaginary group of texts in the center of which the MT, LXX or Sam. Pent. are found, while the other 'members' of that group resemble in some way or other the central representative."[72]   Second, it "refers to a consistent typological characteristic of the text, such as long, expansionistic, short, vulgar, haplographic, corrupt or harmonistic."[73]

---

[69]*Ibid,* p. 63.   Albrektson may have made the transition from the Pharisees to the ultimately triumphant rabbinic movement too easily. Neusner has pointed out the difficulty in attributing the pre-70 C.E. stratum of the Mishnah to a particular group known to us.   Cf. Jacob Neusner, *Judaism: The Evidence of the Mishnah* (Chicago: University of Chicago Press, 1981), pp. 69-71.

[70]Albrektson, p. 63.

[71]Emanuel Tov, "A Modern Textual Outlook Based on the Qumran Scrolls," *HUCA* 53 (1982), 19; (hereafter cited as: Tov, "Outlook").

[72]"Outlook," p. 23.

[73]"Outlook," p. 23. See also Tov, *Septuagint,* pp. 253-275.

Like Gooding, he called for more precise terminology, but more fundamentally, he called for an entirely new framework within which to do textual criticism. So far the new data gained from the discoveries in the Judean Desert have merely been integrated into the old framework of three text-types, with the result that scrolls have been perceived and described in terms of their agreement with one of those text-types. This perception and this description have, in turn, buttressed the old framework, since representatives of all three text-types have indeed been found at Qumran on the basis of this approach.[74]

Tov gave a most instructive historical analogy which is especially pertinent to this study.[75]   In the seventeenth century the established framework allowed for only two recensions, the Massoretic Text and the Septuagint, with the result that even when the western world rediscovered the Samaritan Pentateuch, "no third [recension] could be tolerated next to them." Scholars therefore assigned the "new" text to the Septuagintal recension. They were aided in this misconception by the description of the Samaritan Pentateuch which quickly became accepted: 𝔐 differed from 𝔐 in 6,000 readings, of which 1,900 agreed with 𝔊.   The framework of two recensions caused them to focus exclusively on the notion of agreements between 𝔐 and 𝔊.   It was only with Gesenius' study in 1815[76] that scholars were enabled to recognize 𝔐 as a third recension, though even after 1815 several still referred to one "Samaritan-Alexandrine" text or recension.[77] To state clearly what I take to be the point from Tov's analogy: the established framework governed the perception and description of new data, and that description continued to support the established framework -- a vicious circle.

A new precision in terminology such as Gooding urged would tear down the old framework, for it would preclude the isolation of text-types.

---

[74]Tov, "Outlook," pp. 13, 17-18.

[75]*Ibid.,* pp. 14-15.

[76]See above, note 1.

[77]Traces of this approach still persist today. Despite familiarity with the varieties of texts found at Qumran, Eissfeldt nevertheless wrote: "In 2,000 of the cases mentioned 𝔐 agrees with 𝔊 against 𝔐, and this in itself shows that in 𝔐 and 𝔊 a common text-form appears which deviates from 𝔐" (Otto Eissfeldt, *The Old Testament: An Introduction,* tr. Peter R. Ackroyd [New York: Harper & Row, 1976], p. 695).

Rather, each text -- including 𝕸, 𝐆, and 𝖀[78] -- would then be revealed as an individual *text*, and not as a representative of a text *type*. Our perception would be altered and we would be enabled to recognize that most early texts relate to each other "in an intricate web of agreements, differences and exclusive readings,"[79] and are thus to be seen not as members of a family, but as "individualistic and independent."[80] "Each scroll reflects the idiosyncracies of its own scribe."[81] Scrolls must be evaluated on the basis not only of their <u>agreements</u> with 𝕸, 𝖀, or 𝐆, but also of their <u>disagreements,</u> and especially of their <u>unique</u> readings. Furthermore, agreements in secondary readings are of much greater significance than agreements in original readings for establishing affiliation.[82]

Tov does allow a few exceptions. For one thing, regarding *grouping* of texts, he says:

> The notion of the individuality of the texts must not be maintained *ad infinitum.* One group at least can be identified. ... "proto-Masoretic" ... scrolls represent a textual *approach* that did not allow the insertion of changes after a certain period. They were probably brought to Qumran from outside, possibly from the center where they were copied and where such changes were disallowed, viz., the Temple circles. The authority of scrolls originating in these circles must have been recognized widely, and this situation accounts for the relatively large number of copies of MT (proto-MT) in Qumran and other places in the Judean Desert.[83]

Note that Tov thereby agrees with Greenberg regarding the official nature of scribal activity in the temple and its result in establishing the Proto-Massoretic text as widely authoritative.

Of special significance for this analysis of 4QpaleoExod^m, however, are two other exceptions that Tov makes. First, he does allow that some

---

[78]Tov, "Outlook," p. 24. On p. 26 Tov repeats this idea, but contrast his more nuanced remarks allowing 𝖀 to be called a text-type, earlier on p. 24.

[79]Tov, *Septuagint,* p. 274.

[80]Tov, "Outlook," p. 21.

[81]*Ibid,* p. 20.

[82]See especially "Outlook," pp. 19-22; *Septuagint,* pp. 261-271; and "Determining the Relationship between the Qumran Scrolls and the LXX: Some Methodological Issues," *The Hebrew and Greek Texts of Samuel,* ed. Emanuel Tov (Jerusalem: Academon, 1980), pp. 45-67.

[83]"Outlook," p. 25.

differences are indeed *typological,* such as "some recensional traits" in 𝕾,
i.e. harmonistic variants and other secondary readings, although even in this
case, such variants are not unique to 𝕾,[84] but are characteristic of "a
certain scribal *approach* which is also reflected in other sources."[85] Thus
there is after all "some legitimacy" in applying the term "text-type" for
𝕾[86] -- though none at all for 𝕸 or 𝕲. And second, he does allow for at
least some *grouping,* since he admits that:

> If we do away with the notion of three recensions or text-
> types, one should still be able to find an occasional pair of
> closely connected sources. After all, each scroll was copied
> from another one. Indeed, there seems to be a close link
> between the LXX of Jer. and 4QJer^b. Likewise, 4QpaleoEx^m and
> 4QNum^b are close to the Sam. Pent.[87]

> "some scrolls *do* bear a close resemblance to the LXX or Sam.
> Pent., ...[though] no scroll is as close to the LXX or Sam. Pent. as
> the proto-Masoretic scrolls are to MT. ... 4QpaleoEx^m is close to
> the Sam. Pent., although the degree of closeness cannot be
> determined at this stage."[88]

Thus for Tov 𝕾 was special in that it has some typological features;[89] and
Q was special in that it is close to 𝕾, to a degree that was not yet known.

Before leaving the description of Tov's views, there is one
qualification to make about my analysis of Q. Tov allowed one more
exception in Exodus to his general rejection of typological differences: the
difference in order of Exodus 35-40 in 𝕸 and 𝕲. As will be seen in
Appendices 1 and 2, however, Q is scarcely extant in those chapters, and
when it is, it agrees almost totally with both 𝕾 and 𝕸. Thus it sheds
little light on the question of the wholesale disagreement between 𝕾𝕸 and
𝕲. The contribution of Q is not in chapters 35-40 but rather in chapters
6-32, and particularly to the question of the status of 𝕾.

As Ulrich pointed out in 1984, "no one has presented sufficiently
thorough and comprehensive data to enable us to embrace definitively" any

---

[84]Tov, *Septuagint,* p. 274 and n. 38, and p. 303.

[85]"Outlook," p. 24.

[86] *Ibid.*

[87]Tov, "Outlook," pp. 25-26.

[88]"Outlook," pp. 22-23.

[89]See Tov's very helpful discussion of 𝕾, especially its relationship
with 𝕲, in *Septuagint,* pp. 267-271.

of the preceding theories.[90]   He does suggest that, while Cross "has presented the fullest and the most internally consistent data-base and analysis," Tov has done well to sound a note of caution regarding "the clarity of text-types." Yet for his part, "Tov may turn out to be too reductionist in denying discernible text-types."[91]

The present study may be able to contribute in a limited way to this question of "the clarity of text-types." Since even Tov agrees that the Samaritan Pentateuch may be called a text-type, and that 4QpaleoExod^m is close to $\mathbf{m}$, we can test this notion of text-types, which involves the two aspects of typological characteristics and groupings of texts. *How* close is $\mathbf{Q}^m$ to $\mathbf{m}$? How different is it from $\mathbf{m}$? How much is it like $\mathbf{m}$? How much is it like $\mathbf{G}$? And very important -- how often is it "unique"?[92] If, on the one hand, it agrees with $\mathbf{m}$ in variants that are not only secondary and "unique" but also should be termed "typological," in other words, variants that are so significant that $\mathbf{Q}^m$ should be classified with $\mathbf{m}$; and yet, on the other hand, it agrees with $\mathbf{m}$ and/or $\mathbf{G}$ in other readings, what does that indicate about the nature of a text-type? If even members of one text-type "relate to each other in an intricate web of agreements, disagreements and unique readings,"[93] then what should happen to the notion of text-types? Should it be given up altogether, even for witnesses such as $\mathbf{Q}^m$ and $\mathbf{m}$, or, conversely, should it be broadened to allow other witnesses to constitute a text-type as well?

D. RECENT RECONSTRUCTIONS OF THE ORIGINS OF SAMARITANISM

As the older orthodoxy about three textual recensions has been under attack since the discovery of the Qumran scrolls, so has that about the origins of Samaritanism.

Once again Albright was one who paved the way. Even before the scrolls were discovered he compared the Palaeo-Hebrew script of Hasmonaean coins with the script of early Samaritan inscriptions and

---

[90]Eugene Ulrich, "Horizons of Old Testament Textual Research at the Thirtieth Anniversary of Qumran Cave 4," *CBQ* 46 (1984), 624.

[91] *Ibid.*

[92]The word "unique" can be misleading; see below, Chapter I.F.2.

[93]Tov, "Outlook," p. 26.

concluded that the Samaritan recension could not have antedated the period between 100 B.C.E. and 63 B.C.E.

> ...a relatively late date for the origin of the Samaritan script as such seems highly probable. Moreover, since Shechem and Samaria were conquered by the Jews between 128 and 110 B.C. and were lost to the Romans in 63 B.C., it would be only natural to date the final schism between the sects somewhere in the early first century B.C. It was presumably then or somewhat later that the entire Samaritan Pentateuch was retranscribed into the archaizing "Samaritan" script, which symbolized the refusal of the Samaritans to follow the "modernists" of Jerusalem.[94]

In 1968 Purvis applied Cross's theory of three local texts to the Samaritan Pentateuch and concluded, chiefly on the grounds of script, orthography, and text-type, that Samaritanism as a sect did not originate until ca. 100 B.C.E.[95] As he put the argument, the presence in the caves at Qumran of scrolls with one or more of the following characteristics: the Palaeo-Hebrew script, full orthography, and the Palestinian text-type, shows that the Samaritan recension could not have antedated the Hasmonaean period.

Purvis contended that the distinctive Samaritan script could only be explained as a direct descendant of the Palaeo-Hebrew script being used commonly in Hasmonaean Palestine, as evidenced by the biblical scrolls found at Qumran as well as by the Hasmonaean coins. According to his palaeographical analysis, it was only after the Hasmonaean period that the script began to develop in two different directions: Samaritan, as evidenced by inscriptions from 100 B.C.E. - 600 C.E. as well as later scrolls and codices of the Samaritan Pentateuch; and Jewish, as evidenced by coins and ostraca of the First and Second Revolts.[96]

Similarly, Purvis claimed that the Qumran scrolls show that Samaritan orthography was best explained as a direct development of Hasmonaean orthography. During that period the use of internal *matres*

---

[94]William Foxwell Albright, *From the Stone Age to Christianity: Monotheism and the Historical Process*, 2d ed. with a new introduction (Garden City, NY: Doubleday Anchor Books, 1957), pp. 345-346 n. 12. (Except for the Introduction, this is a reprint of the second edition of 1946.)

[95]James D. Purvis, *The Samaritan Pentateuch and the Origin of the Samaritan Sect*, HSM 2 (Cambridge, MA: Harvard University Press, 1968). Hereafter cited as: Purvis, *Origin.*

[96]*Ibid.*, pp. 18-52.

lectionis was at its height, but this *plene* tendency was to fall out of favor with the rabbis, who chose a less full orthography for their Torah text.[97]

His third argument dealt with the text:

> The Samaritan Pentateuch is a sectarian redaction of a biblical text type which is now known from extra-Samaritan sources. The text used by the Samaritans (the so-called proto-Samaritan) was one of three textual traditions in use during the Hasmonaean period.[98].

> The proto-Samaritan can be understood as a Palestinian text type descended from an Old Palestinian textual tradition. The earliest witness to this Old Palestinian tradition is to be found in those sections of 1 Chronicles 1-9 which preserve Pentateuchal passages in parallel transmission. ... The Palestinian character of the proto-Samaritan is also indicated by its survival in the palaeo-Hebrew script (in 4QEx$^\alpha$) -- the old national script of Palestine. The proto-Samaritan exhibits the development of the Palestinian text type from the fifth to the second centuries B.C.[99]

He pointed out that almost none of the expansions of the Samaritan Pentateuch are due to Samaritan redaction. Instead, they faithfully reflect what he referred to as the Palestinian text-type.[100] As has been hinted above,[101] probably only two changes can be attributed to the Samaritans themselves and can therefore be called "sectarian" (whether even that term should be used is a question that has since been posed to Purvis). These two

---

[97] *Ibid.,* pp. 52-67. Purvis contrasted examples of the defective orthography found in 4QSam^b, which has been dated to the pre-Hasmonaean period, with the fuller orthography appearing in Qumran scrolls which have been dated to the Hasmonaean and Herodian periods. All of his examples had previously been published (pp. 63-67). In the latter category he included 4QpaleoExod^m, giving eight examples from it which had been previously published in Skehan, "Exodus," and Birnbaum, *Hebrew Scripts,* no. 32. In each case mentioned, both 𝔐 and 𝔚 agree in exhibiting shorter orthography. It should be noted, however, that the readings for 𝔚 were according to the edition of von Gall, who deliberately chose orthography in agreement with 𝔐 from the MSS available to him. (See below, Chapter I.F.1.)

[98] *Ibid.,* p. 69; his argument about the text is found on pp. 69-86.

[99] *Ibid.,* pp. 80-81. As indicated above (note 24), 4QEx$^\alpha$ was the original designation for 4QpaleoExod^m.

[100] *Ibid.,* p. 80.

[101] See above, Chapter I.B.

have been mentioned above: the insertion after the Decalogue in Exodus 20 and the twenty-one places in Deuteronomy where, at least from the point of view of the Judean tradition, the imperfective verb יבחר has been altered to the perfective בחר, in order to designate the place of worship as "the place Yahweh *has* chosen."[102]

As Purvis would later suggest,[103] and as a parallel printing of the texts of Exodus 20 in the Samaritan Pentateuch, in 4QpaleoExod^m, and in the Massoretic Text demonstrates clearly, the Samaritans' Scriptures -- even in the one "sectarian" chapter -- are quite close to the Scriptures that others seem to have been using and copying in pre-Hasmonaean and Hasmonaean Palestine. Yet it must be recognized clearly that Purvis' whole approach to the matter was predicated on the theory of the three local texts. The Qumran scrolls that shared "Samaritanlike" characteristics were labeled "Palestinian" and sharply distinguished from "Babylonian" and "Egyptian"

---

[102]It is often claimed that the Samaritans are also responsible for having altered "Ebal" to "Gerizim" in Deut 27:4, which, as we have seen, is also quoted in their Bible in Exodus 20, commanding the Israelites to build an altar when they entered the land (cf. Josh 8:30). (For an older statement of this view see, e.g., James Alan Montgomery, *The Samaritans: The Earliest Jewish Sect* [Philadelphia: John C. Winston, 1907], p. 35; and for a more recent statement, B. J. Roberts, "Samaritan Pentateuch," *IDB* IV [1962], 190.) Yet from a text-critical point of view, it is equally possible that "Gerizim" was in fact the original reading, and that a scribe in the tradition behind the Massoretic Text changed it to "Ebal" in order to preclude the possibility of any legitimation of Samaritan worship. (This is suggested by Otto Eissfeldt, *The Old Testament: An Introduction,* tr. Peter R. Ackroyd [New York: Harper & Row, 1976], p. 695; cf. also p. 216 and n. 9.) In fact, it seems to me to be more reasonable that the tradition should speak of an altar on Gerizim, since according to Deut 27:12-13 the blessing was to be pronounced from Mount Gerizim and the curse from Mount Ebal. When all of the Qumran scrolls of Deuteronomy have been published it will be most interesting to discover whether any of them preserve this verse. And from an archaeological point of view, when more is known of the recently-discovered altar on Mount Ebal, it will be interesting to see what light that might shed on the question. (See Adam Zertal, "Has Joshua's Altar Been Found on Mt. Ebal?" *Biblical Archaeology Review* 11:1 [Jan/Feb 1985], 26-43.)

[103]James D. Purvis, "The Samaritan Problem: A Case Study in Jewish Sectarianism in the Roman Era," in *Traditions in Transformation: Turning Points in Biblical Faith,* ed. Baruch Halpern and Jon D. Levenson (Winona Lake, IN: Eisenbrauns, 1981), pp. 335-337.   Hereafter cited as: Purvis, "Problem."

text-types. It could easily appear that Purvis' theory regarding the origin of the Samaritans stood or fell with Cross's local-text theory. Since there is no documentary proof of a "Babylonian" text-type, it can seem very easy to repudiate claims of a "Palestinian" text-type as well, especially when one reads Talmon's and Tov's attacks on the local-text theory. It is my contention that Purvis' work is best appreciated apart from the local-text theory. If we avoid becoming preoccupied with such issues as whether or not a "Babylonian" text-type was the forerunner of the Massoretic Text we may find that Purvis has given a useful example of the appropriation of the evidence of Qumran for broader historical and religious questions.

Thus Purvis has used the legitimate evidence of 4QpaleoExod^m as well as other data -- namely, that Scriptures very similar to the kind of Torah which the Samaritans use were in common use in Palestine in the Hasmonaean period -- to show that the people who were to become "Samaritans" shared their Scripture with their neighbors at least until *ca* 100 B.C.E., a Scripture which reached the height of its textual and orthographical expansion during the Hasmonaean period.

The implications of Purvis' first work can be used to show two very significant things about the Samaritans. First, the fact that their Torah shared the same characteristics as the Torah of other Israelites in Palestine during the Greek and Hasmonaean periods shows that they were in contact with them and that their religion and their sacred writings were developing in concert with the religion and sacred writings of other Israelites. Accordingly there must have been some sense of solidarity with other Israelites during these periods, and the Samaritans known to us during the Roman period must have been "a community whose self-understanding was not clearly defined until around 100 B.C.E."[104] Second, even when -- to whatever degree -- they did dissociate themselves from the rest of Israel, the fact that their Torah was so similar to that of others in Palestine helps us to see them in their context more clearly and to recognize that their faith and practices were well within the limits of Second Temple Israelite religion.

Other scholars have been reaching similar conclusions concerning the origins and the nature of Samaritanism, but from very different routes. On the basis of literary evidence such as 2 Maccabees, Sirach, Judith, and

---

[104] *Ibid.*, p. 333; Purvis himself has brought out these implications much more clearly in his writings since 1968.

Josephus, as well as of political considerations, Morton Smith dated the existence of the two religious communities from the time of the refusal of the Shechemites ("Samaritans") to participate in the Maccabean revolt.[105]

Coggins[106] used both positive and negative arguments to contend that the Samaritans belonged well within the total spectrum of Judaism, which was characterized by diversity rather than by any "orthodoxy." On the negative side, he demonstrated the lack of any reference to Samaritans in the Old Testament (e.g., in 2 Kgs 17), particularly in writings of the Second Temple period where they have been so frequently alleged (e.g., Haggai), and showed the great difficulties involved in the use of archaeological and literary evidence, particularly that of Josephus. On the positive side, he discussed the Samaritans' own historical traditions, and showed from the nature of Samaritan religion how well it fitted into the religious milieu of the Hasmonaean and Roman periods. Finally, he roundly rejected the use of the word "schism" in connection with the Samaritans.

Dexinger,[107] on the basis of his own interpretation of the literary evidence and the political and economic situation, has dated "the breaking point," "the limits of tolerance," to ca. 100 B.C.E., when John Hyrcanus destroyed Shechem and the Gerizim temple. The Samaritans, for their part, inserted the Gerizim commandment into the Decalogue, either in response to that destruction or perhaps already previously. In either case, they were seeking "to furnish a central article of [their] creed with revelational authority."[108]

Pummer has found no conclusive evidence as to the exact date or the reasons of the final separation but is in basic agreement with this general line of reconstruction.[109]

Yet the work of Cross and of Purvis has been criticized in various ways. Ben-Hayyim asked:

---

[105]Morton Smith, *Palestinian Parties and Politics that Shaped the Old Testament* (New York: Columbia University, 1971), pp. 182-192.

[106]R. J. Coggins, *Samaritans and Jews: The Origins of Samaritanism Reconsidered* (Atlanta: John Knox, 1975).

[107]Ferdinand Dexinger, "Limits of Tolerance in Judaism: The Samaritan Example," in *Jewish and Christian Self-Definition, 2, Aspects of Judaism in the Graeco-Roman Period,* ed. E. P. Sanders with A. I. Baumgarten and Alan Mendelson (Philadelphia: Fortress Press, 1981), pp 88-114, 327-338.

[108]*Ibid,* pp. 108-109.

[109]Reinhard Pummer, "The Present State of Samaritan Studies," *JSS* 21 (1976), 39-61, and 22 (1977), 24-47.

> can one really come to an important historical and social
> conclusion such as the time of the formation of the Samaritan
> sect according to the orthographic form and the script of its
> Holy Writ?[110]

This indicates a weakness in Purvis' original book which he has to some extent corrected in his later writings. The evidence of the Samaritan Pentateuch as compared with the Qumran scrolls should not be seen in isolation from the broader religious, sociological, and historical questions discussed by Coggins and others, as mentioned above.

Macdonald[111] was unpersuaded by Purvis' arguments regarding script and orthography, because of the late dates and the variations of traditions and styles exhibited by extant manuscripts. On the other hand, he did not dispute the first century B.C.E. – C.E. dating of Purvis' earliest inscription. Yet perhaps he was implicitly discounting it because it consists of only twelve letters and is inscribed in stone, making comparison with the script on the leather scrolls from Qumran difficult. Macdonald found Purvis' arguments regarding the text-type much stronger, yet urged caution insofar as our present edition of the Samaritan Pentateuch[112] is not fully reliable.

The responses of Roberts[113] and of Coggins[114] went in the opposite direction from Macdonald's. On the one hand, they both found Purvis' conclusions regarding script and orthography much more convincing than he did. Each made qualifications, however. Regarding script, Roberts cautioned that comparisons between leather and stone are hazardous. Regarding orthography, Coggins cautioned that conclusions based on present editions of the Samaritan Pentateuch must remain somewhat tentative. But on the

---

[110]Z. Ben-Hayyim, Book Review of *The Samaritan Pentateuch and the Origin of the Samaritan Sect* by James D. Purvis (Cambridge, MA: Harvard University Press, 1968), *Biblica* 52 (1971), 253-255.

[111]John Macdonald, Book Review of *The Samaritan Pentateuch and the Origin of the Samaritan Sect* by James D. Purvis (Cambridge. MA: Harvard University Press, 1968), *JJS* 21 (1970), 69-72.

[112]*Der Hebräische Pentateuch der Samaritaner*, ed. August Freiherr von Gall (Giessen: Alfred Töpelmann, 1918).

[113]Bleddyn J. Roberts, Book Review of *The Samaritan Pentateuch and the Origin of the Samaritan Sect* by James D. Purvis (Cambridge, MA: Harvard University Press, 1968), *JTS* 20 (1969), 569-571.

[114]Coggins, Book Review of *The Samaritan Pentateuch and the Origin of the Samaritan Sect* by James D. Purvis (Cambridge, MA: Harvard University Press, 1968), *JSS* 14 (1969), 273-275; and *Samaritans and Jews*, pp. 148-152.

other hand, both were quite skeptical regarding the text, again in contrast with Macdonald. Both expressed grave doubts as to the theory of three local texts, and both lamented the delay of publication, whether of the Qumran scrolls or of a major study of that theory. Roberts suggested that Purvis had too readily accepted and built upon unproven hypotheses.

> Is it actually established that the Qumran 'Samaritan' text-forms are all that close to the Samaritan text? ... The danger is still more obvious when Dr. Purvis without hesitation asserts that there were three recensions of the text ... Further, he would need to remove the prima facie objection to his theory, and one which reflects the centuries-old assessment, that apart from orthography and deliberate changes the text of the Samaritan Pentateuch is virtually the same as the M.T. The treatment demands to be at least as thorough as that devoted to the Samaritan script, but it is not given here. Rather, one is left with the unfortunate impression that Albright and Cross have spoken, and that is that![115]

It is to answer that question -- and to obviate that criticism -- that this study has been undertaken. It is to be hoped that the results of this analysis of 4QpaleoExod^m will contribute indirectly to the question of the origins and the nature of the Samaritan community.

E. DISCUSSIONS OF EDITORIAL AND SCRIBAL PRACTICE IN THE SECOND TEMPLE PERIOD

Since the discovery of the Qumran scrolls, text critics have for the first time been able to "observe at close range, so to say *in situ,* scribal techniques of the Second Temple period."[116]

On the basis of a comparison of some Qumran scrolls with 𝕸, 𝖆, and 𝕲, Talmon has labeled the scribe of this period "a minor partner in the creative literary process," claiming that "mechanical faithfulness to the letter of the sanctified traditional literature" arose no earlier than the first century B.C.E.[117]

---

[115]Roberts, Book Review, pp. 570-571. It is quite true that Purvis devoted much more space to palaeographical than to textual matters.

[116]Talmon, "Text," p. 184.

[117]Talmon, "Study," p. 381.

While Talmon was referring to choice of words and phrases as well as to the order of elements, Skehan drew attention to expansionist tendencies. Skehan pointed out that all of the witnesses to the Torah show evidence of some degree of expansionism of various kinds during the Second Temple period.[118]

The documentary evidence of such scribal practice raises the question of scribal attitudes toward the biblical text and to their task. As Greenberg wrote:

> Piety is not always accompanied by a critical sense. To the devout reader a text giving the substance of the sacred message is not invalidated by slight verbal divergences from other texts. ... Examples are ready at hand of pious indifference to textual considerations among Jews of later ages. ... Just so the verbal and orthographic divergences which rarely affected the meaning, the additional phrases and verses which were based on parallels or traditional interpretations -- these need not have troubled the Qumran pietists any more than they do those of a later day.[119]

After a careful study of the phenomenon of double readings, including Qumran and other textual witnesses and non-biblical literature as well, especially the Qumran *pesharim* and the *ʾal tiqrê* midrashim in rabbinic literature, Talmon concluded that:

> "the combined evidence of Qumran and Rabbinic techniques proves the contention that variant readings in the Biblical textual traditions were viewed with relative equanimity by both groups, and even were perpetuated by diverse manuscriptal and non-manuscriptal devices."[120]

Tov has suggested a new classification of textual witnesses based on "two basically different approaches to the text."[121]   The *conservative* approach in principle "disallowed after a certain period the insertion of changes in the transmitted text." In practice, nevertheless, some changes were made, so that there is more than one conservative text. Tov would include the proto-Massoretic texts and the *Vorlage* of **G**.[122] The *free*

118Skehan, "Text," p. 99.

119Greenberg, "Stabilization," p. 165.

120Shemaryahu Talmon, "Aspects of the Textual Transmission of the Bible in the Light of Qumran Manuscripts," *Textus* 4 (1964), 132.

121Tov, "Outlook," p. 26.

122 *Ibid.*

approach "allowed for orthographic modernization, as well as contextual and grammatical changes, including harmonizations of various types."[123] To this group Tov assigns 𝔐 and several Qumran scrolls, including 4QpaleoExod[m] and 4QNum[b].[124]

As we have seen, various scholars have used adjectives such as "vulgar" vs. "official"[125] or "popular" vs. "conservative"[126] to describe different texts. While it appears that Tov agrees with the description as "official" of the proto-Massoretic texts, certainly "conservative" vs. "free" is, from his point of view, broader, since it can include the *Vorlage* of 𝔊, and from another point of view, less prejudicial.

As Tov himself, however, has strongly affirmed, the Septuagint cannot be described as a whole. On the contrary, each book, and in some cases, each part of a book must be analyzed on its own.[127] Thus I find his characterization of the *Vorlage* of 𝔊 as "conservative" to be puzzling indeed. In this study a recurring question will be: How "conservative" or "free" is 𝔊 in the parts of Exodus where 𝐐 is extant?

𝐐 is the oldest documentation we have on a large scale of the treatment of the text of Exodus by scribes. What light can it shed on the question of the attitudes of scribes to their task and to their *Vorlage?* Did they see themselves as junior partners in the creative endeavor? Can we determine any shifts in attitude? Can it be shown that certain alterations in the text were possible at an earlier date but not later? Throughout chapters II and III such questions as these will be asked. Chapter VI will bring together all the evidence and seek to draw conclusions from the data.

F. METHODOLOGY OF THIS STUDY

1. TEXTS AND EDITIONS USED
𝐐, or 4QpaleoExod[m], has not yet been published. The scroll was reconstructed, deciphered, and edited by Patrick W. Skehan before his death in 1980. When a reading in 𝐐 differed from that in 𝔐 or 𝔐, he also

---

123 *Ibid.*
124 *Ibid.*
125E.g., Greenberg, "Stabilization."
126E.g., Dominique Barthélemy, "Text, Hebrew, History of," *IDBS* (1976), 880.
127E.g., *Septuagint,* pp. 47-49.

collated the readings in **G**, **T**, **S**, and **V**.   Because of the special significance of this scroll, as stated above,[128] Eugene Ulrich and I are checking the decipherment and preparing much more extensive notes as well as a general introduction to the scroll for its publication in *DJD*.   In the present work are discussed only "variants"[129] and such other specific features of the scroll as pertain directly to the questions addressed. For all other matters, see the edition in *DJD*.

The standard critical edition of **Ⱳ**, or the Samaritan Pentateuch, is still that published by von Gall in 1918.[130]   It is an eclectic text and has been much criticized for its methodology.   Von Gall clearly enunciated his own principles for selection among variants in the MSS: he generally preferred defective orthography, he followed exactly the grammatical rules of (Tiberian?) Hebrew, he gave preference to the older grammatical forms, and he compared **Ⱳ** constantly with **G** and **Ⱶ**.[131] Since full orthography and updating of grammatical features are precisely two of the major characteristics of **Ⱳ** and can be expected to have given rise to grammatical phenomena other than those known to us from the Massoretes, such a procedure was clearly misleading. On the other hand, von Gall did include all variants in his apparatus, and it has been possible to determine that very few indeed of his variants have affected the readings involved in the comparison with **Qᵃ**, especially since orthography has not been taken into account.

For **Ⱶ**, or the Massoretic Text, the text of the *Biblia Hebraica Stuttgartensia* has been used as the standard, and references to Cairo MSS have been taken from the apparatus, which was prepared for Exodus by G. Quell.[132]

For **G**, or the Old Greek of the text of Exodus, where **Qᵃ** is extant Professor John Wm Wevers has very kindly provided his critical edition in pre-published form. Thus the establishment of variants has been based on Wevers' text, soon to be published in the Göttingen edition of the Septuagint.

---

[128]See above, Chapter I.B.

[129]The term "variants" as used herein will be defined below, Chapter I.F.2.

[130]August Freiherr von Gall, ed., *Der Hebräische Pentateuch der Samaritaner* (Giessen: Alfred Töpelmann, 1918).

[131]*Ibid,* pp. LXVIII-LXIX.

[132]K. Elliger and W. Rudolph, eds., *Biblia Hebraica Stuttgartensia* (Stuttgart: Deutsche Bibelstiftung, 1967-1977).

Because Wevers' text agrees in the main with that of Rahlfs,[133] I have followed Rahlfs' text for citations of Exodus where $\mathbf{Q^n}$ is not extant. I have consulted the apparatus of Brooke-McLean[134] for variants. For the rest of the Bible, the Göttingen edition has been consulted where it is available.

2. DEFINITIONS OF TERMS AS USED HEREIN

A *variant* is defined in this dissertation as any disagreement among the four texts $\mathbf{Q^n \, \mathfrak{M}\mathfrak{M}G}$ of Exodus in any passage where $\mathbf{Q^n}$ is extant. The determination of variants is not based simply on disagreement with $\mathfrak{M}$, but rather on any disagreement on the part of any one of the four texts with any of the other three texts. This is done in a deliberate departure from the traditional approach of using $\mathfrak{M}$ as the standard, even if it is only called the "base text" and no value judgment is implied.[135]

The evidence of $\mathbf{Q^n}$ is treated with caution. Only those variants are considered which are actually still preserved on the fragments in ink. The evidence of space requirements and reconstruction is not used for determining variants or other statistics, though it is occasionally referred to as supplementary to what is actually extant.

Each variant has a constant reference consisting of chapter-verse-(Hebrew letter) in boldface characters (e.g., **10:24ℵ**). This special reference is consistently used and may be found in the complete list of the variants in chapter-verse order in Appendix 2.

Verse numbering follows that of von Gall's edition of $\mathfrak{M}$, which agrees with that of *BHS* with one extra feature. A small raised [a] or [b] is used as in von Gall's edition to refer to the major expansions that occur in the textual tradition to which $\mathbf{Q^n}$ and $\mathfrak{M}$ belong. If the verse numbering in a Greek edition and/or the *RSV* differ, that number is provided in brackets. A Hebrew letter following the verse number indicates the number in the series of variants within that verse. Thus, for example, **9:19[b]** refers to a major

---

[133]Alfred Rahlfs, ed., *Septuaginta, Id est Vetus Testamentum graece iuxta LXX interpretes*, 2 vols., 9th ed. (Stuttgart: Württembergische Bibelanstalt, 1971).

[134]Alan England Brooke and Norman McLean, eds., *The Old Testament in Greek According to the Text of Codex Vaticanus, Supplemented from Other Uncial Manuscripts, with a Critical Apparatus Containing the Variants of the Chief Ancient Authorities for the Text of the Septuagint*, I, *The Octateuch* (Cambridge: Cambridge University Press, 1906).

[135]As in Tov, "Criteria," p. 430 and n. 4.

expansion, while **9:19ᵇא** indicates the first variant within that expansion between the two texts that preserve it.

This chapter-verse-(Hebrew letter) reference is used consistently throughout the work to identify each variant, which by definition is a place where **Qᵐ** is extant. On the other hand, in contrast to boldface type (e.g., **9:20**), a reference written in lighter type, such as 9:18, refers to a verse in Exodus which exhibits some phenomenon under discussion. In this latter case there is no variant as defined herein: either **Qᵐ** is not extant, or, if it is extant for the word under discussion, there is no variation among the four witnesses, **Qᵐ𝔪𝔐G**. All statistics are based on variants only. Other references are mentioned for comparison only. Once again it must be stressed that "variant" refers to a place where **Qᵐ** is extant and where there is some discrepancy among the four witnesses under investigation.

Purely *orthographical differences* among the three Hebrew witnesses are not included as variants. The orthographical features of the scroll will be fully discussed in the edition in *DJD*.[136] Readings such as the following are considered orthographical in nature and so are excluded from discussion here: מאד\מאדה‎; הם\המה‎; ויאמר\ויואמר\ויאומר‎; אהרן\אהרון‎; אחר\אחרי‎.[137] Similarly, ambiguous forms, such as ידו, which could be singular or plural (defective for ידיו) are also excluded.[138]

Two other features of the scroll should be mentioned because of the role they play in the decipherment and occasionally in the variants. The scribe consistently used dots to show divisions between words. To show divisions between paragraphs he left the rest of the line blank except for a large *waw*, the first letter of the first word of the next section. The rest of the word followed on the right margin of the next line. Such a word is

---

[136]For a sampling already available, see Skehan, "Exodus," pp. 185-187. On p. 183 Skehan stated that the orthograhy of this scroll was a "mild form" of the fuller orthography known from Cave 1. "Its principal peculiarity is the sporadic introduction of the vowel-letter *waw* into forms from which standardized Hebrew orthography would exclude such spelling (זאות, ויאומר, etc.)." See also Purvis, *Origin*, p. 64.

[137]The latter three, strictly speaking, are not orthographical but morphological biforms; since there is no difference in meaning and we cannot be certain about chronological and/or regional differences, they are listed here for convenience.

[138]Cf., e.g., the Qere-Kethib variation את שתי ידיו\את שתי ידו in Lev 16:21.

transcribed here with a *waw* in Palaeo-Hebrew script, ⴕ, to show that it was large and marked a paragraph division; followed by a diagonal slash, \, to indicate a new line; followed by the rest of the word; hence: ⴕ\וידבר. Differences in paragraph divisions are not discussed here; see the edition.

Preferable readings can be determined only with probability.   The degree of likelihood is indicated in the discussion. Only those readings have been labeled preferable where there is a relatively high degree of confidence. Obviously this is a subjective matter. Some principles will be discussed in the following section.

Synonymous variants are those variants for which no preferable reading can be determined even with probability.   They are different legitimate ways of expressing the same idea. Some variants cannot be said to be clearly preferable because of either the fluidity of the Hebrew language or our lack of knowledge of its usage. Others cannot be determined because both the longer and the shorter versions are equally acceptable, and we cannot be sure whether omission or expansion has taken place.

When one of the four texts is said to preserve a particular reading *uniquely,* this must of course be interpreted properly. The word can only mean that only one *of these four texts* has the reading. As Tov has so clearly reminded us, we have access to only a few of the scrolls of Exodus that were in use in the Second Temple period, and so we cannot hope to achieve a correct assessment of the entire picture.

> ...these relationships are necessarily misjudged because of the fragmentary status of the preserved evidence. In other words, we claim that all relations between any two preserved sources, especially agreements, cannot be viewed correctly because these sources are but two constituents of an enormous structure and their exact place in that structure can never be determined. In the light of the uncertainty with regard to the missing constituents of the structure, all emphasis laid on agreements between any two sources is misleading. We are not saying that the agreements and disagreements among MT, Sam. Pent., LXX and Qumran Scrolls must not be examined, but we claim that the results of this examination are of limited value. After all, the mentioned sources are merely individual witnesses of the biblical text, while other witnesses (possibly the majority) have not been preserved. In formulaic terms, relationships among the known sources a, b, c, (e.g., a=b≠c)

must also take unknown sources (d, e, f, n) into consideration.[139]

Thus we are hampered by the fragmentary nature of our knowledge in two different ways. First, Q^a itself is fragmentary, with the result that our investigation of the text of Exodus will necessarily have a random character. All variants to be discussed are in those scraps of leather which happen to have been preserved by the vicissitudes of history and nature.

Second, even the four witnesses $Q^a \mathfrak{m} \mathfrak{M} G$ provide only fragmentary evidence for the text of Exodus. As Tov has pointed out, every formula in this study, such as $Q^a = \mathfrak{m} \neq \mathfrak{M} G$, should be recognized for what it is: a fragmentary -- and tantalizing -- remnant of the actual situation in the Second Commonwealth. In order to advance one small step to offset this lack, the readings of other Qumran scrolls of Exodus have been given where Skehan included them in his notes.

3. CRITERIA USED IN THE EVALUATION OF VARIANTS

The project of evaluating the variants in an effort to determine which readings are preferable has been undertaken in the knowledge that there is no consensus that an *Urtext* ever existed, or that if it did, it is now possible for us to get back to it. Regarding the first, more theoretical question, Talmon has said:

> All we can say is that from the very first stage of manuscript transmission of the Old Testament text the material which is available to us witnesses to a wide variety of textual traditions which seemingly mirror fairly exactly the state of affairs which obtained in the pre-manuscript state of transmission. In other words, the extant evidence imposes on us the conclusion that from the very first stage of its manuscript transmission, the Old Testament text was known in a variety of traditions which differed from each other to a greater or less degree.[140]

Regarding the second, more practical question, Talmon has said:

> The limited flux of the textual transmission of the Bible appears to be a legitimate and accepted phenomenon of ancient scribal tradition and not a matter which resulted from sheer incompetence or professional laxity. This fact, and our ignorance of literary standards and norms practised in the

---

[139]Tov, "Outlook," pp. 26-27 n. 70.
[140]Talmon, "Text," p. 198.

crucial period of the second half-millennium B.C.E., seems forever to proscribe any endeavour to restitute an assumed original of the biblical books.[141]

Yet while he thus discards the notion of an original text of any given book, Talmon himself labors to establish the more original or the preferable text in individual readings.[142] My attempts along this same line should not be interpreted primarily as an argument for or against in the theoretical debate about the existence of an *Urtext.* I would need a much broader base of evidence before I would personally be in a position to make such a general decision. I am seeking to determine only whether in individual variants a preferable reading can be established.

On the other hand, having evaluated the variants involved in this study it does seem to me that none of them <u>requires</u> us to reject the possibility of an *Urtext.* Of the variants which have been judged secondary, it is usually easy to understand how they could have arisen from the reading judged pref-erable. Of the synonymous variants, it is usually easy to imagine that one of them was original and the other arose from that original. The problem is in knowing which is which. In other words, the variants that I have worked with do not seem to raise insuperable problems to the notion of an *Urtext* on a theoretical level. Whether or not it is historically accurate to say that there was an *Urtext,* it at least seems theoretically possible, on the basis of the readings encountered in this study, to imagine that there was one.

As for the practical aspects of the issue, I am well aware of the difficulties involved when we today seek to choose among variant readings; hence the existence of Chapter III, which discusses "synonymous variants" (see below). In matters of variations in grammatical and syntactical matters, phraseology, etc., it often seems impossible at this distance to make a choice. In matters of longer vs. shorter text, the question arises: did Scribe A expand the text here, or did Scribe B shorten it?

Over the centuries several rules have been developed in an attempt to give objective guidance to the textual critic in choosing among variant

---

[141]Talmon, "Study," p. 326.

[142]E.g., Talmon, "Aspects." For his part, Tov expresses the task in this way: "We shall not be able to reconstruct the *Urtext* of any given biblical book, but it is possible, and certainly legitimate, to reconstruct elements of that text, that is, individual readings" (Emanuel Tov, "Criteria for Evaluating Textual Readings: The Limitations of Textual Rules," *HTR* 75 [1982], 429-448; quotation from p. 432 [hereafter cited as: Tov,"Criteria"]).

readings.[143] These have traditionally been of two kinds. <u>External</u> criteria relate to the text in which the variant is found, and include a preference for some texts, most especially 𝕸, over others, and a preference for a reading that is attested broadly. On the other hand, it is generally acknowledged that manuscripts are to be weighed, not counted. Thus when a number of witnesses that are closely related to each other agree in a reading, that seemingly broad attestation counts for much less than if texts which are not so closely related agree.   <u>Internal</u> criteria relate to the variant itself and include preference for the following: the reading which can explain the origin of the others, the shorter reading, and the more difficult reading.

Tov has recently discussed these rules and found them wanting. He rejects the validity of external criteria completely, finds the logic behind some of the internal criteria questionable (especially preference for the shorter reading and for the more difficult reading) and shows that they are applicable in "only a small fraction of the readings which need to be evaluated."[144]   But perhaps his most damaging criticism is that the rules cannot work in the first place: they cannot make the task of the textual critic objective. "The evaluation of readings remains the most subjective part of the textual procedure."[145]

Tov concludes that in this highly subjective task the textual critic has "very little external guidance." There are, however, factors to be taken into consideration in the evaluation, particularly "the language, style, and content of both the immediate context and of the literary unit."[146]   This involves attention to

> the language and vocabulary of the Bible as a whole as well as
> of individual literary units, the exegesis of individual verses,
> chapters, and books, and the general content and ideas of a
> given unit or book, including areas such as biblical history and
> geography. In short, one has to reckon with the whole spectrum
> of disciplines covered by biblical philology. In addition to
> these, the scholar must be aware of the intricacies of the

---

[143]See, for example, the recent listing in the introductory text by Ralph W. Klein, *Textual Criticism of the Old Testament: The Septuagint after Qumran,* Guides to Biblical Scholarship, ed. Gene M. Tucker (Philadelphia: Fortress Press, 1974), pp. 73-84.

[144]Tov, "Criteria," p. 444.

[145] *Ibid.*

[146] *Ibid.,* p. 445.

textual transmission, in particular of the types of errors made
in the course of that transmission.[147]

The main guide for the textual critic is not, Tov concludes, abstract rules,
but one's own common sense.[148] If this seems to some to be an unfortunate
phrase, all the more so in the light of Tov's own very careful and painstaking
work of evaluating readings,[149] his description on the preceding page may do
more justice to his actual approach:

> ...textual evaluation cannot be bound by any fixed rules. It is an
> *art* in the full sense of the word. It is a *habit* which can be
> developed. It is guided by *intuition* based on much experience.
> It is the art of defining the problems, of finding arguments for
> and against the originality of readings.   Indeed, the
> quintessence of textual evaluation is the formulation and
> weighing of these arguments.[150]

In my evaluation of readings I have kept these traditional rules in
mind, but rather than absolutizing them or using them as automatically
applicable I have considered them to be rough "rules of thumb,"
generalizations which need to be held in balance with the specifics of each
reading.   The goal has been not a mechanical, "blanket" use of rules but a
"disciplined, practiced judgment" on the basis of "immersion in the
character of the text."[151]

This "immersion in the character of the text" seeks to find criteria
for evaluation of each reading on its own merits, criteria such as contextual
and grammatical considerations, Hebrew and Greek style in the book of
Exodus and to a lesser extent in the rest of the Torah, the characteristics of
each of the four texts as they emerge during the course of the investigation,
the character of the text of Exodus as it becomes apparent by inference and
deduction, and finally on patterns that emerge, patterns that begin to
suggest that there were some scribal tendencies which may be called

---

[147] *Ibid.*

[148] *Ibid.*, p. 446. In note 56 on that page Tov cites in his defense "the
seventeenth-century scholar Bentley" as quoted in L. Bieler, *The
Grammarian's Craft: An Introduction to Textual Criticism* (Classical Folia,
Studies in the Christian Perpetuation of the Classics; New York: Catholic
Classical Association of Greater New York, n.d.), p. 45.

[149]See, for example, his *Septuagint.*

[150]Tov, "Criteria," p. 445.

[151]Eugene Ulrich has described the art of textual criticism thus in
private conversations.

"typical." Thus there is a certain reciprocal movement during the course of the investigation, movement from the individual reading to the general pattern that has already become apparent, and back again.

An example may be given regarding "the more difficult reading." One problem with the blanket use of this rule is that most scribal errors produce "more difficult readings." It has seemed more helpful to me to distinguish actual errors, which have produced readings that are grammatically or syntactically wrong (to the best of our knowledge from this distance), from readings which appear to be possible but not quite smooth. In the case of errors, one normally attributes the correct reading to the composer or editor and the error to scribes. But in the case of readings that have made a text read more smoothly, one normally attributes the less smooth reading to the composer or editor and the more smooth, more flowing, more consistent reading to a scribe.

This issue is a central one in the evaluation of 𝕸. Scholars have long attributed to the Samaritan Pentateuch such tendencies as these: modernizing grammatical and syntactical features; introducing such features as conjunctions, explicit subjects and objects, signs of the accusative for clarification; creating consistency between, for instance, plural subjects and their verbs.[152] I began my evaluation aware of these traditional claims and determined to check them against the data that would arise in connection with the extant parts of 𝐐ᵐ. I have decided that there is a valid distinction between actual errors, i.e. "[impossibly] difficult readings" due to scribal mistakes, and preferable readings, i.e. "[slightly] more difficult readings" attributable to authors and editors; and that 𝕸 does indeed preserve a scribal tradition that exercised the freedom to make small alterations for the sake of what was to them the smoother reading. This will become clear in the discussions of the individual readings.

Another issue especially crucial in this study has been that of "the shorter reading." The standard text-critical practice is to opt for the shorter reading when no reason for accidental omission can be found, on the theory that whatever freedom scribes did have, freedom to shorten the text

---

152See, e.g., Bruce K. Waltke, "The Samaritan Pentateuch and the Text of the Old Testament," *New Perspectives on the Old Testament,* ed. J. Barton Payne (Waco, TX: Word, 1970), pp. 212-220.

was not among them.[153]   Though I was not convinced of the soundness of
that argument when I began, since the biblical scribes did not leave us
explanations of their principles, I nevertheless launched on this
investigation willing to be guided by my predecessors, in order to test their
approach to variants involving length of text.

Having completed the evaluation of all of the variants, it does seem
that that approach has been to some extent vindicated.   To note how
carefully the text has been treated on the one hand, and on the other to see a
pattern of longer vs. shorter readings emerging, is to feel that -- at least in
Exodus, and at least in these four witnesses -- the wisdom of the
traditional approach has been to a large extent confirmed.

These issues -- the careful treatment of the text and the types of
expansions -- will be discussed fully in Chapter VI, because they pertain to
scribal practices and attitudes. For now, suffice it to say that when a large
proportion of longer readings can be judged to have arisen out of a desire to
enhance the narrative, or to emphasize a point, or to clarify or make more
explicit, then the results of the evaluation confirm the approach taken.

There remain, however, questions about how to deal with these longer
readings, even once they have been labeled expansions. These questions take
on a special significance in the analysis of $\mathbf{Q^a}$ and $\mathbf{m}$, for some forms of
expansionism in these texts were clearly undertaken according to a careful
pattern, and thus with deliberation and purpose, and with an eye to the
entire book of Exodus or even to the rest of the Pentateuch. Furthermore, as
the discussion of these major expansions in Chapter V.A.3 will show, they
were added to a text that was very much like what we call the "proto-
Massoretic" text. Thus we are faced with the fact that the book of Exodus
exists in two forms which differ, not because of random scribal accretions

---

[153]At least one text critic has questioned this practice in recent
years. See James R. Royse, "Scribal Habits in the Transmission of New
Testament Texts," in *The Critical Study of Sacred Texts,* ed. Wendy Doniger
O'Flaherty, Berkeley Religious Studies Series (Berkeley: Graduate
Theological Union, 1979), pp. 139-161. It seems to me that his findings
should be discussed among Old Testament textual critics as well, and I have
been glad to see that Tov cited his article ("Criteria," p. 441). Of course,
findings in New Testament text-critical study are not automatically
transferable to the Old Testament field. Yet as was true in Gooding's
adaptation of Colwell's criteria for text families (see above, section I.C), it
may at least be profitable to bring the matter to discussion.

or alterations, but according to a pattern. How are we to treat such differences?

While Tov states that "at a certain point in time, the literary growth of the biblical books necessarily ended, at least for those who accepted the present canonical form of the books as final," after which point "the actual textual transmission began," he explicitly excepts "the major changes" in 4QNum[b], **Q[m]**, and 𝕾, "whose idiosyncracies were added to the proto-Masoretic base text."[154] He appears to make this exception because he judges that these idiosyncratic major expansions are of a literary character rather than a transmissional nature. He describes this "actual textual transmission" in all other cases thus:

> From this point onwards, scribes merely copied the biblical books, and although in the course of that process many ele-ments were altered, added, and omitted, certainly in the first generations, these changes were limited to mere details.[155]

This brings up the issue again whether there can be a distinction made between "literary" and "transmissional," or "creative" and "mechanical," or "redactional" and "scribal." Were scribal activities restricted in fact to "mere details"? Should changes such as the major expansions be considered literary or scribal?   Can we date these practices to specific eras or centuries? Such issues will be discussed in Chapter VI, concerning scribal practice, when all of the variants have been evaluated and classified and when patterns can be discerned.

Also involved in the matter of preferability of reading is the question: "preferable for whom?"   **Q[m]** has been hidden away for two thousand years, but each of the other texts has been and continues to be the canonical text of a religious community. When one reading is judged "preferable" on text-critical grounds, it must be remembered that the "secondary" reading is in fact "preferable" for one or more particular religious communities. Whether for purely accidental historical reasons or because of an informed preference, this "secondary" reading is part of their Scripture and to be respected on religious and sociological grounds.

---

[154]Tov, "Criteria," p. 431 and n. 5. Note that Tov accepts the *Urtext* theory: "At the beginning of the textual transmission, we thus posit one copy which incorporated the final literary product, and this text may, for the sake of convenience, be called the *Urtext* of the biblical books. This *Urtext,* then, is the ultimate goal of our text-critical analysis" (pp. 431f.).

[155]*Ibid.,* p. 431.

Another aspect of this issue has been: are such major expansions as have been mentioned above limited to $\mathbf{Q}^\mathbf{m}$ and 𝖚, or do either of the other two texts share the same characteristics as well?   If, for example, the text that the Jews have treasured as their canonical text is judged by the same criteria as $\mathbf{Q}^\mathbf{m}$𝖚, will it turn out to have any of these major, "literary" expansions?

Such issues will be taken up again in the final chapter. For now, let us return from these larger issues to the particular question of the "preferable reading." Despite all the effort that has been taken to determine the "contextually most appropriate reading,"[156] it is possible to state the preferable reading only as a matter of probability.   Varying degrees of confidence will be expressed, ranging from "almost certainly" to "probably." Many decisions are debatable, as various arguments seem stronger to various critics. Nevertheless some decisions must be made on the basis of evidence available to us and in harmony with common text-critical theories at this stage in our knowledge.   Whether or not the decisions regarding preferability are deemed acceptable is secondary to the primary goal of presenting all relevant data so that all readers can reach their own decisions.

Turning to the practical matters involved in determining preferability, the process of immersion in the text and context requires the investigation of the style of the rest of the book of Exodus, and sometimes of the Torah, or even of the entire Old Testament. This calls for the use of lexicons, grammatical aids, and concordances. The reference works used are listed in the second section of the Bibliography.

There is no concordance for 𝖚, so that one must work from a concordance for 𝖒, in this case, Mandelkern. I have, however, carefully compared von Gall's edition of 𝖚 with the *BHS* edition of 𝖒, so that I am able to supplement the information in Mandelkern.

Statistics for 𝖒 are based on Mandelkern's concordance. Likewise, statistics for 𝐆 are based on Hatch-Redpath.

4. SURVEY OF THIS STUDY

Chapter II lists all the variants for which the <u>preferable reading</u> can be determined with a fair degree of confidence and discusses the more significant ones.

---

[156]Tov, "Criteria," p. 446.

The preferable readings are arranged in two ways. First, all preferable readings preserved in the same text or group of texts are grouped together, beginning with those preserved in the scroll and continuing in the order 𝕴𝕴𝕴𝕸𝕲 -- i.e., beginning with the text most like the scroll. This outline prepares the way for Chapter IV, where the implications for textual affiliation will be discussed.

Within that major grouping, variants are classified according to the type of preferable reading involved, e.g., shorter, longer, less familiar word. It should be stressed, especially in the light of the preceding section, that this system of classification is not meant to be a substitute for a careful evaluation of all of the evidence, or an appeal to an abstract rule. Rather, each decision about preferability has been made first and on its own terms. Subsequently patterns were sometimes found, and it was deemed helpful to categorize preferable readings preserved by each text or group of texts in order to give indication of the nature of that text or group. This outline prepares the way both for Chapter V, where the character of each text is discussed, and for Chapter VI, where scribal practices are discussed.

Chapter III continues the evaluation of readings, listing those for which the preferable reading cannot be established. These readings have a roughly equivalent claim on preferability. Usually this means that either or any one of them could have been the original. Sometimes it may mean that both of them are most likely secondary.

These synonymous variants are organized in the same way as the preferable readings in Chapter II: first by their attestation, and second by their type. Again, the major outline prepares for Chapter IV on textual affiliation, and the subordinate outline prepares for Chapter V on the character of each text and Chapter VI on scribal practices.

Chapter IV will bring together the evidence from Chapters II and III for the determination of textual affiliation. What patterns, if any, can be recognized in the similarities and dissimilarities among the four witnesses? Are they merely random, or is there some stemmatic relationship? How close is 𝕼ᵃ to 𝕴𝕴𝕴? How close is it to 𝕸? Where does 𝕲 fit in?

Here Gooding's and Tov's reflections regarding the assessment of variant readings[157] will be followed. Secondary readings will be given more

---

[157]See above, I.C.

weight than preferable readings; secondary readings peculiar to the group of texts will be given more weight than secondary readings shared with other texts as well. Secondary readings will be further analyzed to determine whether they point to a causal relationship between the sources or whether they appear to be merely typical exegetical alterations or expansions which various scribes and/or translators may have made independently. Disagreements among texts will be considered as much as agreements. And unique readings of each text will be shown.

Chapter V will bring together whatever new light the analysis of **Q**ᵐ has shed on the nature of each of the four textual witnesses. No attempt is made to discuss the other three witnesses in general, but only as the evidence of **Q**ᵐ has added to our knowledge.

After each witness is discussed individually, an attempt will be made to describe what can be inferred from Chapters II – V regarding the early history of the text of Exodus.

Chapter VI will present analysis of and reflection on the evidence that has been provided regarding editorial and scribal practices in the Second Commonwealth, especially with regard to the degree of freedom which scribes of that period exercised in copying biblical scrolls. Talmon has claimed that scribes had some degree of freedom in choice and order of words and phrases, and Skehan has claimed freedom in expansion and harmonization.[158] Both that freedom and the limits of that freedom need to be investigated.

In this respect we will ask: How deliberate were these changes? Was the scribe operating on a conscious level in this variant, was he intentionally trying to achieve a certain goal? If so, what was that goal? Or does this seem to have been more spontaneous, did he merely use an expression that was familiar to him, almost unconsciously? Or is there another category in between?

Can any patterns be found in the changes, whether conscious or unconscious? Are there consistent concerns or consistent moves that can be detected?

---

[158]See above, I.E.

What does all this suggest about the approach of the scribe toward his text and toward his task? Can we learn anything about his attitude toward the Bible?

Chapter VII will briefly summarize the conclusions about each of the questions dealt with in the study: the nature of each of the four texts; the early history of the text of Exodus; editorial and scribal practice; text-types; and finally, the question which lurks behind this entire investigation: the origins of Samaritanism and its relation to other communities in Palestine during the period known from the Jewish perspective as the Second Commonwealth.

Appendix 1 lists all the passages extant in Q^m. It should be noted that a verse is listed if any portion of it at all, even one letter, appears on the leather.

Appendix 2 lists all the variants in chapter-verse order, showing agreement and disagreement among the four texts. If one reading has been chosen as preferable, the siglum is underlined and the secondary reading is characterized with a symbol. If the readings are considered synonymous variants, that is indicated. This Appendix also serves as an index, since chapters and sections where the variant is discussed are indicated.

Appendix 3 presents a chart which illustrates Chapter IV regarding textual affiliation by showing how the four texts agree with each other in secondary, synonymous, and preferable readings.

Appendix 4 illustrates Chapter V regarding the nature of each of the four texts individually and in comparison with the others by means of a chart showing the types of readings presented by each text.

CHAPTER II

PREFERABLE READINGS

INTRODUCTION

This chapter lists all the variants for which the preferable reading can be determined with a fair degree of confidence and discusses the more significant ones. The exhaustive list of all variants in chapter-verse order is found in Appendix 2.

For a discussion of criteria used in the evaluation of readings, see Chapter I.F.3. As was suggested there, this evaluation was undertaken in accordance with some traditional text-critical methods, such as the search for the preferable reading in individual variants, as well as some traditional text-critical principles, such as the preference, all things being equal, for the shorter reading. This was done in the spirit of experimentation to see whether this approach would be helpful and whether any conclusions could be reached. At least for these four witnesses to the text of Exodus, the results have to a large extent confirmed the general usefulness of these methods and principles. The findings of this chapter will be analyzed in Chapter V to see what can be learned about the nature of each of the four witnesses and the history of the text of Exodus, and in Chapter VI to see what can be learned about the practices of scribes during the Second Temple period.

The preferable readings are presented in categories according to the text(s) that preserves them. Because the emphasis in this study is on the characteristics of the scroll, 4QpaleoExod^m, and on the question of its affiliation with the already-known textual traditions, the preferable readings that it has preserved are presented first, followed by those of the other three in the order of their relationship to the scroll. The outline of this chapter will contribute secondarily to the question of affiliation as discussed in Chapter IV.

In very few cases can the "preferable" or "original" reading of the text of Exodus be determined with certainty. When one text preserves a clear error, as, for example, is the case in 31:4, where 𝕼ᵐ omits one letter and runs together two words, the critic can be quite certain of the preferability of the reading of the other three texts. Such a variant will not even be discussed in this chapter, however, for nothing is learned from this error as to the original text of Exodus. Rather, this will be discussed in Chapter V.A, under the rubric of the character of the text of $\mathbf{Q}^{\pi}$, and in Chapter VI, under the rubric of the nature of scribal practices during the last one or two centuries B.C.E.

At the other end of the spectrum is the much larger group of variants for which it is impossible even to suggest the preferable reading. In this analysis such readings are labeled "synonymous variants," meaning that two or more readings appear to have a similar claim on originality, for they are merely different good ways of expressing the same thing. The significance of synonymous variants lies not so much in the discussion of the original text of Exodus as in the question of affiliation of the texts of Exodus. These variants will be discussed in Chapter III.

In the middle of the spectrum are a host of variants for which the preferable reading can be determined with a high degree of confidence. Many of these will be discussed. Those which are too slight to merit discussion here are merely listed in this chapter in their appropriate classifications. Many of them also appear in lists according to other systems of classification either in Chapter V, where they contribute to the description of the character of the four texts, or in Chapter VI, where they contribute to the description of Second Temple scribal practices.

For most of the variants discussed in the present chapter, it is possible to state the preferable reading only as a matter of probability. Varying degrees of confidence will be expressed, ranging from "almost certainly" to "probably." Much of this is, of course, debatable. Nevertheless some decisions must be made on the basis of evidence available to us and in harmony with common text-critical assumptions at this stage in our knowledge. Whether or not the decisions as to preferability are deemed acceptable is secondary to the primary goal of presenting all relevant data so that all readers can reach their own decisions.

A. PREFERABLE READINGS PRESERVED IN $\mathbf{Q}^{\pi}$

1. $\mathbf{Q}^{\pi}$ = PREFERABLE

There are five cases in Exodus where $\mathbf{Q}^{\pi}$ is judged to preserve uniquely the preferable reading. In four cases the $\mathbf{Q}^{\pi}$ reading is shorter and the longer reading of the other three texts is considered to be a fairly routine expansion; in the fifth, **Qᵐ** preserves an older form.

a. Where **Qᵐ** Preserves the Shorter Text (One Word)

34:1   הלוח]ות אשר [הל(ו)ח(ו)ת הרא(י)ש(ו)(נ)ים אשר   𝖂𝖒G

Qᵐ ≠ 𝖂𝖒G

As far as the sense is concerned, if this shorter reading were found in **𝖒**, there would be little debate as to its originality. It would be pointed out that the extra word is completely unnecessary in the context, since כראשנים appears in the preceding clause and since this occurrence of הלחת is further defined by the words אשר שברת, and that this is precisely the sort of minor expansion to which texts were subjected in an effort to clarify what was already clear.

There is, however, one small complicating factor. In **Qᵐ** the spacing of the column placed כראשנים precisely above the spot where הראשנים would have been written if it had been included. Thus there is a slight possibility that somehow the scribe's attention was drawn to the line above and that he failed to write the second ראשנים that was indeed in his *Vorlage*.

While the possibility must not be totally discounted, it seems more likely that the word was added. The fact that three witnesses agree in the longer reading is not decisive, since, as will become clear, this is the sort of word that frequently was added in for clarification. If this is indeed an expansion, it could easily have taken place early enough in the textual tradition so that all three of the other extant witnesses preserve it in dependence on that one scribe, or else two or three scribes could easily have added it independently.

32:7   רד [רד לך [𝖂𝖒; Βαδιζε καταβηθι το ταχος εντευθεν **G**

Qᵐ ≠ 𝖂𝖒 ≠ **G**

The shortest text is considered the original here because there is no audial or visual similarity in either the Palaeo-Hebrew or the square script which would have given rise to parablepsis. More positively, as will become especially clear in the discussion of secondary readings shared by **Qᵐ** and **𝖂**, some of the scribes who copied the text of Exodus were influenced by parallel passages in Deuteronomy. Presumably a study of Deuteronomy would show that the opposite was also true, so that the texts of both books grew and changed reciprocally. Consider the following:

	Exod 32:7ב		Deut 9:12
Q[?]		רד	☐
ɯ		לך רד	קום רד מהר מזה
m		לך רד	קום רד מהר מזה
G	Βαδιζε καταβηθι το ταχος		Αναστηθι καταβηθι το ταχος
	εντευθεν		εντευθεν

It is important to note that expansion has taken place in three traditions here in Exod 32:7 and possibly in three at Deut 9:12. In Exod 32:7 **Q[?]**, although generally expansionist, is alone in preserving the original, shorter reading. Both **ɯ** and **m** are expansionist here. And although **G** is even longer than **ɯm** here, in Deut 9:12 it preserves exactly the same longer text as **ɯm**. There is no reason, then, to suppose that the expansion occurred during the process of translation into Greek or at a later stage in the Greek transmission. It is just as likely that the additions were made at some stage in the development of the Hebrew *Vorlage* behind the Greek translation.

7:2ᶠⁱⁿ ³[ו]אני • [   ] יש[ראל] ישראל ³ואני מארעו ישראל **ɯmG**

Q[?] ≠ **ɯmG**

Only יש[ר appears before a break in the leather, but the lacuna is small enough to make it virtually certain that מארעו is not in this text.

Although it is impossible to be certain, the weight of the evidence is probably on the side of the originality of **Q[?]**. This scribe makes relatively few errors (see Chapter V.A.); there is no similarity of letters which would have given rise to parablepsis; and מארעו is not necessary to the context, while being a typical expansion.

18:27 וילך אל אל [וילך לו אל אל **ɯm**; και απηλθεν εις **G**   **Q[?]/G/** ≠ **ɯm**

In this passage both the originality and the uniqueness of the reading in **Q[?]** are slightly more questionable than in the previous examples. Despite the general accuracy of this scribe, the possibility of parablepsis is somewhat stronger, given the repetition of the *lamed*. On the other hand, according to Gesenius (119s), this use of the preposition was found especially in colloquial and later style, and by far its most frequent use was with the second person pronoun after imperatives. He does give a few examples of the idiom in the third person, including two in the Pentateuch (here and Gen 21:16), as compared with 9 examples in the Pentateuch in the second person. In all 11 cases ⅏ and 𝕸 agree. Except for this one case from Exodus, all the examples are in Genesis or Deuteronomy.

The lack of the pronoun in 𝕲 can lend no more than slight, if any, support to that in 𝐐ᵃ. Of the 9 cases in the imperative, 𝕲 has the pronoun 5 times, always in Deuteronomy and always plural: υμεις as an emphatic nominative in 1:7,40; 2:13; 5:27; and εαυτοις in 1:13 (in Semitic Greek the third plural reflexive often stood for the second plural; [Bl-D §64(1)]). The 3 times that 𝕲 lacks the pronoun are all in Genesis and all singular: לך in 12:1; 22:2; and 27:43. In the ninth passage שבו לכם פה ⅏𝕸 is rendered καθισατε αυτου (Gen 22:5). Thus even when the context is imperatival, 𝕲 only has the pronoun when it is plural, and not always then.

The two cases of this idiom apart from the imperative are Gen 21:16 and here. In Gen 21:16 the three witnesses line up as here: ותלך ותשב לה ⅏𝕸 corresponds to απελθουσα δε εκαθητο. (Mandelkern does not list occurrences of לו, and BDB under ל 5.h.(b) [reflexive use with verbs of motion] does not list the present reading or any others in Exodus, and gives for the Pentateuch only one reference not listed in Gesenius: Num 22:34, where אשובה לי ⅏𝕸 is rendered αποστραφησομαι.)

Thus, if it seems impossible to draw any certain conclusions, nevertheless the weight of the evidence points in favor of the absence of the pronoun, as in 𝐐ᵃ. If the reading with לו were indeed the original and lost in 𝐐ᵃ by parablepsis, it would apparently represent a rare usage because the context is neither imperatival, colloquial, nor late. The fact that 𝕲 does not have the pronoun says little about its *Vorlage,* precisely because this is such an unusual expression and because it is hard to imagine how it could have been expressed in Greek. In the absence of either imperative or conversation, there would be little point in the emphatic nominative. Thus, 𝐐ᵃ probably retains the preferable reading, and the evidence of 𝕲 is ambiguous.

b. Where 𝐐ᵃ Preserves an Older Form

21:6   אדניו] אדניו 1° ⅏𝕸: ο κυριος αυτου 𝕲   𝐐ᵃ ≠ ⅏𝕸: 𝕲?

The plural form of ⅏ and 𝕸 is an example of the plural of excellence or of majesty (cf. Gesenius 124 i; 145 h) or the intensive plural of rank (cf. *BDB*) which occurs throughout the OT even for human masters. It is used with אדן and בעל consistently in ⅏ and 𝕸 in Exod 21:4,4,6,8,29, and 32, each time with the suffix of the second or third person. In 21:5, with the first person suffix, the consonantal text is ambiguous, but it is pointed by the Massoretes as singular, according to the consistent pattern noted by Gesenius and *BDB* for the first person. $\mathbf{Q^m}$ is extant only here, so that it cannot be checked for consistency. $\mathbf{G}$ renders with the singular in each case, according to the sense. Thus its *Vorlage* cannot be determined.

On the assumption that this is a convention that developed within the Hebrew language, the singular suffix is considered to preserve the older form and to be original.

<u>Summary</u>:   There are five readings, then, where $\mathbf{Q^m}$ appears to be unique in preserving the preferable reading. In one (21:6) $\mathbf{Q^m}$ may well preserve an older form. In the other four $\mathbf{Q^m}$ is shorter. This conclusion should be kept in mind later when we look at the many cases of expansionism in $\mathbf{Q^m}$.

2. $\mathbf{Q^m}$ ய = PREFERABLE
There are two preferable readings preserved by $\mathbf{Q^m}$ and ய alone, both representing small errors on the part of $\mathbf{m}$.

a. *Where Q^mய Preserve the Correct Word*

16:34   אל מ]שה [ய א[ת מ]שה אל משה $\mathbf{m}$; τω Μωυση $\mathbf{G}$ $\mathbf{Q^m}$ய ≠ $\mathbf{m}$; $\mathbf{G}$?
The context here is: צוה יהוה את משה. Of the 40 occurrences of צוה without suffix in Exodus, it is followed in $\mathbf{m}$ by the accusative 38 times, by -ל once (1:22), and by אל only here. ய agrees with $\mathbf{m}$ the other 39 times; only here is there a discrepancy between the two. $\mathbf{G}$ consistently translates with the dative. According to *BHS*, both Cairo and Targ^J read את here. Because of the consistency of style in Exodus, the $\mathbf{m}$ reading is considered a scribal error, perhaps dating to the medieval period, as suggested by the Cairo reading.   The $\mathbf{G}$ *Vorlage* cannot be determined because this variation cannot be reflected in Greek.

18:23   אל מקו]מו [ய על מקמו $\mathbf{m}$; εις τον εαυτου τοπον $\mathbf{G}$
                                    $\mathbf{Q^m}$ய(G) ≠ $\mathbf{m}$
Here the context is: וגם כל העם הזה אל מקמו יבא בשלום. Again the likelihood is that $\mathbf{m}$ preserves a scribal errror, this one facilitated by the loss of the distinction between א and ע, especially late in the Second Temple period. 4QSam^c preserves a case where a scribe wrote ע erroneously

and then corrected it to א.[1]   BDB lists 16 occurrences in 𝔐 of the Torah where על occurs in the sense of "direction towards" with verbs of motion [7.c.(a)]. Of the 16, 𝔚 = 𝔐 10 times, has אל 5 times, and the evidence is mixed in the sixteenth (Gen 38:12: -ל 𝔚ᵉᵈ, אל 10 MSS, על 9 MSS).

Of the 10 𝔚 = 𝔐 agreements, 𝔊 reads επι 4 times, εις 2 times, προς once, dative once, paraphrases once, and reads εως once, in Gen 49:13 (cf. 𝔐ᵃᵖ: Seb nonn Mss Vrs עד!).

Of the 5 cases where 𝔐 reads על but 𝔚 reads אל, 𝔊 reads εις 4 times and προς once. In the sixteenth case mentioned above, Gen 38:12, 𝔊 renders επι. The one occurrence of εως and the frequency of επι point to a literalness of translation and thus lend support to the likelihood that the *Vorlage* of 𝔊 often read אל where 𝔊 has εις. Thus 𝔊 probably supports the reading אל (Qᵃ𝔚) here, against על (𝔐).

Summary: These two cases where Qᵃ𝔚 agree in preserving the preferable reading indicate minor errors in 𝔐. In neither case can the *Vorlage* of 𝔊 be determined with confidence.

3. Qᵃ𝔐 = PREFERABLE
Readings in which Qᵃ and 𝔐 alone preserve the preferable reading include three cases where 𝔚 has a more familiar word and two cases where 𝔚 adds the accusative marker את.

a. Where Qᵃ𝔐 Preserve the Less Familiar Word
There are three variants where Qᵃ𝔐 preserve a less familiar word and 𝔚 has altered it very slightly to a more familiar word.

7:4   [ם]בשפטי[ם 𝔐] במשפטים 𝔚; συν εκδικησει 𝔊   Qᵃ𝔐(𝔊) ≠ 𝔚
The longer word, משפטים, is much more familiar; it occurs 74 times in the 𝔐 of the Torah alone, whereas the shorter word, שפטים, occurs only 4 times. 𝔐's usage of the two plural nouns is quite consistent within the Torah. משפטים is used 31 times, always with the meaning "laws," and almost always occurring with חקים and/or מצוות. שפטים, on the other

---

[1]Eugene Ulrich, "4QSamᶜ: A Fragmentary Manuscript of 2 Samuel 14-15 from the Scribe of the *Serek Hay-yahad* (1QS)," *BASOR* 35 (1979) 1-25, especially pp. 3, 5, 7, 15.

hand, is used each of the 4 times, including here, with the meaning "acts of judgment," and in the context of Yahweh's actions rather than laws. Of these 4 times, 𝖆 agrees with 𝖒 twice (Exod 12:12 and Num 33:4) and has the longer word twice (here and in Exod 6:6, where the context is the same). In this case, then, it is 𝖒 (with **Q**ᵃ) rather than 𝖆 which preserves the consistent usage; and it is the consistent usage which is here considered to be the original, for this is a matter of diction, not merely a minor stylistic feature.

Yet it is readily understandable that 𝖆 has משפטים because of the relatively rare occurrence of שפטים. It is also possible that the visual similarity of the two letters מ and ב in both the Palaeo-Hebrew and the square scripts has contributed to the occurrence of this easier reading. In both verses where 𝖆 disagrees with 𝖒 in having the longer word, the preposition ב immediately precedes the word. Thus the secondary reading may be due to a combination of two factors: a more familiar versus a less familiar word and parablepsis due to visual similarity. Another example of parablepsis in 𝖆 where ב and מ occur together may be in 14:27, where 𝖆 has מערים תוך in contrast to מערים בתוך in 𝖒; out of a total of 18 occurrences of בתוך in the 𝖒 of Exodus, this is the only place where 𝖆 does not agree (except for 39:25, where 𝖆 [and **G**] lack a phrase added by 𝖒 as dittography).

It is likely but not certain that **G** agrees with **Q**ᵃ𝖒. The fact that the translator used the singular instead of the plural does not indicate a different *Vorlage* (see Chapter V.D). HR lists εκδικησις as translating the root שפט 12 times, 9 times in Ezekiel and 3 times in the Pentateuch. The 3 in the Pentateuch (here and Exod 12:12; Num 33:4) all correspond to the noun שפט in 𝖒; in Ezekiel the word translates the noun שפט 4 times, the verb שפט once, שפוט once, and the noun משפט 3 times. In the fourth occurrence in the Torah of 𝖒's שפטים, Exod 6:6, **G** has κρισει; this is the sole case of κρισις for שפט in HR; 35 times in the Torah κρισις corresponds to משפט in 𝖒. On the other hand, in the only two cases in Exodus where 𝖒 reads the plural משפטים, 21:1 and 24:3, **G** reads δικαιωματα. Thus it seems more likely that **G** translates the shorter Hebrew form שפטים and supports the preferable reading.

22:25 שלמת 𝖒] שמלת 𝖆; ιματιον **G**   **Q**ᵃ𝖒 ≠ 𝖆; **G**?

In this case as well **Q**ᵃ and 𝖒 preserve the less familiar word. Because שלמה occurs frequently in 𝖒, as well as in **Q**ᵃ here, it is not considered to be a scribal error, but rather to reflect a dialectal or similar variation in the language. According to M, שמלה occurs 18 times in the Torah, and 12 times in the rest of the OT, while שלמה is found 4 times in the Torah and 12 times in the other books. (The distribution of the two is probably not distinctive enough to warrant estimates as to their chronological or geographic relationship.)   Thus as far as the Torah alone is concerned, the reading of **Q𝕸** is by far the more unusual, and it would not be surprising if **𝕴𝕴** slightly altered it to conform to common usage. Indeed in 3 of the 4 passages in the Torah, **𝕴𝕴** consistently and clearly reads שמלה (Exod 22:8, 25; Deut 29:4). The fourth case (Deut 24:13) is somewhat of a mystery.   The text of vG reads בשלמתו and no variant occurs in the first apparatus, where variants affecting the consonantal text belong.   In the second and third apparatus, however, where punctuation and other marks are recorded, both notes read בשמלתו. One suspects a printing error in the text, a suspicion supported by *BHSap.* **𝕴𝕴**^W בשמלתו (i.e. according to B. Walton's edition), as well as several misprints discovered at random throughout vG.[2]

A possible argument for the originality of שמלה here is that it agrees with the form in the immediately following verse, 22:26, in **Q𝕸𝕴𝕴**. On the other hand, these are not necessarily from the same source, for the first verse gives a case law and the second verse gives a motivation for the law. It may well be that the redactor saw no need to create consistency, whereas a later scribe in the **𝕴𝕴** tradition disagreed.

The **G** reading cannot be used in support of either side, since ιματιον is used for both שמלה and שלמה.

---

[2]The following, discovered at random, appear to be misprints in von Gall's edition of Exodus in the Samaritan Pentateuch:

26:33	דפרכת	for	הפרכת
30:4	לברים	for	לבדים	(contrast note in apparatus 3)
27:3	ו עיו	for	ויעיו
27:9	באתה	for	באמה	(contrast note in apparatus 1)
27:11	לסף	for	כסף	(contrast note in apparatus 3)
27:19^b	לשדת	for	לשרת

The following have also been discovered at random in *BHS* for Exodus:

6:25	פינהס	for	פינחס
37:18	מעדים	for	מעדיה

21:25   כויה[כויה תחת מכוה **m]** מכוה תחת מכוה **w**; κατακαυμα αντι
κατακαυματος **G**   **Q²m ≠ w; G?**

The situation is not so clear here, because both words, כויה and מכוה, are rare in biblical usage. כויה occurs only the 2 times in this one verse, and only in **m**. מכוה occurs 5 times in **m**, but all in one passage, Lev 13:24-28. **w** has מכוה all 7 times. Since it is characteristic of **w** to simplify and create consistency, its reading is here considered secondary. **G** renders κατακαυμα all 7 times, but its evidence is ambiguous.

*b. Where **Q²m** Preserve the Shorter Reading (One Word)*

25:29   קע]ר[תי]ו **m]** pr את **w**; τα τρυβλια αυτης **G**   **Q²m ≠ w; G?**
28:39   הכתנת **m]** pr את **w**; των χιτωνων **G**   **Q²m ≠ w; G?**

These two readings will be discussed in Chapter V.B to shed light on the nature of **w**.

Summary: These five readings where **Q²m** agree in preserving the preferable text include three cases where **w** has made a very slight alteration to a more familiar word and two cases where **w** has added a very minor word. In four readings the difference cannot be detected in Greek and in the fifth the *Vorlage* can be established only with probability.

4. **Q²G** = PREFERABLE

There are no instances preserved in the scroll where **Q²** and **G** alone agree in having the preferable reading.

5. **Q²wm** = PREFERABLE

These are the readings in which all three of the Hebrew texts under consideration agree against the Greek in preserving what is most likely the preferable text. In each case it has been judged that the variant preserved in the Greek is most likely to be attributed to its Hebrew *Vorlage* rather than to the translational process or the transmission of the Greek MSS, because similar variants are also attested among Hebrew MSS in other places. Thus, for instance, since similar differences in length of text and similar differences in word order occur elsewhere between **m** and **w**, it is likely that these differences between **wm** on the one hand and **G** on the other arose at the Hebrew stage.

a. Where Q^a 𝕸𝔐 Preserve the Correct Word

In three cases Q^a 𝕸𝔐 preserve the preferable word whereas **G** preserves a corruption.

18:4 פרעה מח[ר]ב מ[ן] **𝕸𝔐**] εκ χειρος Φαραω **G**   Q^a 𝕸𝔐 ≠ **G**

There is nothing similar elsewhere in Exodus: nowhere else does χειρ render חרב, though it is used 85 times for יד, 7 times for כף, and once each for ימין and חפן. חרב occurs 8 times in Exodus, and is rendered ρομφαια (twice), μαχαιρα (3 times), or paraphrastically with φονος or εγχειρι-διον (once each) in the other 7 locations.

Both words fit the context. The reason for the unusual translation here seems to be not paraphrasis but rather either the auditory similarity between the two words חרב and χειρος or else the fact that יד and/or χειρ occur so frequently in the context. The word יד occurs 4 times in this context in 𝕸 and 𝔐 (18:9,10,10,10) and χειρ occurs 6 times besides here (18:8,8,9,9,10,10), all referring to the same event: the rescue of Israel from the hand of Pharaoh and of Egypt. Since חרב is the much more infrequent word in Exodus as a whole and is otherwise lacking in this chapter (although it does occur just 8 verses previously, in 17:13, regarding the Amalekites), it is more likely to have been the preferable.

17:6 זקני ישראל **𝕸𝔐**] των υιων Ισραηλ **G**   Q^a 𝕸𝔐 ≠ **G**

It should be noted that the *BHS* note is in error here: των υιων does not appear in **G** in addition to, but rather instead of, זקני. An argument could be made for the originality of either word. But since Moses has been ordered to take with him some of the <u>elders</u> when he strikes the rock, it is more significant that they be mentioned in this verse as the eyewitnesses of his action. Moreover, a reason for the change lies at hand. Just before this clause it is stated that the <u>people</u> will be able to drink; perhaps a scribe or translator, distracted by the thought of the result of the miracle, rather than the eyewitnesses, wrote the more common designation, "sons of Israel."

18:21א בע]ע **𝕸𝔐**] υπερηφανιαν **G**   Q^a 𝕸𝔐 ≠ **G**

This verse gives Jethro's qualifications for the men to be chosen as judges. "Unjust gain," as in Q^a 𝕸𝔐, seems to be a more apt object of avoidance by judges than "pride," as in **G**.

Looking first at the context, the other three qualities in the list correspond well, which shows that the translator was endeavoring to render faithfully his *Vorlage:*

אנשי חיל	ανδρας δυνατους
יראי אלהים	θεοσεβεις
אנשי אמת	ανδρας δικαιους
שנאי בצע	μισουντας υπερηφανιαν

The third translation shows a small degree of freedom, but the general sense of the desired quality is retained in Greek. The fourth, however, "pride," fails to retain even the general sense of the Hebrew as it is preserved in **Qᵃ⅏ᵯ**, "unjust gain." Since the context has revealed no reason for supposing that the translator intentionally rendered בצע with υπερηφανια the *Vorlage* may have been different.

This judgment on the basis of the context is supported by the translations of בצע in the rest of the OT. Neither בצע nor υπερηφανια occur again in Exodus; elsewhere in the Torah בצע occurs only once (where it is translated χρησιμον; see below), and υπερηφανια only 3 times (where it translates רום, זדון, and עוז). Apart from Exod 18:21א, the noun בצע occurs 22 times in **ᵯ**. Discounting the 5 cases where the text is questionable, the following words are used in **G**: πλεονεξια 4 times; δωρον and δωροληπτης 1 time each; in the same idiom ωφελεια 2 times and χρησιμον and πλεον 1 time each; πληθος 1 time; ανομια/ανομος 3 times; αδικια 1 time; and, strangely, συντελειας at 1 Sam 8:3 and συντετελεσαι at Ezek 22:13. Thus while general terms such as ανομια are used sometimes, this is the only case where a specific different quality is named. In Prov 28:16 the same expression occurs in **ᵯ**: שנאי בצע; **G** renders ο δε μισων αδικιαν.

Because the other three in the list of qualities given in Exod 18:21 are translated accurately and because בצע is translated more faithfully, if sometimes with a rather general expression, elsewhere, the *Vorlage* of **G** here is judged to have been something other than בצע. Because hating "unjust gain" seems a more appropriate quality for a judge than hating "pride," the reading attested by the three, **Qᵃ⅏ᵯ**, is considered to be preferable to that attested by **G** alone.

b. Where $Q^a\mathfrak{M}$ Preserve the Correct Word and Shorter Reading

Thus we have seen three cases where $Q^a\mathfrak{M}$ together appear to have preserved the correct word against **G**. We turn now to a case where in one reading $Q^a\mathfrak{M}$ preserve the correct word as well as the shorter text.

19:10 לך מ"ם] Καταβας διαμαρτυραι **G** $Q^a\mathfrak{M} \neq$ **G**

This example of influence from elsewhere in the context (19:21) involves both the change of one word and the addition of one word, or perhaps better, the displacement of one word by a two-word phrase. This could have taken place during either the Hebrew or the Greek stage. While it may reflect a desire for consistency within a narrative, a comparison of the two verses will show that there is a limit beyond which this desire did not go:

$Q^a\mathfrak{M}$ ויאמר יהוה אל משה] לך אל] העם   19:10
19:10 ειπεν δε κυριος προς Μωυσην Καταβας διαμαρτυραι τω λαω

□Q^a מ"ם   ויאמר יהוה אל משה רד העד בעם   19:21
19:21 και ειπεν ο θεος προς Μωυσην λεγων Καταβας διαμαρτυραι
       τω λαω

It seems more likely, given the differing content of the two verses, that this change was not done deliberately, but inadvertently by a scribe whose mind was getting ahead of his hand.

c. Where $Q^a\mathfrak{M}$ Preserve the Shorter Reading (A Clause or Phrase)

Now that we have seen four cases involving the change of a word in the **G** tradition against $Q^a\mathfrak{M}$, one of them involving expansion as well, we turn to twelve other readings where $Q^a\mathfrak{M}$ preserve the shorter text against **G**.

34:16א

Q^aשׁ𝕸

ולקחת מבנתיו לב[ניך

G   και λαβης των θυγατερων αυτων τοις υιοις σου

Q^aשׁ𝕸

G   και των θυγατερων σου δως τοις υιοις αυτων,

Q^a

שׁ𝕸

וזנו בנתיו אחרי אלהיהן

G   και εκπορνευσωσιν αι θυγατερες σου οπισω των θεων αυτων

Q^aשׁ𝕸

והזנו את בני[ך אחרי אלהיהן

G   και εκπορνευσωσιν τους υιους σου οπισω των θεων αυτων.

Q^aשׁ𝕸 ≠ G

There are two variants in this verse. The lack of the third line in **Q^a** is discussed in Chapter III.B.4. Though that is considered a synonymous variant, the presence of the second line in **G** offers the opportunity to make a decision regarding preferability. The attestation of **Q^aשׁ𝕸**, the fact that the verse makes better sense without the second line, and the possibility of influence from other passages all lead to the conclusion that this clause is an expansion on the part of **G**.

The other three (or two, as in **Q^a**) lines all deal with the effect of foreign wives on native <u>sons</u>; while mentioning sons could naturally lead a scribe to add the mention of <u>daughters</u> for the sake of symmetry, the rest of the verse as it stands in both שׁ and 𝕸 focuses only on sons and their wives. **G** has attempted to remedy this, it appears, by altering "<u>their</u> daughters" to "<u>your</u> daughters"; yet that alteration was not sufficient, since the fourth line still spoke of "their" causing the sons to sin. B and Syh have, apparently, made one further alteration, changing "sons" from accusative to nominative, thereby achieving symmetry.

There is a close parallel to Exod 34:11-16 in Deut 7:1-5. Since Deut 7:3 forbids both the giving and the taking of daughters in foreign marriages, it may have influenced a scribe in Exodus to create a similar symmetry here. Further afield, there is the fact that Ezra 9:12 also mentions both giving and taking daughters, though the issue in that narrative was only the taking of foreign daughters. This may be a helpful analogy illustrating the tendency of some writers and/or scribes to add parallels.

It seems most likely that the scribe expanded the text here. Thus the shorter reading of **Q° 𝔐** is considered preferable.

9:9ג   בכל ארץ מצ]רים **𝔐]** *εν τε τοις ανθρωποις και εν τοις*
τετραποσιν και εν παση γη Αιγυπτου **G**   **Q° 𝔐 ≠ G**

Some variety of the phrase *εν τοις ανθρωποις και εν τοις* *τετραποσιν* occurs 6 times in **G** in Exodus, all clustered in the narratives of the third and sixth plagues, and only 4 corresponding to the Hebrew witnesses:

8:12 [16]	gnats:	command	–	non hab	**𝔐**;	□**Q°**;	hab **G**
8:13 [17]	gnats:	execution	–	hab	**Q° 𝔐**;		hab **G**
8:14 [18]	gnats:	execution	–	hab	**𝔐**;	□**Q°**;	hab **G**
9:9	1°	boils:	command	–	hab	**Q° 𝔐**;	hab **G**
9:9ג	2°	boils:	command	–	non hab	**Q° 𝔐**;	hab **G**
9:10		boils:	execution	–	hab	**Q° 𝔐**;	hab **G**

All four texts in these passages are replete with repetition of other phrases as well: "all the land of Egypt" most frequently, and other phrases two or three times. There seems to be a desire to heighten the miraculous by making the fulfilment of the plague match the wording of Yahweh's command. It would appear that in this effort the tradition preserved in **G** went further and piled up this stock phrase even higher. There is no indication that this necessarily occurred at the stages of translation or transmission of **G**. Repetition characterizes all four texts, including **𝔐**, and expansionism was a feature of redactional and scribal activity in both languages. Thus **Q° 𝔐** appear to preserve the original here, and **G** a typical addition.

9:8ג   לעיני פרעה **𝔐]** *εναντιον Φαραω και εναντιον των*
θεραποντων αυτου **G**   **Q° 𝔐 ≠ G**

The word *θεραπων* occurs 25 times in **G** between Exod 5:21 and 14:8, always in reference to Pharaoh's servants. Four of these times have no correspondence in **𝔐** or **𝔐**. The four are shown here along with other occurrences of the phrase in their contexts. It should be noted that the evidence of **Q°** is treated cautiously. Though reconstruction indicates that the phrase was not included, the scroll is designated "not extant" unless it can be proven on the basis of actual ink preserved, not on the reconstruction, that the addition could not have been there.

7:9   לפני פרעה   𝔐𝔪: ☐Q^a εναντιον Φαραω
  και εναντιον των θερ. αυτου

7:10a   אל/לפני פרעה   𝔐𝔪: ☐Q^a εναντιον Φαραω
  και των θεραποντων αυτου

7:10b   לפני פרעה Q^a𝔐𝔪;
ולפני עבדיו   εναντιον Φαραω
  και εναντιον των θερ. αυτου

9:8ג   לעיני פרעה Q^a𝔐𝔪;
  εναντιον Φαραω
  και εναντιον των θερ. αυτου

14:5   לב(ב) פרעה   𝔐𝔪: ☐Q^a η καρδια Φαραω
ועבדיו   και των θεραποντων αυτου

14:8   לב פ' מלך מצ'   𝔐𝔪: ☐Q^a την καρδιαν Φαραω βασιλεως Αιγ.
  και των θεραποντων αυτου

Curiously, *BHS* notes the addition in **G** here at **9:8ג** but at none of the other three places.

  This is another case of the addition of a stock phrase from the narrative in the **G** tradition. It is difficult to know whether such additions were made almost unthinkingly or whether a deeper level of interest in the narrative is indicated. In these four additions, for example, there may have been a deliberate attempt to improve the telling of the story.

  In the narratives of the pre-plague sign (7:9-10) and of the plague of boils (9:8-10), in both of which the magicians play a large part, a scribe or translator may have wanted the magicians' presence to be emphasized more from the beginning of the pericope. In the case of the plague of boils, it will be suggested that two different textual traditions have slightly altered the text in two different ways in order to stress the discomfiture of the magicians (see II.D).

  In the other plagues in which the magicians also figured, the presence of the servants is indicated in the Hebrew as well as the Greek traditions: for the first plague, see 7:20 and 22; for the second, the emphasis is not on their presence at Pharaoh's court but rather on their suffering the effects of the plague - whether by the hand of Aaron or their own! (compare 7:28, 29; 8:5, 7 with 8:3 [ETT 8:3, 4, 9,11 with 8:7]); for the third plague, the different construction of the narrative precludes any opportunity to refer to the servants; after the plague of boils, when the magicians are completely disgraced, they are never again mentioned specifically.

As for the last addition (14:8), it may be that at the beginning of the Reed Sea narrative the attitude of Pharaoh's servants is emphasized with a view to justifying the destruction of the entire Egyptian army.

There is no indication as to when these additions took place; they could have occurred during either the Hebrew or the Greek stage of transmission, for they represent the kind of expansionism that characterized all the extant traditions to varying degrees.

7:9 והשלך לפני פרעה 𝔐𝔖] και ριψον αυτην επι την γην
     εναντιον Φαραω **G**   𝐐ᵃ𝔖𝔐 ≠ **G**

Every time ριπτειν occurs in the Torah (16 times, 11 of them in Exodus), it is accompanied by an indication of the direction or destination, except in two verses immediately following this variant: 7:10 and 12. (The parallel passages Exod 32:19 and Deut 9:17 give the direction from which.) In the corresponding passages in 𝔖 and 𝔐 the parallel indication is given as well, except in 7:9, 10, and 12. In the two other occurrences of השלך in Exodus that are not translated with ριπτειν, the destination is likewise given both times in 𝔐 and **G**, but only once in 𝔖. There are five passages in Exodus which are very similar:

4:3aα	השליכהו ארצה	𝔖𝔐;	□𝐐ᵃ	ριψον...επι την γην
4:3aβ	וישליכהו ארצה	𝔖𝔐;	□𝐐ᵃ	ερριψεν...επι την γην
7:9	והשלך לפני פרעה	𝐐ᵃ𝔖𝔐;		ριψον...επι την γην εναντιον Φ.
7:10	וישלך...לפני פרעה	𝐐ᵃ𝔖𝔐;		ερριψεν...εναντιον Φαραω
7:12	וישליכו	𝐐ᵃ𝔖𝔐;		ερριψεν

Thus while it seems to be most usual to indicate the direction or destination of the item thrown, 7:12 indicates that it is not essential in either language. While the phrase "before Pharaoh" is not the direction in which the item is thrown, it does indicate where the action took place. Apparently that was enough originally, in 7:9 and 10; and then in 7:12, when the stage was well set, neither indication was needed. Later a scribe, or perhaps the translator, saw fit to add it the first time in this context but not the two later times.

<u>Summary</u>: Three times in the plague narratives, then, we have discovered that a scribe in the tradition behind **G** has added stock phrases, two of them to improve on the telling of the story. Once in a speech of Yahweh an entire clause has been added. A pattern of expansionism is beginning to emerge which will be reinforced as we look at those instances when **G** adds a single, but significant, word.

d. Where Qᵃ𝔲𝔐 Preserve the Shorter Reading (A Significant Word)

Because of the likelihood that these additions occurred in the Hebrew *Vorlage*, the words are counted according to Hebrew rather than Greek. According to this method of calculating, there are six variants where **G** has added one significant word.

11:9   מופתי 𝔲𝔐] μου *τα σημεια και* τα τερατα **G**   **Qᵃ𝔲𝔐 ≠ G**

σημειον translates אות, while τερας translates מופת. There are three passages in Exodus where **G** is fuller, presenting the two nouns together, in contrast to 𝔐, which reads מופת only: 7:9; 11:9, 10. HR is misleading in that it assigns σημειον to אות 16 times in Exodus but these 3 times to מופת. For these three passages HR should print a dash, indicating that there is no corresponding noun in 𝔐.

The word אות stands without a synonym 28 times in the 𝔐 of the Torah, including 14 times in Exodus and 3 times in Deuteronomy. Never in all 28 passages does 𝔲 or **G** add a second noun. In Deut 11:3 all three traditions present two nouns: אותות and מעשים in 𝔲 and 𝔐; σημεια and τερατα in **G**.

The word מופת occurs 14 times in the Torah: 5 times in Exodus and 9 times in Deuteronomy. In Deuteronomy it follows אות all 9 times in all three traditions, but the situation in Exodus is more complex:

	Qᵃ	𝔲	𝔐	G
4:21	☐	המפתים	המפתים	τερατα
7:3	א[תתי...מופתי	אתתי...מופתי	אתתי...מופתי	σημεια...τερατα
7:9	☐	אות ...מופת	מופת	σημειον...τερας
11:9	מופתי	מופתי	מופתי	σημεια...τερατα
11:10	☐	המפתים	המפתים	σημεια...τερατα

Interestingly, A* and many other witnesses have τερατα alone in 11:10, while in 11:9, our variant, all of the Greek witnesses read both nouns.

One possibility is that the translator added σημειον to clarify the meaning of τερας for his readers in Greek. But this seems much less likely since at 4:21, the very first occurrence of τερας in Exodus and indeed in the Torah, it stands alone.   Furthermore the evidence from Deuteronomy and Exodus shows that מופת attracted אות to itself already during the Hebrew stages, whether compositional, redactional, or scribal; hence it is very likely that both words were in the *Vorlage* of **G** at 11:9. Within the Hebrew tradition it could be that the two words made a set formula that frequently appeared together originally (note that in all 14 occurrences the order of the two nouns remains constant in all three traditions) but that one some-times dropped out by error. The situation could have been the opposite, of course: perhaps either אות or מופת sometimes appeared alone, and as time went on scribes tended to level out the tradition by adding in the other noun for the sake of consistency. In line with the usual assumption in text criticism that consistency and fulness are usually due to scribal tendencies, the latter explanation has been accepted and the shorter reading classified as the more original.

28:3   (ו)הר]א בגדי א[ת א **m M**] την στολην *την αγιαν* Ααρων **G**

                                                   Q⁺ m M ≠ G

The word added in this verse is present in all three traditions in the immediately preceding and following verses, and it will be assumed for the purpose of this chapter that it has entered this verse in the tradition repre-sented in **G** because of influence from one or both of those verses. But there is much repetition in all three traditions:

28:2   ועשית בגדי קדש לאהרן אחיך **m M   Q⁺** ⬚
    και ποιησεις στολην αγιαν Ααρων τω αδελφω σου **G**

28:3   ועשו את בגדי אהרן לקדשו לכהנ(ו) לי **m M**
    και ποιησουσιν την στολην την αγιαν Ααρων εις το αγιον,
    εν η ιερατευσει μοι **G**

28:4   ועשו בגדי קדש לאהרן אחיך ולבניו לכהנ(ו) לי **m M   Q⁺** ⬚
    και ποιησουσιν στολας αγιας Ααρων και τοις υιοις αυτου
    εις το ιερατευειν με **G**

In the face of all that repetition of words and phrases, some of the difficulties involved in determining an "original text" become clear. Is it best to reiterate that all three textual traditions are expansionist in Exodus and to leave it at that? How much repetition, whether for emphasis or pedantry, should be attributed to the succession of composers and redactors throughout the literary history of Exodus, and how much to scribes throughout its textual history? In regard to the one word at issue in the present variant, it may be worth noting that if the text originally included it, it could easily have dropped out along the way because the word appeared both immediately before and immediately after "Aaron." But regarding the larger picture, it may be instructive to compare this passage with its counterpart in the fulfillment section of Exodus, 39:1:

ומן התכלת ... עשו בגדי שרד לשרת בקדש

𝔐𝔊 Q⁰□   ויעשו את בגדי הקדש אשר לאהרן כאשר עוה יהוה את משה

και την καταλειφθεισαν ... εποιησαν στολας λειτουργικας Ααρων ωστε λειτουργειν εν αυταις εν τω αγιω. **G**

In 39:1 at least **G** would seem to deserve its reputation for being not quite so repetitious and expansionist in chapters 36–39 as the 𝔐𝔊 traditions.

      In **28:3** the one word "holy" is considered to be an addition, and the shorter reading of **Q⁰𝔐𝔊** is taken as preferable.

32:13א   𝔐𝔊] ככו[כבי ה]שמים   ωσει τα αστρα του ουρανου
        τω πληθει **G**   **Q⁰𝔐𝔊 ≠ G**

      This simile occurs 6 times in the Torah. In Deut 1:10; 10:22; and 28:62 all three traditions agree in preserving לרב = τω πληθει/εις πληθος, while in Gen 22:17 and 26:4 all three agree in lacking the adverbial modifier. Only here, at the one occurrence in Exodus, is there disagreement. Because ב (of לרב) and מ (of השמים) look somewhat similar in Palaeo-Hebrew and very similar in some square script hands, it is possible that the word was lost by homoioteleuton. Yet since the simile can stand without the modifier in both languages, as the examples in Genesis show, it seems more likely that here the shorter reading was the original and that a scribe, whether in Hebrew or in Greek, added in the stock phrase because it was a common expression.

32:15 כת]בים לֻ(וֹ)חֹת לֻ(וֹ)חַת שׁ‎ 𝕸]‎ πλακες λιθιναι γεγραμμεναι **G**

$$\text{Q}^a\text{ ш } \text{𝕸} \neq \text{G}$$

Of the 13 times that these tablets are mentioned in 𝕸 of Exodus, the modifier occurs 5 times in 𝕸 and 6 times in **G**. The only time there is disagreement is here. This is another example of a routine expansion from the context that could have occurred at any point during either the Hebrew or the Greek stage.

28:43ב עוֹ(וֹ)ן‎ ישׂאו ‎ ш‎ 𝕸]‎ επαξονται προς εαυτους αμαρτιαν **G**

$$\text{Q}^a\text{ ш } \text{𝕸} \neq \text{G}$$

The adverbial phrase "upon themselves" is considered an addition to the text which probably occurred during some stage of the Hebrew *Vorlage* of the Greek. This phrase is not necessary to the expression "bear guilt" either in Hebrew or in Greek, and yet it sometimes occurs in both. Thus it need not be attributed to the translator or to a Greek copyist but may be due to a Hebrew copyist. See, for instance, Lev 16:22, where ш𝕸**G** preserve a similar expression: ונשׂא השׂעיר עליו את כל עונתם ‎ ш𝕸

και λημψεται ο χιμαρος εφ εαυτω τας αδικιας αυτων **G**

In Exod 28:38, however, shortly before the present variant, ш, 𝕸, and **G** have the shorter form of this expression, without the adverbial phrase. It is possible that the disagreement among the Greek MSS as to the preposition in the present variant (προς R[ed]; εφ A[+]) preserves disagreement among Hebrew texts between אל and על.

19:24 ב[ם ‎ יפרץ פן‎ ш𝕸]‎ μηποτε απολεση απ αυτων *κυριος* **G**

$$\text{Q}^a\text{ ш } \text{𝕸} \neq \text{G}$$

Here too the addition of the subject is taken as secondary and attributable as likely to a Hebrew copyist as to the Greek translator. It was common for scribes to add explicit subjects, and it may well have been done here by assimilation to the same clause in 19:22, where all three traditions present the subject.

e. Where Q[a]ш𝕸 Preserve the Shorter Reading (A Small Word)

In two of the variants where Q[a]ш𝕸 preserve the shorter reading the addition in **G** is the very minor one of the word "all":

17:13א עמו ואת‎ ш𝕸]‎ και *παντα* τον λαον αυτου **G**   Q[a]ш𝕸 ≠ **G**
18:13א ה[עם‎ ш𝕸]‎ *πας* ο λαος **G**   Q[a]ш𝕸 ≠ **G**

Summary: In sections 5.b-e we have seen **G** expanded once by a phrase which displaced the original word, four times by a clause or phrase, six times by one fairly significant word, and twice by the word "all." Almost all of these have been in narrative passages.

f. Where **Q²𝖌𝖒** Preserve a Phrase Omitted in **G**

We turn now to a passage where **G** has inadvertently omitted a long phrase; this occurs not in a narrative, but in instruction about the tabernacle furnishings.

25:33   ושלשה גבעים משקדים בקנ]ה האחד[כפתר ופרח **𝖌𝖒]** › **G**

Q²𝖌𝖒 ≠ **G**

The longer reading of the three Hebrew traditions has the same phrase twice, the only difference being the initial *waw* in the second phrase. The repetition is required to show the symmetry of the two sides of the menorah, and such repetition is customarily rendered in Greek as well (cf., e.g., the preceding verse, 25:32, where a similar case of repetition is retained in the Greek, although B* and one other MS suffered from parablepsis). Thus **G** or its Hebrew *Vorlage* has apparently suffered parablepsis here: ופרח 1°⁀2°.

g. Where **Q²𝖌𝖒** Preserve a Word Omitted in **G**

The preceding variant involved the accidental omission of seven words; this next variant involves only one word.

34:11א **Q²𝖌𝖒**   שמור לך את אשר אנכי מצו]ך היום [הנני

G ιδου _____ προξεχε συ παντα, οσα εγω εντελλομαι σοι

Q²𝖌𝖒 ≠ **G**

The longer reading with היום is probably original in this case because the word "today" is such an integral part of this Deuteronomic exhortation. Although this is the only occurrence of the אשר clause in Exodus, it occurs very frequently in Deuteronomy. The following chart shows the variations:

	אשר אנכי מצוך היום	אשר אנכי מצוה אתכם היום
𝖒G	18 times	6 times
𝖒	אשר אנכי מצוך ____ 3 times	אשר אנכי מצוה אתכם ____ 5 times

The proportion is quite different in those verses where the plural accusative is used. In these 5 cases there is a great likelihood of parablepsis due to the final *mem* in both words. In all 8 cases of the shorter reading in 𝕸 other witnesses include "today." All or part of the Greek tradition is involved each time, and 4 of the 8 times other witnesses, including 𝕸ᴹˢˢ 𝖂𝐒, as well.

Thus if it is legitimate to infer anything from Deuteronomy, it is that the tendency of 𝐆 is to include, rather than to lack, "today" in this clause. (Because a study of the word "today" in Deuteronomy would be a major undertaking, I have limited the investigation to this exact clause.)

Hence it appears that the addition of the entire Deuteronomic exhortation belongs to the redactional stage of the text of Exodus, and the loss of the one word in the one tradition belongs to the transmissional stage. Most likely the word was lost already in the Hebrew tradition behind 𝐆, since it is easy to imagine a scribe's eye skipping from הֵיּוֹם to הֵנְנִי thus forgetting the first word. Had a scribe copying a Greek MS succumbed to this problem, his eye would have skipped from σοι to σημερον and he would have forgotten the first word, in this case σοι.

To summarize: after a redactor added the entire Deuteronomic clause in Exodus 34, the word "today" was lost in the transmission of the Hebrew tradition behind 𝐆.

Summary: We have identified eighteen readings in which 𝐆 is secondary: twelve places where 𝐆 alone is expansionist, two where it is haplographic, three qualitative variants where it is secondary, and one place where a qualitative and quantitative change has occurred. In these eighteen readings 𝐐ᵃ𝖂𝕸 all agree in preserving the preferable reading.

6. 𝐐ᵃ𝖂𝐆 = PREFERABLE

The four cases where 𝐐ᵃ𝖂𝐆 together preserve the original reading reveal errors or lapses on the part of 𝕸, one causing the loss of eight words, two causing the loss of one word, and one affecting grammatical form.

a. Where Q⁻ꟿG Preserve Text Omitted in 𝔐 (Eight Words)

22:4[5] **Q⁻**   [כלל]

ꟿ   אחר שלם ישלם משדהו כתבואתה ואם כל השדה <u>יבעה</u> מיטב

G* אחר שלם ישלם משדהו כתבואתה ואם כל השדה <u>יבער</u> מיטב

𝔐   מיטב   אחר

Q⁻ꟿG ≠ 𝔐

Though כל alone of this variant still appears in **Q⁻**, it is in the
third line of a fragment, the other two lines of which agree with 𝔐 except
for one word, where **Q⁻** agrees with ꟿ against 𝔐. The position of כל in
relation to the two lines above is exactly where it should be if restored
according to ꟿG, whereas there is no כל in the vicinity according to the
text as in 𝔐.

The shorter text of 𝔐 (followed by, e.g., *RSV*) mentions only one
basic contingency and provides for maximum restitution. The longer text of
ꟿ and **G** (followed by, e.g., *JB* and *NEB*) mentions two contingencies and
provides for medium restitution ("according to the yield expected," *NEB*) in
the first case and maximum restitution ("from the best part of his own field
or vineyard," *NEB*; cf. also *JB*) in the second. As Childs puts it, "The LXX
reflects the original text which explains the severity of the required
restitution because no judgment can be formed as to the quality of the
entire crop which has been destroyed."[3]

But the question of preferability can be resolved not only on the basis
of the fairness of the stipulations, but also by reference to the text itself.
Whereas ꟿ preserves a discrepancy in its verbs, **G** is consistent:

ꟿ   יבעה ... ובער ... יבעה

G   καταβοσκηση ... καταβοσκησαι ... καταβοσκηση

It is debatable whether בער is to be understood here as meaning "burn" or
"graze over"; the Greek translator understood it in the latter sense, rendering καταβοσκειν, which means "graze over." (בעה, on the other hand,
means "inquire" or "cause to swell, boil up.") But regardless of the meaning
of the verb, the point is that it should be the same in both parts of the
verse, as it is in **G**. Thus **G** appears to preserve uniquely the preferable

---

[3]Brevard S. Childs, *The Book of Exodus: A Critical, Theological Commentary.* Old Testament Library. (Philadelphia: Westminster Press, 1974),
pp. 444 and 449. Hereafter citied as: Childs, *Exodus.*

text, and this reading, when retroverted into Hebrew, as above, explains the reading in 𝕸 as parablepsis: אחר⌒יבער.

The opposite possibility is that the shorter reading as in 𝕸 is the preferable text. In favor of this is the nature of the pericope: the formulation of one case law, of course, easily gives rise to the addition of other cases. This tendency is well illustrated in 𝖎𝖎𝖎 (not, let it be noted, in **Qᵃ** or **G**) in the pericope just preceding this one, 21:28-36 (see the discussion of 21:29 and 21:31 in II.A.7). Yet this solution is unlikely here, since two unrelated traditions, **Qᵃ𝖎𝖎𝖎** and **G**, preserve the longer version. It is difficult to imagine that the same retribution and the same contingency would both be added in two different traditions, with only the difference of one letter, which is an obvious error. It is more likely that 𝕸 retains a case of parablepsis, explained by the two words ending in *resh*.

In conclusion, then, it appears that **G** preserves the original reading, which has been corrupted in two ways. 𝕸 has lost an entire line due to homoioteleuton and 𝖎𝖎𝖎 has changed the second occurrence of יבער to יבעה. Since **Qᵃ** is extant for only the one word כל, it can be assumed that it agrees with 𝖎𝖎𝖎**G** in having the longer reading; whether the error in the verb predated **Qᵃ** cannot be determined. Hence the formula for this variant reflects the fact that **Qᵃ𝖎𝖎𝖎G** all agree against 𝕸 in preserving the longer reading, since that is as much as **Qᵃ** can tell us.

b. *Where Qᵃ𝖎𝖎G Preserve Text Omitted in 𝕸 (One Word)*

In the following two variants 𝕸 has accidentally lost a word.

34:11b **Qᵃ**   והגרגשי]

𝖎𝖎𝖎   את הכנעני והאמרי והחתי ו<u>הגרגשי</u> והפרזי והחוי והיבוסי

𝕸   את האמרי והכנעני והחתי _____ והפרזי והחוי והיבוסי

G τον Αμορραιον και Χαναναιον και Χετταιον και Φερεζαιον και Ευαιον <u>και Γεργεσαιον</u> και Ιεβουσαιον **G**

Qᵃ𝖎𝖎G ≠ 𝕸

For a complete discussion of all of the variations among the 23 passages and in all the textual witnesses in which the list of peoples of Canaan appears, see O'Connell.[4] He concludes that the original list

---

[4]Kevin G. O'Connell, "The List of Seven Peoples in Canaan: A Fresh Analysis," in *The Answers Lie Below: Essays in Honor of Lawrence Edmund Toombs*, ed. Henry O. Thompson (Lanham, MD: University Press of America, 1984), pp 221-241.

consisted of seven peoples (cf. Deut 7:1), including the Girgashites, even though they are included only 3 times in 𝔐, and indeed never appear in 𝔐 of Exodus (cf. 3:8, 17; 13:5; 23:23, 28; 33:2).

The fact that the list varies so widely both in the number of nations included and in their order is due to the pitfalls involved in copying a list consisting of so many names. When one or two names were inadvertently omitted because all seven begin and end in the same way, they would often be added back in again eventually, but frequently in the wrong position because there are so many of them. These difficulties make themselves most clearly felt in the middle of the list, and indeed it is the Girgashites who suffer the most. According to O'Connell, the original list probably had the Girgashites in either the fourth or the fifth place.

Although only the one name is extant in the scroll, the spacing requires that it be reconstructed in the fifth position and that all the other six nations be reconstructed as well. Whether the placement of the Girgashites as in 𝐐ᵃ or as in 𝔐 is preferable is impossible to determine with confidence.

As far as the entire seven-name sequence is concerned, O'Connell concludes that the order as in 𝔐 here occurs 5 out of the 11 times in 𝔐, is peculiar to itself, and is secondary. Judging by the general character of 𝔐, it may be the case that this sequence is the result of standardization which, however, was only partial. Although 𝔐 and 𝐆 agree here as to overall sequence, it is rather different from that sequence which O'Connell concludes was "generally preferred more often" throughout the OT:[5] Canaanites, Hittites, Amorites, Perizites, Girgashites, Hivites, Jebusites (or Girgashites and Perizites reversed). Thus it appears that none of the fully-preserved traditions 𝔐𝔐𝐆 has the more preferable sequence here. The scroll could possibly have had that sequence. At least it was apparently complete and had the Girgashites in one of the two preferred positions.

בֿ7:15	𝐐ᵃ		[(ו)הנה הוא]
	𝔐	הנה הוא יצא	
	𝔐	יצא הנה	
	𝐆	ιδου αυτος εκπορευεται	𝐐ᵃ𝔐𝐆 ≠ 𝔐

The style of Exodus makes it probable that the personal pronoun appeared in the original text. (ו)הנה without suffix occurs 33 times in

---

[5] *Ibid.*, p. 226.

Exodus. In 18 cases הנה(ו) is followed by a noun, in 4 cases by a finite verb; the other 11 cases form the pattern under consideration in this reading: הנה(ו) followed by a present participle.

𝖂 and 𝕸 agree in all 22 cases in the first and second patterns, and they agree in 9 of the 11 cases in this pattern. 𝖂 is consistent in all 11 cases: הנה is followed by a pronoun subsequently followed by a present participle. 𝕸 follows that pattern in 9 cases; only here and in the same clause in 8:16 is the pronoun lacking in 𝕸, even though the next word is a present participle. Three times (4:14; here; and 8:16) the pronoun is in the third person. In 4:14 𝕸 reads הנה הוא יצא exactly as 𝐐ᵃ𝖂 here; in 8:16 it reads הנה יצא, exactly as it reads here.

𝐐ᵃ is extant for only two cases out of the 33, here and at 9:7, where all texts agree.

𝐆 follows the same pattern whenever it translates with ιδου. Of the 11 cases with pronouns and participles, 𝐆 uses (και) ιδου 9 times, and oρα and oδε each once, always followed by the pronoun. In the 3 verses which are so similar in Hebrew (4:14; here at 7:15ב; and 8:16) 𝐆 consistently reads (και) ιδου αυτος εκπορευεται/εξελευσεται.

In summary, then, in all 11 cases of הנה followed by the participle, 𝐆 renders with a pronoun plus participle, as does 𝖂 consistently and 𝕸 in every case but twice. The consistency of this pattern makes it likely that the same pattern originally occurred here in 7:15ב (as well as in 8:16), and that 𝕸's omission is secondary.

c. Where 𝐐ᵃ𝖂𝐆 Preserve the Correct Grammatical Form

Once when 𝕸 exhibits a small error, 𝐐ᵃ𝖂𝐆 preserve the correct form.

17:2א תנה 𝖂] Δος 𝐆; תנו 𝕸   𝐐ᵃ𝖂𝐆 ≠ 𝕸

The longer form of the masc. sg. impv. תנה occurs 23 times in 𝕸 of the OT, including 4 times in the Torah (Gen 30:26; 42:37; Num 11:13; 27:4). In the first 3 cases, all three traditions agree as to the singular. At Num 27:4 the note in *BHS* advises: "l[ege] c[um] 𝖂GV תנו," whereas here it merely informs: "mlt Mss 𝖂GSTᴶV תנה." The phrase is similar there (תנה/תנו לנו) and here (ויאמרו תנה/תנו לנו); thus from the point of view of auditory repetition a mistake from the singular to the plural may be more likely. Yet from the point of view of meaning, the 𝕸 reading in Num 27:4 is not necessarily incorrect, for the addressees could easily be interpreted as plural (Moses, Eleazar, the leaders and all the congregation, v 2) or singular (Moses seen as paramount). Here, however, **m** is in error, since only Moses is addressed.

Another factor contributing to confusion could be the visual similarity between ה and ו in Hasmonaean and Herodian hands, especially if the two short words had been written together as one word, as often was done with a short sense unit; especially in the middle of a word the second stroke of the ה could easily have been overlooked by the next scribe.

In conclusion, then, the notes in *BHS* might better be reversed: whereas at Num 27:4 **m**'s reading is debatable, here it is an error.

Summary: Thus we have seen four readings where **Q°mG** appear to preserve the original; in one **m** has a minor error involving an incorrect verbal form, and in three a minor lapse, involving the loss of eight words once and of one word twice.

7. **Q°mG** = PREFERABLE

The eight readings where **Q°mG** agree against **m** in preserving the preferable reading include two where **m** has made a specific law more generally applicable, one where **m** has added a phrase and altered a verbal form, three where **m** has added a word or brief phrase, one where **m** has made the text more specific by changing an adverb to a place name, and one where **m** has altered the grammatical form.

a. *Where* **Q°mG** *Preserve the More Specific Meaning*

Two variants belong together because they are in one pericope which **m** has altered.

21:29   יסקל[ור הש[ו **mG]**   הבהמה תסקל **m**   **Q°mG** ≠ **m**

21:31   **Q°**   א[ו בת י]גח
         m   או בן יכה או בת
         m   או בן יגח או בת יגח
         G   εαν δε υιον κερατιση η θυγατερα   **Q°mG** ≠ **m**

These two variants belong to the legal pericope in 21:28-36, throughout which **m** consistently broadens the application of the laws: from an ox which gores to any animal which kills (vv 28-32); from the death of an ox or ass to that of any animal (vv 33-34); and from the killing of one ox by another to the killing of any animal by any other animal (vv 35-36). Four times 𝔐 adds "or any animal" after "ox," nine times it substitutes "animal" for "ox," and five times it substitutes "kill" for "gore" (cf. also 22:3; 23:4). Whereas the expansionism characteristic of this tradition often tends to make the text more specific, here the intent is the opposite, because this is a legal section, i.e., to expand in order to make the law more generally applicable. It should be noted that in the second variant 𝔐 actually has fewer words, since it does not repeat the verb as 𝔐 does, although the passage in general has been expanded and modified.

Waltke[6] treats the change from נגח to נכה in isolation from the other changes in this pericope, and hence classifies it as a replacement of "rare and lively expressions with customary and prosaic expressions." Reading the pericope as a whole suggests that this change was motivated not by the greater familiarity of the verb נכה, as Waltke suggests, but rather by the exegetical desire to extend the application of the law.

The same phenomenon of extending the application of the laws is found occasionally in 𝔐 and 𝕲 as well as in 𝔐, e.g. in 21:33 ("ox or ass"), 21:37 [22:1] ("ox or sheep"), 22:3[4] ("ox or ass or sheep" 𝔐; "ox or sheep" 𝕲); even in this last verse 𝔐 still adds "or any animal." In 22:9[10] all three texts agree in the fullest form: "ass or ox or sheep or any animal."

As fragmentary as the scroll is, there are three indications that in this entire pericope 𝐐ᵃ agrees with 𝔐 and 𝕲 against 𝔐: space requirements in v 28 (see the edition in *DJD*) and these two variants. Here then is another example of the priority of 𝐐ᵃ in relation to 𝔐 although it clearly belongs in the same family (cf., e.g., II.A.1 and 3).

b. *Where 𝐐ᵃ𝔐𝕲 Preserve the More Difficult Reading*

In one variant 𝔐 seems to have altered the text for the sake of the easier reading and/or for the sake of harmonization, and then to have expanded for the sake of clarification.

---

[6]Bruce K. Waltke, "The Samaritan Pentateuch and the Text of the Old Testament," in *New Perspectives on the Old Testament,* ed. J. Barton Payne (Waco, TX: Word, 1970), p. 220. Hereafter cited as: Waltke, "SP."

19:12 **Q͏ᵃ**   סבי]ב   לאמור

ɯ   והגבלת את ההר סביב ואל העם תאמר

m   והגבלת את העם סביב   לאמר

G   και αφοριεις τον λαον κυκλω   λεγων

Q͏ᵃmG ≠ ɯ

The *Hip⁽il⁾* of this verb occurs only one other time in Exodus, at 19:
23, and only one other time in the entire OT, a problematic reading. The *Qal*
occurs only three times (Deut 19:14; Josh 18:20; Zech 9:2), always referring
to an inanimate object. In Exod 19:23 the command in all four texts, including **Q͏ᵃ**, is to set bounds for the <u>mountain</u>. Here, in **mG** the command is to
set bounds for the <u>people</u> and then to speak to them; but in **ɯ** Moses is commanded to set bounds for the <u>mountain</u> and then to speak to the <u>people</u>. The
fragmentary scroll no longer lets us know which object it contained.

It is difficult to determine which of the two objects is the original
here, because the verb occurs so rarely in the OT and has by definition a
two-directional reference. It is easy to understand how a scribe might have
either erred or intentionally amended in either direction.

One possibility is that the reading with עם in **mG** is the original,
modified to ההר in the harmonizing tradition behind **ɯ** so that it would agree
with 19:23. (It is possible that **Q͏ᵃ** represents the first stage in that tradition. If its full reading were והגבלת את <u>ההר</u> סבי]ב לאמור, it would have
undergone the first change, from העם to ההר, but the further changes would
not yet have been made.)   Then, perhaps at a later stage, for the sake of
greater clarity ואל העם was added and לאמר changed to תאמר.   Arguments
against this scenario include the usage of the verb (above) and the usage of
סביב in the Torah -- ca. 50 times -- always used with inanimate objects
rather than people.

Another possibility is that the original read simply: והגבלת את ההר
סביב לאמר; this would have agreed with 19:23 and could have been the
reading, for example, in **Q͏ᵃ**. This object could have been changed to עם in
the tradition(s) behind **m** and **G** on the basis of the meaning, namely, that
the <u>people</u> were then addressed in a warning not to overstep the boundary, or
perhaps by inadvertent error. In the tradition behind **ɯ**, on the other hand,
the object would have been retained, but the addition of the prepositional
phrase would have been added for clarity, necessitating the change in the
verbal form. An argument against this reconstruction is that both **m** and **G**
(and quite possibly **Q͏ᵃ**) agree, making it somewhat less likely that this is a
secondary reading. As will be seen in Chapter IV.C., **m** and **G** never agree

on secondary readings, though it is possible that two scribes made the same changes independently, either deliberately or by mistake.

On balance, then, it seems more likely that 𝕸 and 𝕲 (and Qᵃ?) preserve the original reading, which in this case is also the more difficult reading, and that this is a typical case of harmonization and clarifying expansion in the tradition represented by 𝖘 alone, and not shared by Qᵃ. Thus for the part of the variant which is extant in the scroll, Qᵃ is judged to belong with 𝕸 and 𝕲 in preserving the original.

c. Where Qᵃ𝕸𝕲 Preserve the Shorter Reading

Three times Qᵃ𝕸𝕲 preserve the shorter reading when 𝖘 has expanded somewhat.

19:25 Qᵃ𝕸𝕲   אל ה]עם   וירד משה
       𝖘𝕸[MSS]𝕿[JP]   וירד משה מן ההר אל העם   Qᵃ𝕸𝕲 ≠ 𝖘

Based on the standard text-critical assumption that in the absence of extenuating circumstances such as similar letters or polemical statements texts tend to expand rather than shrink at the hands of successive scribes, such an innocuous phrase as this is considered a routine expansion in the 𝖘 tradition. The fuller clause appears in all three traditions in 19:14. The fact that 𝕸[MS] as well as 𝕿[JP] [𝕸ap] contain the expansion here should be understood as a completely independent expansion on the part of a like-minded scribe or scribes.

6:27 ב   ממצרים 𝕸𝕲]   מארץ מצרים 𝖘𝕸[MSS]𝕾B+   Qᵃ𝕸𝕲 ≠ 𝖘

It appears that ארץ is a routine expansion in 𝖘. 𝕸[MSS] 𝕾 B+ have the longer reading as well, but this could have been added by scribes almost unthinkingly, independently of each other; hence this is not very significant for textual affiliation. Regarding textual history, it illustrates continuing expansionist tendencies within the Qᵃ𝖘 tradition, with 𝖘 expanding beyond Qᵃ.

29:33   Qᵃ𝕸   את ידם] לקדש אתם   אשר כפר בהם ל]מלא
                           𝖘   אשר כפר בם למלא בם את ידם לקדש אתם
       εν οις ηγιασθησαν εν αυτοις τελειωσαι   τας χειρας αυτων
       αγιασαι αυτους 𝕲   Qᵃ𝕸/𝕲/ ≠ 𝖘

This is most likely a minor addition typical of 𝖘 for the sake of greater clarification, which occurred in the 𝖘 tradition after the stage

represented by **Qᵃ**. Note that 𝕴𝕸 both have the fuller form just four
verses earlier:

29:29   □**Qᵃ**   𝕴𝕸   [𝕸] בהם [ולמלא <u>בם</u> את ידם   למשחה בם

χρισθηναι αυτους εν αυτοις και τελειωσαι _____ τας χειρας
αυτων **G**

d. Where **Qᵃ𝕸G** Preserve the Simpler Designation

15:27   [ו]שם **𝕸G]**   ובאילים ו𝕴**GᴹˢTᴶ**Philo   **Qᵃ𝕸G** ≠ 𝕴

In this reading **Qᵃ** and **G** agree with 𝕸 in preserving the simpler
reading, while 𝕴, along with three other witnesses (see 𝕸ᵃᵖ), has made the
place name explicit. It is difficult to understand why the scribe felt the
need to spell out the name again, since the immediately preceding word is
Elim!

e. Where **Qᵃ𝕸G** Preserve the Correct Grammatical Form

In the final variant of this section 𝕴 presents an altered verbal form.

10:10   [י]יה **𝕸G]**   יהיה 𝕴   **Qᵃ𝕸G** ≠ 𝕴

The jussive (imperative in Greek) is required, at least according to
Tiberian Hebrew, in this exclamation, which may have already been altered
from an original curse to a euphemistic form, or else is to be understood as
sarcasm.[7]

Though the ending of the word is not visible in **Qᵃ**, only the one letter
is missing from the leather. The first letter of the next word is extant and
space for only one letter is available.

This use of the regular (i.e., longer) form of the imperfect instead of
the shorter jussive may be a part of a larger pattern in 𝕴 as contrasted
with 𝕸. According to Waltke, 𝕴 has a tendency to substitute the longer
form of the imperfect where 𝕸 preserves the short form with *waw*-
consecutive, which Waltke explains as the older usage.[8]   Purvis adds that
"the apocopated forms of *lamed he* verbs are sometimes rejected in favor of
longer forms."[9]

---

[7]Cf. Childs, *Exodus*, p. 126: "'I would just as soon wish God's blessing
on you as to let your children go with you!'"; and p. 130.

[8]Waltke, "SP," pp. 214-215.

[9]James D. Purvis, "Samaritan Pentateuch," *IDBS*, p. 774.

Of the ten occurrences of יהי in 𝕸 in the Pentateuch, 𝔐 agrees only three times (Gen 1:3,6,14).   Three times 𝔐 reads ויהי (Gen 33:9; Exod 7:9 [☐𝐐ᵃ]; Deut 33:24), once יהיו (Deut 32:38), and three times יהיה (Gen 30:34; 49;17; and Exod 10:10).   Thus the jussive form is preserved only in the three occurrences in Genesis 1.

G translates with imperative eight of the ten times. Only at Exod 7:9 and Deut 33:24 does **G** have the future indicative, thus agreeing formally with 𝔐 at those two verses and disagreeing formally with 𝔐 at the other five verses where 𝔐 disagrees with 𝕸.

𝐐ᵃ is extant only in this one case, but as far as it goes its evidence suggests that the trend toward the longer form of the imperfect and/or the longer form of the *lamed he* verb continued during or even after the Qumran period. Once again **𝐐ᵃ** agrees with 𝕸**(G)** against 𝔐 in a preferable reading, showing that 𝔐 continued to develop after **𝐐ᵃ** was copied.

Summary: We have seen eight instances where **𝐐ᵃ𝕸G** appear to preserve the original reading against 𝔐. Of these, 𝔐 has made the text more general twice, harmonized and then clarified once, expanded three times, made the text more specific once, and altered a grammatical form once.

B. PREFERABLE READINGS PRESERVED IN 𝔐

1. 𝔐 = PREFERABLE
There are no variants where 𝔐 uniquely preserves the preferable reading.

2. 𝔐𝕸 = PREFERABLE
There are five variants where 𝔐𝕸 appear to preserve the original against **𝐐ᵃ**. In the first **𝐐ᵃ** has added one word; in the other four **𝐐ᵃ** has a slightly different word or form.

a. Where 𝔐𝕸 Preserve the Shorter Original (One Minor Word)

9:8א   לאמר קחו] קחו 𝔐𝕸; λεγων Λαβετε **G**   **𝐐ᵃ** = **G** ≠ 𝔐𝕸
There are 48 occurrences of לאמר in 𝕸 of Exodus; none of these are omitted in **G**.   On the other hand, **G** has λεγων 15 times in Exodus when there is no corresponding לאמר in 𝕸.   Before 1952 it would have been

assumed without question that the translator or an early Greek copyist added the 15. Now Q^a shows that we need to bear in mind that G's *Vorlage* might well have already been expanded at the Hebrew stage. On the other hand, since this is such a minor and such a typical addition it could have happened at any stage; by itself it gives no indication of textual affiliation. At 8:16[20] Q^a is the only one of the three witnesses that adds לאמר; at 32:7א Q^a ⱮG all add it.

b. *Where ⱮⱮ Preserve the Preferable Text and Q^a Has a Slightly Different Word or Form*

In five variants ⱮⱮ together preserve the preferable word or form while Q^a reflects a slight alteration.

7:18   היאר [בת]ון] ביאר] Ɱ Ɱ; εν τω ποταμω G Q^a ≠ Ɱ Ɱ (G?)

The simpler preposition is taken as preferable because of its broader attestation.

In 7:18, where a commandment is given to Moses, Ɯ agrees with Ɱ in having the simpler preposition. The major expansion preserved in Q^aƜ, 7:18[b], reports Moses' fulfilment of the commandment; within the expansion Ɯ retains the simpler form. Q^a has the longer form in both places. In 7:18, then, ⱮⱮ together are preferable; in 7:18[b] ב Ɯ is secondary in that it has the major expansion but is preferable to Q^a in that it has the simpler preposition. This second variant is included here for the sake of comparison; it is not counted as a case where ⱮⱮ share a preferable reading:

7:18[b]   ב[תון היאר] [בת]ון] ביאר Ɯ; > ⱮG Q^a ≠ Ɯ ≠ ⱮG

One cannot be at all confident as to the *Vorlage* of G. Of the 18 occurrences of בתוך in Exodus, G has εν 3 times, a form of μεσος 9 times (εις [το] μεσον 4 times, εν μεσω twice, ανα μεσον twice, and μεσον once), and the remaining six phrases are paraphrased or omitted in G. Thus it would appear somewhat more likely that G's *Vorlage* read ב- but it is quite possible that it read בתוך. Other extant Hebrew witnesses might shed some light on the G *Vorlage*. Of these 18 occurrences of בתוך, Ɯ also has בתוך 16 times; once (39:25) ⱮG correctly lack the phrase against the dittographic repetition in Ɱ; and once Ɯ has תוך rather than בתוך, probably because the preceding word ends in *mem*, a letter which is similar in appearance to *beth* in both the Paleo-Hebrew and the square scripts. Q^a is not extant in any of these 18 places.

In 7:18, then, 𝖀 agrees with 𝕸 in preserving the preferable preposition against 𝐐ᵐ. In 7:18ᵇ ב 𝖀 agrees with 𝐐ᵐ in having a major expansion against 𝕸. 𝐐ᵐappears to preserve a slightly further development beyond 𝖀 -- or to reflect a collateral development -- in both sentences, by presenting a fuller form of the preposition.

10:21א   וידבר/ו] ויאמר 𝖀𝕸; Ειπεν δε 𝐆   𝐐ᵐ ≠ 𝖀𝕸(𝐆)

In this case of a minor difference in the choice of the verb, the root which occurs in all three traditions is taken as original. 𝐆 is listed as almost surely supporting אמר, because in the overwhelming number of occurrences of אמר in 𝕸 of Exodus λεγειν and ειπειν correspond to it (λεγειν 90 times out of 107, and ειπειν 190 times out of 213), whereas λαλειν is used to correspond to דבר (62 out of 65 times). For a discussion of the variations between 𝖀 and 𝕸 regarding these two verbs, see Chapter V.B.

31:5   𝐐ᵐ   [בכל מלאכת]
        𝖀𝕸   לעשות בכל מלאכה
        𝐆   εργαζεσθαι κατα παντα τα εργα   𝐐ᵐ ≠ 𝖀𝕸; 𝐆?

The reading in 𝐐ᵐ is judged to be secondary because of the agreement of 𝖀 and 𝕸. But it is impossible to be sure how to interpret the fragmentary evidence of 𝐐ᵐ.

First, מלאכת may be a plural and may in fact agree with 𝐆.   There are three arguments against this, however. The general orthographic tendency of 𝐐ᵐ would be to have the *mater lectionis* in a plural form. Further, if we may learn anything from the usage in 𝕸 and 𝖀, there are only two occurrences of the plural of this word in the entire OT in 𝕸 (1 Chr 28:19 and Ps 73:28), and no occurrences of the plural in Exodus in 𝖀. Finally, 𝐆 translates with the plural of this word 17 times in Exodus, as against only 9 translations with the singular. It becomes less likely to suppose that 𝐆 reflects a *Vorlage* different from 𝖀𝕸 17 out of 26 times.

A second possibility is that מלאכת is a construct form; if so, since this is the end of a sentence in 𝖀𝕸 and 𝐆, it may reflect a scribal error. Third, it may be a construct form which was not in fact the last word of the sentence in 𝐐ᵐ. Exod 35:33 is the parallel verse to 31:5. There 𝐐ᵐ is not extant, but 𝖀𝕸𝐆 agree in reading:

לעשות בכל מלאכת מחשבות...

...και ποιειν εν παντι εργω σοφιας.   (note the singular!)

It may well be that this is one case where $\mathbf{Q}^{m}$ has expanded slightly to make two parallel verses agree exactly, even though 𝕸 has not done so in this instance.

Thus the secondary reading of $\mathbf{Q}^{m}$ could be a plural, an error, or an expansion from the parallel passage in the second part of the tabernacle account. Only in the first case is there any possibility that it agrees with **G**, and even that is unlikely. Most likely it stands alone against the other three witnesses in a secondary reading.

23:31א   ו[ש]מתי (vid)] ושתי 𝔐𝕸; και θησω **G** $\mathbf{Q}^{m}$ ≠ 𝔐𝕸; **G**?

There is some doubt about the reading in $\mathbf{Q}^{m}$, but Skehan reconstructed as above, with the note that the broken letter read as מ could be neither ש nor א. It appears that a scribe who saw in his *Vorlage* the less common word שית ("put, set"), which occurs only 7 times in Exodus, inadvertently wrote the more common word with the same meaning, שים, which occurs about 50 times in Exodus. The less common word also gave difficulty to scribes in the later Samaritan tradition: cf. ושאתי in three MSS (𝕸ᵃᵖ; hence Skehan's reference to א.)

The *Vorlage* of **G** is uncertain, because τιθεναι is used 13 times in Exodus and 17 times in the rest of the Torah for שים, and only this one time in Exodus and once in the rest of the Torah (Gen 3:15) for שית.

In conclusion, ושתי is considered the preferable reading. It is the less common word, explains the variant in $\mathbf{Q}^{m}$, and is attested by both 𝔐 and 𝕸.

Summary: These five readings where 𝔐𝕸 agree in preserving the original can tell us almost nothing about **G**. In four of the five the *Vorlage* of **G** cannot be determined with any confidence; even in the fifth case the addition is so slight and so characteristic of all of the traditions that no affiliation can be assumed. They do show some insignificant variants in $\mathbf{Q}^{m}$: one instance of the simple addition of לאמור and four minor differences involving דבר\אמר and individual letters of other words. In these five minor variants 𝔐 agrees with 𝕸 against $\mathbf{Q}^{m}$ in preserving the preferable reading.

3. 𝔐**G** = PREFERABLE

There is no instance in the extant portions of $\mathbf{Q}^{m}$ where 𝔐 and **G** alone agree in preserving a preferable reading.

4. 𝖀𝔐G = PREFERABLE

The extant portions of **Qᵐ** preserve six very minor variants where it alone is secondary. Two are additions of לאמור and -ו, one involves synesis, and three are errors involving one letter each plus one run-on word. In these six instances 𝖀𝔐G all agree in preserving the preferable reading.

a. Where 𝖀𝔐G Preserve the Shorter Reading

In both of these cases it is assumed that the shorter reading was the more original, and that additions made frequently elsewhere in the other three witnesses are made only by **Qᵐ** here.

8:16[20]   משה 𝖀𝔐G] משה [לאמור]   **Qᵐ ≠ 𝖀𝔐G**

This word is frequently added in the various witnesses. As we saw in section II.B.2 regarding **9:8א**, **G** reads λεγων 15 times in Exodus where there is no corresponding לאמר in **𝔐**. A comparison of 𝖀 with **𝔐** shows that 𝖀 has לאמר only 4 times where **𝔐** lacks it (20:22; 30:34; 32:7; and 33:1). Where **Qᵐ** is extant, it alone adds לאמור here, agrees with **G** in adding it at **9:8א**, and agrees with 𝖀 and **G** at **32:7א**. This is not to suggest that לאמר was never added in the developing **𝔐** tradition, but merely that comparison shows that it happened less often. At all of the 48 occurrences of the word in **𝔐** in Exodus, both 𝖀 and **G** have it as well.

7:15א   הנה 𝖀𝔐G] והנה   **Qᵐ ≠ 𝖀𝔐G**

Again the shorter reading attested by the three traditions is considered preferable (cf. also 𝖀 and **𝔐** in the parallel passage in 8:16 [☐**Qᵐ**]).

b. Where 𝖀𝔐G Preserve the Preferable Grammatical Form

In one variant 𝖀𝔐G preserve what is almost certainly the preferable form of a word, while **Qᵐ** presents a slightly altered form.

12:6   אתו 𝖀𝔐G] אותם   **Qᵐ ≠ 𝖀𝔐G**

This pericope gives instructions regarding the passover lamb mixing plural and singular forms. The sentence in v 6 gives a command with a plural verb: כל קהל עדת ישראל [**Qᵐ** אותם] אתו ושחטו. It appears that the reading in **Qᵐ** is an example of synesis, where the scribe, most likely unconsciously, construed the object to conform with the collective subject and plural verb. The next verse continues with a series of plural verbs: "they shall take..., they shall put..., they shall eat..."; the last verb is

followed again by the accusative singular אתו in 𝖜𝖒 [□𝐐ᵃ]; **G** renders
that pronoun with the plural αυτα [Rᵉᵈ; αυτο A⁺ Syh etc., one more
example of A's having been revised back to the developing 𝖒 tradition]. In v
6 the singular is considered original, as the (slightly) more difficult reading
represented in all three traditions. In v 7 **G**'s reading would be considered
another example of synesis during the translation process, which a more
literally-minded scribe revised.

c. Where 𝖜𝖒**G** Preserve the Correct Reading

The three cases of error on the part of **𝐐ᵃ** will be merely listed here,
and discussion reserved for Chapter V.A.

28:11א	יפתח] תפתח 𝖜𝖒**G**	**𝐐ᵃ** ≠ 𝖜𝖒**G**
28:41	והלבשתם אתם (וה[ ] והלבשת אתם 𝖜𝖒**G**	**𝐐ᵃ** ≠ 𝖜𝖒**G**
31:4	לעשות בזהב] לעשוב[זהב 𝖜𝖒**G**	**𝐐ᵃ** ≠ 𝖜𝖒**G**

Summary: These six instances where all three traditions preserve the
preferable reading against **𝐐ᵃ** alone shed much more light on the nature of
𝐐ᵃ than on the nature of the other three. Hence the significance of these
will be discussed in Chapter V.A.

C. PREFERABLE READINGS PRESERVED IN 𝖒

In sections A and B we discussed readings where **𝐐ᵃ** and/or 𝖜
preserved the original. In sections C and D we will consider those readings
where neither **𝐐ᵃ** nor 𝖜 preserve the more original. Section C will discuss
first those readings where 𝖒 alone is original and then where 𝖒 is joined
by **G**.

1. 𝖒 = PREFERABLE

The readings where 𝖒 alone is clearly preferable include several
passages where **G** disagrees with 𝖒 and several where the **G** *Vorlage* cannot be determined.

a. Where 𝖒 Preserves the Shorter Reading and Preferable Word

Two variants that belong together apparently involve the addition of
one word followed by a slight alteration for harmonization.

10:24א,ב

Q²ᵐ	ויקרא]פרעה למשה ולאהר(ו)ן ויאמר
𝕸	ויאמר ויקרא פרעה אל משה
𝕸²ᴹˢˢ	ויקרא פרעה אל משה ואהרן ויאמר
G	και εκαλεσεν Φαραω Μωυσην και Ααρων λεγων

א (ל\ל\א):   **Q²ᵐ ≠ 𝕸; G?**

ב (אהרן):   **Q²ᵐG ≠ 𝕸**

The subject of the mention of Aaron's name is treated extensively in Chapter VI.A.1.g, with other issues relating to scribal practice in late antiquity. The conclusion is that whatever trend there may have existed to add Aaron's name into the text of Exodus, it seems to have taken place in two separate periods: first during the period of literary development and then much later after the **Q²ᵐ** tradition had gone its separate way.

Thus it no longer seems possible automatically to assume that **𝕸** preserves the original here in 10:24ב and that Aaron has been added in the other witnesses either independently or because of textual affiliation. Instead, we must look at other factors. The question arises whether the lack of the second name could be a simple scribal error in **𝕸**, and in fact every second letter in the two words is repeated, which could possibly have given rise to parablepsis: ולאהרן ויאמר.

A factor pointing in the opposite direction, to the preferability of the shorter reading would be the three occurrences of Aaron's name in the paragraphs preceding this one (Exod 10:3,8,16), and more particularly the similarity of context between 10:24 and 10:8, where Pharaoh says the same thing to both Moses and Aaron together. These verses in the close context may have influenced scribes independently to name Aaron here as well.

But the decision to designate the shorter reading as the original rests chiefly on the variation in the prepositions. **𝕸** reads אל with its one object; **Q²ᵐ** read -ל and -ול with their two objects; the *Vorlage* of **G** cannot be determined. It is likely that אל was the original, and that after Aaron's name was inserted the prepositions were harmonized.

It appears that Exod 8:21 underwent similar expansion and subsequent harmonization, and that **𝕸** documents a transitional stage in the process:

𝕸	ויקרא פרעה אל משה ולאהרן
ᵐ	ויקרא פרעה למשה ולאהרן

A similar addition and harmonization seems to have occurred at Lev 10:6 with the names of Eleazar and Ithamar (see the discussion of Exod 24:1, 9 in Chapter V.A.3).

Exod 8:4; 9:27; 12:31, on the other hand, preserve agreement between 𝔐𝔲 and 𝔐 in the identical clause: both witnesses name the two men, Moses and Aaron, with the preposition ־ל.

Returning to Exod 10:24, note the different treatment in the two MSS of 𝔐 which added Aaron's name here: they did not add a second preposition at all.

To summarize: the disagreement in the prepositions is taken to indicate that Aaron's name was inserted later. Thus the two variants belong together and 𝔐 is considered to preserve the original in both: אל משה. Although the preposition(s) in the *Vorlage* of **G** cannot be determined, it apparently did have Aaron's name. Hence **G** is secondary as far as the addition is concerned.

b. *Where 𝔐 Preserves the Shorter Reading (One Word)*

In three variants 𝔐 preserves the shorter text where **Qᵃ**𝔲**G** have added one word.

9:7   ממקנה בני ישראל 𝔲TᴹˢTᴶSG(απο παντων...)]
        ממקנה ישראל 𝔐   **Qᵃ**𝔲**G** ≠ 𝔐

The addition of בני appears to be a case of routine expansion that is virtually meaningless for the narrative and that was probably done almost without thinking on the part of various scribes. **Qᵃ**𝔲𝔐**G** all have the same phrase in its fuller form, וממקנה בני ישראל, in the preceding verse. In a similar context in 9:4 **G** includes the addition, but 𝔲 and 𝔐 (and A⁺, apparently having been revised toward the 𝔐 tradition) lack it (as does 𝔲 in 9:5ᵇ).

22:3[4]   שנים ישלם [שנים] אחד 𝔲] שנים ישלם 𝔐; διπλα αυτα (> A⁺)
           αποτεισει **G**   **Qᵃ** 𝔲 ≠ 𝔐; **G**?

The addition of אחד in the **Qᵃ**𝔲 tradition appears to be for the sake of greater clarity, as also in two other verses in the same chapter:
22:6 שנים אחד ושלם 𝔲; שנים ישלם 𝔐; αποτεισει διπλουν **G**; □**Qᵃ**
22:8 שנים אחד ישלם 𝔲; שנים ישלם 𝔐; αποτεισει διπλουν **G**; □**Qᵃ**

Since 𝔐 has the shorter reading all 3 times and **G** twice, this is considered the original. The rendering in **G** may be a good translation of the shorter Hebrew. On the other hand, the fact that A revised the Greek in 22:3 to omit αυτα may indicate that that word in this one verse was understood in the same sense as אחד: a translator or early scribe had added αυτα to make it clear that the penalty was to pay double for <u>each</u> animal stolen. Thus the evidence of **G** is here considered ambiguous.

32:7א   לא[מ]ור **שּׁG]** > **𝕸**   **Q²שּׁG ≠ 𝕸**

The fact that this routine addition occurred in the three texts other than **𝕸** should not by itself be taken as indicating any relationship among the three, for it is the type of expansion typical of most scribes of the period (cf. **9:8א** at II.B.2 and **8:16[20]** at II.B.4).

c. Where 𝕸 Preserves the Shorter Reading (A Morpheme)

Besides the four preceding variants where **Q²שּׁG** added one word, there are also three variants where the same witnesses added a morpheme.

32:13ב   ל[ל]ם(ו)ונחל[וה לע](ו) **שּׁＳ]** ונחלו לעלם **𝕸**; και καθεξουσιν αυτην
εις τον αιωνα **G**   **Q²שּׁG ≠ 𝕸**

This is probably a case of independent expansion on the part of various scribes and perhaps also the Greek translator, who supplied the accusative object for the sake of completeness. Since the object is clear from the immediately preceding context and thus does not need repetition (indeed the verb just before this, אתן, has no suffix) and since the following word would not appear to give rise to omission, the shorter reading is considered original.

Providing verbs with accusative suffixes is a typical kind of expansion in the textual traditions in Exodus. A similar addition occurs only in **שּׁ** in 24:8: ויזרקהו (ויקח משה את הדם) **שּׁ**; ויזרק **𝕸**; (λαβων δε Μωυσης το αιμα) κατεσκεδασεν **G**; □**Q²**. The other places where **שּׁ** adds an accusative suffix to a verb when it is lacking in **𝕸** are: 2:6; 13:13//34:20; 21:2; 22:1, 8; 32:20bis; 34:34; cf. 15:22. **G** agrees with **שּׁ** against **𝕸** in 34:20; 21:2; 32:20bis (Red; 1° > A⁺; 2° > A⁺); 34:34). Some examples of the same phenomenon in **G** alone include 7:9 (αυτην Red; > B⁺); 15:25; 16:15 (αυτο Red; > A⁺); and 22:26.

17:2ב   ומה **שּׁ𝕸mltMSSTMSTJＳ]** מה **𝕸**; και τι **G**   **Q²שּׁG ≠ 𝕸**

Moses asks two separate questions, and there is no need to connect them. The abrupt, staccato style fits the narrative better.

32:27   עברו 𝕸 [𝔊𝗎 ועב]רו   Q⁻𝗎𝔊 ≠ 𝕸

This is the second in a series of four imperatives, and it comes after
a slight break (the Massoretes put the *athnach* just before it). Thus it
seems equally natural with or without the conjunction. The possibility of
haplography cannot be ruled out, since it immediately follows ירכו. But on
balance the asyndetic reading can be taken as probably the original.

d. Where 𝕸 Preserves the Preferable Idiom

In one case 𝕸 preserves what appears to be the original idiom, which
is altered in Q⁻𝗎.

25:20   אל אחד[ד𝗎 אחד א]ל אחיו אל איש 𝕸; εις αλλ̄ηλα 𝔊
                                                   Q⁻𝗎 ≠ 𝕸; 𝔊?

Waltke[10] classifies this variant concerning the cherubim's wings
with those cases of 𝗎's "replacing rare constructions with more frequently
occurring constructions." He uses the adjectives "rare and lively" vs.
"customary and prosaic" and "banal" and quotes Geiger's adjectives "lively"
vs. "more sober, and seemingly more regular." (See Chapter II.A.7, where I
question his classification of the changes in Exod 21:28-36 in this category.) In support of Waltke's interpretation is the fact that whereas 𝗎 (and
Q⁻ insofar as it is extant) agrees with 𝕸 in using איש אל/את אחיו when
referring to humans (10:23; 16:15; 32:27; cf. 32:29), it uses אחד אל אחד
and אחת אל אחת in reference to non-humans, e.g., cherubim, curtains, and
frames in the tabernacle.

But there is another factor that may play an equal or greater role: the
motive of standardizing parallel passages. This is one of 6 passages in
which 𝗎 and 𝕸 differ as they do here. The other 5 disagreements occur in
26:3ᵇⁱˢ, 5,6,17, regarding the curtains and frames. 𝕸 reads אשה אל אחתה
all 5 times in chapter 26, where the command is given, but in the
corresponding 5 times in 36:10,10,12,13,22, where the execution is given, it
reads אחת אל אחת. 𝗎, on the other hand, reads אחת אל אחת consistently
every time in both passages. This would appear to be secondary
standardization on the part of 𝗎, motivated by a desire similar to that so
obvious in the plague narratives, to make the command and the execution
match. Since Q⁻ is not extant in any of these verses, we cannot confirm at
what stage this standardization took place.

10Waltke, "SP," p. 220.

In the case of the cherubim the situation is different, in that 𝔐 reads consistently איש אל אחיו while ⅏ reads consistently אחד אל אחד (here for the command and at 37:9 for the execution). 𝔔^{m} is extant only here for the command. Yet since this passage regarding the cherubim occurs just two paragraphs before the lengthy instructions regarding the curtains and frames, which ⅏ was to standardize, it may be that the same desire arose here in anticipation of those 5 readings. If the motivation for the present variant was indeed as much for standardization as for "banality," then we would expect 𝔔^{m} to have had the same phrase it has here also in the ten places in chapters 26 and 36, for that trend would have begun early enough to have affected both 𝔔^{m} and ⅏. If, however, this variant is to be seen as arising from a different motive than was the case for those ten, the standardization may have postdated the copying of 𝔔^{m}.

With the more limited evidence from 𝔊, it is impossible to know how its *Vorlage* read, although one might tend to think that this 𝔔^{m}⅏ reading postdated the translation into Greek. 𝔊 several times uses a phrase with **αδελφος** when the subjects are human beings (10:23; 32:27; cf. 32:29), but once even with humans it renders differently (**ετερος τω ετερω** in 16:15). The relevant passages in chapters 36 and 37 are lacking in 𝔊, so we cannot compare its translations when 𝔐 differs. In chapter 26, however, where ⅏ and 𝔐 disagree as they do here, 𝔊 has variations of **ετερα τη ετερα** in verses 3bis,6,17, but **αλληλαις εις εκαστην** in 26:5. Thus 𝔊 is not considered to support either reading here.

e. *Where 𝔐 Preserves a Minor Syntactical Inconsistency*

The final variant in this section where 𝔐 alone is preferable affects the number of a verb.

17:12 ויהיו ידיו ⅏**TT^{J}S]** και εγενοντο αι χειρες 𝔊; ויהי ידיו 𝔐
𝔔^{m}⅏/𝔊/ ≠ <u>𝔐</u>

Waltke[11] gives 5 examples of the tendency of ⅏ to correct verbs to agree with the number of the subject, including one in Exodus: 4:29, where another singular verb is corrected to the plural. The fact that 𝔔^{m} shares this reading with ⅏ indicates that this tendency began early in the 𝔔^{m}⅏ tradition. The evidence of 𝔊 cannot be used in the question of textual

[11] Waltke, "SP," p. 218.

affiliation, since a translator would have rendered with plural regardless of his *Vorlage*.

Summary: Thus this section shows 𝕸 standing alone in ten original readings. It preserves the slightly shorter reading in seven, the original preposition in one, the original idiom in one, and a minor syntactical inconsistency in one.

2. 𝕸𝔊 = PREFERABLE

𝕸 and 𝔊 together preserve the preferable reading in fourteen variants. Those preferable readings, however, tell little about the nature of the relationship between 𝕸 and 𝔊. It is the secondary readings, rather, that illustrate the tendencies of the tradition shared by 𝐐ⁿ and 𝖅. The most noteworthy group in this category is composed of those major expansions in 𝐐ⁿ and 𝖅, significant additions to the text for the sake of harmonization of various kinds. Of somewhat less import are those cases of agreement between 𝕸 and 𝔊 against 𝐐ⁿ and 𝖅 in smaller variants. While any one of these secondary readings could have arisen independently in both 𝐐ⁿ and 𝖅, taken together and with the major expansions, they contribute to the emerging pattern of agreement such that 𝐐ⁿ and 𝖅 clearly belong to the same textual tradition. Also to be investigated, however, are the many cases of smaller variants where 𝐐ⁿ disagrees with 𝖅. These disagreements reveal the complexities involved even in establishing textual traditions. For a full discussion of these questions, see chapters IV and V.

a. *Where 𝕸𝔊 Preserve the Shorter Reading (Major Expansion)*

There are eleven variants in this category. In nine of the following passages both 𝐐ⁿ and 𝖅 preserve lengthy expansions to the narrative, and in two they preserve expansions which are short in length but major in exegetical significance, against both 𝕸 and 𝔊, which lack the expansions. These expansions will be discussed at length in Chapter V.A and B, where they will be used to describe the nature of 𝐐ⁿ and 𝖅. At that time minor differences between the two witnesses will also be investigated to see what can be learned of the chronological development within the 𝐐ⁿ𝖅 tradition.

The verse numbering is that of von Gall. Some expansions have no special verse number because of their brevity, although they are qualitatively significant.

7:18^b   hab 𝔐] › 𝔐𝔊   Q^a𝔐 ≠ 𝔐𝔊

7:29^b   hab 𝔐] › 𝔐𝔊

8:19^b   hab 𝔐] › 𝔐𝔊

9:5^b   hab 𝔐] › 𝔐𝔊

9:19^b   hab 𝔐] › 𝔐𝔊

10:2^b   hab 𝔐] › 𝔐𝔊

18:25𝔐   // Deut 1:9-18 𝔐]   aliter et brevius 𝔐𝔊

27:19^b   hab 𝔐] › 𝔐𝔊

32:10   hab 𝔐] › 𝔐𝔊

In the following two readings both **Q^a** and 𝔐 preserve an expansion which, though short, is nevertheless exegetically significant.   They will likewise be discussed in Chapter V.A.

24:1   ר[נדב ואביהוא אלעזר ו]איתמ   𝔐 נדב ואביהוא] נדב ואביהוא אלעזר ו[איתמ]ר   𝔐𝔊

24:9   נדב ואביהוא אלעזר וא]יתמר   𝔐 נדב ואביהוא] נדב ואביהוא אלעזר וא[יתמר   𝔐𝔊

b. Where 𝔐𝔊 Preserve the Shorter Reading (Five Words)

One variant, where **Q^a**𝔐 add five words from the immediate context, represents a transition between the major expansions just mentioned and the brief expansions in the following section.

10:5 **Q^a** 𝔐   ואכל את] כ[ל] עשב הארץ ואת כל [פרי העץ הצמח לכם מן השדה

𝔐𝔊   העץ הצמח לכם מן השדה   ואכל את כל

Q^a𝔐 ≠ 𝔐𝔊

This is considered an addition in **Q^a**𝔐 because the two otherwise unrelated traditions 𝔐 and 𝔊 lack it and because there is no obvious occasion for parablepsis.   (It is true that there are two possibilities for parablepsis involving the two כל's, but neither seems likely.   First, a scribe's eyes might well have skipped from the first כל to the second if פרי were not in the *Vorlage* but were a later addition; but without פרי the two parallel phrases would not have been symmetrical. Alternatively, פרי could have been in the *Vorlage,* כל‿כל lost by parablepsis, and then פרי later lost by both 𝔐 and 𝔊; this would be somewhat surprising.)

This verse occurs in the words of Moses and Aaron to Pharaoh, threatening the eighth plague, that of locusts. Similar passages occur two more

times later in the narrative of the same plague, where $\mathbf{Q^m}$ is not preserved.
In 10:12, where Yahweh instructs Moses to stretch out his hand to bring the
locusts, $\mathbf{ш}$ agrees with $\mathbf{G}$ in a reading that is longer than the text in $\mathbf{m}$; and
in 10:15, where the results are described, $\mathbf{шmG}$ all have the full reading:

10:12 $\mathbf{шG}$ ויאכל את כל עשב הארץ ואת כל פרי העץ אשר השאיר הברד

$\mathbf{m}$ ויאכל את כל עשב הארץ את כל   אשר השאיר הברד

10:15 $\mathbf{шmG}$ ויאכל את כל עשב הארץ ואת כל פרי העץ אשר הותיר הברד

$\mathbf{m}$, then, mentions trees in the threat in 10:5 and plants in the instructions
in 10:12; then in the results in 10:15 it combines plants and the fruit of
trees. If these two shorter readings are to be considered preferable, then
the dramatic effect was achieved by having two prior statements each
predicting a different result, and the statement of the results combining
those two.

It appears that scribes in both the $\mathbf{Q^mш}$ and $\mathbf{G}$ traditions expanded
earlier sentences of prediction by using phrases occurring later in the
description of the results. The $\mathbf{ш}$ tradition (including $\mathbf{Q^m}$, if we may
assume that $\mathbf{Q^m}$ also had the longer reading in 10:12) did so more consistently than the $\mathbf{G}$ tradition.[12]

Here then is a case where the $\mathbf{Q^mш}$ tradition expands with a few
words taken from a bit later in the same narrative, apparently for the sake
of a different kind of dramatic effect, emphasizing at each stage the gravity
of the damage done by the locusts as well as the correspondence between
the prediction and the fulfilment of the plague. It is not considered a major
expansion because it is fairly short, the words are taken from the close
context, and no major exegetical move seems to be reflected. It should be
carefully noted that a case of this same sort of expansion occurs also in $\mathbf{G}$
as well as in $\mathbf{ш}$ just seven verses later.

---

[12]The longer reading here in 10:5 was reproduced in the major expansion of $\mathbf{ш}$ in 10:2[b], where the words of Moses to Pharaoh in 10:3b-6a are
first spoken by Yahweh to Moses (see Chapter V.A.3.a regarding the series of
major expansions in $\mathbf{Q^mш}$). The repetition in $\mathbf{ш}$ in 10:2[b] cannot be taken as
an argument in favor of its preferability in 10:5, since scribes made certain
that the major expansions exactly matched the text they were taken from.
What it does argue for is that $\mathbf{Q^m}$ also had the longer reading in 10:2[b] (it is
no longer extant in that part of the major expansion) since it still preserves
it in 10:5.

*c. Where **MG** Preserve the Shorter Reading (One Word)*

There are two variants where **MG** preserve the shorter reading and **Q^a Ш** add one word.

17:13ב ואת עמו

Q^a ויחלש] יהשוע [את] עמלק ויכם לפי [חרב

Ш ויחלש יהושע את עמלק ואת עמו ויכם לפי חרב

M ויחלש יהושע את עמלק ואת עמו ____ לפי חרב

και ετρεψατο Ιησους τον Αμαληκ και παντα τον λαον αυτου (> B*+) ______________ εν φονω μαχαιρας **G**

Q^a Ш ≠ MG

The shorter reading of **MG** is considered preferable because it makes good sense following the earlier verb, **ויחלש** (defeat), because the two traditions agree against the one tradition represented by **Q^a Ш**, and because no occasion for accidental omission of **ויכם** is obvious.

This reading does provide a good example of actual parablepsis committed and then corrected by the same scribe: the two *waw*'s beginning **ואת** and **ויכם** caused the scribe to skip over the two short words in between. But he apparently noticed his own mistake and corrected it by inserting the two missing words just above the line. This mistake indicates that the added word **ויכם** was already in his *Vorlage,* since it was the *waw* of that word that caused the parablepsis. Here we have clear evidence that the tradition represented in **Q^a** and **Ш** antedated the copying of **Q^a**. Incidentally, there is only one other corrected error extant in **Q^a**, and both occurred in the same column, just three lines apart (see Chapter V.A.).

It should be noted that the free translation of **לפי חרב**, "by the mouth of the sword," as **(εν) φονω μαχαιρας**, "with slaughter of the sword," occurs also at Num 21:24; Deut 13:16; and 20:13. At Gen 34:26, on the other hand, the translation is literal: **εν στοματι μαχαιρας**. This provides a good example of the freedom of the translator(s) in some instances (see Chapter V.D. for more examples of freedom along with examples of literalness).

8:20[24] מאד [ערב כבד **Ш**] ערב כבד **M**; η κυνομυια πληθος **G**; *gravissima* **V** **Q^a Ш ≠ MG**

This reading is included here with some hesitation. One's first inclination on seeing an adverb heightening a description in **Q^a Ш** but lacking in **MG** is to write it off as a typical expansion of scribes, even more so when it occurs in the plague narratives where desire to heighten the miraculous is quite understandable. A study of the plague narratives shows, however, that 𝕸 describes plagues and similar phenomena with this adverb 5 times (9:3, 18, 24; 10:14, 19) and that except for here 𝖀 has the word only in those same 5 verses.[13] In the entire book of Exodus 𝖀 and 𝕸 agree in having the word 12 times; only here is there disagreement. Furthermore, a case could be made for parablepsis here (see the immediately preceding example), since the two words in a row consist of 3 letters and end in *daleth*.

Since, therefore, this is not a word that 𝖀 characteristically adds, the longer reading could well be taken as preferable. Perhaps somewhat arbitrarily, the shorter reading has been tentatively designated the original, because of the agreement of 𝕲 with 𝕸. In 11 out of the 12 occurrences of מאד in 𝕸, 𝕲 renders with σφόδρα(-ος); in the twelfth, at 19:16, 𝕲 renders μέγα. Since neither word occurs here, 𝕲 appears to support the shorter reading of 𝕸.

Summary: Once again, these fourteen cases of agreement between 𝕸 and 𝕲 in lacking expansions shared by 𝗤ᵐ and 𝖀 reveal very little about any specific relationship between 𝕸 and 𝕲. It is to be expected that texts agree in preserving the original: that only means that they go back to a common heritage in the distant past. It is when texts share striking secondary readings that the question of their affiliation arises.

D. PREFERABLE READINGS PRESERVED IN 𝕲

In this final section we will consider those readings in which 𝕲 appears uniquely to preserve the preferable reading against the three Hebrew witnesses. The findings here will play a significant role in the discussion in Chapter IV regarding textual affiliation and also in Chapter V.D regarding the nature of 𝕲 and in V.E regarding the history of the text of Exodus.

---

[13]Plus an additional 2 times in the major expansions 9:5ᵇ and 9:19ᵇ, but only where it is directly repeating a מאד in the preceding paragraph in 𝕸. For more on major expansions, see Chapter V.A.

a. Where G Preserves the Shorter Reading (Major Expansion)

There is one variant where **G** alone preserves the shorter reading and **Q⁰ ɯ 𝔪** all add a major expansion.

32:9 ויאמר יהוה]אל מש[ה ראיתי את העם הנה והנה עם קשה ערף הוא

Q⁰ ɯ 𝔪 ⊬ G   **ɯ 𝔪] ⟩ G**

This is a major expansion presumably brought in from the book of Deuteronomy and as such represents the only case discovered in this study where **𝔪** can be clearly seen to share this phenomenon with **Q⁰** and **ɯ** (cf. Chapter V.A, B, and C). The reason for its uniqueness may be merely that this is the only passage where we have a control. If such expansion occurred elsewhere early enough to have affected all four witnesses being investigated here, there is no clue at all as to whether it should be attributed to a literary or a transmissional stage in the development of the text. All other cases of major expansions from Deuteronomy that have been discovered have been confined to the single tradition behind **Q⁰** and **ɯ** and have not affected either of the other witnesses. There have, however, been a few cases of moderate or minor expansion or alteration which is at least influenced by passages in Deuteronomy (see below for examples).

In Exod **32:9** the shorter reading is taken as preferable for two reasons. On the negative side, there is no reason to suspect parablepsis in **G**, since the only thing the insertion shares with the beginning of the following sentence is the initial *waw*.[14]   On the positive side, Exodus 32 was fertile soil for expansion from Deuteronomy and for alteration under its influence because of the fairly extensive parallel narrative in Deuteronomy 9. The story of the golden calf (Exodus 32) is summarized in Deut 9:8-21. This is one of two major expansions from Deuteronomy 9 which can be detected in **ɯ**. The other occurs in the very next verse, **32:10**; **Q⁰** shares it with **ɯ**, but neither **𝔪** nor **G** does (see Chapter V.A). **G**, however, preserves a smaller expansion from Deut 9:12 in Exod **32:7ב** (see Chapter II.A.1; cf. also **32:11ב** and **32:13א**, also apparently influenced by Deuteronomy). For these reasons the shorter reading of **G** is considered almost certainly preferable, and in this one case **𝔪** can be seen to share a major expansion from Deuteronomy with **Q⁰** and **ɯ**.

---

[14]Quell had already tentatively suggested that this sentence was an addition from Deut 9:13 (*BHS* [4p]).

It appears, then, that an early scribe imported Deut 9:13 into his text of Exodus. From this distance two reasons suggest themselves for this expansion. The scribe may have wanted to sharpen the contrast between the Israelites as "a stiff-necked people" (32:9) who should be consumed and Moses' descendants whom God would make into "a great nation" (32:10). Although the phrase "stiff-necked people" occurs nowhere else in the OT, it does occur in the vicinity of this story both in Exodus (33:3,5; and 34:9) and in Deuteronomy (9:6).

A second possible reason lies in the fact that this is the only state-ment in Yahweh's speech to Moses in the narrative in Deuteronomy which is lacking in **G** in Exod 32:7-10. The scribe may have wished to make Yahweh's speech complete. Note, however, that the influence did not go in the other direction: Deut 9:12-14 has not been supplemented with the extra state-ments in Exod 32:7-10. This one-sided activity may suggest that such expansions were very much a personal, perhaps even idiosyncratic phenomenon. It may well be that this major expansion was made by one scribe working alone, and that from that one moment it entered the text which later divided into the two traditions we now know as **Q⁺ɯ** and **ɯ**.

If the motivation of the scribe is not entirely clear, his method is. The scribe brought the entire sentence from Deuteronomy, only changing אלי to אל משה, as required by the different context. Otherwise the texts are identical in all four places: in Exod 32:9 and Deut 9:13 in **ɯ** and **ɯ**, except that both **ɯ** and **ɯ** have לאמר in Deuteronomy; presumably scribes in both traditions added that minor word in Deuteronomy after this sentence had been inserted in Exodus. Thus it appears that the scribe very deliberately and carefully copied the sentence so that it would be exactly reproduced. Whether he copied from his memory or by opening a scroll of Deuteronomy cannot be determined.

b. *Where **G** Preserves the Shorter Reading (One or Two Words)*

In six cases where **G** preserves the shorter reading **Q⁺ɯɯ** add a word or phrase; in one case **ɯ** adds one word and **Q⁺ɯ** add a major expansion.

20:19ᵃ   hab **ɯ**]   דבר אתה עמנו ונשמעה **ɯ**;   Λαλησον συ ημιν **G**

                                                  Q⁺ɯ ⊁ **ɯ** ⊁ **G**

This reading represents a transition between the preceding variant, which was a major expansion, and the following ones, which are short expansions. Here **G** disagrees with **𝕸** in that **𝕸** added one word to the preferable text, but agrees with **𝕸** in not having added the major expansion preserved in **Q**ᵃ𝖝. The major expansion will be discussed in Chapter V.A.

Here it is enough to note that the shorter reading of **G** preserves the contrast of the original narrative much better than does the longer reading of **𝕸**. The emphasis is on the question: Who is to speak to us, Yahweh or Moses?   The addition of "and we shall hear" would appear to have been added later by a scribe with liturgical or homiletical interests under the influence of the covenant ceremony.

9:20 [ו]את מקנה[ו] את עבדיו **𝖝𝕸**] τα κτηνη αυτου **G**   **Q**ᵃ𝖝𝕸 ⊬ **G**

If the roles of **𝕸** and **G** were reversed, and it were **𝕸** that had the shorter reading against the other three witnesses, few would doubt that the longer reading with "his slaves" is a case of exegetical expansion. The context describes precautions taken -- or not taken -- before the seventh plague, hail. While the command in verse 19 does not specifically mention bringing slaves in from the field, it does threaten death to any human being left outside;   and verses 22 and 25, reporting Yahweh's command and describing the results, again mention hail falling on everything in the fields from human to animal.   Verses 20 and 21 describe the responses to the threat in verse 19 of those who feared Yahweh and those who did not.   In both 20 and 21, where **G** lacks "slaves," 𝖝 and **𝕸** agree in adding "slaves" to the mention of animals either taken inside or left in the field.   If only one instance were involved, the repetition of the word "slaves" and of the את in verse 20 might lead one to think of parablepsis on the part of **G**. But that becomes much less likely when the same thing happens in two verses in a row and when a clear motivation for the addition is present: that of internal harmonization within the narrative.

Qᵃ is extant only in verse 20, and of the addition it preserves only the *waw* - and even that one letter is not totally clear! Yet the fact that there is any letter at all attached to the את indicates that the entire phrase must have been included on the scroll.

Thus we are presented with evidence that **G** preserves a preferable shorter reading in opposition to these three extant Hebrew witnesses. We will now consider other examples of the same phenomenon more briefly; their implications will be discussed in Chapter V.D and E.

18:1ב [עמו וליׂשׂראל למשה **ⅢⅢ**] Ισραηλ τω εαυτου λαω **G**

Qᵃ ⅢⅢ ≠ G

Again the context seems to have cried out for a scribe to add Moses' name for the sake of emphasis and completeness. Jethro has just been identified as Moses' father-in-law, and in the following verses his trip to visit Moses and to bring his family will be described. Here, then, it did not seem enough to say that Jethro heard what Yahweh had done for Israel, although that is the topic of the verse as a whole. The personal relationships prompted a scribe to add Moses' name as the prime recipient of Yahweh's acts, since that was what chiefly concerned Jethro. But this particular bit of exegetical expansion did not affect the **G** tradition.

34:2   **Qᵃ ⅢⅢ**   סיני הר אל בב(ו)קר ועלי[ת לבקר נכון (Ⅲ והיה) והוי

και γινου ετοιμος εις το πρωι και αναβηση _____ εις το
ορος το Σιναι **G**   **Qᵃ ⅢⅢ ≠ G**

The בב(ו)קר is taken with some hesitation as a case of a clarifying expansion shared by the three Hebrew witnesses. It is not likely that it was lost in the process of translation because it was perceived as too repetitious. Most of the Greek translation of the narrative and legal portions of Exodus reveals that repetition was generally retained and occasionally perpetrated. The possibility of parablepsis in the Greek transmission clouds the issue. Yet the nature of the reading makes it likely that the shorter text was original, and that a scribe felt that the second verb should receive a time designation as well as the first, to make Yahweh's command totally precise.

32:29ב   **Qᵃ ⅢⅢ**   ברכה היום עלי[כם ולתת

δοθηναι εφ υμας _____ ευλογιαν **G**   **Qᵃ ⅢⅢ ≠ G**

Although the comparison here is not so clear as one would like, nevertheless in the light of the above examples we may with some degree of confidence assign originality to **G**. Complicating factors include the presence of other variants earlier in the verse, especially the fact that the first verb is imperative in **ⅢⅢ** and **Ⅲ** but aorist indicative in **G**, and the possibility of homoioteleuton because two words in a row end with *mem*. On the other hand, the word "today" appears earlier in the sentence in all four witnesses, and on either understanding of the verb the repetition does not seem necessary. Thus the shorter reading of **G** is considered probably preferable. (For a case where **G**'s lack of the word "today" is taken as probably secondary, see the discussion of **34:11א** in II.A.5.)

28:40   ולבני אהרן תעשה כ(י)תנת ‏[ועשית להם‏] אבנטים
         ‏[ומגבעו‏]ת תעשה להם **Q⁴𝔪𝔐**

και τοις υιοις Ααρων ποιησεις χιτωνας και _____ ζωνας
και κιδαρεις ποιησεις αυτοις **G**

Q⁴𝔪𝔐 ≠ G

The verb "make, do" is a frequent addition in the various witnesses of Exodus. **𝔐** never preserves the word when it is lacking in **𝔪**. (**Q⁴** provides no further data on this word.) **G** has the verb 13 times when it is lacking in **𝔐**. **𝔪** has the verb 4 times when it is lacking in **𝔐**. One of those times (36:8 [37:1**G**]) the evidence of **G** is ambiguous, twice (26:20 and 27:19) **G** agrees with **𝔐** in not having the verb, and once (12:17) **𝔪** seems to have conflated two readings, ושמרתם as in **𝔐** and ועשיתם as in **G**. In 2 of these 4 readings a case could be made for loss of the word by parablepsis because of the repetition of letters: תעשה עשרים (26:20) and עשו עשר (36:8).

While the evidence is thus quite mixed, still it may be fair to say that since the tendency is for **𝔪** or **G** to have the word when it is absent in **𝔐**, probably due more often to expansionism than to parablepsis, it seems more likely that the shorter reading in **G** is the original. תעשה already appears twice in the verse, before and after this point. Did a scribe add the third verb – in a different form, ועשית – and indirect object so that each of the three accusative objects would have its own verb and indirect object? It seems much less likely that such labored parallelism was original to the text.

9:10 **Q⁴𝔪𝔐**   ויקחו את פיח הכבשן ‏[ויעמדו‏] לפנ[י‏] פרעה
και ελαβεν την αιθαλην της καμιναιας _____ εναντιον φ. **G**

Q⁴𝔪𝔐 ≠ G

Since it is hard to see how parablepsis could have occurred and since the passage is able to stand without the extra verb, this is considered a case of expansion on the part of the Hebrew traditions witnessed in **Q⁴𝔪𝔐**. But it may be that the expansion was motivated by something other than the mere desire for harmonization or completeness that we have seen so often. As I have suggested for a variant two verses before this, **9:8ג** (see Chapter II.A.5), there may have been a polemical desire on the part of scribes to heighten the confusion of the magicians. The tradition preserved in **G** added explicit references to the servants of Pharaoh 4 times, including at 9:8, perhaps with the aim of emphasizing their involvement in the contest between Pharaoh and Yahweh and hence their defeat.   It may be that a tradition preserved in the three Hebrew witnesses emphasized the defeat of the magicians in a different way, with a word play.   Verse 11 states: ולא יכלו החרטמים לעמד לפני משה מפני השחין.

Perhaps a scribe wanted to heighten the contrast between the victory of Moses and the humiliation of the magicians by adding the same word in the previous sentence: Moses and Aaron <u>were</u> able to stand before Pharaoh, although the magicians could not stand before Moses.

In support of this suggestion is the fact that apart from these two verses the verb עמד in all of its forms occurs in only two places in the entire plague narrative: in 9:28, where Pharaoh tells Moses that he will let them go and they need <u>stay</u> no longer; and in 9:16, where Yahweh's message for Pharaoh is that he has been allowed to <u>stand</u> for one purpose only: that he might see Yahweh's power. The magicians can no longer stand, because of their suffering from the boils. Pharaoh can still stand, but only so that he may be a defeated witness of Yahweh's greater power. Thus 9:10 is the only reference to Moses and Aaron standing before Pharaoh; it is as if the stage is being explicitly set for the magicians no longer to be able to stand before Moses.

Whether or not it was such a motive that moved the scribe to add the verb, it still seems that the effect of the word would have been obvious enough that no scribe would have deliberately left it out. And, as stated above, no reason suggests itself for an accidental omission. Hence the word appears to have been added: late enough in the history of the text so that the *Vorlage* of **G** lacked it, but early enough so that all three Hebrew witnesses have it.

<u>Summary</u>: **G** appears to have preserved the original text in eight readings. In six cases **Q⁰ⅢⅢ** add a word or phrase; in one **Ⅲ** adds one word and **Q⁰Ⅲ** add a major expansion from Deuteronomy; in the last case **Q⁰ⅢⅢ** agree in adding a major expansion from Deuteronomy. To anticipate the discussion in Chapter V.D and E somewhat: whereas **G** is clearly expansionist much of the time, occasionally it seems clearly to preserve the shorter, preferable reading. Thus its history appears to be much more complex than may have been expected.

CONCLUSION

In Chapter II we have looked at those readings where we could with some degree of confidence assign preferability to one or more of the witnesses. Of the total of 174 variants, preferability has been established -- always with qualifications! -- in 85 cases.

Of the 85 readings discussed in this chapter, $\mathbf{Q}^{a}$ exhibits 42 preferable readings: 5 uniquely and 37 more in conjunction with one or more other witnesses. $\mathbf{m}$ exhibits 0 preferable readings uniquely but 35 in conjunction with one or more other witnesses. $\mathbf{m}$ exhibits 66 preferable readings: 10 uniqely and 56 in conjunction with one or more other witnesses. $\mathbf{G}$ exhibits 40 preferable readings: 8 uniquely and 32 in conjunction with one or more other witnesses.

We now turn in Chapter III to those readings where it seems impossible to establish a preferable or original text.

CHAPTER III

SYNONYMOUS VARIANTS

INTRODUCTION

This chapter lists all the variants for which no preferable reading can be determined.[1] These are entitled "synonymous variants," meaning that they are different legitimate ways of expressing the same idea. Some variants cannot be said to be clearly preferable because of either the fluidity of the Hebrew language or our lack of knowledge of its usage. Others cannot be determined because both the longer and the shorter versions are equally acceptable, and we cannot be sure whether omission or expansion has taken place.

Some might say that most variants are synonymous, simply because there probably never was an *Urtext;* rather there were parallel formulations of the same text from the beginning.[2] Devoting a chapter here to synonymous variants does not necessarily signal rejection of any *Urtext*. But it does at least reflect a recognition of our limitations at this distance from the early days of the text.

Even if there was one *Urtext* which left the final editor's table to meet its fate at the hands of successive scribes, there remains the difficulty of establishing the moment in time that distinguishes editorial work from scribal work. The book of Exodus is full, for example, of repetition in all four witnesses under scrutiny here. Which instances of repetitiousness are to be attributed to an original composer, whether in oral or written form, which are to be attributed to one of the several redactors through the centuries, and which to scribes and translators? How would repetition at a literary stage look different from repetition at a transmissional stage?

Because of these difficulties, it is necessary to be cautious in discussing preferability of readings. In the previous chapter were listed

---

[1]See Chapter I.F.3 for a discussion of the criteria and problems involved in the evaluation of readings.

[2]E.g., Talmon; see Chapter I.C. for a discussion of his and others' views on this issue; and see Chapter I.F.3 for a discussion of my approach to the evaluation of readings and its relationship to the question of an *Urtext*.

those readings where a decision about preferability could be made with some confidence. In this chapter are discussed those readings where it seems best to leave the question open and simply label them synonymous variants.

Yet if synonymous variants do not lead us closer to a preferable *Urtext*, they do have their value. On the hypothesis that there was an original *Urtext*, establishing synonymous variants gives us two (or more) equally good candidates for that *Urtext*. Alternatively, on the hypothesis that there were parallel texts from the beginning, establishing synonymous variants gives us two (or more) of those parallel "original" texts.

Furthermore, synonymous variants are significant in the area of textual affiliation. Hence these variants are also discussed in the same order and the same categories as the preferable readings in Chapter II. If it is impossible to choose between readings, it is at least possible to classify them according to agreement and disagreement of the witnesses. The evidence of these synonymous variants will be collated in Chapter IV to determine whether and in what ways each of the various witnesses is related to each of the others.

A. SYNONYMOUS VARIANTS PRESERVED BY **Q**

1. SYNONYMOUS VARIANTS PRESERVED BY **Q** ALONE

There are twelve instances of synonymous variants where **Q** is alone in its reading. Eight of these are quite minor, each involving only one or two grammatical features or "all"; one involves variation within a phrase, and three involve a fairly significant difference in length of text.

Each of these is discussed elsewhere in Chapter III, depending on which, if any, of the other three witnesses agree together against **Q**. The entire list is presented and organized according to type in Chapter IV.A.1, and the section of Chapter III where each is discussed is also indicated there.

2. SYNONYMOUS VARIANTS SHARED BY **Q** ⅢⅢ

There are twelve synonymous variants shared by **Q** ⅢⅢ. Two involve a different order; in one **Q** ⅢⅢ are shorter and in three they are longer; one involves a different word, and five a different form of a word.

a. Different Order

Two variants shared by **Qᵃ ᴍ** preserve a different order. One involves ten verses, the other only two words.

30:1-10 post 26:35 ᴍ] post 29:46 **mG**   **Qᵃ ᴍ ≅ mG**

It should be noted that parts of only three words from these ten verses are extant in **Qᵃ**, and that the fragment on which they are preserved contains no words from any other pericope. Thus it is only as a result of reconstruction that it has been determined that the scroll agrees with **ᴍ** in the position of this paragraph. Nevertheless the placement seems assured by the margins and spacing of cols. xxix–xxxii and xxxv; for a full discussion of the reconstruction see the edition in *DJD*.

Although there are 21 cases where **ᴍ** and **m** disagree on the order of individual words and phrases, and one case where one verse is placed differently (cf. Chapter V.B), this is the only time where the placement of an entire paragraph is affected. Neither order seems obviously superior or inferior to the other judging from context, nor is it obvious that or why anyone would have deliberately transposed these ten verses from one of these positions to the other.

A case could be made in favor of either order. Placing the pericope in chapter 26 makes sense in light of the spatial arrangement of the tabernacle. In all traditions, these subjects are treated in the following order:

26:31-35	veil between the holy place and the holy of holies, the <u>mercy seat behind the veil</u>, and the table and lampstand outside the veil
≅ **Qᵃ ᴍ** 30:1-10	*altar* of incense, which is to be put <u>before the veil,</u> <u>before the mercy seat</u>
26:36-37	screen for the door of the tent
27:1-8	*altar* (sc. for burnt offerings)
27:9-19	court
27:20-21	lamp to burn continually

The references to the veil and to the mercy seat in 26:31-35 as well as in **30:1-10** make this placement seem logical, as does the complementarity between the treatment of the altar of incense and the other altar in 27:1-8.

On the other hand, reference to daily burning on the other altar in 29:38-42 could have occasioned the introduction of the incense altar five verses later, at **30:1-10** according to 𝔐's counting. In all traditions, the subjects are dealt with in the following order:

29:1-37	ordination of priests
29:38-42	<u>daily</u> burnt offerings on the offering <u>altar</u>
29:43-46	Yahweh's meeting with the people there and
	sanctification
≅ 𝔐𝔊 30:1-10	<u>daily</u> burning on the incense <u>altar</u>
30:11-16	census, ransom, and atonement money
30:17-21	laver
30:22-33	anointing oil for consecration
30:34-38	incense

But neither of these orders is fully satisfying. We would logically expect the instructions for the incense altar to be given in chapter 25, along with the other articles of furniture for the most holy place and the holy place, before attention shifts to matters of overall construction. (Reference to a sketch of the tabernacle will facilitate understanding here.)

» 25:10-22	ark, mercy seat, cherubim
» 25:23-30	table, plates, dishes, bread of Presence
» 25:31-40	lampstand, lamps, snuffers, trays
26:1-6	curtains of fabric
26:7-10	curtains of goats' hair
26:11-13	clasps; hanging the curtains
26:14	covering of rams' skins and goatskins
26:15-25	frames
26:26-30	bars
26:31-33	veil separating most holy place from holy place
26:34	mercy seat in the most holy place
26:35	<u>table and lampstand outside veil</u> !
26:36-37	screen and pillars for door of tent

This survey of the contents of chapters 25 and 26 shows two things. First, a logical ordering would call for the incense altar to appear with the ark, the table, and the lampstand, to complete the furniture of the two inner rooms (see the arrows). Second, in connection with the veil that separates the two rooms, only the table and lampstand are mentioned as being outside the veil (26:35). It appears that Q⁴ 𝔐 tried to rectify this by placing the instructions for the incense altar here; verse 6 of this disputed pericope commands the placing of the altar before the veil. But again the logical arrangement would have called for the altar to have been described previously, and for 26:35 to refer to all three items belonging together in the one room.

Two more factors should be mentioned here. **G** lacks any reference to the actual construction of the incense altar, yet it does mention its placement twice in the final chapter of Exodus. Thus the incense altar appears as follows:

Instructions: **30:1-10** given in chapter 30, 𝔐**G**; given in chapter 26, **Qᵃ**𝔴
Construction: given in 37:25-28, 𝔴𝔐 (□**Qᵇ**); lacking in **G**
Placement: lacking in 26:35 in 𝔴𝔐**G** (□**Qᵇ**);
                 mentioned in 40:5 and 26 in 𝔴𝔐**G** (□**Qᵇ**)
In lists: included in 30:27[30:28𝔴], 31:8, 35:15, 39:38 in 𝔴𝔐 (□**Qᵇ**);
                 included in 30:27 in **G**, but only one altar is mentioned
                 in the other three lists in **G**

It should be noted that in the account of the construction, 𝔴𝔐 (□**Qᵇ**) place the incense altar in an order which seems logical:

37:1-9	ark, mercy seat, cherubim
37:10-16	table, plates, dishes, bowls, flagons
37:17-24	lampstand, lamps, snuffers, trays
<u>37:25-29</u>	<u>incense altar, anointing oil, incense</u>
38:1-7	altar of burnt offering
38:8	laver
38:9-20	court

A similar order is followed in the lists in 𝔴𝔐 (30:27; 31:8; 35:15; 39:38) and twice in chapter 40: 40:1-8 and 40:18-33; note that in these last two passages **G** shows basic agreement with 𝔴𝔐.

The final factor is a smaller grammatical feature. Regarding the other altar, that for burnt offerings, in 27:1 𝔐 gives instructions to build את המזבח, which was to be overlaid with bronze. 𝔴 and **G**, on the other hand, lack the definite article, and 𝔴 lacks the את (□**Qᵇ**). It has been argued[3] that the incense altar is not from the original P, but from a later stratum, P₂. Driver bases this on two factors: the absence of the incense altar in chapter 25 and the definite article with the altar of burnt offering in 27:1; 30:18,20; 40:7,32; etc., making it sound as if there were only one altar. (He does not refer to any of the evidence of 𝔴 and **G** noted above, perhaps due to the nature of the commentary series.)

---

[3] See, e.g., S. R. Driver, *The Book of Exodus* (Cambridge: Cambridge University Press, 1953; 1st ed., 1911), pp. 291 and 328.

Taken in conjunction with all of the other factors, the variation in the definite article appears at first to be of significance, as if 𝕸 in 27:1 preserved a memory of a time when there was only one altar in Exodus, and 𝕾 and 𝕲, both known to strive for consistency elsewhere, altered the verse to allow for the fact that the other altar had been received into the tradition. Yet this argument is weakened, it seems to me, when the other articles of furniture are also taken into account: when the ark, table, and lampstand are first mentioned (25:10, 23, and 31; the same is true for the incense altar, 30:1) they also are indefinite.   Furthermore, elsewhere 𝕾𝕸𝕲 agree in referring to the bronze altar as simply "the altar" (e.g., 29:12,36,38; 30:18, 20; 40:32 [G 38:27];   40:7 𝕾𝕸 [verse lacking in 𝕲]). It seems more likely that the disagreement in 27:1 is merely a matter of grammar, where 𝕾 and 𝕲 preserve the usual Hebrew usage.

All of the other anomalies remain, however. The instructions for the incense altar appear in chapter 26 in 𝐐ᵃ𝕾 and in chapter 30 in 𝕸𝕲; neither placement seems right. The account of the construction is given -- and in a logical position -- in 𝕾𝕸 but does not appear in 𝕲.   The altar is included in four lists in 𝕾𝕸 but apparently in only one list in 𝕲. It is not mentioned with the other furniture of the holy place in chapter 25 or in 26:35. Yet it is mentioned in similar contexts in 40:5 and 26. Thus there does seem to be good reason to question the originality of the tradition of the incense altar. Yet it remains difficult to classify this question: is it a matter of the literary history of Exodus or of its textual transmission? When Driver attributes this tradition to P$_2$ rather than to P proper he is treating it as a literary issue. But all of the evidence cited above would appear rather to date from the history of the transmission of the completed work.

All of these peculiarities show how complex is the relationship among the three textual traditions and the two accounts, that of the instructions and that of the construction of the tabernacle. For a complete picture, the discrepancies which have been mentioned need to be considered in the context of the entire tabernacle account, chapters 25-31 and 35-40. Gooding, for instance, discusses some of what has been mentioned here in conjunction with yet more peculiarities.[4]   Because of the fragmentary

---

[4]D. W. Gooding, *The Account of the Tabernacle: Translation and Textual Problems of the Greek Exodus,* Texts and Studies, N.S. VI (Cambridge: University Press, 1959), esp. pp. 66-69.   Hereafter citied as: Gooding, *Tabernacle.*

nature of **Q**ᵐ, this study, focusing on **Q**ᵃ as it does, can contribute only to
the question of the different order of **30:1-10**, to which smaller question we
will now return.

It would be possible to draw five mutually exclusive conclusions
regarding the two different positions of **30:1-10**: (1) the first order is
logically preferable and thus reflects (a) the original intention of author or
redactor, or (b) a secondary modification by a scribe to bring better order
into the text; or similarly, (2) the second order is (a) original or (b)
secondary; or differently, (3) a pericope that occurs in different places in
different texts is often considered to be a secondary addition that was
accepted into different places by different scribes. Since neither order
seems correct, neither can be chosen as preferable; it may well be that
both reflect insertions of a secondary pericope.

The real point for this study is that this is the only instance of a
major difference in order between **ɰ** and **ɱ**, and that **Q**ᵃ sides with **ɰ**.
Further, of the parts of three words out of this pericope that are preserved
on the scroll, על קר[נתיו, and ל[דורתיכם, all from v 10, there is no
deviation from the text presented by **ɰ** with the exception of the <u>waw</u> in
the last word, a purely orthographic difference.   (On the other hand, all
three Hebrew witnesses agree on the second plural suffix of that word, as
opposed to the third plural of **G**; see III.A.5.)

26:10 ללא[ו]ת חמשים 1° **ɰ**] חמשים ללאת **ɱ**; αγκυλας πεντηκοντα **G**
                                                         Qᵃ**ɰ**/**G**/ ≅ **ɱ**

There are 23 instances where **ɰ** and **ɱ** differ in the order of their
material (see Chapter V.B). Only one of these is major, involving ten verses
(30:1-10); one involves one verse (29:21); and 21 involve only a word or
phrase. **Q**ᵃ is extant in only two of these 23 instances: the preceding
variant, **30:1-10**, involving ten verses; and this variant, **26:10**, involving
only one word.

When this same phrase, "fifty loops," is repeated later in the same
verse, **Q**ᵃ**ɰɱ** all agree in having ללאת (ו)חמשים, and **G** has
πεντηκοντα αγκυλας. In 36:17, the fulfilment of the instruction in
26:10, **ɰɱ** both agree in reading חמשים ללאת (ו) in the first half and
ללאת (ו)חמשים in the second half (**G** lacks 36:10-34).

The main point is that in the two variants involving different order
where **Q**ᵃ is extant, one major and one minor, **Q**ᵃ agrees with **ɰ** against **ɱ**.

b. Q⁺ɰ Are Shorter

There are two synonymous variants where **Q⁺ɰ** are shorter than **ɱ𝐆**.

29:2

Q⁺ɰ	סלת	ולחם מצות וחלות[מצות בללות בשמן] ו[ר]קיקי מצות
ɱ	סלת	ולחם מצות וחלת מצת בלולת בשמן ורקיקי מצות מַשְׁחִים בַּשֶּׁמֶן
𝐆		και αρτους αζυμους πεφυραμενους εν ελαιω και λαγανα
		αζυμα <u>κεχρισμενα εν ελαιω</u>· σεμιδαλιν

Q⁺ɰ ≅ ɱ𝐆

According to **ɱ** three unleavened items are mentioned here: bread, cakes mixed with oil, and wafers smeared or spread with oil. The translation of **𝐆** agrees basically but freely with **ɱ**; apparently its having only one noun, αρτους, for both לחם and חלות, is due either to a deficiency in Greek vocabulary or a lack of imagination on the part of the translator, rather than to a shorter *Vorlage*. (Compare the same phenomenon in 29:23 and the repetition of αρτον in Lev 8:26, apparently representing a different solution.) **ɱ** and **𝐆** both mention oil with two baked items, whereas **Q⁺ɰ** call for oil only with the cakes, not with the wafers.

This variant is difficult to judge. There are four arguments for the reading in **Q⁺ɰ**. Two relate to this verse on its own: the usual text-critical bias in favor of the shorter reading and the fact that there are no words so similar that they would readily give occasion to haplography. The other two arguments reach further afield: first, the fact that oil is mentioned only with cakes in 22:23 in **ɰɱ𝐆 [☐Q⁺]**, which agrees with the shorter reading here (cf. Lev 8:26 in **ɰɱ𝐆**, in the narrative of the execution of this command in Exod 29:2); and second, the fact that there was a readily available source for the phrase if it were added (even by two different scribes independently) from elsewhere in the Torah: in the description of the peace offering in Lev 7:12, where the same expression occurs in **ɰɱ𝐆** (διακεχρισμενα).

There are three arguments for the reading in **ɱ𝐆**: its attestation in two unrelated traditions, the fact that the disputed phrase is only related to but not identical to the earlier phrase, and the repetition in the verse. מצות occurs three times in **ɱ** and בשמן twice; although this would not be a clear case of homoioteleuton or homoiarchton, it may be that the repetition of those words created confusion in the mind of a scribe in the **Q⁺ɰ** tradition, so that he forgot where he was in the list of similar items. An argument in favor of the antiquity of the longer reading, though not its preferability, is the haplography in **G**A: ελαιω 1°⌒2°; this presupposes the presence of the longer text.

In view of these conflicting arguments, this is taken as a synonymous variant. The important point is that in this case **Qᵃ ɰ** agree against both **m** and **G** in a shorter reading!

9:8ב השמ[מ]ים **ɰ]** השמימה **m**; εις τον ουρανον **G**   **Qᵃ ɰ** ≅ **m**; **G**?

Of the five variants involving the locative *he*, this is the only time **Qᵃ** and **ɰ** agree. **Qᵃ** consistently lacks the *he* in all five variants, whereas **ɰ** lacks it only once and **m** lacks it three times. (Though it is not counted as a variant because **Qᵃ** is not extant, just two verses later **ɰ** again lacks the *he* and **m** has it in exactly the same expression.) But it would be misleading to note without further comment that **ɰ** lacks the *he* only here in **9:8ב.** The fact is that an overall reading of the entire book of Exodus comparing **ɰ** with **m** shows that **ɰ** very frequently lacks the locative *he* when **m** has it. (For an important exception to this general impression, see **27:9; 27:11א**; and **36:23**, which involve the *he* with the points of the compass.)

Because no pattern can be discerned either within **ɰ** or **m** or in the disagreements between them, it does not seem possible to claim that either tradition represents an earlier or later stage. Rather, both traditions seem to treat this grammatical feature in a rather random fashion. Thus neither reading can be declared preferable. It is more important to notice that this is the one case where **Qᵃ** agrees with **ɰ** against **m** in a minor grammatical feature in which **Qᵃ** agrees three out of five times with **m** against **ɰ**.

c. *Qᵃ ɰ Are Longer*

As there are two synonymous variants where **Qᵃ ɰ** preserve a shorter text, so there are also two where they preserve a slightly longer text.

18:20 אש]ר הדרך **ɰ]** הדרך **m**; τας οδους, εν αις **G**   **Qᵃ ɰ/G/** ≅ **m**

Note that in the immediately following parallel clause **ɰ m G** all agree in having the **אשר.**

18:21ב ושרי מאות **ɰ G]** שרי מאות **m**   **Qᵃ ɰ/G/** ≅ **m**

In these two variants involving longer readings it is not possible to be sure that **Qᵃ ɰ/G/** are expansionist; it is equally possible that **m** has accidentally lost the text.

d. Different Word

There is only one case of a synonymous variant where $\mathbf{Q^a}$ 𝔚 preserve a different word.

7:14   וידבר\[†] 𝔚] ויאמר 𝔐; Ειπεν δε **G** $\mathbf{Q^a}$ 𝔚 ≅ 𝔐(**G**)

At 10:21א $\mathbf{Q^a}$ stands alone in reading וידבר\ו against ויאמר in 𝔚𝔐 and Ειπεν δε in **G** (see Chapter II.B.2). There ויאמר is taken as the preferable reading since it is supported by the three separate traditions (for the statistics on **G**, see the discussion). Here, however, because 𝔚 agrees with $\mathbf{Q^a}$ the reading is with some hesitation considered a synonymous variant.

e. Different Form of a Word

In five synonymous variants $\mathbf{Q^a}$ 𝔚 preserve a different form of a word.

26:26   בריחי עעי שטים 𝔚] בריחם עעי שטים 𝔐; μοχλους εκ ξυλων ασηπτων **G** $\mathbf{Q^a}$ 𝔚 ≅ 𝔐; **G**?

It should be noted that the absolute plural בריחם occurs 9 times in 𝔐 of Exodus, always spelled defectively; 𝔚, on the other hand, always spells it *plene*.

According to the Massoretic convention as codified by Gesenius (§128o), items made of a certain material were in the construct state, e.g., Exod 25:31; 26:11 (𝔚𝔐). Whether this practice was common among all writers of Hebrew is another question. Many instances in the tabernacle account are ambiguous as far as the consonants are concerned, e.g., 25:10, 17; 26:7 (𝔚𝔐); and 25:23: שלחן עעי שטים (𝔚𝔐). Sometimes, however, even in 𝔐, the item is in the absolute state, e.g., 25:18: שנים כר(ו)בים כרסי זהב (𝔚𝔐); (contrast with 26:6: חמשים קרסי זהב [𝔚𝔐]; i.e., the number can precede the construct state). In 36:31, the fulfilment of the instruction in 26:26, 𝔚 and 𝔐 agree in reading בריחי עעי שטים.

Because of this uncertainty this reading is considered a synonymous variant.

22:6   וגנב 𝔚] ו[נגנב 𝔐; και κλαπη **G** $\mathbf{Q^a}$ 𝔚 ≅ 𝔐; **G**?
32:11א   יחר 𝔚] יחרה 𝔐; θυμοι **G** $\mathbf{Q^a}$ 𝔚 ≅ 𝔐; **G**?

In these two synonymous variants involving different verbal forms $\mathbf{Q^a}$ agrees with 𝔚 against 𝔐. The *Vorlage* of **G** cannot be determined; the verb in **22:6** is in the passive (of κλεπτειν), as are both forms in Hebrew (cf. 22:11, where κλαπη corresponds to the *Nifʿal* יגנב [ɯɯ]); in 32:11א θυμοι, as a contract verb, could be either indicative or subjunctive.

22:26א היא [... א]הי ɯ] הוא ... הוא ɯ; τουτο ... τουτο **G**

                                                Q^a ɯ ≅ ɯ; **G**?

31:13   א]הי ɯ] הוא ɯ; εστιν **G** Q^a ɯ ≅ ɯ; **G**?

All three of these pronouns have been pointed by the medieval Massoretes as feminine. The antecedent in **22:26א** is שלמה (Q^aɯ) or שמלה (ɯ), both feminine nouns. In **31:13** the antecedent is אות, which is usually masculine elsewhere (e.g. Exod 4:8; 8:19), but is treated in Ezekiel (4:3) and in P (e.g., Exod 31:17; cf. also Josh 24:17) as feminine.

According to Gesenius (§ 32 1) ɯ has the correct gender of this pronoun throughout the Pentateuch, whereas ɯ has the masculine orthography for feminine in all but eleven places in the Pentateuch, but consistently points as feminine. Note that Q^a agrees with ɯ in having the more difficult form of the noun (**22:25**; see II.A.3) but agrees with ɯ in having what we now consider to be the correct form of the pronoun. Visually, the difference in the pronoun is, of course, an extremely minor one, since the *waw* and *yod* were often almost indistinguishable in Hasmonean and Herodian square scripts.

Though present understandings of orthography and grammar point to the feminine, the strong witness of ɯ for the masculine cautions us to leave the question open as to which reading was preferable when and for which group(s) of Hebrew writers.

Summary: Of these twelve synonymous variants shared by Q^aɯ, only one, involving a different placement of ten verses, seems major in itself. Yet taken together they contribute to the pattern which began emerging in Chapter II and which shows that Q^a and ɯ are both members of one textual tradition of the book of Exodus.

3. SYNONYMOUS VARIANTS SHARED BY Q^aɯ

There are fourteen instances where Q^a agrees with ɯ in a synonymous variant against ɯ. Two involve a difference of one word, in four readings Q^aɯ are longer, in four they are shorter, and four readings involve a different form of a word.

a. Different Word

Two synonymous variants shared by **Q⁰Ⅲ** involve a different word.

13:6   ימים ששת **ⅢG**   **Ⅲ]** ש[בעת י[מ]ים   **Q⁰Ⅲ ≅ ⅢG**

An equally convincing argument could be made for the originality of either reading. Since indeed no leaven was to be eaten for a total of seven days, the original could well have been "seven." On the other hand, it was also true that no leaven was to be eaten for the six days preceding the feast; thus the original could logically have been "six." In either case, a scribe and/or translator could easily have "corrected" the number to its opposite: to "six" in order to set off the seventh day as the feast day; or to "seven" in order to make this verse agree with 12:15 and 13:7, where all four texts consistently have "seven." Thus no final decision can be made as to preferability in this reading.

Furthermore, the question of affiliation is also difficult. While **Ⅲ** and **G** agree, it is by no means clear that they are affiliated. If "six" is original, then they agree because they are ultimately related to the original tradition. If "six" is secondary, nevertheless such "correcting" of texts can easily have been done independently by different scribes and/or translators. On the other hand, there may be some slight weighting in favor of affiliation in the fact that the same relationship occurs in Gen 2:2, where **Ⅲ** and **G** (and **S**) have "six," whereas **Ⅲ** has "seven." Again, such "correcting" could have been carried out independently in all three text traditions; but possibly the consistency suggests a more concerted effort that affected more than one tradition.

A similar question arises with regard to the agreement of **Q⁰** and **Ⅲ**. If "seven" is the original, then nothing is proven regarding their affiliation. If "seven" is secondary, then the weight would shift toward the side of affiliation if this were one case of many agreements between **Q⁰** and **Ⅲ**.

10:11   **Q⁰Ⅲ**   לא כן לכו נא
        Ⅲ   לכן לכו נא
        G   μη ουτως· πορευεσθωσαν δε   **Q⁰Ⅲ/G/ ≅ Ⅲ**

This reading has been classified as a synonymous variant, and the *Vorlage* of the **G** reading as not determined, because of the ambiguity in the use of לא כן and לכן in the Hebrew traditions as well as in their rendering in **G**.

In at least 9 cases **G** reads ουχ (ουδ) ουτως where **𝕸** has (ו)לבן(ו).
In 3 of these cases (1 Sam 3:14; 2 Kings 21:12; and Job 20:2) it is difficult
to understand the importation of the negative idea, and one is thus inclined
to prefer the reading לכן and to postulate visual or auditory confusion in the
Hebrew stage underlying the **G** tradition. But in 6 cases it is quite easy to
interpret the phrase as refuting the preceding idea and introducing
positively the succeeding one. In Gen 4:15, for example, Yahweh could be
understood as saying: "No, no one will kill you, for (לכן) there will be a
warning of seven-fold vengeance on your forehead." Likewise in Gen 30:15
Rachel could be saying: "No, I am not trying to steal your mandrakes; (לכן)
Jacob may sleep with you tonight in exchange for them." (In both cases **𝖲**
agrees with **𝕸**.) Similar interpretations could be given for 1 Kings 22:19; 2
Kings 1:4,6; or Jud 11:8. In the case of the last, however, whereas A⁺ read
ουχ ουτως, B⁺ read δια τουτο. (The same variation occurs in Jud 8:7,
where the negative may be somewhat more obscure but is at least
defensible.) This variation within the **G** tradition could point to a varying
degree of literalness in rendering the same *Vorlage*, לכן, or to differing
Vorlagen. In the case of all 6 passages, it may be that ουχ ουτως
represents a perfectly acceptable translation of לכן or that an original לכן
had been corrupted to לא כן already in the Hebrew tradition underlying the
G translation.

Of the 4 occurrences of לא כן in the **𝕸** Pentateuch, **𝖲** agrees with **𝕸**
3 times. Only in the present reading, Exod 10:11, do the two traditions
disagree. In all 4 cases **G** translates ουχ (μη) ουτως. In all 4 passages
the idea is, as above, one of refuting the preceding notion and introducing
the following one: No (לא כן)! Jacob must not put his right hand on Ephraim,
but on Manasseh (Gen 48:18); Moses is not like other prophets (Num 12:7);
the Israelites are not to go to soothsayers as the Canaanites do (Dt 18:14).
Similarly in the present passage: I will not let your children go, because
you have an evil purpose in mind; rather only the men are to go. Following
the evidence of **𝕸** in the passages with לכן discussed above, however, it
seems possible that the original Hebrew could have read either the more
expected לא כן or the less familiar but equally possible (and perhaps
colloquial? see BDB) לכן.

We are left then, with ambiguity both as to the preferable reading and
the affiliation of **G**. But at least among the Hebrew texts the affiliation is
clear for this reading: **Qᵃ𝕸** ≅ **𝖲**.

b. *Q^a𝔪 Are Longer*

In four readings **Q^a𝔪** are longer than **𝔐**; these are slight differences, it is true, but must be considered as part of the total picture.

22:24 בעני   העני [𝔪 ; עני 𝔐; τω πενιχρω **G**   **Q^a𝔪/G/ ≅ 𝔐**
For discussion, see **22:24א**, III.A.5.

13:5 החתי והן[חתי [𝔪**G** ; 𝔐   **Q^a𝔪/G/ ≅ 𝔐**

28:4 וכתנת [𝔪 ; כיתנת 𝔐; και χιτωνα **G**   **Q^a𝔪/G/ ≅ 𝔐**

There is so much variation regarding the conjunction in lists of nouns that these are both considered synonymous. **G** translates freely enough in this matter that its evidence is ambiguous. It is, however, perhaps worth noticing that at **28:4** B⁺ lack this same και out of a series of five conjunctions. On the other hand, both **𝔐** and **𝔪** lack the conjunction for the next noun, and **G** (including B) has και there.

28:23 שתי 2° [𝔪 ; > 𝔐; clause lacking **G**   **Q^a𝔪 ≅ 𝔐 ≠ G**

c. *Q^a𝔪 Are Shorter*

In four synonymous variants **Q^a𝔪** preserve the slightly shorter reading.

27:9 תימנה נג[ב [𝔪 ; נגבה תימנה 𝔐; το προς λιβα **G**   **Q^a𝔪 ≅ 𝔐; G?**

27:11א צפון [𝔪 ; צפונה 𝔐; τω προς απηλιωτηνδπ   **Q^a𝔪 ≅ 𝔐; G?**

36:23 נגב תימ[נה [𝔪 ; נגבה תימנה 𝔐;
          36:10–34 lacking **G**   **Q^a𝔪 ≅ 𝔐 ≠ G**

No clear pattern is discernible for the use of the locative *he* with points of the compass. In each of these three readings, all of them following the word לפאת, **𝔐** has one *he* that **Q^a𝔪** lack. Yet in the two readings (27:9; 36:23) in which two directions are named, **Q^a𝔐𝔪** all agree in having the *he* after the second direction. In 26:18; 27:13; and 38:13, furthermore, **𝔐𝔪** agree in reading a *he* following both directions in this same construction with לפאת (**Q^a** agrees in 27:13 and is not extant in 26:18 or 38:13). Thus the several variations are all acceptable and no reading can be considered preferable.

Whereas preferability cannot be established, it is nevertheless possible to recognize that 𝔐 has a greater tendency to lack the locative *he* in this construction while 𝔐 tends to have it: cf., e.g., 26:20; 27:12; 38:9, 11, 12. In the four readings where **Qᵃ** is extant and there is variation in the text, it agrees with 𝔐. In 36:23 **Qᵃ𝔐** both lack the first *he;* but more strikingly, in 27:9 and 11א **Qᵃ𝔐** lack a *he,* whereas just two verses later **Qᵃ𝔐** have the *he* after both directions. 𝔐 has the *he* in all four verses.

26:8 ת(ו)יריע **𝔐]** היריעות 𝔐; ταις ... δεppεσι **G**   **Qᵃ𝔐** ≅ 𝔐/G/

At this point in the instructions regarding curtains it seems somewhat preferable to refer to them with the article. In favor of the reading in 𝔐/G/ is the possibility of haplography in **Qᵃ𝔐** due to the *he* at the end of the preceding word. In favor of the reading in **Qᵃ𝔐** is the tendency of 𝔐 to have (add?) the article when it is lacking in 𝔐 (cf., e.g., 26:3//36:10, with this same noun following a number, but where parablepsis is unlikely; and 36:15, parallel to the present variant at **26:8**). In the face of these conflicting arguments this is judged a synonymous variant.

d. Different Form of a Word

Four synonymous variants shared by **Qᵃ𝔐** involve a different form of a word.

6:30 אלי ישמע **𝔐]** ישמעני 𝔐; εισακουσεται μου **G**   **Qᵃ𝔐** ≅ 𝔐; G?

This is considered a synonymous variant because both Hebrew forms are acceptable and the preferability of both can be defended. This is the only place in Exodus where 𝔐 and 𝔐 have any disagreement regarding the suffix with ישמע. The form that appears in **Qᵃ𝔐** is by far the more frequent in Exodus and in the entire OT. The only time that ישמעני appears in 𝔐 of Exodus is in 6:12. The imperfect of this verb occurs with accusative suffix only 5 times in 𝔐 in the OT (including ני-, as here at Exod 6:30 in 𝔐: in Exod 6:12 in 𝔐𝔐 and Mic 7:7 in 𝔐).

On the other hand it is precisely the single other place in Exodus where the form with the suffix occurs, 6:12, which is the closest parallel of this verse. Both verses occur in P, one before and one after the genealogy of Moses and Aaron; thus 6:30 repeats 6:12 in order to resume the narrative after the genealogy. Both verses are printed, along with the other occurrence of this verb in the context, 6:9; the objects of the verb are underlined:

6:9   ⅏𝔪   (וידבר משה כן אל בני ישראל) ולא שמעו <u>אל משה</u>

       G   ... και ουκ εισηκουσαν <u>Μωυση</u>

6:12   ⅏𝔪   הן בני ישראל לא שמעו <u>אלי</u> ואיך ישמע<u>ני</u> פרעה

                                     ואני ערל שפתים

       G   Ιδου οι υιοι Ισραηλ ουκ εισηκουσαν <u>μου</u>,

          και πως εισακουσεται <u>μου</u> Φ; εγω δε αλογος ειμι.

6:30   ⅏   הן אני ערל שפתים ואיך ישמע<u>ני</u>   פרעה

       𝔪   הן אני ערל שפתים ואיך ישמע <u>אלי</u> פרעה

       G   Ιδου εγω ισχνοφωνος ειμι, και πως εισακουσεται <u>μου</u> Φ;

To defend the originality of ⅏ one could argue that the unusual form should be preferred since it is grammatically acceptable; and particularly in light of the literary function of the verse one could prefer that form which appears in the earlier verse. To defend the originality of 𝐐ᵃ𝔪 one could argue that the agreement of two witnesses shows that ⅏ has -- characteristically -- harmonized the parallel passages. Is consistency to be attributed to the author or redactor, or to a later scribe?

The evidence of G is ambiguous, since it translates with the same phrase regardless of what stands in ⅏ or 𝔪.

Thus 𝐐ᵃ𝔪 agree against ⅏ in a synonymous variant in which the *Vorlage* of G cannot be determined.

18:6א   אל משה 𝔪] למשה ⅏; Μωυση G   𝐐ᵃ𝔪 ≅ ⅏; G?

Both prepositions are used elsewhere following ויאמר, and while אל may occur more frequently with this verb at least in the 𝔪 of Exodus, neither can be said to be preferable. The variant is so minor that the agreement of 𝐐ᵃ and 𝔪 can only be said to be significant if a larger pattern is found.

18:16 בא[ו](ו)] ⅏; בא 𝔪; (και) ελθωσι G   𝐐ᵃ𝔪 ≅ ⅏G

22:26 אני 𝔪] אנכי ⅏; ειμι G   𝐐ᵃ𝔪 ≅ ⅏; G?

<u>Summary</u>: These fourteen synonymous variants shared by 𝐐ᵃ and 𝔪 against ⅏ and sometimes against G are all minor. In the face of the clear evidence of positive affiliation between 𝐐ᵃ and ⅏, these agreements between 𝐐ᵃ and 𝔪 in synonymous variants might in themselves point to

nothing more than a tendency of texts in different traditions to agree with each other in minor features. But taken as part of a larger pattern in which **Qᵃ** and **𝕸** share only one secondary reading but six preferable readings against **𝖬**, these fourteen shared synonymous variants may take on a new significance. See Chapter IV.A.3 for discussion.

4. SYNONYMOUS VARIANTS SHARED BY **QᵃG**

There are three instances in the extant parts of **Qᵃ** where it shares a synonymous variant with **G**.

10:26   נשאר **G]** תשאר **𝖬𝕸**   **QᵃG** ≅ **𝖬𝕸**

The *Hipʿil* imperfect of **Qᵃ** corresponds to the middle future of **G**. Both the first plural active/middle of **QᵃG** and the third singular passive of **𝖬𝕸** fit the context well. It is not certain, of course, that there is any causal relationship between the readings of **Qᵃ** and **G**. Just two verses before, at 10:24ג, **G** uniquely has an active form in a similar context against the passive of **Qᵃ𝖬𝕸**.

18:21ג ושᵃ]רי חמשים **G]** שרי חמשים **𝖬𝕸**   (III.B.2) **Qᵃ/G/** ≅ **𝖬𝕸**
18:16א א[ב]ו] באו **𝖬**; בא **𝕸**; και ελθωσιν **G** (III.B.2) **Qᵃ/G/** ≅ **𝖬𝕸**

Summary: These three synonymous variants shared by **Qᵃ** and **G**, involving one verbal form and two conjunctions, are too few and too insignificant to indicate any affiliation between the two witnesses.

5. SYNONYMOUS VARIANTS SHARED BY **Qᵃ𝖬𝕸**

There are 35 synonymous variants shared by **Qᵃ𝖬𝕸** against **G**. In six **Qᵃ𝖬𝕸** are longer, six suggest that an entire pericope existed in two different forms, two provide conflicting representations, four involve the order of words or phrases, eight involve the choice of a word or phrase, seven involve different forms of a word or a suffix, and in two there may have been either omission, expansion, or transposition.

a. *Qᵃ𝖬𝕸 Are Longer*

In six synonymous variants **Qᵃ𝖬𝕸** are longer than **G**; in three of these the difference is substantial, affecting an entire pericope.

36:21–24 hab 𝔖𝔐] > 36:10–34 G   **Qᵃ𝔖𝔐 ≅ G**

These twenty-five verses which are lacking in **G** tell of the joining together of the linen curtains; the making and joining of the curtains of goats' hair; the making of the covering of rams' skins and goatskins; and the construction of the frames and bars. Thus the account of the construction of the tabernacle in **G** has the making and the dimensions of the linen curtains (G 37:1–2 [H 36:8–9]) and continues immediately with the making of the veil and its four pillars, the screen for the door and its five pillars (G 37:3–6 [H 36:35–38]).

The instructions for the items in these twenty-five verses are included in **G**, as in 𝔖𝔐, in 26:3–30. Furthermore, the rest of the account of the construction in **G** shows knowledge of these features (e.g., the immediately following pericope, G 37:7–18 [H 38:9–20]). It is not (as seems possible in the case of the incense altar; see the discussion of **30:1–10** in III.A.2) a question of a tradition lacking all knowledge of these items, but rather of a tradition lacking the detailed account of their construction, while yet including very detailed accounts of the construction of other features.

Since the question of this pericope must be studied along with the larger issue of the entire account of the tabernacle in chapters 25–31 and 35–40 in the three different traditions, the question of preferability is outside the scope of this study. It is enough here to state that **Qᵃ** agrees with 𝔖𝔐 against **G** in preserving the longer text, at least to the extent of these four verses, **36:21–24**, dealing with the construction of the frames.

37:9–16 hab 𝔖𝔐] aliter G [38:8–12]   **Qᵃ𝔖𝔐 ≅ G**

The entire section 37:1–24 [38:1–17 G], which tells of the construction of the ark, table, and lampstand, is somewhat longer in 𝔖𝔐 and somewhat shorter in **G**. **Qᵃ**, which is partially extant in one of the verses relating to the cherubim and all seven verses relating to the table, agrees with 𝔖𝔐 except for one variant in **37:13**, where **Qᵃ** appears to be in error (see Chapter V.A.5). The evidence of **Qᵃ** thus contributes nothing to the question of preferability or of development of the text, which must be studied in conjunction with the entire tabernacle account. For the purposes of this study, then, this reading is counted as a synonymous variant.

28:23–29 hab 𝔖𝔐] hab vv 29, 29a (ex 23–28) G   **Qᵃ𝔖𝔐 ≅ G**

This variant is in the paragraph about the breastpiece of judgment.

Qᵃᛗᛗ give a great deal of detail about gold rings and cords and such matters to explain how the breastpiece is to be attached to the ephod in vv 23-28, and then in v 29 give the purpose of all of this, that Aaron is to wear it in the holy place to remind Yahweh of the names of the tribes of Israel. **G**, on the other hand, first gives the purpose of the breastpiece (v 29) and then a much shorter explanation of the attachment (29a).

Qᵃ is partially extant in verses 23, 24, and 26-28; to the extent that it is preserved it agrees with **ᛗ** completely and with **ᛃᛃ** in all but one word (see **28:23** in III.A.3.c).

To complicate matters, **ᛃᛃᛗ** have the longer form in both the instructions (**28:23-29**) and in the account of the making of the breastpiece (39:16-21) except that the purpose of the breastpiece (**28:29**) is not repeated in chapter 39. **G**, on the other hand, has the shorter form in the instructions (**28:29-29a**) but the longer form in the account of the making of the breast-piece (36:23-29).

Because this variant is closely related to all of the variations in the entire tabernacle account, chapters 25-31 and 35-40, and because **Qᵃ** exhibits such exact agreement with **ᛗ**, the evidence of **Qᵃ** cannot contribute to the question of preferability here, other than to testify to the antiquity of the reading in **ᛃᛗ**.

28:11ב   מ(ו)ס[בת [משב]צות ז[הב תעשה אתם   **ᛃᛗ]** > **G**   **Qᵃᛃᛗ ≅ G**

This command to make settings of gold filigree for the two stones in the ephod occurs, but without mention of its purpose of serving as a setting for the stones, two verses later, in 28:13 in **ᛃᛗG** (□**Qᵃ**):

ועשית משבצת זהב   και ποιησεις ασπιδισκας εκ χρυσιου καθαρου.

In the account of the execution of the command, **ᛃᛗG** (□**Qᵃ**) read:

מסבת משבצת זהב   (39:6)

συμπεπορπημενους και περισεσιαλωμενους χρυσιω   (36:13).

Viewing the accounts in **ᛃᛗ** on their own merit, the fact that the word מסבת, which explains the function of this gold filligree, occurs in **ᛃᛗ** at this verse, **28:11**, and also at the execution, in 39:6, but is lacking later in the instructions, at 28:13, might suggest that the preferable reading in **28:11** includes this command. The earlier verse, then, would have given instructions for the engraving and the settings of the stones, two tasks appropriately mentioned together, before the placement of the stones in the ephod, dealt with in verse 12. It seems likely that the following verses, 28:13-14, originally read: "And you shall make two chains...and you shall

attach the corded chains to the settings"; the reference to the settings presumably prompted a later scribe to insert instructions to make them.

The evidence of **G**, however, complicates matters by having the command only at the latter verse, and by having the counterpart in the execution
in entirely different language.

This is one more variant which must be considered as a part of the
entire tabernacle account.   The evidence of **Qᵐ** contributes little to the
issue of preferability; it does make clear that the reading of **𝕸𝕸** was
indeed ancient.   In conclusion, then, this is another synonymous variant
where **G** stands alone.

32:2 נשי[כם בניכם ובנתיכם] **𝕸𝕸**] τῶν γυναικῶν υμῶν καὶ
θυγατέρων **G**   **Qᵐ𝕸𝕸 ≅ G**

In this verse Aaron instructs the Israelites to bring the gold rings
from the ears of their wives, sons, and daughters to him. The word for "your
sons" could easily have dropped out either by parablepsis, because there are
three words in a row ending in ־יכם, or it could have been omitted deliberately or accidentally because of some objection to males wearing earrings.
Or it could perhaps just as well have been added to fill out the reference to
the family members. Gen 35:4 refers to rings that were in "their" ears,
using the masculine plural suffix, apparently referring to the males and
females of Jacob's household. (Exod 32:3 also refers to the rings that were
in "their" ears, with the masculine plural suffix in Hebrew; the gender of
αυτων is of course ambiguous. Cf. Exod 35:22.) Yet if it is a gloss for
completeness, it was not entirely successful, since no corresponding reference to the adult males was added.

Here then is an instance where **G** is shorter by one word than
Qᵐ𝕸𝕸. It cannot, however, be determined which reading is preferable.

9:16 אולם[ו **𝕸𝕸**] καὶ **G**   **Qᵐ𝕸𝕸 ≅ G**
אולם(ו) occurs 19 times in **𝕸**, but only here in Exodus. **G** renders
with an adversative (e.g., αλλα, πλην, ου μην δε αλλα) 13 times, εαν
δε and εαν μη once each, and twice (Gen 28:19; Jud 18:29) misunderstands
it as part of a proper name! Only once is there something akin to the και
here at Exod 9:16: δε at Jb 13:4; and that could be explained by parablepsis
(ואתם אולם). In light of the entire OT, then, it would appear that if this
word had been in the *Vorlage* here the translator would have rendered it
somehow even if he had not understood it. Thus one possibility is that the

shorter reading in **G** is the original, and that after the tradition behind **G** separated a scribe in the tradition behind **QᵃⅢ𝔐** added אולם for the sake of greater precision.

An argument against the preferability of the shorter reading may be the need in the context for such an adversative. And there remains the fact that since this is the only occurrence of the word in Exodus we cannot be sure how this particular translator would have dealt with אולם had it been in his *Vorlage*. It could be that unlike the translators of Genesis and Judges (see above) he would have felt free to skip lightly over a strange word, rendering with an all-purpose και.

This must be considered, then, a synonymous variant.

b. *Different Form of a Pericope*

Having seen six variants where **QᵃⅢ𝔐** are longer than **G**, three of them affecting entire pericopes, we turn now to six variants which seem to indicate that one pericope existed in two distinct formulations. Here the length is not so much the issue; rather, there are a series of all sorts of different readings within one pericope.

18:9-11	**QᵃⅢ𝔐**	**G**
9א:	ו[יחד]	εξεστη δε
	לישר[אל ... העילו]	αυτοις ... εξειλατο αυτους
		και εκ χειρος Φαραω
10א:	אתכם	τον λαον αυτου
	אשר העיל א[ת העם מתחת יד מצרי(י)]ם	
11:	כי בדבר אש]ר	ενεκεν τουτου οτι
		QᵃⅢ𝔐 ≅ G

Although only six variants are listed from these verses, a comprehensive view of the passage shows that there were two parallel formulations of this pericope. Hence all of these variants are considered together as part of one larger reading. But of the many places where **G** differs from **QᵃⅢ𝔐**, **Qᵃ** is extant only in these six. (See Appendix 2 for the specific designation of each variant.) Presumably **G** faithfully translated one form of this narrative, and **QᵃⅢ𝔐** have preserved the parallel tradition. Since both formulations are quite repetitive, it appears likely that scribes in both traditions were adding phrases and clauses, but in different forms and different positions in the text. Most of the variants appear in the other tradition elsewhere. For instance, αυτοις/αυτους of 18:9ב agree with the suffix of ויעלם in 18:8; τον λαον αυτου (18:10א) agrees with את העם in 18:10ב; and what looks like an expansion in **Qᵃ 𝔐𝔪**, 18:10ב, finds its partial counterpart in what looks like an expansion in **G** at the end of 18:8.

Since, therefore, both traditions are repetitious but consistently different, there is little hope of determining a preferable or original text; rather, this entire pericope is considered a synonymous variant.

In the light of the larger picture, then, it is no longer necessary to suppose that the translator erred in **18:9א**, taking the root חדה as חרד. That is, of course, possible. But it is equally possible that the two different Hebrew traditions had two different roots. "Rejoiced" as in **Qᵃ 𝔐𝔪** and "was amazed, terrified; trembled" would both be fitting responses for Jethro upon hearing what Yahweh had done.

By the same token, both versions of the second clause in 18:11 may more or less faithfully preserve two parallel versions of the narrative. **Qᵃ** is only extant for the beginning of the difficult clause and sheds no light on the verb.

In summary, all six variants are considered part of one large synonymous variant affecting at least four verses, 18:8-11.

c. Conflicting Representations

25:23	עצי שטים 𝔐𝔪] χρυσιου καθαρου **G**	**Qᵃ 𝔐𝔪** ≅ **G**
25:24	ועפית [א(ו)תו זהב טהור 𝔐𝔪] > **G**	**Qᵃ 𝔐𝔪** ≅ **G**

These two variants belong together. In **Qᵃ 𝔐𝔪** Moses is told to build the table (for the "bread of the Presence") out of acacia wood and to overlay it with pure gold. In **G**, however, the table is to be built out of pure gold, and there is thus no mention in the following verse of an overlay. The same variation in the material of the table occurs in the account of the execution of these instructions, along with variation in the amount of detail given. In 37:10-11 **𝔐𝔪** repeat 25:23-24 word for word except for necessary changes such as verbal tenses (**Qᵃ** agrees to the extent that it is preserved), whereas the corresponding section in **G**, 38:9, states only that they made the table out of pure gold, omitting the measurements.

Gooding[5] interpreted this variation as another example of abbreviation by the translator which misrepresented the facts, in line with

---

[5]Gooding, *Tabernacle*, p. 28.

his contention that the translator's *Vorlage* was very much like 𝕸. But it may be worth pointing out that the translator did refer to acacia wood overlaid with gold in the case of the instructions concerning the ark (25:10), the poles (25:28), and the incense altar (30:1). In the account of the construction of the ark (G 38:1 [H 37:1]) 𝔊 does not mention the wood, as 𝖘𝕸 do, but does refer to overlaying with gold, as opposed to construction out of gold, as with the table; the same is true for the construction of the poles (G 38:11 [H 37:15]). In the case of the altar for burnt offerings, as well as for its poles, 𝔊 agrees with 𝖘𝕸 in giving instruction for acacia wood overlaid with bronze (27:1-2 and 6). Yet whereas in 𝖘𝕸 the account of its construction (38:1-2, 6) agrees completely and explicitly with the instructions, in 𝔊 the poles are not mentioned and the altar is referred to as "the bronze altar" (38:22). This need not necessarily be interpreted as analogous to the variant regarding the table, for it is not a detailed account but rather could be understood as a simple reference to the way the altar appeared, which was of importance since in 𝔊 (as opposed to 𝖘𝕸) the point is made that the bronze used was that from the censers involved in the revolt of Korah (cf. Numbers 16). In contrast to the incense altar, which was overlaid with gold, the offering altar was (overlaid with) bronze. (There is one factor complicating this interpretation, it is true: 𝔊 preserves the instructions for the gold-overlaid incense altar but not the account of its construction. Nevertheless, since the golden altar does appear in 30:1 and 40:5 in 𝔊, the tradition of 𝔊 seems to have known of this altar, and the above interpretation can stand.)

Returning to the specific issue of the table, it appears that there are several possibilities. Gooding could be right, that this is a case of careless abbreviation, even though there are other examples of accuracy, and even though this "carelessness" appears in both instruction and construction. Others would argue that the entire account of the tabernacle reflects systematic expansion in Hebrew (and, some would add, in Greek), and that the translator had a shorter *Vorlage* than has been preserved in Hebrew. In this particular case, however, it must be remembered that 𝐐ᵃ𝖘𝕸𝔊 all give details of the size of the table, its molding, frame, rings, poles, and utensils, in chapter 25. Thus in this one passage it would not seem to be question of abbreviation, but of two conflicting representations of the table. Was it overlaid with gold, like its poles and like the ark and the incense altar? Or was it constructed of gold, like the lampstand, the mercy seat and the cherubim?

This difference between **(𝔔^a 𝔪)𝔐** and **𝔊** in the conception of the table does not seem to be borne out in the rest of the OT. **𝔐** and **𝔊** agree in referring to the table in the temple as golden in 1 K 7:48 (contrast 2 Chr 4:19, where both lack mention of the material; but cf. 1 Chr 28:16, where both refer to gold) and as "pure" (**טהר, καθαρος**) in Lev 24:6 and 2 Chr 13:11. Again, these are merely references to the table, not instructions for making it. And in the same context the altar is also referred to as golden. For both reasons, these passages should not be taken to mean that the table was necessarily all of gold.

While it is possible, then, that the translator merely abbreviated his Hebrew *Vorlage,* this seems unlikely since the rest of the two verses, 25:23-24, is not at all abbreviated in **𝔊** but gives all the same details as **𝔪𝔐**. Furthermore, since **𝔪𝔐** present a consistent picture of the table as made of wood and **𝔊** presents a consistent picture of the table as made of gold, it seems that the different textual traditions had different conceptions of the material of the table, while agreeing regarding its measurements and other aspects. Since some articles of the furnishings are made of gold and some are made of wood overlaid with gold, and since the rest of the OT neither clarifies the issue nor shows a pattern of disagreement between **𝔐** and **𝔊** outside of Exodus, this must be considered a synonymous variant. There seems to be no way for us to reach behind these two conflicting representations.

d. Different Order of Words or Phrases

There are four readings where the traditions preserve different word order: the first involves phrases; the other three involve individual words.

19:11 לעיני כל]העם על הר ס[יני **𝔪𝔐]** επι το ορος το Σινα
εναντιον παντος του λαου **𝔊** **𝔔^{a}𝔪𝔐 ≅ 𝔊**

This simple transposition of phrases could have arisen because one of the phrases is a slightly later addition that got inserted in different places by different scribes, or because a scribe who was writing from dictation got an entire thought in his mind and then wrote it down in a different order. A third possibility is that the order preserved in **𝔔^{a}𝔪𝔐** is the original, and that the transposition occurred in the early stages of the Greek transmission: because of the two initial *epsilon*'s in **επι** and **εναντιον.** Because of the uncertainty, however, it is included here with those variants which point to a special relationship among the three apart from the Greek.

10:25   ו]עלות נב[ח]ים 𝘂𝗺Ⅿ] ολοκαυτωματα και θυσιας **G**

$$Q^{m}\,\text{𝗺Ⅿ}\,\approx\,\textbf{G}$$

This variant involving different word order should be considered in conjunction with another variant, 18:12, involving the difference between singular and plural, which will be counted in a later subsection; and with the two other passages in Exodus where the same two words appear together in Greek. Only in the first two verses is **Q**ᵐ extant.

18:12   עו)לה וז]ב[ח]ים   ολοκαυτωματα και θυσιας

24:5   נבחים שלמים ... עו)לת   ολοκαυτωματα και...θυσιαν σωτηριου

32:6   שלמים ... עו)לת   ολοκαυτωματα και...θυσιαν σωτηριου

נבח = θυσια are generic terms for sacrifice; עלה = ολοκαυτωμα represent a subdivision and refer specifically to burnt offering; שלמים is usually translated "peace offerings." Twice (18:12 and 10:25) the words occur in an immediate pair, and twice (24:5 and 32:6) they occur in parallel clauses but separated only by "and" plus a verb. All four verses occur in narrative passages rather than in pericopes giving cultic legislation.

In all four cases the Hebrew witnesses agree among themselves, but each of the four phrases is different. In three cases, the Hebrew order has עלה (עלות) first, but here in 10:25 it is second. Three times the Hebrew has עלות, but once it has עלה. The variation in the Hebrew word(s) for the other member of the pair is greater still. Thus there appears to be fluidity in the Hebrew usage, which suggests strongly that although none of these Hebrew witnesses agrees with **G** in these two variants, the Hebrew *Vorlage* of **G** probably was different from the Hebrew that has been preserved.

Although in all four cases the Greek order is ολοκαυτωμα first and θυσια second, the Greek does fluctuate between singular and plural. Further, θυσιαν appears with σωτηριου whether the Hebrew has נבחים or not. Thus the translator seems to have exercised a degree of license while at the same time rendering faithfully the meaning of his *Vorlage*.

It should be noted that Hatch-Redpath's listings for 10:25 are misleading. Whereas in six out of eight times in Exodus ολοκαυτωμα = עלה, only at this verse is it said to equal נבח; and whereas in four out of ten times in Exodus θυσια = נבח, only at this verse and at 29:42 is it said to equal עלה. For both words here it would have been more accurate to indicate that **G** reflects a different word order from that in Ⅿ.

In conclusion, then, since the Hebrew order in this phrase seems to be fluid, rather than being a set cultic phrase, and since **G** in general appears faithfully to reflect its *Vorlage*, it appears that in these two verses **G** is mirroring a Hebrew text that was different from that preserved in **Qᵃ𝔐𝔪**. Its *Vorlage* presumably had a different order in 10:25, and plural as opposed to singular in 18:12.

As for the question of preferability, in both cases the fluidity in the four Hebrew phrases shows that various forms of this expression were possible. In 10:25 Moses makes general demands of Pharaoh for animals for sacrifices; these could be mentioned in either order. In 18:12 Jethro brings offerings to God. Although the combination of a singular and a plural looks strange because we are accustomed to thinking of them in abstract terms and hence both in plural, it may well fit the story for Jethro to bring one burnt offering and several sacrifices. Thus both of these are considered to be synonymous variants.

9:9   בג   את(ו)אבבעל(ו) פ(ו)רח ל[ש]ח[ין ל(ו)פ פ(ו)רח אבבעל(ו)את   𝔪𝔪] ελκη φλυκτιδες αναζεουσαι **G**
    Qᵃ𝔪𝔪 ≅ **G**

The order of words in **Qᵃ𝔪𝔪** reads "boils breaking out into blisters," whereas that in **G** reads "sores, blisters breaking out." In the following verse, 10, 𝔪𝔐**G** all have the word order that **G** has here in 9 (□**Qᵃ**). Thus **G** is consistent in both verses, while 𝔪𝔪 fluctuate. This gives rise to the suggestion that either אבבעות or שחין might be a gloss which was inserted in different places in the two verses and in the various traditions. The first might have been a technical term of significance to a learned scribe, while the latter might have been a more common word inserted as explanation.

It is, of course, possible that no variant is reflected in verse 9 at all, and that the translator simply exercised freedom in word order. In any case, this is certainly not an instance where one of these readings could clearly be preferred to the other.

6:27   ג   משה ואהר(ו)ן   𝔪𝔪] Ααρων και Μωυσης **G**   **Qᵃ𝔪𝔪** ≅ **G**

The two brothers are named together 34 times in Exodus; 31 times Moses is mentioned first and twice Aaron is mentioned first, 𝔪𝔐**G** agreeing those 33 times; only here in 6:27 is there disagreement. Interestingly, even at 7:7, which gives their respective ages, Moses is named first in spite of the fact that he is described as three years younger.

The two clauses that name Aaron first are in the immediate context: 6:20, in the middle of their genealogy, reports that Jochebed bore Aaron and

Moses;   and 6:26, immediately following the genealogy, resumes the
narrative with the words: ...הוא אהרן ומשה אשר אמר יהוה להם,   or
ουτος Ααρων και Μωυσης....   There follow two sentences describing
Yahweh's command and their fulfillment of it, and then the final summary:
הוא משה ואהרן, or αυτος Ααρων και Μωυσης.

One could argue that the order in 31 out of 34 cases in Exodus is also
preferable here, that the agreement of **Qᵃ𝔪𝔐** favors that order, and that
the reading preserved in **G** was the inadvertent result of the influence of
the two exceptional cases in the preceding context. The two clauses with
הוא/ ουτος/αυτος would form an inclusio around the two-sentence
resumption of the narrative, with the first clause retaining the order proper
to the genealogy, based on age, and the second clause shifting to the order
proper to the Exodus narrative, based on leadership. Thus the transition
from chronological priority to priority of role would be complete.

Alternatively one could argue as follows. First, the two clauses of
such an inclusio would have the same order. Second, Aaron should be
mentioned first because this paragraph is still properly following the order
of the genealogy and also because this verse, 27, describes the two as those
"who spoke to Pharaoh," which activity it is precisely the point of the P
narrative here to attribute to Aaron. Third, it is the unusual order that has
a better claim to preferability. Thus the reading in **G** is the original.

Faced with these conflicting arguments this reading is considered a
synonymous variant in which **G** alone disagrees with **Qᵃ𝔪𝔐**.

e. Different Word or Phrase

In eight synonymous variants **G** preserves a word or phrase that
differs from the reading of **Qᵃ𝔪𝔐**. The first six involve designations of
individuals: God and Jethro.

16:33	יהו]ה 𝔪𝔐]	του θεου **G**	**Qᵃ𝔪𝔐** ≅ **G**
19:8	יהו[ה 𝔪𝔐]	τον θεον **G**	**Qᵃ𝔪𝔐** ≅ **G**
32:30	יהוה 𝔪𝔐]	τον θεον **G**	**Qᵃ𝔪𝔐** ≅ **G**
18:1א	אלה[ים 𝔪𝔐]	κυριος **G**	**Qᵃ𝔪𝔐** ≅ **G**
20:1	אל[הים 𝔪𝔐]	κυριος **G**	**Qᵃ𝔪𝔐** ≅ **G**

These five readings represent all of the variants that involve disagreement in the designation used for God. In each case **G** alone differs
from the three Hebrew witnesses, but there is no reason to suppose that the

variation did not occur in Hebrew MSS.   Similar variations can be found among Hebrew witnesses.   For instance, at **18:1א** a Cairo text reads יהוה against 𝕸.   Elsewhere in Exodus where **Q^m** is not extant, 𝖲𝖺𝗆 and 𝕸 disagree six times (אלהים 𝖲𝖺𝗆; יהוה 𝕸 3:4;   יהוה 𝖲𝖺𝗆; אלהים 𝕸 6:2;   אדני יהוה 𝖲𝖺𝗆; האלהים 𝖲𝖺𝗆; יהוה 𝕸 9:30;   יהוה אלהיך 𝖲𝖺𝗆; יהוה 𝕸 13:5, 11;   יהוה 𝖲𝖺𝗆; האלהים 𝖲𝖺𝗆; יהוה אלהים 𝕸 22:8; cf. also 11:3; 15:2, 17; 22:19; 23:17; 29:10, 25; 34:23; 40:27).

Thus the fact that θεος is used in Exodus in **G** ca. 110 times when אלהים appears in 𝕸 but ca. 45 times when יהוה appears in 𝕸 should not be taken to mean that it was necessarily the translator who created the variant. Rather, he may have been faithfully reproducing his *Vorlage*, which differed from 𝕸.   There is variation of all kinds affecting the three traditions.

All five of these are considered synonymous variants because there are so many factors that may have been involved in the use of the names and titles of God that we can no longer determine preferability.   For instance, at **18:1א** a modern reader would expect to read that the priest of Midian heard what Yahweh -- not God -- had done for Israel (cf. 18:1b, 8-11; in these instances **G** agrees with 𝖲𝖺𝗆𝕸 in reading κυριος/יהוה).   Yet an Israelite author or editor may have had his own reasons for writing "God," as appears in the three Hebrew texts at **18:1א**, whether for theological or literary purposes, e.g., as part of an editorial introduction to the narrative (cf. 18:12, the conclusion of one section of the narrative; here again **G** agrees with 𝖲𝖺𝗆𝕸 in reading θεος/אלהים).

As we can no longer reconstruct with certainty the literary history of the various sources and redactions, so we cannot be sure about the trans-missional history either.   Scribes used a variety of methods to protect the name of God by warning the reader not to pronounce it, including writing the tetragrammaton in Palaeo-Hebrew characters, writing only dots instead of any characters, or, later, pointing with the vowels of אדני.   In Greek a very common method was to render κυριος rather than transliterating.   In both languages the word "God" was sometimes simply substituted.   All of these as well as other methods have been documented in the early texts.[6]   But it

---

[6]Patrick W. Skehan, "The Divine Name at Qumran, in the Masada Scroll, and in the Septuagint," *BIOSCS* 13 (1980) 14-44; Albert Pietersma, "Kyrios or Tetragram: A Renewed Quest for the Original Septuagint," in *De Septuaginta: Studies in Honour of John William Wevers on his Sixty-fifth Birthday* (Mississauga, Ontario: Benben Publications, 1984), pp. 85-101.

is impossible to determine precisely what happened at each individual passage and in each textual tradition.

In the light of all of these factors and questions, these five readings are considered synonymous variants, for in each passage an argument could be made for both texts. Rather than coming to dubious conclusions regarding preferability, it is better merely to record the statistics: in all five variants regarding the designation for God **G** stands alone against **Q⁺𝔪𝔐**.

18:14 משה[חתן 𝔪𝔐] Ιοθορ **G**   **Q⁺𝔪𝔐 ≅ G**

This individual is referred to by name and/or title 15 times in this chapter, and in all but this one case the three witnesses agree in the designation used. The scroll is at least partially extant in 9 of the 15 cases, and to the extent that it is preserved, it agrees with the other three witnesses except in this one case. The designations in which all traditions agree are:

Jethro, the priest of Midian, Moses' father-in-law	(v 1)
Jethro, Moses' father-in-law	(vv 2,5,12)
Jethro	(vv 9,10)
Moses' father-in-law	(vv 12,17)
his father-in-law	(vv 7,8,15,24,27)
your father-in-law, Jethro (Jethro, your father-in-law **G**)	(v 6)

The only variations among the Greek MSS concern the order of the phrases or the lack of a personal pronoun.

The overwhelming agreement in these designations throughout the narrative shows that all of the scribes or translators involved were content to copy what they read without doctoring the text for simplicity, for less repetition, or for greater explicitness. Thus we are left with two equally acceptable designations, both of which occur twice in the context, with no motive for intentional change at this one passage, and we must be content to classify these as synonymous variants. The important point is that **Q⁺𝔪𝔐** agree with each other against **G**.

Having seen six synonymous variants involving proper names of individuals, we turn now to two involving designations of Israelites more generally.

16:31 בית ישראל 𝕨𝕸] οι υιοι Ισραηλ **G**; בני ישראל 𝕸ᴹˢˢ𝕋ᴹˢ𝕾

Q°𝕨𝕸 ≅ **G**

בני ישראל occurs 118 times in Exodus; בית ישראל only twice, and בית יעקב once; only here does υιος correspond to בית in Exodus. οικος Ισραηλ never occurs in **G** of Exodus, while οικος Ιακωβ occurs twice. The unusual texts other than the present variant read as follows:

19:3	לבית יעקב 𝕨𝕸	τω οικω Ιακωβ **G**	□Q°
20:22	אל בני ישראל 𝕨𝕸	τω οικω Ιακωβ **G**	□Q°
40:38	כל בית ישראל 𝕨𝕸	παντος Ισραηλ **G**	□Q°

Thus if this is a case of visual confusion of letters, reading בני for בית or vice versa, whether by a scribe or a translator, then this is the only time out of 118 occurrences in Exodus that such confusion occurred. On the other hand, note that the confusion extends to other witnesses in the 𝕸 tradition. Furthermore, 4QSamᵃ preserves an agreement with **G** against 𝕸 at 2 Sam 6:5:[7] בני ישראל 4QSamᵃ **G**   בית ישראל 𝕸

Thus whichever was the original text, the secondary reading could easily have originated, probably by accident, at the Hebrew stage.

The rarity of the phrase בית ישראל in Exodus (2 times) and in the Torah (6 more times; all 8 are assigned by BDB to P or H) and the fact that this is its first occurrence in the Torah may argue in favor of its originality here. Since the entire verse 16:31 may be a later insertion into the earlier narrative, explaining the name "manna," a redactor or glossator may perhaps have used a term which is somewhat anachronistic in the wilderness context. Thus it may be that בית was the original term and that a scribe or the Greek translator conformed to his usual designation for the people deliberately or, more likely, unconsciously, simply because there was nothing special to him about this passage.

On the other hand, if the verse is a later insertion the style of Exodus may be irrelevant; the redactor or glossator may have used either phrase, depending on his own style. Thus this reading is considered a synonymous variant, since it is no longer possible to determine which was original. It is no longer possible to take for granted that where **G** differs it is necessarily secondary; the variation within the 𝕸𝕋𝕾 tradition could be used as an

---

[7]Eugene Ulrich, *The Qumran Text of Samuel and Josephus,* HSM, 19 (Missoula, MT: Scholars Press, 1978), p. 84.

argument in either direction; and the style of Exodus is less significant if the entire verse is somewhat later.

22:24א **Q**ᵃ   אם כסף תלוה את ע[מי את] העני עמכה

ℳ   אם כסף תלוה את עמי את   עני עמך

ⅿ   אם כסף תלוה את עמי את   העני עמך

G   εαν δε αργυριον εκδανεισης τω αδελφω τω πενιχρω

παρα σοι   **Q**ᵃℳⅿ ≅ **G**

Since the laws in this section deal with one's relations with other individuals, and since there is a clear analogy in 23:11: ואכלו אביוני עמך, "that the poor of your people may eat," it is likely that the original here was: אם כסף תלוה (?את) (?ה)עני עמך. A scribe in the tradition behind **G** may have inserted אחי, while a scribe in the tradition behind **Q**ᵃℳⅿ may have written עמי either in error for עני or as an added clarification; in either case at a later stage both עני and עמי were retained in a conflation of readings.

Later the definite article could have been added to עני to make it clear that the following word should be read as "with you," or alternatively the article could have been removed, reading it as in the construct state, "the poor person of your people," or simply by accidental analogy with את עמי. This might best explain how these two variants arose and how the difficult reading preserved in **Q**ᵃℳⅿ might have arisen.

Because of all of the uncertainties, and because none of these extant texts may represent the original, both of these are considered synonymous variants:
22:24א, regarding עמי as opposed to את, is classified here: **Q**ᵃℳⅿ ≅ **G**;
22:24ב, regarding the definite article, is listed in III.A.3: **Q**ᵃⅿ/G/ ≅ ℳ.

f. Different Form of Word or Suffix

Seven synonymous variants shared by **Q**ᵃℳⅿ involve a difference in the form of a word or suffix.

6:27א   להוציא ℳⅿ] και εξηγαγον **G**   **Q**ᵃℳⅿ ≅ **G**

Verses 26-27 are two parallel statements which form a transition from the genealogy of Moses and Aaron to the resumption of the narrative. In verse 26 is the clause:

Qᵃℳⅿ ...אשר אמר יהוה להם הוציאו את בני ישראל...

G ...οις ειπεν αυτοις ο θεος εξαγαγειν τους υιους Ισραηλ...

In v 26 the Greek infinitive is a legitimate, if somewhat free, rendering of the Hebrew imperative. In verse 27, however, the verb appears to be not a free translation of the Hebrew preserved in 𝐐ᵃ𝐦𝐌, but rather to translate a different *Vorlage,* ויוציאו:

𝐐ᵃ𝐦𝐌   הם המדברים אל פרעה מלך מצרים להוציא את בני ישראל...

ουτοι εισιν οι διαλεγομενοι προς Φαραω βασιλεα Αιγυπτου και εξηγαγον τους υιους Ισραηλ...

(In the other four instances of להוציא in Exodus, 𝐆 renders much more literally, which argues in favor of a different *Vorlage* here: ωστε εξαποστειλαι 6:13;   εξαγαγειν 8:14;   ωστε εξαγαγειν 12:42; εξαγαγων 14:11.)

In 6:27א, whereas the infinitive, as in 𝐐ᵃ𝐦𝐌, gives the topic or the purpose of their speaking with Pharaoh, the aorist indicative, as in 𝐆, gives the second of two activities: they spoke and they led out.   This latter construction might be considered preferable as far as content and style are concerned, since it completes the parallelism of the two verses better. According to the first verse they were commanded to bring out the Israelites; according to the second verse they succeeded in doing so. If this parallelism is indeed more pleasing, it may result either from the intention of the one who composed this transition or from a later scribe.   It is considered here a synonymous variant since it is impossible to determine which construction is earlier. (For the two other variants in this verse, apparently also occasioned by the parallelism of vv 26–27, see 6:27ב in II.A.3 and 6:27ג in III.A.5.)

10:24ג   יעג 𝐦𝐌] υπολειπεσθε 𝐆   𝐐ᵃ𝐦𝐌 ≅ 𝐆

The difference between third singular imperfect in *Hopʿal,* "will be detained," and second plural present imperative in middle, "leave behind," is slight enough that one might suspect merely free translation.   This is counted as a variant, however, because of the several other cases of minor differences in *binyan,* mood, person, and number of verbs, some affecting both Hebrew and Greek witnesses (e.g., 10:10; 10:26; 16:32; 22:6). Both forms are permissible in the context.

16:32   האכ]לתי אתכם 𝐦𝐌] εφαγετε υμεις 𝐆   𝐐ᵃ𝐦𝐌 ≅ 𝐆

Compare 10:24ג and the other variants mentioned there.

18:6ג   עמה [בנ[יה מ‎ᴍ] υιοι σου μετ αυτου **G**   **Qᵃᴍᴍ ≅ G**

It makes equally good sense for the message to be that Jethro is bringing <u>your</u> wife and <u>her</u> two sons with <u>her</u>, or that he is bringing <u>your</u> wife and two sons with <u>him</u>.

30:10   רתיכם](ו)ד[ל מ‎ᴍ] εις τας γενεας αυτων **G**   **Qᵃᴍᴍ ≅ G**

27:10   ועמד[יו מ‎ᴍ] και οι στυλοι αυτων **G**   **Qᵃᴍᴍ ≅ G**

18:12   ע(ו)לה ות[ב]חים מ‎ᴍ]

          ολοκαυτωματα και θυσιας **G**   **Qᵃᴍᴍ ≅ G**

See III.A.5.c for discussion of 18:12 and 10:25 together.

g. Longer, Shorter, or Transposition?

10:6א,ב   ובתי כל עבדיך וב[תי מ‎ᴍ] και αι οικιαι των θεραποντων σου και πασαι αι οικιαι **G**   **Qᵃᴍᴍ ≅ G**

Two occurrences of כל are involved here: did the original lack one or both? Is this a case of expansion, omission, or transposition?

    Summary: Thus we have seen 35 synonymous variants which **Qᵃᴍᴍ** share against **G**. Perhaps only nine of these could be said to be of significance individually -- those involving an entire pericope. Yet all of them together contribute substantially to the pattern of a significant tendency for **G** to stand alone against **Qᵃᴍᴍ**. The meaning of this pattern will be discussed in Chapter IV.A.5.

6. SYNONYMOUS VARIANTS SHARED BY QᵃᴍG

    There are only two synonymous variants shared by the three witnesses **QᵃᴍG** against **ᴍ**. Each involves only one word.

7:10   לפני פרעה 1° 4QExodᵇᴍG] אל פרעה **ᴍ**   **QᵃᴍG ≅ ᴍ**

This reading is considered a synonymous variant because a case could be made for the preferability of either לפני or אל. Both are permissible following the verb "go," though Moses (and Aaron) are elsewhere consistently said to "go" (בא or לך) אל Pharaoh. ᴍ and ᴍ agree each time: 3:11,18; 5:23; 7:15,26; 9:1; 10:1,3; ᴍ has אל also in the major expansions at 7:18ᵇ, 29ᵇ; 8:19ᵇ; 9:5ᵇ, 19ᵇ.

לפני could be considered preferable because it is the unusual usage and because it is preserved by the three witnesses -- as well as by 4QExod^b -- together against 𝕸. This could be countered, however, with the fact that לפני occurs 3 other times in verses 9-10 with the verb השליך (twice before "Pharaoh" and once before "his servants"), which could have influenced a scribe to write that preposition here as well. If this is a case of a move toward consistency, deliberate or unconscious, would it have been toward consistency of preposition with "go," or toward consistency of preposition in these two verses?

It is best to leave this as a synonymous variant, noting the agreement of 𝐐ᵃ4QExod^b𝖲𝐆 against 𝕸.

18:6ב אני 𝕸 [𝖲𝐆 הנה   𝐐ᵃ𝖲𝐆 ≅ 𝕸

Both words are acceptable, provided that the preceding ויאמר be understood appropriately. If it is taken impersonally (cf. ανηγγελη), then a third party is announcing Jethro's coming to Moses, with the word הנה, as in 𝐐ᵃ𝖲𝐆. If it is taken as Jethro's speaking through a messenger, then the messenger has gone ahead and is speaking in Jethro's name, with the word אני, as in 𝕸.

Summary: Thus 𝐐ᵃ𝖲𝐆 share only two synonymous variants against 𝕸, both of them quite minor. These few minor agreements can tell us little specific about affiliation between the 𝐐ᵃ𝖲 tradition and the 𝐆 tradition. Probably they only point to the many possibilities of slight variations among texts with the potential that arises for agreement among essentially unrelated texts.

7. SYNONYMOUS VARIANTS SHARED BY 𝐐ᵃ𝕸𝐆

27:11ג ווי [𝕸𝐆 וויהם 𝖲   𝐐ᵃ𝕸𝐆 ≅ 𝖲

Note that 𝖲 and 𝕸 differ in the same way in 27:10 (and compare a similar phenomenon at the execution in 38:17).

26:24 ויחד(י)ו [𝕸 יחדו 𝖲; και κατα το αυτο 𝐆   𝐐ᵃ𝕸𝐆 ≅ 𝖲

Summary: Thus there are only two synonymous variants where 𝐐ᵃ𝕸𝐆 agree against 𝖲. As has been seen in Chapter II.A.7, it is more often the case that these three witnesses agree in an original reading against 𝖲.

B. SYNONYMOUS VARIANTS PRESERVED BY 𝔐

1. SYNONYMOUS VARIANTS PRESERVED BY 𝔐 ALONE

There are thirteen instances of synonymous variants where 𝔐 is alone in its reading. Ten of these are quite minor, each involving only one or two grammatical features; one involves a slightly different expression, and two involve a minor difference in length of text.

Each of these is discussed elsewhere in Chapter III, depending on which, if any, of the other three witnesses agree together against 𝔐. The entire list is presented and organized according to type in Chapter IV.B.1.

2. SYNONYMOUS VARIANTS SHARED BY 𝔐𝔪

There are seven synonymous variants shared by 𝔐 and 𝔪. All of them are very minor, involving one locative *he,* two definite articles, two conjunctions, and two verbal forms.

21:13 שם] שמה 𝔐𝔪; εκει G   Qᵃ ≅ 𝔐𝔪; G?

Of the five variants concerning the locative *he* this is the only time when 𝔐 and 𝔪 agree. Qᵃ consistently lacks the *he* in all five cases. The presence or absence of the locative *he* is considered to be a synonymous variant because there is such lack of discernible consistency within each of the two complete witnesses of the Hebrew text of Exodus, 𝔐 and 𝔪, as well as such frequent disagreement between them and among 𝔐 MSS (see, e.g., for שם versus שמה, 16:33; 21:33; 26:33; 29:42, 43; 30:6, 18, 36; and 40:30). Thus although 𝔐𝔪 agree in this one instance against Qᵃ, that may be more by accident than by affiliation. G uses εκει for both שם and שמה; hence its *Vorlage* cannot be determined. (See 9:8ב for agreement between Qᵃ𝔐 in lacking the locative *he* against 𝔪. See 27:9; 27:11א; and 36:23 for agreement between Qᵃ𝔪 in lacking the *he* against 𝔐.)

18:13ב Qᵃ   [ערב]   מן בוקר
        𝔐   מן הבקר ועד הערב
        𝔪   מן הבקר עד הערב
        G   απο πρωιθεν εως εσπερας   Qᵃ ≅ 𝔐𝔪; G?

Each of the three Hebrew texts reads slightly differently, though as far as Qᵃ is extant 𝔐 and 𝔪 agree against it. Each form is possible and occurs elsewhere in Exodus in 𝔪. For example, in the very next verse, 18:14, where Qᵃ is not extant, 𝔪 lacks the articles but 𝔐 has them.

29:22 ב‫...‬ הי[ו]תרת] י[ו](ו)תרת הכבד Ш𝔐; του λοβου του ηπατος 𝔊   Qᵃ ≅ Ш𝔐; 𝔊?

There are 11 references to the appendage of the liver, occurring in 3 forms: the construct state here and in Lev 8:16, 25; 9:19 in Ш𝔐; with על (i.e., היותרת על הכבד) in Lev 3:4, 10, 15; 4:9; 7:4 in Ш𝔐; and similarly with מן in Lev 9:10. Although Ш and 𝔐 agree here and each time in Leviticus, they disagree in the only other passage in Exodus, at 29:13: Ш has the construct as also here, while 𝔐 has על.

𝔊 uses the genitive as here 5 times and επι 6 times (επι and απο appear once each in MS variation), but there is no strict correlation with the readings in Ш𝔐 at each passage. In Exod 29:13, the one place where Ш and 𝔐 disagree, 𝔊 has the genitive, superficially agreeing with Ш against 𝔐.

Because the other constructions occur as virtually synonymous, it is assumed that there is no grammatical error here in Qᵃ, but rather that it read either על or מן. These readings are taken as synonymous variants, and 𝔊 is considered ambiguous because of its fluidity in rendering this expression.

18:21ג ושרי חמשים 𝔊] שרי חמשים Ш𝔐   Qᵃ/𝔊/ ≅ Ш𝔐

18:16א ו[ב]א[ ] באו Ш; בא 𝔐; και ελθωσιν 𝔊   Qᵃ/𝔊/ ≅ Ш𝔐

In both of these cases of synonymous variation regarding the conjunction, the evidence of 𝔊 is taken as ambiguous because of its relative freedom to render such minor elements. Whatever slight significance these two cases of agreement between Ш and 𝔐 against Qᵃ might have had is vitiated by the facts that at 18:21ב, earlier in the same list of nouns, Ш agrees with Qᵃ against 𝔐 in having the conjunction, and that in 18:16 𝔐 agrees with Qᵃ against Ш in the number of the verb (= variant ב). Such minor disagreements show some of the complexities involved in the question of affiliation.

8:14[18] ה[כ]נים[ ] ויהי הכנם Ш; ותהי הכנים 𝔐;
και εγενοντο οι σκνιφες 𝔊   Qᵃ ≅ Ш𝔐; 𝔊?

According to Gesenius plurals of names of animals (here, "gnats") frequently take feminine singular verbs as collectives. If this is a Massoretic convention it seems also to have been followed by Ш at least in this case; however, given the uncertainties of our knowledge of non-Massoretic Hebrew, it seems wise to consider the variation in this verb a synonymous variant. The point is that **Q⁻** stands alone against the other two.

10:26   נשאר **G**] תשאר **ᵤᵤ𝕸**   (III.A.4)   **Q⁻G ≅ ᵤᵤ𝕸**

Summary: These seven synonymous variants shared by **ᵤᵤ** and **𝕸** are very minor. Rather than showing any specific affiliation between **ᵤᵤ** and **𝕸** against **Q⁻**, they perhaps point instead to the fact that members of the same family may exhibit many minor disagreements, and that members of different families may exhibit many minor agreements.

3. SYNONYMOUS VARIANTS SHARED BY ᵤᵤG

There are only three synonymous variants shared by **ᵤᵤ** and **G**. The first two have appeared above.

13:6   ש[ב]בעת י[מ]ים **𝕸**] ששת ימים **ᵤᵤG**   (III.A.3)   **Q⁻𝕸 ≅ ᵤᵤG**

18:16ב   ו[ב]א[ו] **ᵤᵤ**; בא **𝕸**; και ελθωσι **G**   (III.A.3)   **Q⁻𝕸 ≅ ᵤᵤG**

32:11ב   ו[בגרוע חזק]ה] ובגרוע נטויה **ᵤᵤG**; וביד חזקה **𝕸**
                                                              Q⁻ ≅ ᵤᵤG ≅ 𝕸

These readings are classified as synonymous variants because each one is possible, attested elsewhere, and defensible. **Q⁻** has the more difficult reading because it is so rare; but even its combination, "strong arm," is attested in **𝕸** once: at Jer 21:5. **ᵤᵤG** are suspect because of their tendency to be influenced by parallel passages in Deuteronomy; yet the reading "outstretched arm" is attested by two different traditions. Not only does **𝕸** stand alone but also, regardless of its reputation, it likewise has been influenced by Deuteronomy (see the discussion of **32:9** [II.D and IV.A.5.a] and cf. Deut 9:26 quoted below).

The readings of **𝕸** and **ᵤᵤG** are found combined -- "strong hand and outstretched arm" -- in Deuteronomy (never in Exodus): 5 times in **ᵤᵤ𝕸G** (at Deut 4:34; 5:15; 7:19; 11:2; and 26:8) and 2 additional times in **G**, where **ᵤᵤ𝕸** have only "strong hand" (at 6:21 and 7:8).

"Strong hand" is the slightly more common expression in Exodus, occurring 3 times in **ᵤᵤ𝕸G** (3:19; 6:1 [1°]; 13:9; □**Q⁻**). "Outstretched arm" occurs only once in **ᵤᵤ𝕸G** of Exodus: at 6:6, in combination with "great judgments." In Exod 6:1, however, where **ᵤᵤ𝕸** curiously repeat "strong hand" in two parallel clauses, **G** presents the more expected "strong hand // outstretched arm."

　　　But the most significant parallels to this reading in Exod 32:11 are two verses in the parallel narrative in Deut 9. The three complete clauses are printed here with disagreements underlined:

Ex 32:11　**Qᵃ**　　　　　ו[בזרוע חזקה]　　　　　　　　אשר הוע]את

　　　　　　ɰ　　אשר הוצאת　　ממצרים בכח גדול　ובזרוע נטויה

　　　　　　m　　אשר הוצאת מארץ מצרים בכח גדול　וביד　חזקה

　　　　　　G　ους εξηγαγες εκ γης Αιγυπτου εν ισχυι μεγαλη και
　　　　　　　　εν βραχιονι υψηλω

Deut 9:26　**ɰ**　＿＿＿＿＿＿＿　בידך החזקה　＿＿＿＿＿＿　אשר הוצאת ממצרים

　　　　　　m　＿＿＿＿＿＿＿　חזקה　ביד　＿＿＿＿＿＿　אשר הוצאת ממצרים

　　　　　　G　ους εξηγαγες εκ γης Αιγυπτου εν τη ισχυι σου τη
　　　　　　μεγαλη και εν τη χειρι σου τη κραταια και εν τω
　　　　　　βραχιονι σου τω υψηλω

Deut 9:29　**ɰ**　אשר הוצאת ממצרים בכחך הגדול ובגרועך הנטויה

　　　　　　m　אשר הוצאת　　בכחך הגדל　ובגרעך　הנטויה

　　　　　　G　ους εξηγαγες εκ γης Αιγυπτου εν τη ισχυι σου τη
　　　　　　μεγαλη και εν τω βραχιονι σου τω υπηλω

In Deut 9:26 and 29 **ɰ** and **m** agree on the various expressions used in each verse. **G** agrees with **ɰm** in v 29, but inserts into v 26 the two other expressions from v 29. (**G** makes the same additions in Deut 3:24; cf. also 26:8.) **G**^(B+) make the expansionism reciprocal by adding "strong hand" from v 26 into v 29!

　　　A reading of the two parallel pericopes, Exod 32:11-14 and Deut 9:25-29, will show that they include different ideas and order them differently, which means that either Deut 9:26 or 29 -- or both -- could have influenced various scribes at Exod 32:11. Thus it seems unfair to assume on the one hand that scribes in both the **ɰ** and **G** traditions were influenced at Exod 32:11 by Deut 9:29, but on the other hand that scribes in the **m** tradition were completely uninfluenced by Deut 9:26. Of course the agreement in both Exod 32:11 and Deut 9:29 of the first element, "great power," greatly strengthens the likelihood of influence in **ɰG**;　but that is at least partially offset by the agreement between the two of them against **m** alone.

The **Qᵃ** reading, "strong arm," could reflect simply a lapse on the part of a scribe, due to the similarity and frequent juxtaposition of the two phrases.   Another possibility is that it is indeed the original reading, attested, as we have seen, in Jer 21:5 in **𝕸**, where the combination "outstretched hand and strong arm" is found. If the more difficult reading of **Qᵃ** was original, perhaps scribes in the **𝖒𝕸𝐆** traditions all altered it to a phrase which was both more usual and present in the parallel pericope in Deuteronomy.   Thus the unique reading of **Qᵃ** would be the original, more difficult expression which would explain the two variations in the other witnesses.

In conclusion, then, we have three readings, each possible and defensible. **𝖒** and **𝐆** are the only two of the four witnesses which agree.

Summary: These three synonymous variants shared by **𝖒** and **𝐆** can tell us little in themselves about any positive affiliation between these two.

4. SYNONYMOUS VARIANTS SHARED BY 𝖒𝕸𝐆

There are four synonymous variants shared by all three of the witnesses being studied, **𝖒𝕸𝐆**, against **Qᵃ**.   Each involves a shorter reading in **Qᵃ**, which could be haplographic or could be the original.

10:21ב **Qᵃ**   ויט משה   [מצר]\ים

      𝖒   מצרים וימש החשך ויט משה

      𝕸   מצרים וימש חשך ויט משה

      𝐆   Αιγυπτου, ψηλαφητον σκοτος. εξετεινεν δε Μωυσης

                                                  Qᵃ ≅ 𝖒𝕸𝐆

At first glance this might appear to be a clear case of parablepsis on the part of **Qᵃ** (וי⌃וי).   The clause at issue, however, is an unusual one in the plague narratives: is "that one may feel [the] darkness" perhaps somewhat poetic for this context? A comparison with Jb 12:25 may suggest an expansion in Exodus from that book:

      𝕸 ימשש וחשך   ψηλαφησαισαν σκοτος **𝐆**

Admittedly there are very few cases of expansion that have been discovered in Exodus from a book farther afield than Deuteronomy.   The motivation would be similar to what we have seen in other sections of the plague narrative, however: heightening the dramatic impact of the story.   (It is also possible that there was some mediating influence from Deuteronomy.

A clause in Deut 28: 29 combines two very rare words to threaten punishment: "you shall grope at noonday, as the blind grope in darkness." The verb used twice for "to grope" is the same as that used here in Exod 10:21, and the unusual and ominous noun for "darkness," אפלה, appears also in Exod 10:22, the next verse. This is another case of the plagues against the Egyptians being expressed with the same words as the threats of judgment for Israel.)   Even if there were influence from Job, however, it could well have occurred during the literary development of Exodus so that it would be considered to belong to the preferable text, which Q^n lost by parablepsis.

Because of the uncertainty, this is considered a synonymous variant. It is listed here as a case of agreement among 𝖚𝖒𝔊 because they all have the longer text. Note, however, that 𝖚 has the definite article which 𝔪 lacks: perhaps this too is best taken as a synonymous variant, since the article seems almost required by the context.

31:13-14 Q^n כי]אות הי]א ל]כם מחלל]יה

𝖚𝖒𝔊   כי אות היא (הוא 𝔪) ביני ובינ(י)כם לדרתיכם לדעת
                כי אני יהוה מקדשכם
                14ושמרתם את השבת

                כי קדש היא (הוא 𝔪) לכם מחלליה
                                        Q^n ≅ 𝖚𝖒𝔊

While it is quite possible that this is a case of parablepsis in Q^n (היא⌢היא), it is also possible that the shorter reading is preferable and has been expanded under the influence of Ezek 20:12, 20.   The shorter reading makes good sense. Since most of these words occur in various combinations elsewhere in the paragraph, 31:12-17, little is lost to the context by their lack at this position. Only one idea receives less emphasis by the lack: that of sanctity, but even it is mentioned in verse 15, and sufficient other positive motivation is given in the context for the keeping of sabbath, including its sign character, the covenant, and the creation story.

Because of the conflicting possibilities -- parablepsis, or expansion from Ezekiel -- this reading is considered a synonymous variant.

ב34:16

Qᵃ ᛧᛗ

G   και λαβης των θυγατερων αυτων τοις υιοις σου   ולקחת מבנתיו לב]ניך

Qᵃ ᛧᛗ

G   και των θυγατερων σου δως τοις υιοις αυτων,

Qᵃ

ᛧᛗ   וזנו בנתיו אחרי אלהיהן

G   και εκπορνευσωσιν αι θυγατερες σου οπισω των θεων αυτων

Qᵃ ᛧᛗ   והזנו את בני]ך אחרי אלהיהן

G   και εκπορνευσωσιν τους υιους σου οπισω των θεων αυτων.

Qᵃ ≅ ᛧᛗG

There are two variants in this verse. In the first (א34:16) **G** has an added clause (line two above; see Chapter II.A.5), while in the second (ב34:16) **Qᵃ** lacks a clause that ᛧᛗ both have (line three above).   Only four words from the verse are represented, and they are on two separate fragments. But since לב]ניך is followed immediately by והזנו on the same fragment, it is clear that **Qᵃ** lacked וזנו בנתיו אחרי אלהיהן at this point.

Probably most would agree that the second line of the verse, which is in **G** only, is an addition, whether for the sake of symmetry or under the influence of Ezra 9 and/or Deut 7:3 (see II.A.5).

It is more difficult, however, to know how to judge the third line, which is lacking only in **Qᵃ**. The shorter reading, consisting of only the first and the fourth lines, makes good sense on its own, and yet could be considered ripe for expansion.   Furthermore, a possible source for the expansion lies very close at hand, in the immediately preceding verse: 34:15 reads ...וזנו אחרי אלהיהם...   For all three of those reasons, the shorter reading might be preferable.

There is, however, the possibility of haplography: וזנו ̑והזנו. And one argument against the expansion in **G** cannot be made here: there **G** stands alone in having the longer reading; here ᛧᛗG all agree in having the longer reading. Hence this reading joins the synonymous variants where **Qᵃ** stands alone in its ambiguity.

9:9א

Qᵃ ≅ ᛧᛗG

על כל ארץ [על ארץ ᛧᛗG

The probability that the word כל was added in ᛧᛗG, as happened so commonly in all of the traditions, is tempered by the possibility that it was lost by parablepsis (ל‸ל). Because of this uncertainty the reading is considered a synonymous variant.

    <u>Summary</u>: These four synonymous variants shared by ᴟꟽG against Qᵃ are difficult to judge. If in fact these are original readings in Qᵃ where the other three all have the expanded texts, then these would join those four readings discussed in Chapter II.A.1, where Qᵃ alone has the shorter prefer- able reading, and there would be even more evidence that Qᵃ somehow managed to preserve the pristine text in some places in spite of its proclivity in many other places to expansionism. It would then be the case that these eight expansions either occurred so early or else gained such wide circulation that the three other witnesses all have them, although they exhibit little other evidence of affiliation.

    On the other hand, if these four readings result from parablepsis on the part of Qᵃ or its *Vorlage,* then they indicate only that the other three witnesses share original readings, which, as we have seen, cannot prove anything about specific affiliation, but only highlight the distinctiveness of Qᵃ.

C. SYNONYMOUS VARIANTS PRESERVED BY ꟽ

1. SYNONYMOUS VARIANTS PRESERVED BY ꟽ ALONE

    There are fourteen instances of synonymous variants where ꟽ is alone in its reading. Eleven of these are quite minor, each involving only one or two grammatical features; two involve variation in wording; and one involves different word order.

    Each of these is discussed elsewhere in Chapter III, depending on which, if any, of the other three witnesses agree together against ꟽ. The entire list is presented and organized according to type in Chapter IV.C.1.

2. SYNONYMOUS VARIANTS SHARED BY ꟽG   (III.A.2)   Qᵃᴟ ≅ ꟽG

30:1-10   post 26:35 ᴟ]   post 29:46 ꟽG

29:2   סלת ᴟ] pr משחים בשמן ꟽG

Summary: These two synonymous variants shared by 𝔐 and 𝔊 cannot prove much about a positive affiliation between the two traditions, since there is no pattern of agreement in secondary readings.

D. SYNONYMOUS VARIANTS PRESERVED BY 𝔊 ALONE

There are 35 instances of synonymous variants where 𝔊 is alone in its reading. In all of these the three Hebrew witnesses agree with each other. In six 𝔊 is shorter, six suggest that an entire pericope existed in two different forms, two provide conflicting representations, four involve the order of words or phrases, eight involve the choice of a word or phrase, seven involve different forms of a word or a suffix, and in two there may have been either omission, expansion, or transposition. Perhaps only nine of these could be said to be of significance individually -- those involving an entire pericope. Yet all of them together contribute substantially to the pattern of a significant tendency for 𝔊 to stand alone against Q° 𝔪 𝔐.

These readings have all been discussed together in one section, Chapter III.A.5. The entire list is presented and organized according to type in Chapter IV.A.5.

E. SYNONYMOUS VARIANTS PRESERVED DIFFFERENTLY IN EACH

This chapter on synonymous variants would not be complete without a final section showing those few readings where none of the four witnesses agree with each other.

17:16   Q°   עד דור ודו]ר
         𝔪   מדר ודר
         𝔐   מדר דר
         𝔊   απο γενεων εις γενεας   Q° ≆ 𝔪 ≆ 𝔐 ≆ 𝔊

The variations of this phrase are possible and attested elsewhere. The form with עד as in Q° occurs 4 times in 𝔐: Is 13:20 and Jer 50:39 (and cf. Ps 100:5 and Joel 2:2);   𝔊 translates with εως and δια.

The reading with -מ, as in both 𝔪 and 𝔐, has only one close counterpart, in Is 34:10: מדור לדור 𝔐; εις γενεας 𝔊.

For several similar versions of the reading with **απο** in 𝔊, see Ps 9:27 [10:6H]; 32:11 [33:11H] in MSS BS; 76:9 [77:9H]; and 84:6 [85:6H]; each of these corresponds to **לדר ודר** in 𝔐 (but cf. also Ps 12:8).

There are only three occurrences of this idiom in the Torah:

	𝔪	𝔐	𝔊
Exod 3:15	לדר ודר	לדר דר	γενεων γενεαις
Exod 17:16	מדר ודר	מדר דר	απο γενεων εις γενεας
Deut 32:7	דור ודור	דור ודור	γενεας γενεων

Whereas 𝔪 has the conjunction all 3 times, 𝔐 has it only once. (𝔔^{m} is extant only at 17:16) Yet some form of the phrase occurs 38 times in the rest of the OT; except for the 2 times when it has the preposition -ל and the 3 times when the second noun is plural, the only times 𝔐 lacks the conjunction are precisely these two times in Exodus.

𝔊 could reflect any of the three Hebrew versions, but it is perhaps even more likely that it reflects a fourth. **לדר ודר** is the form that most frequently occurs in 𝔐 (19 times); it is rendered by a wide variety of Greek phrases, but the idiom with **απο** always corresponds in its 4 other occurrences to **לדר ודר** (see above). The next most frequent form in 𝔐 is **דר (ו\ל)דר**; it occurs 7 times.

Thus each of the four readings is taken as different. Since each of them is attested elsewhere, each is considered equally possible here. Since each is preserved here by only one of the witnesses, this is considered a synonymous variant.

18:16א,ב ו[ב]א] באו 𝔪; בא 𝔐; και ελθωσι 𝔊 𝔔^{m} ≅ 𝔪 ≅ 𝔐 ≅ 𝔊

34:13 ואשריו] ואשריהם 𝔪; ואת אשריו 𝔐; και τα αλση αυτων 𝔊
𝔔^{m} ≅ 𝔪 ≅ 𝔐; 𝔊?

29:22א ואת [...] את האליה 𝔪; והאליה 𝔐; > 𝔊(vid.)
𝔔^{m} ≅ 𝔪 ≅ 𝔐; 𝔊?

<u>Summary</u>: These four synonymous variants where none of the texts agree with any other show the potential that exists for slight variation with little or no change in meaning.

CONCLUSION

Thus we have seen 80 readings which, because the contending texts have a roughly equivalent claim on preferability, have been classified as synonymous variants. This total should be compared with that in Chapter II: there we saw 85 readings in which preferability could, albeit with varying degrees of confidence, be established.

The significance of Chapter III will be brought out as we look at the question of textual affiliation in Chapter IV.

CHAPTER IV

TEXTUAL AFFILIATION

INTRODUCTION

This chapter presents the data for the determination of affiliation among the four witnesses 𝐐ᵐ ⅲ𝔪𝐆 to the text of Exodus. The main divisions of the chapter are the same as in Chapters II and III, again beginning with the major concern of this work, the nature and affiliation of the scroll. Within those divisions the order of presentation of readings follows the order of their significance for the question of affiliation.

Appendices 3 and 4 present two charts which show graphically what Chapters IV and V deal with in lists and prose. Appendix 3 should be consulted while reading Chapter IV. It shows how the texts agree with each other in secondary, synonymous, and preferable readings.

The first subdivision in each section lists all instances of agreement in secondary readings, presented in order of significance. First to be listed is the most noteworthy evidence for textual affiliation: agreement of two or three texts in significant readings which are clearly secondary, e.g., those major expansions which are preserved in both 𝐐ᵐ and ⅲ. These are followed by readings which, though probably or even clearly secondary, are the type which various scribes could well have made independently. They will be listed by type, beginning with the more significant cases such as exegetical expansions (e.g., explicit subjects or objects) and syntactical tidying (e.g., creating agreement between subject and verb). Such agreements have greater probability for affiliation if they occur in the majority of cases but probably do not show affiliation if no pattern can be established. They will be followed by readings which are of minimal significance for the question of affiliation, e.g., minor additions such as "and" and "all."

The second subdivision presents the readings termed "synonymous variants," where two or more readings appear to have a similar claim on originality, for they are merely different good ways of expressing the same thing. While we cannot say that one reading is preferable to another, we can see how the witnesses agree and disagree among themselves and gain more evidence as to affiliation.   These readings are listed in the order in which they were discussed in Chapter III.

The third subdivision gives total agreements in preferable readings. These are of only minor significance for the question of textual affiliation.[1] After all, it is to be expected that the various witnesses will agree in preserving the original or preferable text, and as a matter of fact all four witnesses do agree in most of the book of Exodus. Only when one or more texts disagree is a reading even discussed in this work. Agreements in preferable readings cannot bear great weight for proving family relationship other than that all the texts go back to a common heritage, but they may in fact depend upon real affiliation even if we cannot prove it. That is, just as an erroneous or secondary reading in one text will cause erroneous or secondary readings to appear in texts dependent upon it, so too original readings in one text, where other traditions have errors or secondary developments, will cause original readings to appear in texts dependent upon it. Each section, therefore, will end with a brief reference to the number of agreements in preferable readings. Full information on these readings is given in Chapter II.

There is a negative side of textual affiliation which is also given attention in this chapter. Each witness not only agrees with other texts but also preserves some unique readings, whether preferable, synonymous, or secondary variants. These unique readings set the boundaries to the affiliation of that witness. All unique readings are accounted for in this chapter. Unique secondary readings and synonymous variants are listed together for each witness, and the total of unique preferable readings is given, with reference to the section of Chapter II where they are discussed.

A special caution is necessary where **G** appears to agree with one or two other texts, especially in secondary or synonymous variants. As Tov has put it:

> In many instances...it cannot be determined whether a certain deviation in the LXX reflects a Hebrew variant, even if the deviation agrees exactly with a variant reading extant in an ancient Hebrew source. This caution applies particularly to deviations in the area of grammar, in which the analysis of

---

[1]This has been frequently pointed out by Emanuel Tov. See, e.g., "Determining the Relationship between the Qumran Scrolls and the LXX: Some Methodological Issues," *The Hebrew and Greek Texts of Samuel*, ed. Emanuel Tov (Jerusalem: Academon, 1980), p. 48.

translation technique, as well as complicated Hebrew evidence, does not allow for satisfactory decisions. As a result, certain agreements between the LXX and a particular scroll cannot be taken into consideration in evaluating the relationship between the two.   At least, they should be separated from the other data.[2]

Many of the agreements [between the Septuagint and the Samaritan Pentateuch] are ambiguous for text-critical purposes. The two sources should not be analyzed in the same manner, because the reconstruction of the Hebrew *Vorlage* of the LXX is a matter of conjecture. Many of the agreements between the LXX and the Sam. Pent. reflect common exegesis, especially contextual exegesis, and in many cases there are no criteria for determining whether the exegesis reflected in the LXX derived from the translator or his *Vorlage*. In such cases the nature of the agreement cannot be evaluated for text-critical purposes.   This applies especially to differences between MT and the Sam. Pent. in grammatical categories such as number, person, verbal forms, etc.... For example, it cannot be determined whether the plural form of the LXX for MT ומקלכם in Ex. 12:11 derived from a variant like ומקליכם in the Sam. Pent. or whether it reflects the technique, also known elsewhere in the LXX, of adapting the number of nouns to that of the words with which they are connected. Similarly, in Ex. 24:2, the plural verb of MT (יעלו) is reflected in the singular in both the LXX and Sam. Pent. (יעלה) in agreement with its subject (העם).   The same applies to some two hundred instances of an added και and *waw* in the LXX and the Sam. Pent. and some hundred instances of its omission.[3]

By listing all agreements in each section, I hope to enable readers to draw their own conclusions as to which agreements can be considered significant. For myself, I have used diagonal slashes (/**G**/) to indicate doubt regarding any causal relationship between **G** and one of the Hebrew witnesses.

---

[2]Tov, *Septuagint,* pp. 261-262.
[3]Tov, *Septuagint,* pp. 269-270.

A. THE TEXTUAL AFFILIATION OF $\mathbf{Q}^{a}$

1. UNIQUE, NON-AFFILIATED, READINGS IN $\mathbf{Q}^{a}$

a. Secondary Readings

(1) $\mathbf{Q}^{a}$ +

7:15א	והנה [הנה ɰ𝕸G	(IIB4)	$\mathbf{Q}^{a} \neq$ ɰ𝕸G
8:16[20]	אל משה] לאמור [אל משה ɰ𝕸G	(IIB4)	$\mathbf{Q}^{a} \neq$ ɰ𝕸G

(2) $\mathbf{Q}^{a}$ 2v

10:21א	וידבר/‡ [ויאמר ɰ𝕸; Ειπεν δε G	(IIB2)	$\mathbf{Q}^{a} \neq$ ɰ𝕸(G)
7:18	בת]וך [ביאר ɰ𝕸;		
	εν τω ποταμω G	(IIB2)	$\mathbf{Q}^{a} \neq$ ɰ𝕸(G?)
12:6	אתו [אותם ɰ𝕸G	(IIB4)	$\mathbf{Q}^{a} \neq$ ɰ𝕸G
23:31	וש[מתי (vid) [ושתי ɰ𝕸; και θησω G	(IIB2)	$\mathbf{Q}^{a} \neq$ ɰ𝕸; G?
31:5	מלאכה [מלאכת ɰ𝕸; τα εργα G	(IIB2)	$\mathbf{Q}^{a} \neq$ ɰ𝕸; G?

(3) $\mathbf{Q}^{a}$ X (VA5)

28:11א	יפתח [תפתח ɰ𝕸G	(IIB4)	$\mathbf{Q}^{a} \neq$ ɰ𝕸G
28:41	ו]הלבשתם [והלבשת ɰ𝕸G	(IIB4)	$\mathbf{Q}^{a} \neq$ ɰ𝕸G
31:4	לעשוב]זהב [לעשות בזהב ɰ𝕸G	(IIB4)	$\mathbf{Q}^{a} \neq$ ɰ𝕸G

Thus $\mathbf{Q}^{a}$ stands alone in ten secondary readings. All of them are very minor, and most represent actual errors or other almost unconscious lapses or additions.

b. Synonymous Variants

(1) Q Is Shorter

31:13-14

Q   כי]אות הי[א ל]כם מחלל]יה

⅏𝔐G   כי אות היא (הוא 𝔐) ביני וביני(י)כם לדרתיכם לדעת

כי אני יהוה מקדשכם

¹⁴ושמרתם את השבת

כי קדש היא (הוא 𝔐) לכם מחלליה

(IIIB4) Q ≅ ⅏𝔐G

10:21ב   ⅏𝔐G מצרים וימש (ה)חשך ויט [[מצר]\ים ויט

(IIIB4) Q ≅ ⅏𝔐G

34:16ב   ⅏𝔐; וזנו בנתיו אחרי אלהיהן [pr והנו

pr και εκπορνευσωσιν αι θυγατερες

σου οπισω των θεων αυτων G   (IIIB4) Q ≅ ⅏𝔐G

9:9א   ⅏𝔐 על כל ארץ [על ארץ   (IIIB4) Q ≅ ⅏𝔐G

21:13   שם] שמה ⅏𝔐; εκει G   (IIIB2) Q ≅ ⅏𝔐; G?

18:13ב   ⅏𝔐 הבקר ... הערב [בוקר [ ]ערב

πρωιθεν ... εσπερας G   (IIIB2) Q ≅ ⅏𝔐; G?

34:13   ואת אשריו ⅏; ואשריהם [ואשריו 𝔐;

και τα αλση αυτων G   (IIIE)   Q ≅ ⅏ ≅ 𝔐; G?

(2) Q Is Longer

29:22א   והאליה ⅏ את האליה [ואת]... 𝔐;

> G(vid.)   (IIIE)   Q ≅ ⅏ ≅ 𝔐; G?

29:22ב   י)(ו)תרת [הי]ותרת ⅏𝔐;

τον λοβον G   (IIIB2) Q ≅ ⅏𝔐; G?

(3) <u>Different Word and Longer</u>   (IIIE)

17:16   עד דור ודו]ר [מדר ודר 𝔚; מדר דר 𝔐;

     απο γενεων εις γενεας **G** Q^a ≅ 𝔚 ≅ 𝔐 ≅ **G**

(4) <u>Different Word</u>   (IIIB3)

32:1l בו   ו]בגרוע חנ]קה [ובגרוע נטויה 𝔚**G**;

        וביד חזקה 𝔐 Q^a ≅ 𝔚**G** ≅ 𝔐

(5) <u>Different Form of Word</u>

8:14[18]   ויהי ה]כ]ב]נים [ותהי הכנ(י)ם 𝔚𝔐;

     και εγενοντο οι σκνιφες **G**   (IIIB2) Q^a ≅ 𝔚𝔐; **G**?

In these twelve readings Q^a clearly disagrees with the other two Hebrew witnesses; in six of the readings Q^a clearly disagrees also with **G**, but in six readings the *Vorlage* of **G** cannot be determined. Eight of these are quite minor, each involving only one or two grammatical features or כל; one involves variation within a phrase, and three involve a fairly significant difference in length of text.

c. *Preferable Readings*   (IIA1)

Q^a uniquely preserves the preferable reading in five instances. In four cases Q^a is shorter by one word, and in one case it preserves an older form. All of these are fairly minor variants.

d. *Conclusion*

Thus there are 27 readings where Q^a preserves a unique reading. Of these, ten are secondary, of which three are actual errors. These 27 variants range from something as minor as the presence or absence of a *yod* to the presence or absence of a passage of fourteen words. They show that regardless of any affiliation Q^a may prove to have with any of the other texts, it nevertheless stands alone in 24 readings which are not errors, a relatively large number. Thus this first conclusion about the textual affiliation of Q^a is a negative one: in 27 readings, mostly but not all minor, it does not agree with any of the other witnesses studied here.

2. READINGS SHARED BY **Qᵃ** AND 𝔐

a. *Agreement in Secondary Readings*

(1) Qᵃ𝔐 ++   (VA3) **Qᵃ𝔐 ≠ 𝔐G**

7:18ᵇ   hab 𝔐] > 𝔐G

7:29ᵇ   hab 𝔐] > 𝔐G

8:19ᵇ   hab 𝔐] > 𝔐G

9:5ᵇ   hab 𝔐] > 𝔐G

9:19ᵇ   hab 𝔐] > 𝔐G

10:2ᵇ   hab 𝔐] > 𝔐G

18:25𝔐   // Deut 1:9-18 𝔐] aliter et brevius 𝔐G

27:19ᵇ   hab 𝔐] > 𝔐G

32:10   hab 𝔐] > 𝔐G

20:19ᵃ   hab 𝔐] דבר אתה עמנו ונשמעה 𝔐;

         Λαλησον συ ημιν **G**   (IID; VA3) **Qᵃ𝔐 ≠ 𝔐 ≠ G**

These are the major **Qᵃ𝔐** expansions where a passage from
elsewhere in Exodus or Deuteronomy is interpolated, or where a passage
from the same context in Exodus is repeated with minor variations to fit the
sense. These will be discussed in Chapter V.   At this point it is enough to
state that wherever **Qᵃ** is extant, it preserves the same major expansions
that 𝔐 presents, with the single exception of the specifically "Samaritan"
expansion concerning the altar on Mount Gerizim in Exodus 20.   There are
two other readings included here although they represent a sub-category:

24:1   𝔐] ואביהוא אלעזר ו[איתמ]ר

        ואביהוא 𝔐G   (VA3) **Qᵃ𝔐 ≠ 𝔐G**

24:9   𝔐] ואביהוא אלעזר וא[י]תמר

        ואביהוא 𝔐G   (VA3) **Qᵃ𝔐 ≠ 𝔐G**

(2) Qᵃ𝔪 +

10:5	כל 𝔪G [שו]כל עשב הארץ ואת כל] פרי	(IIC2) Qᵃ𝔪 ≠ 𝔪G
17:13	לפי 𝔪G [שו]ויכם לפי בג17:13	(IIC2) Qᵃ𝔪 ≠ 𝔪G
8:20[24]	כבד 𝔪G [שו]כבד[מאד	(IIC2) Qᵃ𝔪 ≠ 𝔪G
22:3[4]	שנים 𝔪; [שו]אחד]שנים	
	διπλα αυτα G	(IIC1) Qᵃ𝔪 ≠ 𝔪; G?

The first expansion is moderately significant, clearly indicating affiliation. In the last three cases, the expansion consists of only one word. While they could have been added by different scribes independently, taken together with the other features shared by both witnesses, they assume greater importance than they would alone.

(3) Qᵃ𝔪 2ν   (IIC1)

10:24א	למשה [שו]אל משה 𝔪; Μωυσην G	Qᵃ𝔪 ≠ 𝔪; G?
25:20	איש אל אחיו [שו]אחד א[ל אחד 𝔪;	
	εις αλληλα G	Qᵃ𝔪 ≠ 𝔪; G?

These are likewise cases of rather slight differences, yet the fact that Qᵃ𝔪 share them as part of a larger pattern of common variants strongly suggests that these reflect common development as well.

Thus there are 18 secondary readings shared by Qᵃ𝔪 against 𝔪G. Twelve are major expansions and represent typological characteristics of this textual tradition; one moderate expansion consists of five words, while three smaller expansions involve one word each, of varying significance. The two alterations are minor in themselves and take on significance only as part of the larger pattern.

b. Agreement in Synonymous Variants   (IIIA2)

(1) Different Order

30:1-10	post 26:35 שו] post 29:46 𝔪G	Qᵃ𝔪 ≈ 𝔪G
26:10	חמשים ללאת [שו]° 1 ללא[ות חמשים 𝔪;	
	αγκυλας πεντηκοντα G	Qᵃ𝔪/G/ ≈ 𝔪

(2) 𝐐ᵃ 𝔐 Are Shorter

29:2	סלת 𝔐] pr משחים בשמן 𝔐G	𝐐ᵃ 𝔐 ≅ 𝔐G
9:8ב	הש[מ]ים 𝔐] השמימה 𝔐; εις τον ουρανον G	𝐐ᵃ 𝔐 ≅ 𝔐; G?

(3) 𝐐ᵃ 𝔐 Are Longer

18:20	הדרך אש[ר 𝔐] הדרך 𝔐;	
	τας οδους, εν αις G	𝔐 𝔐/G/ ≅ 𝔐
18:21ב	ושרי מאות 𝔐G] שרי מאות 𝔐	𝔐 𝔐/G/ ≅ 𝔐

(4) Different Word

| 7:14 | וידבר\[†] 𝔐] ויאמר 𝔐; Ειπεν δε G | 𝐐ᵃ 𝔐 ≅ 𝔐(G) |

(5) Different Form of a Word

26:26	בריחם עצי שטים 𝔐] בריחי עצי שטים 𝔐;	
	μοχλους εκ ξυλων ασηπτων G	𝐐ᵃ 𝔐 ≅ 𝔐; G?
22:6	ו]נגנב 𝔐] וגנב 𝔐; και κλαπη G	𝐐ᵃ 𝔐 ≅ 𝔐; G?
32:11א	יחר 𝔐] יחרה 𝔐; θυμοι G	𝐐ᵃ 𝔐 ≅ 𝔐; G?
22:26א	הי[א...הוא 𝔐] הוא...היא 𝔐; τουτο...τουτο G	𝐐ᵃ 𝔐 ≅ 𝔐; G?
31:13	א]היא 𝔐] הוא 𝔐; εστιν G	𝐐ᵃ 𝔐 ≅ 𝔐; G?

Only the first of these twelve synonymous variants is of major significance in itself, involving as it does a different placement of ten verses. But the other eleven take on somewhat more importance, first, because there are so many of them, and second, as part of the larger pattern of agreement between 𝐐ᵃ and 𝔐 in secondary and synonymous readings.

c. *Agreement in Preferable Readings*   (IIA2a)

There are only two very minor instances of preferable readings shared only by 𝐐ᵃ and 𝔐. These point to slight lapses on the part of the 𝔐 tradition.

d. Conclusion

Of the four witnesses being compared, only the first two are clearly related in ways that indicate a significant period of common development during which specific secondary readings arose.

It should be noted that for the sake of neutrality this tradition is designated by its two extant witnesses, $\mathbf{Q^m}$ 𝖆𝖆, rather than by such terms as "Palestinian" or "Proto-Samaritan." The first term has been criticized because it suggests that this tradition was originally or peculiarly attached to a certain location and that others were not, which has not been proven. The second term has the disadvantage of constantly drawing attention to the group that ultimately preserved it in its advanced, "sectarian" form, and thus drawing attention away from the more important fact that this was a tradition apparently used by more than one group.

By the same token, it is unfortunate that we have no better term with which to refer to what is called the "Proto-Massoretic" or even "Proto-Rabbinic" tradition. The use of the siglum 𝖒 should be construed only as referring to the most advanced, "sectarian" form of that tradition.

The clearest evidence of close affiliation between $\mathbf{Q^m}$ and 𝖆𝖆 is the fact that in all major expansions preserved by 𝖆𝖆, where $\mathbf{Q^m}$ is extant it preserves that expansion as well, with only the one exception regarding the altar on Mount Gerizim (see above). Full discussion is saved for Chapter V, where these major expansions will be analyzed to determine the character of the two witnesses. But besides the twelve major expansions, $\mathbf{Q^m}$ also shares with 𝖆𝖆 six secondary readings ranging from moderate to minor, as well as one major and eleven minor synonymous variants.

The conclusion to this section is that $\mathbf{Q^m}$ and 𝖆𝖆 belong to the same textual tradition. This is based on the fact that they share 32 readings against 𝖒𝐆: eighteen secondary readings, twelve synonymous variants, and two preferable readings.

Yet while $\mathbf{Q^m}$ and 𝖆𝖆 clearly belong to a single tradition, there are nevertheless significant smaller differences between them. A major task of this investigation is to clarify the pattern of commonalities and of differences between the two and thus to shed light on the history of this textual tradition.

The first limitation to the affiliation of $\mathbf{Q^m}$ and 𝖆𝖆 has already been presented in the preceding section, IV.A.1: the 27 variants in which $\mathbf{Q^m}$ preserves a unique reading. We turn now to the relationship between $\mathbf{Q^m}$

and **𝕸**, which will further -- and perhaps even more significantly -- modify
our understanding of the **Q^a𝕸** tradition.

3. READINGS SHARED BY **Q^a** AND **𝕸**

a. Agreement in Secondary Readings

There are no secondary readings shared only by **Q^a𝕸** in the extant
parts of **Q^a**.

b. Agreement in Synonymous Variants   (IIIA3)

(1) Different Word

13:6   ששת ימים **𝕸]** ש[בעת י[מ]ים **𝕊G**   **Q^a𝕸 ≅ 𝕊G**

10:11   ουτως **G** μη **𝕊**; לכן **𝕸]** לא כן   **Q^a𝕸/G/ ≅ 𝕊**

(2) **Q^a𝕸** Are Longer

22:24 בל   העני **𝕸]** עני **𝕊**; τω πενιχρω **G**   **Q^a𝕸/G/ ≅ 𝕊**

13:5   והןחתי **𝕸G]** החתי **𝕊**   **Q^a𝕸/G/ ≅ 𝕊**

28:4   וכתנת **𝕸]** כיתנת **𝕊**; και χιτωνα **G**   **Q^a𝕸/G/ ≅ 𝕊**

28:23   שתי 2° **𝕸]** > **𝕊**; clause lacking **G**   **Q^a𝕸 ≅ 𝕊 ≠ G**

(3) **Q^a𝕸** Are Shorter

27:9   נגבה תימנה **𝕸]** נג[ב תימנה **𝕊**;
          το προς λιβα **G**   **Q^a𝕸 ≅ 𝕊; G?**

27:11 א   צפון **𝕸]** צפונה **𝕊**; τω προς απηλιωτην **G**   **Q^a𝕸 ≅ 𝕊; G?**

36:23   נגב תימנה **𝕸]** נגבה תימ[נ]ה **𝕊**;
          36:10-34 lacking **G**   **Q^a𝕸 ≅ 𝕊 ≠ G**

26:8   היריעות **𝕸]** יריע(ו)ת **𝕊**;
          ταις ... δερρεσι **G**   **Q^a𝕸 ≅ 𝕊/G/**

(4) <u>Different Form of a Word</u>

6:30   ישמע אלי m] ישמעני w;

      εισακουσεται μου G Q^am ≅ w; G?

18:6א   אל משה m] למשה w; Μωυση G Q^am ≅ w; G?

18:16ב   א[ב](ו)] באו w; בא m; (και) ελθωσιν G Q^am ≅ wG

22:26ב   אני m] אנכי w; ειμι G Q^am ≅ w; G?

These fourteen synonymous variants shared by Q^am are all rather minor and it is only the large number of them that lends them significance. They are an important reminder that although Q^a and w belong to the same textual tradition, as the secondary readings shared by Q^a and w demonstrate, still a textual tradition can be composed of texts which differ at many smaller points from each other; and further, that in those differences one text may agree with some consistency with a text in a completely different tradition.

c. *Agreement in Preferable Readings*   (IIA3)

There are five instances where Q^am share an original reading. In three of these they preserve the less familiar word against w, which has substituted a more familiar word; in the other two they preserve the shorter reading against w, which has added the accusative marker את. These five readings suggest that although Q^a belongs to the same tradition as w, it represents a somewhat earlier stage in that tradition.

d. *Conclusion*

The evidence of the agreement between Q^a and m necessitates a modification of the conclusion of IV.A.2. At that point the affiliation of Q^a and w was obvious, because of their agreement in secondary readings both large and small and in synonymous variants both large and small. Now it has become clear that there is some relationship between Q^a and m as well -- not in secondary readings, but in synonymous variants. The five preferable readings shared by Q^a and m help to clarify the nature of this relationship.

It appears that Q^a belongs to the same tradition as w, but that it represents a collateral line of that tradition. In major variants Q^a almost always (for the single exception, see Chapter V.B) agrees with w, but in smaller variants Q^a can go in one of three different directions: it can agree with 𝕝𝕝𝕝, it can agree with 𝕞, or it can stand on its own. As the agreement with 𝕞 in preferable readings shows, **Q²** is not only in a collateral line of the family, but it also represents an earlier stage in the history of the family.

It is unfortunate that we have only these two major Hebrew witnesses to compare it with, 𝕝𝕝𝕝 and 𝕞; it will be most interesting in the future to have the opportunity to compare it systematically with the other Qumran scrolls of Exodus, of which there are reportedly fourteen.

Meanwhile, we turn to the next section, to find that **Q²** almost never agrees only with **G** against the others.

4. READINGS SHARED BY **Q²** AND **G**

a. Agreement in Secondary Readings

● **Q²/G/ +**   (IIB2)

9:8א   לאמור **G]** > 𝕝𝕝𝕞   **Q²G ≠ 𝕝𝕝𝕞**

This is the only case where **Q²** agrees with **G** in a secondary reading, and this expansion is so minor and so typical of most texts that it is of little value by itself in determining textual affiliation.

b. Agreement in Synonymous Variants   (IIIA4; IIIB2)

10:26   נשאר **G]** תשאר 𝕝𝕝𝕞   **Q²G ≅ 𝕝𝕝𝕞**

18:21ג   וש]רי חמשים **G]** שרי חמשים 𝕝𝕝𝕞   **Q²/G/ ≅ 𝕝𝕝𝕞**

18:16א   ו[ב]א **]** באו 𝕝𝕝; בא 𝕞; και ελθωσιν **G**   **Q²/G/ ≅ 𝕝𝕝𝕞**

The extant parts of the scroll preserve only these three instances where **Q²** and **G** alone agree in a synonymous variant. By themselves they probably indicate nothing about affiliation between **Q²** and **G**.

c. Agreement in Preferable Readings
There are no preferable readings in which only **Q²** and **G** agree.

d. Conclusion
This evidence indicates that there is no significant affiliation between **Q²** and **G**.

5. READINGS SHARED BY **Qᵇ**, **𝖲**, AND **𝔐**

a. Agreement in Secondary Readings   (IID)   **Qᵇ𝖲𝔐 ≠ G**

(1) Qᵇ𝖲𝔐 ++

32:9   ויאמר יהוה]אל מש[ה ראיתי את העם הזה והנה עם קשה ערף הוא

     𝖲𝔐] › G

(2) Qᵇ𝖲𝔐 +

9:20   ]ואת מקנה[ו את עבדיו 𝖲𝔐] τα חνחזא αυτου G

18:1ב   ]ולישראל[למשה 𝖲𝔐] Ισραηλ G

34:2   בב)ו(קר 𝖲𝔐] › G

32:29ב   היום 𝖲𝔐] › G

28:40   ]ועשית[להם 𝖲𝔐] και G

9:10   ]ויעמדו 𝖲𝔐] › G

These seven cases where **G** preserves the original against **Qᵇ𝖲𝔐** demonstrate that, although **G** is rightly described as expansionist in general, this description holds for only some of its text. In other places **G** has uniquely preserved the preferable and shorter text. There was a period of time, then, after the tradition behind **G** had separated, when the traditions behind **Qᵇ𝖲𝔐** continued to expand together before they too separated.

b. Agreement in Synonymous Variants   (IIIA5) **Qᵇ𝖲𝔐 ≅ G**

(1) Qᵇ𝖲𝔐 Are Longer

36:21-24 hab 𝖲𝔐] › 36:10-34 **G**

37:9-16 hab 𝖲𝔐] aliter **G** [38:8-12]

28:23-29 hab 𝖲𝔐] hab vv 29, 29a (ex 23-28) **G**

28:11ב   ]מ)ו(ס[בת]משב[צות נ]הב תעשה אתם 𝖲𝔐] › **G**

32:2   ]ובנתיכם בניכם נשי[כם 𝖲𝔐] των γυναικων υμων και θυγατερων **G**

9:16   ]א[ולם ו 𝖲𝔐] και **G**

(2) A Series of Six Variants Indicating a Different Form of a Pericope

18:9א   ו[יחד 𝔐𝔖] εξεστη δε G

18:9ב   ליש[ר]אל ... העילו 𝔐𝔖] αυτοις ... εξειλατο αυτους G

18:9ג   [מצרים 𝔐𝔖] + και εκ χειρος Φαραω G

18:10א   אתכם 𝔐𝔖] τον λαον αυτου G

18:10ב   פרעה אשר העיל א[ת העם מתחת יד מצרי(י)]ם 𝔐𝔖] Φαραω G

18:11   כי בדבר אש]ר 𝔐𝔖] ενεκεν τουτου οτι G

(3) Conflicting Representations

25:23   עצי שטים 𝔐𝔖] χρυσιου καθαρου G

25:24   וצפית] א(ו)תו זהב טהור 𝔐𝔖] > G

(4) Different Order of Words or Phrases

19:11   העם כל]לעיני על הר ס[יני 𝔐𝔖] επι το ορος το Σινα
εναντιον παντος του λαου G

10:25   נב[ח]ים ו[עלות 𝔐𝔖] ολοκαυτωματα και θυσιας G

9:9ב   ל[ש[חין פ](ו)רח אבעבע(ו)]ת 𝔐𝔖]
ελκη φλυκτιδες αναζεουσαι G

6:27ג   משה ואהר(ו)]ן 𝔐𝔖] Ααρων και Μωυσης G

(5) Different Word or Phrase

16:33   יה]ו[ה 𝔐𝔖] του θεου G

19:8   יהו[ה 𝔐𝔖] τον θεον G

32:30   י]הוה 𝔐𝔖] τον θεον G

18:1א   אלה[ים 𝔐𝔖] κυριος G

20:1   אל[הים 𝔐𝔖] κυριος G

18:14   חתן [משה 𝔐𝔖] Ιοθορ G

16:31   בית ישראל 𝔐𝔖] οι υιοι Ισραηλ G; בני ישראל 𝔐^Mss 𝔗^Mss 𝔖

22:24א   את ע]מי 𝔐𝔖] τω αδελφω G

(6) Different Form of Word or Suffix

6:27א   להוציא ‎𝖀𝕸] και εξηγαγον **G**

10:24ג   יעג ‎𝖀𝕸] υπολειπεσθε **G**

16:32   האכ]לתי אתכם ‎𝖀𝕸] εφαγετε υμεις **G**

18:6ג   בנ]יה[עמה ‎𝖀𝕸] υιοι σου μετ αυτου **G**

30:10   ל]ד(ו)רתיכם ‎𝖀𝕸] εις τας γενεας αυτων **G**

27:10   ועמד]יו ‎𝖀𝕸] και οι στυλοι αυτων **G**

18:12   ע(ו)לה ות]ב[חים ‎𝖀𝕸] ολοκαυτωματα και θυσιας **G**

(7) Longer, Shorter, or Transposition?

10:6א,ב   ובתי כל עבדיך וב]תי ‎𝖀𝕸] και αι οικιαι των θεραποντων
σου και πασαι αι οικιαι **G**

Of these 35 synonymous variants where only **G** differs from the other three witnesses, three variants where **G** is shorter involve an entire pericope each, all in the tabernacle account; and six other variants belong together and constitute an extended and related set, in a narrative section. These nine are the most significant. Eight show the existence of two parallel formulations of entire pericopes and the ninth affects the presence or absence of a whole section.

Of the other 26 synonymous variants, from the standpoint of content, eight involve proper names of individuals or the designation of the people of Israel or some group thereof. Four occur in the account of the tabernacle. Two of these are of some significance, affecting the representation of the table.

From the standpoint of text, five of these 26 involve shorter vs. longer readings; ten involve choice of word or phrase; and four involve order of words or phrases. Seven others involve slight differences in the forms of words or their suffixes.

None of these 26 is in itself striking, although the designations for God and the order of the names of Aaron and Moses are of some significance in terms of the content of the text.

More important, all 35 together lend considerable weight to the picture that is emerging: there is clearly affiliation among **Q²𝖀𝕸** which points to a period of development shared by the three after the tradition behind **G** had separated (and possibly had been translated). This affiliation of **Qᵃⅲⅲ** does not necessarily or always mean that they have preserved the preferable text. Rather, each of the various traditions has faithfully preserved some parts of the text and corrupted other parts; and in many passages both preserve equally defensible readings.

c. *Agreement in Preferable Readings*   (IIA5)   **Qᵃⅲⅲ ≠ G**

There are eighteen readings in which **Qᵃⅲⅲ** preserve the preferable reading against **G**. These include preservation of the correct word in three cases, of the shorter text in twelve cases, of the correct and shorter text in one case, and of the longer original text in two cases. These eighteen readings show more about **G** than about **Qᵃⅲⅲ**: **G** has developed in significant ways on its own, apart from the other three.

d. *Conclusion*

Thus we have seen that **Qᵃⅲⅲ** agree in preserving not only eighteen preferable readings but also seven secondary readings and 35 synonymous variants against **G**. The readings where the three Hebrew witnesses agree together against **G** suggest that after the tradition behind **G** had separated from the tradition behind them, there was a period of time during which these three (and no doubt many others) developed together before the tradition behind **Qᵃ** and **ⅲ** broke off. Thus there are many commonalities among these three as opposed to **G** that appear to have nothing to do with the process of translation into Greek, but rather indicate that the tradition behind the Greek did not continue to share in that period of the common history of the other texts. The most striking of these are those that have to do with length of text: the seven readings where **Qᵃⅲⅲ** together seem to have expanded, while **G** preserves the shorter text; and the synonymous variants involving different length or different order of text.

The combination of secondary, synonymous, and preferable readings shows that the tradition behind **G** separated from that behind the other three early enough to preserve uniquely some original readings as well as to develop its own character as expansionist in other readings.

6. READINGS SHARED BY Qᵃ, 𝔪, AND G

a. Agreement in Secondary Readings　　　(IIC1)　Qᵃ𝔪G ≠ 𝔐

(1) Qᵃ𝔪G +

10:24 בﬞ   ולאהר(ו)ן 𝔪G] > 𝔐

9:7   ישראל 𝔪G] בני ישראל 𝔐

32:7א   לא[מור 𝔪G] > 𝔐

32:13 בﬞ   ונחל[וה 𝔪G] ונחלו 𝔐

17:2 בﬞ   מה 𝔪G] ומה 𝔐

32:27   ועב]רו 𝔪G] עברו 𝔐

(2) Qᵃ𝔪G 2v

17:12   ויהי 𝔪G] ויהיו 𝔐

All seven of these secondary readings shared by Qᵃ𝔪G represent such minor changes and are so typical of scribal activity in any period that they need not point to any textual affiliation at all. Rather, they indicate that of these four witnesses, 𝔐 tends uniquely to preserve the preferable text in very minor matters; and that the other three tend to expand and harmonize slightly.

Because we have so much other evidence of affiliation between Qᵃ and 𝔪, it is appropriate to suggest that these examples of harmonizing and expanding may well have occurred during the period when the Qᵃ𝔪 tradition was a recognizably distinct family. Yet because we have little evidence of any positive affiliation between the Qᵃ𝔪 tradition and the G tradition, these examples cannot be used to suggest any such relationship.

b. Agreement in Synonymous Variants　　　(IIIA6)　Qᵃ𝔪G ≅ 𝔐

7:10   אל פרעה 𝔐 4QExodᵇ𝔪G] 1° לפני פרעה

18:6 בﬞ   אני 𝔐 𝔪G] הנה

These synonymous variants are so slight that they can prove nothing about positive textual affiliation.

c. Agreement in Preferable Readings   (IIA6)   Q^aⱮG ≠ Ɱ

There are four cases where **Q^aⱮG** preserve the preferable reading against **Ɱ**, one involving a grammatical form and three involving parablepsis on the part of **Ɱ**.   They cannot be used to suggest any affiliation other than the most general, descent from a common heritage, among **Q^aⱮG.**

d. Conclusion

Thus we have found no compelling evidence of specific textual affiliation between **Q^aⱮ** on the one hand and **G** on the other hand.

It may be appropriate, nevertheless, to suggest that these agreements between **Q^a** and **Ɱ** contribute secondarily to the larger pattern already clearly demonstrating close affiliation between those two witnesses.   In the absence of any such larger pattern for all three, **Q^aⱮG**, however, these minor agreements tell us little about any positive relationship including all three.

7. READINGS SHARED BY Q^a, Ɱ, AND G

a. Agreement in Secondary Readings   (IIB1)   Q^aⱮG ≠ Ɱ

No instances have been found where **Q^aⱮG** agree together against **Ɱ** in a secondary reading, meaning that **Ɱ** is never uniquely preferable where **Q^a** is extant.

b. Agreement in Synonymous Variants   (IIIA7)   Q^aⱮG ≅ Ɱ

The three texts share only two synonymous variants against **Ɱ**:

27:11ב   וי וו **ⱮG]** וויהם **Ɱ**

26:24   )](י)ויחד **Ɱ]** יחדו **Ɱ**; και κατα το αυτο **G**

c. Agreement in Preferable Readings   (IIA7)   Q^aⱮG ≠ Ɱ

There are eight instances where **Q^aⱮG** preserve the preferable reading against **Ɱ**. All of these indicate more about the nature of **Ɱ** than they do about specific textual affiliation among **Q^aⱮG**, for they are cases where **Ɱ** has made a law more generally applicable (twice), added a phrase and altered a verbal form (once), expanded (three times), made the text more explicit (once), and smoothed the text (once).   In all of these cases, then, **Q^aⱮG** are only related in the negative sense, i.e., they have all refrained from tampering with the older text.

The significant point here is that once again we have evidence of the priority of **Q**ᵃ as compared with ⅲ in the history of the tradition to which they both belong.

d. Conclusion

The priority of **Q**ᵃ as compared with ⅲ is shown chiefly by the agreement of **Q**ᵃ with 𝕸𝕲 against ⅲ in original readings. It is reinforced by the fact that there is no instance where ⅲ preserves the preferable text against **Q**ᵃ𝕸𝕲.

B. THE TEXTUAL AFFILIATION OF ⅲ

1. UNIQUE, NON-AFFILIATED, READINGS IN ⅲ

a. Secondary Readings

(1) ⅲ 2v +

19:12   סבי[ב לאמ(ו)ר 𝕸𝕲]

        סביב ואל העם תאמר ⅲ   (IIA7)   **Q**ᵃ𝕸𝕲 ≠ ⅲ

(2) ⅲ +

19:25   מן ההר ⅲ + [משה 𝕸𝕲]   (IIA7)   **Q**ᵃ𝕸𝕲 ≠ ⅲ

6:27ב   ממצרים 𝕸𝕲] מארץ מצרים ⅲ   (IIA7)   **Q**ᵃ𝕸𝕲 ≠ ⅲ

29:33   למלא 𝕸𝕲] + בם ⅲ   (IIA7)   **Q**ᵃ𝕸/𝕲/ ≠ ⅲ

25:29   קע[ר]תי[ו 𝔐] pr את ⅲ;

        τα τρυβλια αυτης 𝕲   (IIA3)   **Q**ᵃ𝔐 ≠ ⅲ; 𝕲?

28:39   הכתנת 𝔐] pr את ⅲ; των χιτωνων 𝕲   (IIA3)   **Q**ᵃ𝔐 ≠ ⅲ; 𝕲?

(3) ⅲ 2v

21:29   הבהמה תסקל 𝕸𝕲] הש[ור יסק]ל ⅲ   (IIA7)   **Q**ᵃ𝕸𝕲 ≠ ⅲ

21:31   יגח או בת יגח ⅲ; יכה או בת [א]ו בת י[גח 𝔐;

        κερατιση η θυγατερα 𝕲   (IIA7)   **Q**ᵃ𝕸𝕲 ≠ ⅲ

15:27   וּ[שם] **mG**[וּבאילים **ɯ**   (IIA7) **Q͏ᵃmG** ≠ **ɯ**

7:4   [מ]בשפטי **m**[במשפטים **ɯ**;
       συν εκδικησει **G**   (IIA3) **Q͏ᵃm(G)** ≠ **ɯ**
21:25 כויה **m**[מכוה **ɯ**; κατακαυματος **G**   (IIA3) **Q͏ᵃm** ≠ **ɯ**; **G**?
22:25 שלמת **m**[שמלת **ɯ**; ιματιον **G**   (IIA3) **Q͏ᵃm** ≠ **ɯ**; **G**?

10:10 [י]יה **mG**[יהיה **ɯ**   (IIA7) **Q͏ᵃmG** ≠ **ɯ**

Thus **ɯ** stands alone in thirteen secondary readings. None is clearly an error, though three substitute more familiar for less familiar words, which could have occurred by accident. Five are the result of expansion, and four that are qualitatively secondary seem to reflect exegetical work on the text (19:12; 21:29; 21:31; 15:27).

b. Synonymous Variants

(1) ɯ Is Longer

27:11ב ווי **mG**[וויהם **ɯ**   (IIIA7) **Q͏ᵃmG** ≅ **ɯ**
27:9   נג[ב תימנה **m**[נגבה תימנה **ɯ**;
        το προς λιβα **G**   (IIIA3) **Q͏ᵃm** ≅ **ɯ**; **G**?
27:11א צפון **m**[צפונה **ɯ**;
        τω προς απηλιωτην **G**   (IIIA3) **Q͏ᵃm** ≅ **ɯ**; **G**?
36:23   נגב תימ[נה **m**[נגבה תימנה **ɯ**;
        36:10-34 lacking **G**   (IIIA3) **Q͏ᵃm** ≅ **ɯ** ≁ **G**

(2) ɯ Is Shorter

28:23   שתי 2° **m**[> **ɯ**; clause lacking **G**   (IIIA3) **Q͏ᵃm** ≅ **ɯ** ≁ **G**
22:24ב העני **m**[עני **ɯ**; τω πενιχρω **G**   (IIIA3) **Q͏ᵃm/G/** ≅ **ɯ**
13:5   החתי **mG**[וה]חתי **ɯ**   (IIIA3) **Q͏ᵃm/G/** ≅ **ɯ**

28:4   וכתנת 𝕸] כיתנת 𝕾;
και χιτωνα G   (IIIA3) Qᵃ𝕸/G/ ≅ 𝕾

26:24   ויחד(י)ו 𝕸] יחדו 𝕾;
και κατα το αυτο G   (IIIA3) Qᵃ𝕸/G/ ≅ 𝕾

29:22א   ואת...] את האליה 𝕾; והאליה 𝕸;
> G (vid.)   (IIIE) Qᵃ ≅ 𝕾 ≅ 𝕸; G?

(3) Different Word and Longer

17:16   עד דור ודו]ר מדר ודר 𝕾; מדר דר 𝕸;
απο γενεων εις γενεας G   (IIIE) Qᵃ ≅ 𝕾 ≅ 𝕸 ≅ G

(4) Different Word

10:11   לא כן 𝕸] לכן 𝕾; μη ουτως G   (IIIA3) Qᵃ𝕸/G/ ≅ 𝕾
22:26ב   אני 𝕸] אנכי 𝕾; ειμι G   (IIIA3) Qᵃ𝕸 ≅ 𝕾; G?

(5) Shorter and Different Morpheme

34:13   ואשריו] ואשריהם 𝕾; ואת אשריו 𝕸;
και τα αλση αυτων G   (IIIE) Qᵃ ≅ 𝕾 ≅ 𝕸; G?

(6) Different Morpheme

18:6א   אל משה 𝕸] למשה 𝕾; Μωυσει G   (IIIA3) Qᵃ𝕸 ≅ 𝕾; G?
6:30   ישמעני 𝕸] ישמע אלי 𝕾;
εισακουσεται μου G   (IIIA3) Qᵃ𝕸 ≅ 𝕾; G?

In these sixteen synonymous variants 𝕾 clearly disagrees with the other two Hebrew witnesses; in three of the readings 𝕾 clearly disagrees also with G, but in the other eleven the *Vorlage* of G is somewhat ambiguous. None of the sixteen is significant, which means that where 𝕾 does have synonymous variants of any import, it agrees with at least one other of the three witnesses.

c. Preferable Readings (IIB1)

There are no readings where 𝔪 uniquely preserves the preferable form.

d. Conclusion

Thus 𝔪 exhibits thirteen unique secondary readings, sixteen unique synonymous variants, and no unique preferable readings, for a total of 29 unique readings. The point to be reiterated here is that even though 𝔔^{m} and 𝔪 belong to the same textual tradition, there are many disagreements between them, most of them minor. The sixteen unique synonymous variants of 𝔪 show that 𝔔^{m} and 𝔪 have developed separately to some extent, and the thirteen unique secondary readings of 𝔪 together with its complete lack of unique preferable readings might indicate that 𝔪 represents a later stage in the tradition than 𝔔^{m}. This question will be taken up in Chapter V.B and E.

2. READINGS SHARED BY 𝔪 AND 𝔐

a. Agreement in Secondary Readings (IIA1)

(1) 𝔪𝔐 +

32:7ב רד] לך רד 𝔪𝔐; Βαδιζε καταβηθι το ταχος εντευθεν 𝔊 — 𝔔^{m} ≠ 𝔪𝔐 ≠ 𝔊

18:27 וילך] + לו 𝔪𝔐; και απηλθεν 𝔊 — 𝔔^{m}/𝔊/ ≠ 𝔪𝔐

(2) 𝔪𝔐 2v

21:6 אדונו] אדניו 𝔪𝔐; ο κυριος αυτου 𝔊 — 𝔔^{m} ≠ 𝔪𝔐; 𝔊?

None of these three secondary readings shared by 𝔪𝔐 is very significant because they are so characteristic of texts in general and could have arisen independently.

b. Agreement in Synonymous Variants　　　(IIIB2)

(1) ШМ Are Longer

21:13　　שם] שמה ШМ; εκει G　　　　　　　　　Q^a ≅ ШМ; G?

18:13ב　הבקר ... הערב [בוקר] [ערב　ШМ;
　　　　πρωιθεν ... εσπερας G　　　　　　　　　　Q^a ≅ ШМ; G?

(2) ШМ Are Shorter

29:22ב　י(ו)תרת [הי]ותרת ШМ; του λοβου G　　　Q^a ≅ ШМ; G?

18:21ג　שרי חמשים [וש]רי חמשים G] ШМ　　　Q^a/G/ ≅ ШМ

18:16א　ו[ב]א [באו Ш: בא М; και ελθωσιν G　　　Q^a/G/ ≅ ШМ

(3) Different Form of a Verb

8:14[18]　ותהי [ויהי ШМ; και εγενοντο G　　　　　Q^a ≅ ШМ; G?

10:26　　תשאר [נשאר G] ШМ　　　(IIIA4)　Q^{a}G ≅ ШМ

　　　These seven synonymous variants all involve minor grammatical features and are too slight to suggest any specific positive textual affiliation between Ш and М.

c. Agreement in Preferable Readings　　　(IIB2)　Q^a ≠ ШМ

　　　There are five instances where ШМ agree against Q^a in preserving the preferable reading, of which four involve a minor alteration and one a minor expansion. In four of these the *Vorlage* of G cannot be determined; in one G and Q^a both add לאמור. All five variants are so minor that they indicate little about positive affiliation of Ш and М. Presumably both of them merely preserved the preferable text.

d. Conclusion

　　　None of the fifteen variants where ШМ agree can bear much weight in the question of affiliation between them. The conclusion is that there is no specific affiliation between these two witnesses. Further, the fifteen serve as a reminder of the fact that many minor agreements may exist between members of different families (ШМ), and that many minor disagreements may exist between members of the same family (Q^{a}Ш).

Neither agreements nor disagreements in minor variations can prove or disprove much about textual affiliation.

3. READINGS SHARED BY 𝔐 AND 𝔊

a. *Agreement in Secondary Readings*   (IIA3) Q̲ᵃ𝔐 ≠ 𝔐𝔊

There are no clearly secondary readings shared only by 𝔐 and 𝔊 in the extant parts of **Qᵃ**.

b. *Agreement in Synonymous Variants*

13:6   בעת[ש **𝔐**] ששת 𝔐𝔊   (IIIA3) Q̲ᵃ𝔐 ≅ 𝔐𝔊

32:11בל [ובזרוע חזק]ה ו[בזרוע נטויה 𝔐𝔊;

         וביד חזקה **𝔐**   (IIIB3) **Qᵃ** ≅ 𝔐𝔊 ≅ 𝔐

18:16בל [א[בל](ו)(ו)] באו 𝔐; בא **𝔐**; (και) ελθωσιν 𝔊   (IIIA3) Q̲ᵃ𝔐 ≅ 𝔐𝔊

26:8   ת(ו)יריע[**𝔐**] היריעות 𝔐;

         ταις...δερρεσι 𝔊   (IIIA3) Q̲ᵃ𝔐 ≅ 𝔐/𝔊/

These four synonymous variants shared by 𝔐 and 𝔊 cannot be used to demonstrate affiliation between the two traditions, because the readings could be original, or if not, they could have arisen independently, as more than one scribe desired to correct the text (13:6 and 18:16בל) or was influenced by the parallel in Deuteronomy (32:11בל).   Since there are only four such agreements, the likelihood of any causal relationship decreases.

c. *Agreement in Preferable Readings*   (IIB3) Q̲ᵃ𝔐 ≠ 𝔐𝔊

There is no instance in the extant portions of **Qᵃ** of a preferable reading shared only by 𝔐 and 𝔊.

d. *Conclusion*

These four instances of agreement between 𝔐 and 𝔊 are too minor and too few to prove any causal relationship.   Thus they cannot in themselves demonstrate affiliation between the two witnesses.

In light of the traditional view that 𝔐 and 𝔊 share a close relation-ship,[4] it is appropriate to pause to review the evidence. Qᵃ𝔊 share only four agreements: one minor expansion and three minor synonymous variants

---

[4]See Chapter I.C, especially p. 25 and n. 77.

(see Chapter IV.A.4). ⅢG also share only four agreements: all synonymous variants, one of which (שׁשׁת instead of שׁבעת) may reflect a causal relationship. QᵃⅢG together share thirteen agreements: six minor expansions and one slight alteration, two minor synonymous variants, and four preferable readings, three involving parablepsis on the part of 𝔐 (see IV.A.6). These are strikingly meager results. Yet no definite conclusions should be drawn because the data are based only on the random fragments of the scroll.

4. READINGS SHARED BY Ⅲ, 𝔐, AND G

a. *Agreement in Secondary Readings*   (IIA1) Qᵃ ≠ Ⅲ𝔐G

• Ⅲ𝔐G +

7:2   ישׂר]אל [+ Ⅲ𝔐G מארצו

34:1   הלוח]ות [+ הרא(י)שׁ(ו)(י)נים + Ⅲ𝔐G

These two readings where Qᵃ seems uniquely to preserve the preferable text represent such minor expansions on the part of Ⅲ𝔐G that they can indicate little about any causal relationship.

b. *Agreement in Synonymous Variants*   (IIIB4) Qᵃ ≅ Ⅲ𝔐G

31:13-14

Qᵃ   כי]אות הי]א ל]כם מחלל]יה

Ⅲ𝔐G   כי אות היא (הוא 𝔐) ביני וביני(י)כם לדרתיכם לדעת

                 כי אני יהוה מקדשכם

            ¹⁴ושמרתם את השבת

          כי קדש היא (הוא 𝔐) לכם מחלליה

10:21בֹ   מצר]\ים ויט [מצרים וימש (ה)(חשׁך ויט Ⅲ𝔐G

34:16בֹ   והגנו [pr וזנו בנתיו אחרי אלהיהן ;Ⅲ𝔐

        pr και εκπορνευσωσιν αι θυγατερες σου

         οπισω των θεων αυτων G

9:9א   על כל ארץ [על ארץ Ⅲ𝔐G

These four synonymous variants shared by 𝔪𝔐G do not necessarily demonstrate any relationship among those three traditions, but rather shed light on the nature of **Qᵃ**. Unfortunately that light is too dim to clear up the question: in these three instances where it has the shorter text, does **Qᵃ** preserve the original reading or is **Qᵃ** haplographic?

c. Agreement in Preferable Readings   (IIB4)   **Qᵃ ≠ 𝔪𝔐G**

There are six instances where 𝔪𝔐G preserve preferable readings against **Qᵃ**. One involves a grammatical form, two involve the shorter reading, and three involve errors on the part of **Qᵃ**. None are significant enough to show any causal relationship among the three witnesses.

d. Conclusion

The two secondary and six preferable readings shared by 𝔪𝔐G are too minor, and the four synonymous variants are too inconclusive, to prove much about affiliation of 𝔪𝔐G.

C. THE TEXTUAL AFFILIATION OF 𝔐

1. UNIQUE, NON-AFFILIATED, READINGS IN 𝔐

a. Secondary Readings

(1) 𝔐 -   (IIA6)

22:4[5] **Qᵃ**   [כל]

       𝔪   אחר שלם ישלם משדהו כתבואתה ואם כל השדה <u>יבעה</u> מיטב

       G*   אחר שלם ישלם משדהו כתבואתה ואם כל השדה <u>יבער</u> מיטב

       𝔐   מיטב   אחר

                                          Qᵃ𝔪G ≠ 𝔐

34:11 בל   𝔪; והחתי והגרגשי והפרזי והחוי [והגרג]שי [ ]

             και Χεττaιον και 𝔐; והחתי והפרזי והחוי

             Φερεζαιον και Ευαιον και Γεργεσαιον G   **Qᵃ𝔪G ≠ 𝔐**

7:15 בל   𝔪 הוא [יעא 𝔪G] יעא 𝔐   **Qᵃ𝔪G ≠ 𝔐**

(2) 𝔐 +

20:19ᵃ   𝔐: [𝔴 hab דבר אתה עמנו ונשמעה

       G λαλησον συ υμιν   **Qᵃ𝔴 ≠ 𝔐 ≠ G**

(3) 𝔐 X

16:34   𝔐: משה ש[וה] 𝔴 א[ת מ]שה אל
       G τω Μωυση   (IIA2)   **Qᵃ𝔴 ≠ 𝔐; G?**

18:23   𝔐: על [𝔴 אל] אל; G εις   (IIA2)   **Qᵃ𝔴(G) ≠ 𝔐**

17:2ﬡ   𝔐 תנו [𝔴G] תנה   (IIA6)   **Qᵃ𝔴G ≠ 𝔐**

     Thus 𝔐 stands alone in seven secondary readings. Presumably only one was done deliberately: the addition of one word. Five of them are minor, two involving accidental omission of one word and three involving an error affecting one letter. The seventh, the omission of eight words, has substantially changed the content of the passage, yet it probably arose as the result of parablepsis.

b. Synonymous Variants

(1) 𝔐 Is Shorter

18:20   𝔐: [𝔴 הדרך אש]ר הדרך
       G τας οδους, εν αις   (IIIA2)   **Qᵃ𝔴/G/ ≅ 𝔐**

18:21ב   𝔐 [𝔴G] ושרי מאות שרי מאות   (IIIA2)   **Qᵃ𝔴/G/ ≅ 𝔐**

29:22ﬡ   [... ואת] את האליה 𝔴 :𝔐; והאליה
       ≻ G (vid.)   (IIIE)   **Qᵃ ≅ 𝔴 ≅ 𝔐; G?**

(2) 𝔐 Is Longer

9:8 ב   𝔐: [𝔴 הש[מ]ים] השמימה
       G εις τον ουρανον   (IIIA2)   **Qᵃ𝔴 ≅ 𝔐; G?**

(3) Different Order

26:10   חמשים ללאת [ש 1° ללא[ת]ות חמשים   𝕸;

αγκυλας πεντηκοντα **G**   (IIIA2)   **Q^a ш/G/ ≅ 𝕸**

(4) Different Word and Shorter

17:16   מדר דר [ש מדר ודר ; עד דור ודו[ר]   𝕸;

απο γενεων εις γενεας **G**   (IIIE)   **Q^a ≅ ш ≅ 𝕸 ≅ G**

(5) Different Suffix and Longer

34:13   ואשריו [ש ואשריהם ; ואת אשריו   𝕸;

και τα αλση αυτων **G**   (IIIE)   **Q^a ≅ ш ≅ 𝕸; G?**

(6) Different Word

32:11ב   ובגרוע נטויה [ו[בגרוע חזק[ה   **ш G**;

וביד חזקה   𝕸   (IIIB3)   **Q^a ≅ ш G ≅ 𝕸**

18:6ב   אני [ש G הנה   𝕸   (IIIA6)   **Q^a ш G ≅ 𝕸**

7:10   לפני פרעה 1° 4QExod^b [ш G   אל פרעה   𝕸   (IIIA6)   **Q^a ш G ≅ 𝕸**

7:14   וידבר\[†] ש [ויאמר   𝕸; Ειπεν δε **G**   (IIIA2)   **Q^a ш ≅ 𝕸(G)**

(7) Different Form of Word

22:6   וגנב ש [ו[נ]גנב   𝕸; και κλαπη **G**   (IIIA2)   **Q^a ш ≅ 𝕸; G?**

32:11א   יחר ש [יחרה   𝕸; θυμοι **G**   (IIIA2)   **Q^a ш ≅ 𝕸; G?**

26:26   בריחי ש [בריחם   𝕸; μοχλους **G**   (IIIA2)   **Q^a ш ≅ 𝕸; G?**

22:26א   היא [...] הי[א] ש [הוא ... הוא   𝕸;

τουτο ... τουτο **G**   (IIIA2)   **Q^a ш ≅ 𝕸; G?**

31:13   הי[א] ש [הוא   𝕸; εστιν **G**   (IIIA2)   **Q^a ш ≅ 𝕸; G?**

In these sixteen readings 𝕸 clearly disagrees with the other two Hebrew witnesses. In four of the readings 𝕸 clearly disagrees also with

G; but in eleven readings the *Vorlage* of **G** is somewhat ambiguous. None of the sixteen is significant, which means that in synonymous variants of any import, 𝔐 agrees with at least one other of the three witnesses.

c. *Preferable Readings*   (IIC1)

𝔐 preserves the preferable reading in ten instances. In four cases 𝔐 is shorter by one word, in three by a morpheme; once it preserves the correct word; once it preserves the original idiom; and once it preserves a minor syntactical inconsistency. All of these are fairly minor.

d. *Conclusion*

Thus there are 33 variants where 𝔐 preserves a unique reading. Of these, seven are secondary (including three actual errors), sixteen are synonymous, and ten are preferable. These 33 variants range from something as minor as the difference between a *waw* and a *yod* to the presence or absence of the name of Aaron or of the Girgashites or eight words in a law. None of these is significant in itself. This total, 33, should be compared with the total unique readings of **Q**ᵃ (27) and Ш (29).

2. READINGS SHARED BY 𝔐 AND **G**

a. *Agreement in Secondary Readings*   (IIA2)   **Q**ᵃ Ш ≠ 𝔐**G**

No readings have been found where 𝔐 and **G** clearly agree in preserving a secondary reading against an original in **Q**ᵃ Ш.

b. *Agreement in Synonymous Variants*   (IIIA2) **Q**ᵃ Ш ≅ 𝔐**G**

30:1-10   post 26:35 Ш] post 29:46 𝔐**G**

29:2   סלת Ш] pr משחים בשמן 𝔐**G**

The difference in placement of ten verses is a fairly major variant. Taken with so many other variants shared by **Q**ᵃ and Ш it seems significant for their affiliation. But since 𝔐 and **G** share so little other than clearly preferable readings, not too much weight can be placed on these two cases of agreement in synonymous variants for their affiliation.

c. *Agreement in Preferable Readings*   (IIC2)   **Q**ᵃ Ш ≠ 𝔐**G**

There are fourteen variants where 𝔐**G** clearly share the preferable reading against **Q**ᵃ Ш, eleven involving major expansions, one a moderate

expansion, and two involving expansions of one word each. While these
variants clearly demonstrate the character and the affiliation of Q^n and ɯ,
all that they demonstrate about ɯ and G is that they go back to a common
heritage.

d. Conclusion

Since there are no instances of agreement in secondary readings, and
only two in synonymous variants, there is no evidence of any positive
affiliation between ɯ and G.   The fourteen instances of agreement in
preferable readings give evidence only that they are both descendants from
a common heritage and do not belong to the Q^n ɯ family.

D. THE TEXTUAL AFFILIATION OF G

UNIQUE, NON-AFFILIATED, READINGS IN G

a. Secondary Readings   (IIA5) Q^a ɯɯ ≠ G

(1) G 2v

18:4   פרעה מח[ר/ב] ɯɯ] εκ χειρος Φαραω G

17:6   זקני ישראל ɯɯ] των υιων Ισραηλ G

18:21א   בצ]ע[ɯɯ] υπερηφανιαν G

(2) G 2v +

19:10   לך ɯɯ] Καταβας διαμαρτυραι G

(3) G +

34:16א ־ לב[ני]ך ɯɯ] + και των θυγατερων σου δως τοις υιοις
         αυτων G

9:9ג   בכל ארץ מצ]רים ɯɯ] *εν τε τοις ανθρωποις και εν τοις
         τετραποσιν και εν παση γη Αιγυπτου* G

9:8ג   לעיני פרעה ɯɯ] εναντιον Φαραω *και εναντιον των
         θεραποντων αυτου* G

7:9   והשלך לפני פרעה [𝔐ₘ κα ριψον αυτην *επι την γην* εναντιον Φαραω **G**

11:9   מופתי [𝔐ₘ μου *τα σημεια και* τα τερατα **G**

28:3   את בגדי א[הר(ו)ן [𝔐ₘ την στολην *την αγιαν* Ααρων **G**

32:13א   ככו[כבי ה]שמים [𝔐ₘ ωσει τα αστρα του ουρανου
             τω πληθει **G**

32:15   ל(ו)חת כת]בים [𝔐ₘ πλακες *λιθιναι* καταγεγραμμεναι **G**

28:43ב   ישאו עו(ו)]ן [𝔐ₘ επαξονται *προς εαυτους* αμαρτιαν **G**

19:24   פן יפרץ ב]ם [𝔐ₘ μηποτε απολεση απ αυτων *κυριος* **G**

17:13א   ואת עמו [𝔐ₘ και *παντα* τον λαον αυτου **G**

18:13א   ה]עם [𝔐ₘ *πας* ο λαος **G**

(4) G –

25:33   ושלשה גבעים משקדים בקנ[ה האחד] כפתר ופרח [𝔐ₘ ⟩ **G**

34:11א   היום [𝔐ₘ ⟩ **G**

     Thus **G** stands alone in eighteen secondary readings. In twelve variants **G** alone is expansionist, twice it is haplographic, three times it is qualitatively secondary, and once a qualitative and quantitative change has occurred. None of these secondary readings is major in itself (contrast the major expansions in the **Qᵃ𝔐** tradition), yet there is a clear pattern of expansionism in phrases and individual words.

b. Synonymous Variants   (IIIA5; IVA5; IIIE)
     There are 35 synonymous variants preserved uniquely by **G** against **Qᵃ𝔐ₘ**. In six **G** is shorter, six suggest that an entire pericope existed in two different forms, two provide conflicting representations, four involve the order of words or phrases, eight involve the choice of a word or phrase, seven involve different forms of a word or a suffix, and in two there may have been either omission, expansion, or transposition. Perhaps only nine of these could be said to be of significance individually -- those involving an

entire pericope. Yet all of them together contribute substantially to the pattern of a significant tendency for **G** to stand alone against Q^a 𝔖 𝔐.

The entire list of these readings is presented and organized according to type in Chapter IV.A.5.b. As stated in the discussion there, the only synonymous variants that are significant in themselves are the three that involve an entire pericope each and the six that belong together and point beyond themselves to suggest the existence of two parallel formulations of a pericope. Few of the other 26 synonymous variants are significant alone, but the pattern shows that **G** belongs to a tradition different from that of Q^a 𝔖 𝔐.

Finally, **G** stands alone in one synonymous variant in which none of the other three witnesses agree either (see IIIE), for a grand total of 36 unique synonymous variants.

c. *Preferable Readings*   (IID)

G uniquely preserves the preferable reading in eight instances. In six cases **G** is shorter by one or two words; in one case 𝔐 adds one word and Q^a 𝔖 add a major expansion from the parallel narrative in Deuteronomy; in the last case Q^a 𝔖 𝔐 agree in adding a major expansion from the parallel narrative in Deuteronomy.

d. *Conclusion*

There are 62 variants where **G** preserves a unique reading.

Of the 36 unique synonymous variants, only nine are of any significance in themselves.

Of the eighteen unique secondary readings, twelve involve expansion. All eight preferable readings, on the other hand, are cases where **G** is shorter. Thus it is misleading to characterize **G** as expansionist, unless it is also made clear that in some places **G** actually preserves the preferable shorter reading. This seeming paradox is best explained by positing that after the tradition behind **G** separated from the tradition behind Q^a 𝔖 𝔐, both traditions continued to expand separately, in different patterns. This point will be elaborated in Chapter V.E.

These 62 unique readings in **G** are based on a total of 121 readings where its *Vorlage* can be determined with some degree of confidence. In other words, in about half of the readings where **G** disagrees with one of the three witnesses, it disagrees with all three of them.

The number 62 should be compared with the number of unique readings in the other three witnesses: **Qᵃ** exhibits 27, **ɰ** 29, and **m** 33 unique readings, each based on a total of 165 readings. **G** is thus further removed from the other three than any of them is from each other. Once again it is clear that the tradition behind **G** was the first to have separated from the tradition behind the other three.

Yet although **G** is more different from **m** than **ɰ** is, these findings nevertheless support Tov's contention that:

> The Hebrew text presupposed by the LXX basically represents a tradition which is either close to that of MT or can easily be explained as a descendant or a source of it.[5]

Yet perhaps the last word in this section should be a reiteration of the fact that **G** preserves eight preferable readings, all of them shorter readings. While it is certainly true that **G** is expansionist in some places, it is also true that **G** preserves the pristine, shorter text in other places. In Tov's words, if in some readings **G** represents a tradition that is a *descendant* of the tradition behind **m**, in others it is a *source* thereof.

E. NO AGREEMENT   (IIIE)

17:16   **m**; עד דור ודו[ר] מדר ודר **ɰ**; מדר דר **m**;

        απο γενεων εις γενεας **G**   **Qᵃ** ≅ **ɰ** ≅ **m** ≅ **G**

18:16א,ב   **m**; בא **ɰ**; באו **Q**; ו[ב]א] και ελθωσι **G**   **Qᵃ** ≅ **ɰ** ≅ **m** ≅ **G**

34:13   **m**; ואת אשריו] ואשריהם **ɰ**; ואת אשריו **m**;

        και τα αλση αυτων **G**   **Qᵃ** ≅ **ɰ** ≅ **m**; **G**?

29:22א   ...[ואת] את האליה **ɰ**; והאליה **m**;

        > **G** (vid.)   **Qᵃ** ≅ **ɰ** ≅ **m**; **G**?

These synonymous variants suggest the number of slight variations possible among four texts in one word or phrase. They also reflect another limitation to the question of textual affiliation. Regardless of a close relationship between two texts, **Qᵃ** and **ɰ** in this case, they may disagree in many small details. Affiliation is not determined by such minor variations as these.

---

[5]Tov, *Septuagint,* p. 261.

CONCLUSION

This chapter has brought together the findings of Chapters II and III regarding secondary, synonymous, and preferable readings in order to determine relationships among the various witnesses to the text of Exodus. Each subsection has closed with its own conclusion, and the chart in Appendix 3 shows the numerical results graphically.

Some major findings need to be reiterated. Negatively, very little evidence indeed has surfaced to support the notion of a relationship between $\mathfrak{M}$ and $\mathfrak{G}$, whether or not $\mathbf{Q^n}$ is included. In fact, $\mathfrak{G}$ has shown itself to be much further removed from the other three witnesses than any of them is from each other. While it is expansionist in many places it also preserves the shorter preferable reading in others; in Tov's words, it is sometimes a descendant, sometimes a source of the tradition behind $\mathfrak{m}$.

But our major question concerned $\mathbf{Q^n}$: what was its relationship to $\mathfrak{M}$? Should it be grouped with $\mathfrak{M}$ as another member of that text-type? The answer is clearly affirmative because of all the significant agreements between them. On the other hand, the definition of "text-type" must be kept flexible enough to allow for the large number of agreements between $\mathbf{Q^n}\mathfrak{m}$ against $\mathfrak{M}$, and between $\mathfrak{M}\mathfrak{m}$ against $\mathbf{Q^n}$, as well as to allow for the large number of unique readings on the part of both $\mathbf{Q^n}$ and $\mathfrak{M}$.

Finally, the fact that $\mathfrak{M}$ preserves no original readings and that $\mathbf{Q^n}$ often agrees with $\mathfrak{m}$ against $\mathfrak{M}$ in preferable readings suggests that $\mathbf{Q^n}$ represents a somewhat earlier stage in the development of the tradition than $\mathfrak{M}$.

Now that we have looked at the four witnesses in all possible groupings, in the following chapter we will look at each of the four individually.

CHAPTER V

NEW LIGHT FROM 4QpaleoExodᵐ

ON THE CHARACTER OF THE WITNESSES TO EXODUS

INTRODUCTION

This chapter discusses in turn each of the four witnesses studied in this work, with a fifth section on the history of the text of Exodus. The object is to determine what new insights can be gained from the analysis of Q^m concerning the nature, characteristics, and history of each of the four texts. While Q^m will be described as fully as possible, no attempt will be made to describe the other three in general; rather, only those aspects of the three which have been newly illuminated from the analysis of Q^m will receive attention. Thus the first section will be disproportionately long.

This chapter builds directly on the three preceding chapters, using the information gained about preferable readings, synonymous variants, and textual affiliation to determine the nature of each text individually and in comparison with the others.

The charts in Appendices 3 and 4 present a graphic summary of the findings of those three chapters and should be referred to while reading this chapter. They show the number of secondary, synonymous, and preferable readings presented by each of the four texts; the types of synonymous and secondary readings; and the number of readings both preserved uniquely and shared with the other texts.

The chart in Appendix 4 relates especially to the nature of each text in itself and answers the following questions. How many times does it preserve the preferable reading? How many times does it preserve secondary readings? What kind of secondary readings are they: quantitative (expansions or omissions), qualitative (different words or forms), or actual errors? Of the synonymous variants, how often does this text have the longer, shorter, or qualitatively different reading? Of both the secondary and synonymous readings, how many are major variants and how many are relatively insignificant?

The total number of readings analyzed is the same for all three Hebrew texts: 165. Thus all of the statistics for **Qᵐ𝔐** can be compared and contrasted with each other without further ado. This is unfortunately not the case for **G**, since the total number of its readings is only 121. The difference depends on our inability to determine what the Hebrew *Vorlage* was in 44 of the readings. Because of this difference in the data base, in this chapter the percentages of secondary and preferable readings are also given for each of the four texts.

The chart in Appendix 3 is self-explanatory. It provides a visual summary of the results of Chapter IV and shows how frequently each text agrees with each of the others.

This chapter closes with a brief discussion of the history of these four texts of Exodus, inferred from all that has gone before: characteristics of each individual text and agreement among the various texts.

Once again it must be stressed that everything that is said about the nature of the individual texts and about their history and affiliation is necessarily of a random nature. This is due, first, to the fragmentary nature of the overall evidence that remains and, second, to the fragmentary nature of this individual scroll.

This investigation is not a comprehensive study of the text of Exodus as it was used in the Second Commonwealth. It is a study of only four texts, as they have come down to us in different ways. Most of the other texts that were used have been lost to us. Due to the position that three of them have held for two thousand years we sometimes think of them as if they had formed a triumverate already during Hellenistic or at least by Hasmonaean days. But we do not know that. In fact, the finds from Qumran, at least as they are interpreted by such scholars as Talmon and Tov,[1] tend to argue against such a neat picture and in favor of the existence in those days of many more texts than these three. Thus our picture is necessarily partial and our statistics are skewed.[2]

Nor is this work a comprehensive study of the text of Exodus. It is based, rather, on the evidence of the scroll, which is dependent upon the random scraps of leather which happen to have been preserved. The value of the scroll is that it represents a stage in the transmission of Exodus sometime between 225 B.C. and 68 A.D. Whereas each of the other three

---

[1]See above, Chapter I.C regarding the debate about text-types.
[2]See above, Chapter I.F.2, and Tov, "Outlook," pp. 26-27 n. 70.

witnesses is from a much later period, having been subjected to copying and corruption for centuries more, the Q^n tradition froze at one point and stopped developing.

The advantage provided by its age is not without cost, however, as is obvious throughout the entire analysis and even in the definition of the term "variant" as used in this work. Only when Q^n is extant are all four texts compared and variants isolated.[3]   Thus a "variant" is by definition a place where two things are true: Q^n is extant and there is a variation among the four witnesses under investigation. And since the descriptions in this chapter are based largely upon the evidence of the variants, they are necessarily random as well. They are, furthermore, subject to correction when other Qumran scrolls have been published and analyzed.

With this caution in mind, then, what new light can the random evidence of Q^n shed on each of the four witnesses of Exodus?

A. THE CHARACTER OF Q^n

1. PREFERABLE, SYNONYMOUS, AND SECONDARY READINGS

Of the 165 readings which have been analyzed so far, 80 have been classified as synonymous variants, meaning that preferability cannot be determined. Of the remaining 85 readings, Q^n preserves the preferable reading 42 times and the secondary reading 43 times.

Based on the total 165 readings, Q^n has the preferable reading in 25.5% of the cases, the secondary reading in 26%, and a synonymous variant in 48.5% of the cases.

Based on the 85 readings where preferability can be established with some degree of confidence, Q^n has roughly 50% each of preferable and secondary readings.

The foregoing figures relate to all of the preferable and secondary readings preserved in Q^n, regardless of whether and which other texts share the same readings.

---

[3]The distinction between "variants" and other passages in Exodus is shown in the designation of the reference: a variant is always referred to with boldface characters (e.g., **32:9**; contrast 32:9, which would refer to another part of the verse, where either Q^n is not extant or else there is no variation among the four texts).

Of the 27 variants that $\mathbf{Q^m}$ preserves uniquely, 5 are preferable (19%), 10 are secondary (37%), and 12 are synonymous (44%). Based on the 15 readings where preferability can be established with some degree of confidence, $\mathbf{Q^m}$ has the preferable reading 33% of the time, and the secondary reading 67% of the time.

2. TYPES OF SECONDARY READINGS AND SYNONYMOUS VARIANTS

Of the 43 secondary readings preserved in $\mathbf{Q^m}$, 10 are unique to $\mathbf{Q^m}$:

- only 2 expansions are unique to $\mathbf{Q^m}$:

    the conjunction and לאמור

- 5 slight alterations:

    ב־ for בת[ו]ך, ושתי for וש[מתי, מלאכה for מלאכת

    וידבר for ויאמר, and 1 example of synesis, אתו for אותם

- 3 clear errors, each involving one or two letters only.

Each of these 10 variants could easily have resulted from carelessness and preoccupation of the scribe.

Thus it is clear that of the readings which are clearly secondary and are unique to $\mathbf{Q^m}$ there is no pattern at all, there are no readings of any great significance, and there is nothing that indicates a concerted effort to alter the text in any way. The unique aspects of $\mathbf{Q^m}$, insofar as they are secondary, are the result of error, carelessness, or almost unconscious scribal moves, rather than exegetical and/or expansionist motives.

Of the 43 secondary readings preserved in $\mathbf{Q^m}$, it shares 33 with at least one other witness. The most significant of these are the 12 major expansions of the $\mathbf{Q^m}$ய tradition, which will be discussed in the following section, V.A.3, and the one major expansion preserved in $\mathbf{Q^m}$யℳ, which will be discussed in V.C.3.

The remaining 20 secondary readings shared with at least one other witness break down thus:

- 17 expansions:

    כל עשב הארץ ואת כל פרי;

    a second object (את עבדיו, ולאהרון, למשה);

    a verb or clause (ויעמדו, ויכם, ועשית להם);

    a number (אחד);

    an adverb (מאוד);

    a designation of time (once each: היום, בבוקר);

    a minor word (twice לאמור, once בני);

    an accusative suffix (once);

and the conjunction (2 times).

- 3 alterations: 1 verb altered to fit the syntax,
    1 altered preposition, and 1 altered prepositional phrase.[4]

Turning to the synonymous variants preserved in **Qⁿ**, those variants for which preferability cannot be established, we find that of the total of 80, **Qⁿ** shares 68 with at least one other witness:

- **Qⁿ** is longer in 3 involving the length of entire pericopes;
- 6 indicate the existence of one pericope with two different formulations;
- 6 involve difference in order (1 involves a paragraph of ten verses, 1 a phrase, and 4 involve one word each);
- 2 affect the representation of the table;
- in 6 **Qⁿ** is shorter (משחים בשמן, 4 locative *he*'s, and 1 definite article);
- in 12 **Qⁿ** is longer (מוס[בת [משב]צעות]הב תעשה אתם, (ו)אולם, אשר, שתי, בניכם, 1 definite article, and 6 conjunctions);
- 2 involve כל;
- 14 involve the difference of one word (לא כן, שבעת, וידבר, אל, לפני, ע[מי, בית, חתן] משה, הנה, and 5 variations in the designation for God);
- 11 involve different forms of a word (7 in verbs, 1 in a noun, and 3 in pronouns);
- 6 involve difference in grammatical features (1 construct state, 1 preposition instead of verbal suffix, 3 differences in noun suffixes, and ווי instead of וויהם).

Besides the 68 synonymous variants shared with other witnesses, **Qⁿ** uniquely preserves the following 12 synonymous variants:

- 7 where **Qⁿ** is shorter (1 passage of 14 words; 1 four-word clause; 1 two-word clause; כל; 1 locative *he*; 1 definite article; and 1 את);
- 3 where **Qⁿ** is longer (1 conjunction, 1 definite article, and את);
- 2 differences in words (ו[בגרוע חזק]ה and עד);
- 2 differences in forms of words (1 verbal gender, 1 noun suffix).[5]

---

[4]See Chapter IV.A for details and affiliation.

[5]To catalogue each of the synonymous variants gives a total of 14 rather than 12, which indicates the complexities involved in counting such minor variants, where one word or short phrase will involve two variations.

Thus of the synonymous variants unique to $\mathbf{Q}^{\mathbf{m}}$, 3 are of some interest. There are two shorter readings where it is possible that $\mathbf{Q}^{\mathbf{m}}$ alone does not expand from Ezekiel (31:13-14) or from Job (בו10:21). Similarly, in the case of a two-word phrase, ו[בגרוע חזק]ה, where there is variation in both words, it is possible that $\mathbf{Q}^{\mathbf{m}}$ is the only one of the four witnesses studied that does not reflect influence from the parallel passage in Deuteronomy (see the discussion of בו32:11 in Chapter III.B.3). Alternatively, of course, it is possible that $\mathbf{Q}^{\mathbf{m}}$ or its *Vorlage* is guilty of haplography in the first two cases and of writing one wrong word in the last case.

These cases of secondary and synonymous variants in $\mathbf{Q}^{\mathbf{m}}$ must be viewed along with its preferable readings. The 42 preferable readings in $\mathbf{Q}^{\mathbf{m}}$ are all listed and discussed in Chapter II.A. Only the 5 preferable readings that are unique to $\mathbf{Q}^{\mathbf{m}}$ are worthy of note again here: they include one case where $\mathbf{Q}^{\mathbf{m}}$ preserves an older form and four cases where $\mathbf{Q}^{\mathbf{m}}$ is shorter by one word: הראישונים, מארעו, לו, and לך. These reflect minor exegetical expansions on the part of other texts. While none of these is striking in itself, the five of them together serve as a reminder that even a text which belongs to a generally expansionist tradition may still preserve some shorter, preferable readings. In this way, then, $\mathbf{Q}^{\mathbf{m}}$ may be compared to $\mathbf{G}$ (see V.D.).

3. THE RELATIONSHIP OF $\mathbf{Q}^{\mathbf{m}}$ WITH ⱴ

a. *Major Expansions in the $\mathbf{Q}^{\mathbf{m}}$ⱴ Tradition*

There are twelve major expansions preserved in both $\mathbf{Q}^{\mathbf{m}}$ and ⱴ. These are the "typological" variants which persuaded Tov to put $\mathbf{Q}^{\mathbf{m}}$ into the same "text-type" as ⱴ.[6] These are of four kinds: major cases of repetition within the plague narratives; major interpolations from parallel passages in Deuteronomy; a statement added to introduce a paragraph within the instructions for the tabernacle; and the addition of the names of two sons of Aaron.

(1) Major Cases of Repetition within the Plague Narratives

Six of the twelve major expansions where $\mathbf{Q}^{\mathbf{m}}$ is extant (7:18[b]; 7:29[b]; 8:19[b]; 9:5[b]; 9:19[b]; 10:2[b]) belong to the first sub-category: major cases of

---

[6]Tov, *Septuagint,* p. 274 and n. 38, and "Outlook," pp. 22-23 and 25-26; see above, Chapter I.C.

repetition within the plague narratives.   Since $\mathbf{Q}^\mathbf{n}$ is fragmentary it will help to look at the complete list of these major expansions that occur in 𝔐. The following chart shows the number and nature of the plague, the verse reference of the expansion in 𝔐 if there is one, whether or not it can be determined from the extant parts of the scroll that $\mathbf{Q}^\mathbf{n}$ agrees with 𝔐, and the nature of the expansion. In conjunction with what are normally considered the ten plagues is listed also the pre-plague sign, which follows the same form as several of the plagues.

Number	Type	𝔐	$\mathbf{Q}^\mathbf{n}$?	Nature of Expansion
Sign	Serpent	no exp	$\mathbf{Q}^\mathbf{n}$	
* 1	Blood	7:18^b	$\mathbf{Q}^\mathbf{n}$	repeats command to show execution
* 2	Frogs	7:29^b	$\mathbf{Q}^\mathbf{n}$	repeats command to show execution
		8:1^b	□	repeats command to show execution
* 3	Gnats	no exp	$\mathbf{Q}^\mathbf{n}$	
* 4	Flies	8:19^b	$\mathbf{Q}^\mathbf{n}$	repeats command to show execution
* 5	Plague	9:5^b	$\mathbf{Q}^\mathbf{n}$	repeats command to show execution
* 6	Boils	no exp	$\mathbf{Q}^\mathbf{n}$	
* 7	Hail	9:19^b	$\mathbf{Q}^\mathbf{n}$	repeats command to show execution
* 8	Locusts	10:2^b	$\mathbf{Q}^\mathbf{n}$	precedes execution with command
* 9	Darkness	no exp	□	
*10	Firstborn	11:3^b	□	(1) precedes execution with command;
		11:3^b	□	(2) repeats command in 4:22 to show execution

There are nine expansions, the last plague having two. Although $\mathbf{Q}^\mathbf{n}$ is extant in only six of these expansions, there is good reason to believe that it originally had all nine. Even though no words from any of the other three expansions are preserved, the reconstruction of the columns calls for all of them to have been there.[7] Thus the chart represents a minimalistic view.

If we look at the content of these expansions we see that there are three kinds. Roughly speaking, the first type, represented by the first six expansions, could be described as follows.   ($\mathbf{Q}^\mathbf{n}$)𝔐𝔪G have a command from Yahweh to Moses. 𝔪 and G leave the reader to infer that Moses carried out the command, since the narrative then proceeds with the results of his having done so. $\mathbf{Q}^\mathbf{n}$𝔐, however, leave nothing to inference, but rather show that Moses fulfilled the command word for word, by repeating the

---

[7]See the edition in *DJD*.

words from Yahweh's command and changing nouns, pronouns, and verbal forms as necessary.

In the second type, the expansion precedes the execution that is already in $(\mathbf{Q^n})$ⅢⅢ𝕘 by repeating the words in the same way, but this time to show that Yahweh had indeed commanded what was carried out. There are two in this group: $10:2^b$ and the first part of $11:3^b$. ($11:3^b$ is actually two expansions, though von Gall has given only the one reference.[8])

The third type (the second part of $11:3^b$) harks back to the command in 4:22-23 to tell Pharaoh that if he refuses to let the Israelites go Yahweh will kill his firstborn, repeating that so that its execution is literally carried out. Since this last type is of a qualitatively different nature, we will leave it aside for the moment and concentrate on the first two types.

There are three questions to ask about these expansions in the plague narratives. First, what exactly did the scribe do?   Second, why did he do it? Third, why didn't he expand all of the plagues?

To answer the first question, about the scribe's method, one of these expansions is written out as an example on the following page, so that we can see more clearly exactly what he did. This is an example of the first type of expansion, those that follow a command to show its fulfilment. The first three lines are from $8:16-19^a$ and give Yahweh's command: the two full lines show Ⅲ and ⅢⅢ respectively; the top -- partial -- line shows what is extant in $\mathbf{Q^n}$. The last two lines are from $8:19^b$, and give the execution of the command: the full line shows ⅢⅢ; and the bottom -- partial -- line shows what is still extant in $\mathbf{Q^n}$. Small differences (other than orthographical) are underlined for easier recognition.

Let us compare first the three texts of the command, $8:16-19^a$. There are several small differences between Ⅲ and ⅢⅢ where $\mathbf{Q^n}$ is not extant. First, Ⅲ lacks the pronoun which ⅢⅢ has. In the corresponding passage in ב15:7 $\mathbf{Q^n}$ agrees with ⅢⅢ against Ⅲ; it was decided that the longer reading is probably preferable on the basis of the usual style in Exodus (see Chapter II.A.6). Second, Ⅲ has a locative he lacking in ⅢⅢ. For a similar case see the discussion of ב 9:8 in Chapter III.A.2; there $\mathbf{Q^n}$ⅢⅢ have השמים where Ⅲ has השמימה.   Third, Ⅲ lacks the את of ⅢⅢ. As will be mentioned in Chapter V.B.4, ⅢⅢ often has את where Ⅲ does not. In many of these cases there is a similar phrase very close by that has the את in both Ⅲ and ⅢⅢ, so

---

[8]The two parts are separated by the sentence in the second half of 11:3 in Ⅲ𝕘 which sounds very much like a gloss.

𝔔ᵐ ¹⁶   [לאמר]

𝔐   השכם בבקר והתיצב   ¹⁶ויאמר יהוה אל משה

𝔚   השכם בבקר והתיצב   ¹⁶ויאמר יהוה אל משה

𝔚   ¹⁶ᵇויבא משה ואהרן

𝔔ᵐ [אליו]

𝔐   לפני פרעה הנה ___ יוצא המימה ואמרת אליו כה אמר יהוה

𝔚   לפני פרעה הנה הוא יצא המים ואמרת אליו כה אמר יהוה

𝔚   אל פרעה ויאמרו אליו כה אמר יהוה

𝔔ᵐ [אמ]ר

𝔔ᵐ מש[לח את עמ]י

𝔐   שלח ___ עמי ויעבדני ¹⁷כי אם אינך משלח את עמי הנני משליח

𝔚   שלח את עמי ויעבדני ¹⁷כי אם אינך משלח את עמי הנני משלח

𝔚   שלח את עמי ויעבדני כי אם אינך משלח את עמי הנני משלח

𝔔ᵐ [עמי הנני]

𝔔ᵐ הער]וב ומלא]ו

𝔐   בך ובעבדיך ובעמך ובבתיך את הערב ומלאו בתי מצרים את הערב

𝔚   בך ובעבדיך ובעמך ובבתיך את הערב ומלאו בתי מצרים את הערב

𝔚   בך ובעבדיך ובעמך ובבתיך את הערב ומלאו בתי מצרים את הערב

𝔔ᵐ ומל]או בתי מצרי]ם

𝔔ᵐ [המה עליה ¹⁸ו]הפליתי

𝔐   וגם האדמה אשר הם עליה ¹⁸והפליתי ביום ההוא את ארץ גשן

𝔚   וגם האדמה אשר הם עליה ¹⁸והפליתי ביום ההוא את ארץ גשן

𝔚   וגם האדמה אשר הם עליה והפליתי ביום ההוא את ארץ גשן

𝔔ᵐ ביו]ם ההוא את אר]ץ

𝔐   אשר עמי עמד עליה לבלתי היות שם ערב למען תדע כי אני יהוה

𝔚   אשר עמי עמד עליה לבלתי היות שם ערב למען תדע כי אני יהוה

𝔚   אשר עמי עמד עליה לבלתי היות שם ערב למען תדע כי אני יהוה

𝔔ᵐ [למען תדע כי אני יה]וה

𝔐   בקרב הארץ ¹⁹ᵃושמתי פדת בין עמי ובין עמך למחר יהיה האת הנה

𝔚   בקרב הארץ ¹⁹ᵃושמתי פדות בין עמי ובין עמך למחר יהיה האות הנה

𝔚   בקרב הארץ ושמתי פדות בין עמי ובין עמך למחר יהיה האות הנה

𝔔ᵐ [למחר יהיה ה]אות

that one suspects that 𝕾 has added it the second time for consistency. And that is also the case here: cf. the משלח את עמי later in the same line.

But those three are the only differences, other than orthographical, between 𝔐 and 𝕾 in those four verses. Which is to say that the agreement is very close. This example shows clearly why it is often said that 𝕾 is merely an expanded version of 𝔐.

In the extant parts of Qᵇ there is only one difference other than orthographical, and here it is unique: in 8:16[20] it adds לאמר (see Chapter II.B.4). Once again, however, this is a very minor difference.

We turn now to a comparison of the last two lines with each other: the major expansion as it appears in 𝕾 and Qᵇ. In this instance there are no variants at all between the two. This is not the case in all the expansions; see below, V.A.3.b.

Now let us compare the major expansion, the fulfillment in Qᵇ𝕾, with the command in 𝔐𝕾. Here we can see in action a scribe who was deliberately expanding on his *Vorlage*. His method was to copy the words of the command exactly, letter-for-letter, with just a few changes. Note that when 𝕾 of the source disagrees with 𝔐 of the source, 𝕾 of the expansion agrees exactly with 𝕾 of the source against 𝔐. This pattern persists in all of these expansions, including those passages which involve greater variation between 𝕾 and 𝔐, such as:

7:29ᵇ//7:26 (דבר 𝕾; אמר 𝔐);

9:5ᵇ//9:1 (דבר 𝕾; אמר 𝔐);

10:2ᵇ//10:5 (עשב הארץ ואת כל פרי 𝕾; > 𝔐
     [see Chapter II.C.2.b regarding 10:5]);

11:3ᵇ//11:6 (בכל ארץ מערים 𝕾; במערים 𝔐).

The first change involved the freedom to make <u>omissions</u>. The scribe deemed it unnecessary to repeat the very beginning, the instructions relating specifically to Moses' behavior: "Get up early in the morning and take your stand." He summarized that with the words "And Moses went." Then, because "<u>before</u> Pharaoh" fitted with "take your stand" but not with "went," he changed the pronoun to "<u>to</u>." He also decided to omit the explanatory note as to where Pharaoh was to be found -- "behold he will be going out toward the water" -- because this too was to guide Moses' actions.

Here is a part of the answer to the second question asked above: What was the scribe's <u>motive</u> in creating these expansions? Since he could practically ignore Yahweh's instructions to <u>Moses</u> in his expansion, it seems that the only thing that was important to repeat were Yahweh's words to Pharaoh. We will come back to this later.

Continuing with the scribe's method, it seems that to whatever extent a principle may have already been operative for scribes in this period, to the effect that the Word of God could not be abbreviated, it applied -- for this scribe at least -- only to the first occurrence of the words. If he wanted to repeat the words of Scripture he was free to summarize peripheral matters the second time. But even his summary used words that were in the context. There were two commands following the pattern printed above (8:16 and 9:13); a third was much more detailed, but began with לך אל פרעה (7:15); two other commands followed a shorter pattern, with the simple command בא אל פרעה only (7:26 and 9:1). When the scribe wanted to summarize the longer commands, he used this simpler pattern, בא (לך) אל פרעה, with the result that that is what appears in all five expansions.

The second change involved the freedom to make additions and alterations. The instructions were directed only to Moses -- only he was addressed, and all three verbs are in the singular. Yet our scribe has added Aaron to the action: "Moses and Aaron went ... and they said ...." (The first verb has not been made plural; but a singular verb is common if the verb precedes a plural subject.)   As the example shows, since the rest of the text is a message from Yahweh to Pharaoh, only the introduction needed to be altered in order to include Aaron. Only one other alteration was needed in all of this group of expansions: **7:18ᵇ** altered "Yahweh has sent me" (7:16) to "Yahweh has sent us." Note that the expression in 7:17, "I will strike with my staff which is in my hand," was not altered. Were the staff and hand seen as belonging to Yahweh, or as an extension of Yahweh's power, or was it merely that only one man could logically hold it in his hand?

Was this a case of tendentiously adding Aaron so that he would be a more active participant in the plague narratives?   At first it seems so, since four other major expansions in the plague narratives add his name and make the verb plural in exactly this way (contrast **7:18ᵇ** with 7:15; **7:29ᵇ** with 7:26; **9:5ᵇ** with 9:1; and **9:19ᵇ** with 9:13).[9] In all five cases the first

_____

[9]The expansions that do not add Aaron's name are all somehow different from the pattern of these five: in 8:1ᵇ Moses is relaying a command to Aaron as he was instructed; the first part of 11:3ᵇ is the command that precedes the execution already in the text; and the second part of 11:3ᵇ reports the fulfilment of the command in 4:22-23, before Aaron had joined Moses. For **10:2ᵇ** see below.

verb was allowed to remain in the singular (ויבא or וילך), then Aaron's name was joined to Moses', and then the following verb was written in the plural (ויאמרו). Was the scribe deliberately enhancing the prestige of Aaron?

But this theory runs into difficulty in 10:2[b], which is one of the two exceptions where the expansion has to give the command, since it is the fulfilment that is already in the text. In other words, the scribe's *Vorlage* reported Moses' speaking to Pharaoh with no explicit instructions as to what to say; he therefore added an expansion to make the command explicit. In this case, then, 10:1 has the beginning of a command in ⱮⱮ𝔾: בא אל פרעה;[10] but 𝔪𝔾 never spell out what Moses is to say when he gets to Pharaoh. Then 10:3-6, which is in 𝔪𝔾 as well as in Ɱ, has Moses talking to Pharaoh -- but Moses is not alone; 10:3 reads in ⱮⱮ𝔾: ויבא משה ואהרן אל פרעה ויאמרו אליו. When the scribe wrote the expansion, 10:2[b], then, he phrased it in the singular, to continue on as 10:1 had begun: ואמרת אל פרעה. If 10:1-3 is an early reading -- and it must be fairly early to be preserved in 𝐐ᵃⱮ𝔪𝔾 -- then that pattern had already been set before our scribe set to work:

(1) Yahweh commands Moses with verbs in the singular (10:1);
(2) Moses and Aaron fulfill the command, and the second verb is plural (10:3).

If this is true, then there was no *Tendenz* on the part of the scribe who created the major expansions; in the same way that he went from 8:19[b] to verses already in his *Vorlage*, such as 7:26, to find the simpler verb בא to summarize השכם...והתיצב..., so also he went to 10:1 and 3 to find the pattern that had already been established concerning Moses' and Aaron's collaborating. Once again, then, it does not appear that any particular textual tradition can be credited with a bias in favor of Aaron or of priests in general. Whatever insertion of Aaron's name for the purpose of increasing his prestige ever did occur, in principle it pre-dated the division of any of our four texts.[11] The only effect of the major expansions in (𝐐ᵃ)Ⱨ was to

---

[10]Rather perversely, the scroll is never extant where it could show that it did or did not have Aaron's name in the major expansions, except for one ambiguous variant (see below, Chapter V.A.3.b, regarding 7:18[b]א). It is extant in 10:1, however, where it agrees with ⱮⱮ𝔾 in the singular imperative בא.

[11]See the discussion of the treatment of Aaron's name in Chapter VI.A.1.g.

make this phenomenon more obvious, since it now occurred six times instead of only once.

In light of all this, then, it would seem most likely that the same scribe who created these expansions added Aaron's name as a part of the process. There is, however, one complicating factor. Q^a is extant in only one place that could shed any light at all on whether or not it made Aaron's participation explicit: at 7:18^{b}א -- and that is ambiguous. It is impossible to tell whether or not Aaron's name was ever on the scroll, but the second verb in that opening series is ויאמר, i.e., singular. (See the discussion below: V.A.3.b.[1].) In any event that variant does not affect the evaluation of what was involved in Aaron's having been added other than to mean that it happened in a stage later than that represented by Q^a. Regardless of when the addition was made, it was legitimated by the pattern in 10:1-3.

This, then, was the method of our scribe: exact reproduction of all of the words of Yahweh to Pharaoh, with a narrative introduction that could be (1) greatly condensed and (2) altered to include Aaron. Yet for both of these changes the scribe had an exact pattern to follow elsewhere in the plague narrative.

I have deliberately spoken of our scribe in the singular, because it seems probable that only one person was involved. The expansions that we have seen thus far are so uniform and are in such a restricted section of Exodus that they appear to be the work of one man, and in a very short period of time, perhaps a day or two, or however long it took to copy five chapters. On the other hand, judging from the fact that these expansions were preserved, he may have been carrying out the wishes of his community. At the very least, some community or communities liked what he had done and adopted it later.

The second question is: Why did the scribe do this? Or perhaps, why did his community ask him to do it? It is often assumed that the motivation for these expansions was the pedantic refusal of the scribe to allow any command of Yahweh to remain unfulfilled explicitly. And this may indeed have been the case. It should be noted, however, that it is equally possible that the motivation was not so much a pedantic one, but perhaps a dramatic and/or liturgical one. Yahweh's very precise instructions regarding when and where Moses was to speak to Pharaoh were, as we have seen, not repeated at all. Are we to infer that Moses actually met Pharaoh in his audience room in the afternoon, rather than by the water early in the morning? No -- the point of these expansions is not to emphasize Moses' strict obedience to Yahweh. The point is to emphasize Yahweh's threats to Pharaoh. This is a narrative of warfare between two deities. Various scribes used various means to heighten the tension and to highlight the victory of Yahweh. Some scribes made minor changes to enhance the sub-plot of the conflict between Moses and the magicians (see 9:8a and 9:10). This particular scribe decided to make major expansions to enhance the central plot of the conflict between Yahweh and Pharaoh.

Perhaps the texts which contained these expansions were designed for use in instruction of children or in liturgical settings, where public recitation of command and of fulfillment would be assigned to different readers. Perhaps the celebration of the Exodus from Egypt included readings designed for maximum dramatic effect; there may even have been provision for audience participation of some kind. Comparison could be made with the development of the celebration of the story of Esther and Purim, including such devices as noisemakers to drown out the sound of Haman's name. This possibility is mentioned only as a reminder that not all textual developments need necessarily to be attributed to scribes working as individuals and intending their work to be used only by learned men for study. The needs of the entire community, including children and women, including instruction and worship, may occasionally have influenced the activities of scribes.

The scribe's method was exact reproduction of Yahweh's words to Pharaoh; his motivation was somehow related to the importance of the verbal aspect of the battle between the two deities.

Here is the answer to the third question, the choice of the scribe: Why did he leave some plagues unexpanded? The chart shows that only seven plagues received major expansions. On the other hand, plagues #2 (frogs) and #10 (firstborn) each received two; but the second of each is exceptional. In 8:1^b what is repeated is an instruction to Aaron; note that this is the only expansion that does not fit the pattern, since no public words of Yahweh are involved. The second expansion in 11:3^b will be discussed below.

What do the three plagues and the preliminary sign -- all lacking a major expansion -- have in common? None of them have a speech from Yahweh to Pharaoh. All four of them involved, instead, an action on the part of Aaron or Moses: with the staff (7:9; 8:12[16]), ashes (9:8), or the hand (10:21).[12]

If we look further we will find more instances of this pattern. Within the individual plague narratives there is often more than one command, and hence more than one opportunity for expansion. In 7:19; 9:22; and 10:12 Yahweh commands Moses to act or to instruct Aaron to act -- rather than to speak to Pharaoh -- and none of them received any attention from our scribe. Actually, his *Vorlage* already mentioned fulfilment in each of these cases, if we may judge from the fact that it is in all three traditions (7:20; 9:23; 10:13).

To summarize: (1) there are no commands of Yahweh to speak to Pharaoh -- or reports of Moses' speaking to Pharaoh -- that have not been expanded; (2) there are seven commands to speak to Aaron or to perform an action which have not been expanded; three of them already have their fulfilment explicit in all the traditions; (3) there is only one exception, 8:1[b]: here the command to speak to Aaron was repeated in a major expansion. It seems safe to conclude that the interest of our particular scribe was in the words of Yahweh to Pharaoh; repeating them enhanced the narrative of the battle between the two.

In thinking about the purpose and number of these expansions, a negative point arises. While it is unclear how soon the idea of *ten* plagues arose (cf. the ambiguous relationship of the pre-plague sign to the plagues, the likewise ambiguous relationship of the slaying of the firstborn, and the varying representations in Pss 78 and 105), it is quite clear that these expansions were not related to any pattern of ten. The best count would give nine expansions, and these do not correspond to nine plagues, since two plagues have been given two expansions. Perhaps we should conclude that, if the notion of *ten* was in the scribe's mind, he did not have the freedom to tamper with the text in any way other than to repeat; i.e., he could not invent a speech of Yahweh against Pharaoh to insert in the three plagues that had none. It was too late to improve the text *that* much. The other possibility, and perhaps the more likely one, is that he was not even thinking in terms of *ten*.

---

[12]According to Childs (*Exodus*, p. 131), those involving the staff or hand are assigned to P, and that involving ashes is divided between J and E. The three belonging to P, incidentally, feature Aaron prominently without any help from Q⁴ ⅲ expansionism.

Thus these two types of major expansions -- the simplest -- involved exact copying with minor changes according to a pattern already in the *Vorlage*. They seem to have been motivated by a desire to repeat word-for-word all of Yahweh's words to Pharaoh; with one exception, none of Yahweh's other commands were repeated. It seems appropriate to assign all of these expansions to one scribe working at one time because they are so alike. Though his work is not distinctive enough to suggest anything about where he lived or what stream of religious tradition he represented, we can at least place him after **G** and **𝔐** had each separated from **Q**ᵐ𝔪, but early enough in the tradition for **Q**ᵐ to share it with 𝔪.

We turn now to the third type of expansion in this section, the second part of what von Gall designated as 11:3ᵇ. According to the reconstruction, **Q**ᵐ had both parts (see above in the explanation of the chart). This is important, since the second part involved repeating 4:22-23, threatening Pharaoh's firstborn. This is qualitatively different from the other expansions discussed in this section; whereas they copied a paragraph immediately following or immediately preceding, 11:3ᵇ copied text from seven chapters earlier, indicating a much broader scope of attention on the part of a scribe, a desire to harmonize the narrative of the plagues and exodus as a whole.

There is one other expansion similar to this one, at 6:9ᵇ, shortly before the plague narrative begins. There is no way at all to determine whether it was in **Q**ᵐ, since the first extant column begins only in 6:25. This expansion reaches forward in the narrative and repeats 14:12, so that the Hebrews are explicitly reported to have said the words they claim to have said while still in Egypt: "Let us alone and let us serve the Egyptians, since it is better for us to serve the Egyptians than to die in the wilderness." Since 6:9ᵇ reflects a desire and a method similar to that in 11:3ᵇ, which the reconstruction includes in the scroll, it seems quite likely that both of these more far-reaching expansions were done by one scribe and therefore that if one of them was in **Q**ᵐ, both were. That conclusion is supported by the fact that the major expansions from Deuteronomy, which show a similar broader view, are extant in the scroll (see below).

If it is the case that these two were in **Q**ᵐ, then we could date them to the same general period as the first two types, even though they are qualitatively different, simply because they were all in **Q**ᵐ. We still would not know whether the same scribe made these as well, however.

The <u>motive</u> and the <u>method</u> of these two expansions again relate closely to each other. Both were taken from a relatively distant section of Exodus and were inserted in exactly the right place to enhance the literary structure of the Exodus narrative. The threat of the killing of Pharaoh's firstborn, which was found in 4:22 just before the story about Moses' firstborn, was inserted just at the beginning of the narrative of the plague in which the threat to Pharaoh's firstborn was carried out; thus the parallel between the firstborn sons of Pharaoh and of Moses was explicitly drawn. Here again Yahweh's threats to Pharaoh were repeated.

The complaint of the people, which was found in 14:12 to show their "great fear" at the approach of the Egyptian army, was inserted in 6:9^b, where the text referred to their refusal to listen to Moses in Egypt "because of their broken spirit and their cruel bondage." This expansion differed in two ways. It required a forward rather than a backward step in Exodus, and it repeated human words rather than Yahweh's. Yet it served to enhance the tension between the unbelief of the people and the power of Yahweh to save them. Whether threats of Yahweh to Pharaoh or unbelieving complaints of the Hebrews, all of these expansions heighten the glory of Yahweh and emphasize the process whereby Egyptians and Israelites alike came "to know that I am Yahweh."

The scribe who made these two expansions was not only concerned that a unit of nine chapters be harmonized. He also had an acute sense of literary parallels that were rather far removed in his text, and he did his work skillfully enough to emphasize those parallels.

(2) Major Interpolations from Parallel Passages in Deuteronomy

Q^a shares three major interpolations from Deuteronomy with 𝖒. The first two have been carefully analyzed by Tigay,[13] who has printed the relevant portions of the texts of Deuteronomy, 𝖒 of Exodus, and 𝕸 of Exodus, and indicated redactional additions and changes. His study should be consulted for understanding of these two major expansions.

18:25𝖒 // Deut 1:9-18 𝖒] aliter et brevius 𝖒𝐆   **Q**^{a}𝖒 ≠ 𝖒𝐆

Tigay shows that this expansion was made for the purpose of harmonizing two versions of the narrative. Whereas in the Exodus version

---

[13]Jeffrey H. Tigay, "An Empirical Basis for the Documentary Hypothesis," *JBL* 94 (1975), 329-342.

Jethro suggested that Moses choose judges from among the people, Deut 1:9-18 mentions only Moses' action. A scribe has carefully conflated the two versions to make one harmonious succession of events.[14]

20:19ª hab 𝕸] › 𝕸𝕲   𝐐ª𝕸 ≠ 𝕸𝕲

$\mathbf{Q}^a$ is extant only in **20:19ª**, but as Skehan has reconstructed the scroll the "companion piece," **20:21ᵇ**, must also have been present, both on the basis of column spacing and because they belong so closely together in content and method.[15] The first comes from Deut 5:24-27, while the second comes from Deut 5:28b-29; 18:18-22; and 5:30-31. Thus the story of the Sinai theophany has been greatly supplemented. The plea of the people that Moses act as mediator lest they die receives much more emphasis, as does Moses' position as prophet.

But then the scribe reached further than the parallel passage to the promise of "a prophet like you" in Deuteronomy 18. If the major expansions in the plague narratives tended to emphasize Aaron's prophetic role, these two expansions more than compensate by stressing Moses' prophetic role and that of the prophet to come.[16]

32:10 ובאהר(ו)ן התאנף יה[ו]ה מאד להשמידו ו[י]תפלל משה בעד א[הר](ו)ן
𝕸] › 𝕸𝕲   𝐐ª𝕸 ≠ 𝕸𝕲

This expansion should be viewed together with that in the preceding verse, **32:9**, which is preserved not only in 𝐐ª𝕸 but also in 𝕸 (see below, Chapter V.C.3). Both are now found in the same narrative in Exodus and come from the same narrative in Deuteronomy, although the subject of each is different. Whereas **32:9** presents a part of Yahweh's speech in Deuteronomy that was missing in Exodus, **32:10** presents a part of the narrative that was missing: Yahweh's profound anger against Aaron and Moses' intercession to save Aaron's life.

The complete text of Deut 9:20 reads as follows, with those words which have been omitted or changed underlined:

ובאהרן התאנף יהוה מאד להשמידו <u>ואתפללה</u> <u>גם</u> בעד אהרן <u>בעת ההיא</u>

As we have seen with the major expansions in the plague narratives, the scribe copied very carefully (whether from memory or from a scroll of

---

[14] *Ibid.,* pp. 333-335.

[15] See Chapter I.B.

[16] For the details of the scribe's methods, see Tigay, pp. 336-340.

Deuteronomy) and made only those changes which suited his purpose: the change from first to third person narration and the change in perspective from Moses' final sermon ("at that time") to more general storytelling.

Regarding the specific motivation, if there was only one, of the scribe, we can only speculate. Did he merely want to supplement one narrative with another? Or did he specifically want to emphasize Aaron's sin and need of Moses' intercession, perhaps for theological and/or political reasons relating to tensions between prophets and priests? Or was his motive more strictly literary: did he see how prominently Aaron's leadership in this sin was already featured in the narrative in Exodus (see 32:1,2,3,4,5,21,22,24, 25,35!) and feel that the story needed more balance by referring also to the threat of judgment for Aaron? Was there also a theological motive? Since Aaron's initiative was so emphasized, did it seem inconsistent of God that 3,000 should die yet Aaron be saved? Was the mention of Moses' intercession necessary to show Yahweh's justice?

(3) An Introduction to a Paragraph

There is one case of a statement having been added into the account of the tabernacle, presumably to introduce a new section of the instructions.

27:19ᵇ   ועשׂ]ית בגדי תכלת וארגמן ותולעת שני ¹⁷לשרת בהם בקדשׁ
𝔐Gᶠⁱʳ] > 𝔐G   Qᵃ𝔐 ≠ 𝔐G

This is a very strange expansion because it seems so unnecessary and because (in 𝔐 at least) it has been put in the wrong place: yet, judging from the absence of a note in von Gall's apparatus, all of the MSS he used agree in having it and in its position. It occurs just after a lengthy section (27:9-19) about the pillars, hangings, and measurements of the court; verse 19 specifies that the utensils and pegs are to be of bronze. The expansion immediately precedes a paragraph (27:20-21) about oil to keep the lamp burning continually. The next verse begins chapter 28, which is devoted to the subject of the priests' clothing. Thus this introduction was placed two or three verses too early. But not only is it misplaced, it is superfluous as well, since the subject of the priests' clothing is already introduced in 28:2.

Although only three letters are still visible on the scroll, their placement on one fragment with words from the two preceding lines seems

---

¹⁷Von Gall's edition reads לשׁדת for what should clearly be לשׁרת.

to indicate that **Qᵐ** did have this entire sentence, and in the same position as it is in 𝔐. This is supported by the fact that none of the next several sentences (until 28:2) begins with ועשית. It does seem strange that what is obviously the beginning of a new division in the text has not been signaled according to the custom of this scribe. He usually marked paragraph divisions by leaving a space at the end of one line except for a large *waw*, and then continuing the next word at the right margin of the next line. Here, however, ועש[is clearly visible at the right margin. Incidentally, this can scarcely be the ועשית at the beginning of verse 19ᵃ, since the two lines above it have the words שש מ[שזר, which is from 27:18, and עבוד[תו, which is from verse 19ᵃ.

While the position of this word is thus fixed relative to 27:19ᵃ, it is just possible that it was not followed by 27:20-21, but rather by 28:1 or 28:2; or that it was in fact the beginning of 28:2, i.e., that 27:20-21 and 28:1 were lacking. The next fragment has the first two words of 28:3; it could possibly represent the left side of the same line that ועש[begins. In that case, **Qᵐ** would not have had the two verses about the oil for the lamp or the instructions to bring Aaron and his four sons for priestly service. Note that although 𝔐𝔐𝔊 agree in having them, both could easily have been later additions: the lamp is completely out of place here (its description is in 25:31-40), and the sentence naming the five priests sounds suspiciously like a gloss. Finally, neither passage occurs in the second part of the tabernacle account (chapters 35-40), though the oil for the lamps is included in lists in 35:8,14,28; and 39:37. Thus there is the slight possibility that **Qᵐ** preserves a shorter reading where 𝔐𝔐𝔊 have all inserted two later expansions and where 𝔐 has added a third as well.

While we cannot be as certain about the presence and position of this expansion in **Qᵐ** as we can be regarding the other major expansions, the clear agreement of **Qᵐ** with 𝔐 in all other typological features where it is extant (eleven major expansions and the different placement of the pericope about the incense altar, 30:1-10) tips the scales here, so that it should be considered likely that **Qᵐ** agreed with 𝔐 here as well. The one argument against that conclusion is that this is so different from the other typological features, which were neither superfluous nor misplaced. This expansion may possibly have arisen somewhat later in the tradition so that it did not affect **Qᵐ**.

Perhaps this statement was originally a marginal rubric at 28:1 or 2, to assist in quicker location of the passage, which was later mistakenly added into the text proper. In that case, it is perhaps misleading to group it with the major expansions, since all the others reflect careful scribal deliberation. Possibly it should be classified rather as the result of a scribal lapse. Yet it does retain significance as far as textual affiliation is concerned, since it is one more piece of evidence -- albeit questionable -- of the close relationship between Q^a and 𝕸.

Regardless of the history of this expansion, it is still worth noting that all of the words come from other passages in Exodus: the wording is quite different from 28:2-5, 43, but allowing for differences in word order it is almost the same as 39:1:

ומן התכלת והארגמן ותולעת השני עשו בגדי שרד לשרת בקדש
ויעשו את בגדי הקדש אשר לאהרן כאשר צוה יהוה את משה.

Since 39:1 is the introduction to the chapter in the fulfilment half of the tabernacle account that corresponds to chapter 28 in the instructional half, it appears that a scribe went to 39:1, took what he deemed appropriate -- and made such changes as he deemed appropriate, e.g., dropping the articles -- for the preliminary reference to the clothing.

Summary: This major expansion differs from the others in two ways. First of all, it is qualitatively different in that it reflects none of the careful and skillful editorial work of the other major expansions, but seems to have resulted from some sort of scribal lapse. Second, it is not definite that Q^a agreed with 𝕸 in the presence and/or position of this expansion. The pattern of agreement in all other major expansions and in the major difference in order (30:1-10, which is also in the tabernacle account!) can provide only ambiguous support to the probable evidence of the leather fragment, because it is precisely this major expansion which does not fit the pattern of scribal craft.

If Q^a did have the expansion, then it agrees with 𝕸 here as in other major features. If it did not have the expansion, then it seems to reflect a text that was prior not only to 𝕸 but also to 𝕸𝔾, since it would then lack two discrete glosses added in 𝕸𝔾.

(4) Aaron's Sons

24:1

Q²Ɱ   אתה ואהר(ו)ן נדב ואביהוא אלעזר ו[איתמ]ר ושבעים מזקני ישראל

ⱮG   ושבעים מזקני ישראל   אתה ואהרן   נדב ואביהוא

24:9

Q²Ɱ   משה ואהר(ו)ן נדב ואביהוא אלעזר וא[יתמר ו]שבעים מזקני]ישר[אל

ⱮG   ושבעים מזקני ישראל   משה ואהרן   נדב ואביהוא

Q²Ɱ ++

These expansions are included in a sub-category with the longer expansions because, as short as they are, they nonetheless indicate significant exegetical work on the text. The names of the two younger sons of Aaron, Eleazar and Ithamar, appear together in only two passages in Ɱ of Exodus: at 6:23, in the genealogy of Aaron and Moses; and at 28:1, where Moses is told to prepare Aaron and his four sons for service as priests. Eleazar is mentioned also in 6:25, as the genealogy continues with his fathering Phinehas. Ithamar is mentioned also in 38:21, as the one directing the work of the Levites. All of these passages are ascribed to P.

Lev 10:1-7 tells the story of the death of the two older sons, Nadab and Abihu, as the result of their having offered "unholy fire." Lev 10:12-20 then reports that their place was taken by the younger sons, Eleazar and Ithamar. A comparison of the prepositions and the passive participles used in this pericope suggests that the names of Eleazar and Ithamar were added as part of a gradual process of expansion. In the second and third mention of their names, at Lev 10:12 and 16, the three traditions agree:

10:12   ⱮⱮG   וידבר משה אל אהרן ואל אלעזר ואל איתמר בניו הנותרים

10:16   ⱮⱮG   ויקצף על אלעזר ועל איתמר בני אהרן הנותרים

But at the first mention of their names, at Lev 10:6, there is disagreement. It seems likely that the two names were a later insertion into the text and that the three witnesses represent three stages in the gradual process of expansion. Ɱ represents the stage when the names have been inserted but no attempt has been made to smooth the text; a scribe in the Ɱ tradition has tidied the prepositions; and the G tradition has added the participle from 10:12 (or 16):

10:6 𝕸   ויאמר משה אל אהרן   ולאלעזר   ולאיתמר בניו

     𝔚   ויאמר משה אל אהרן ואל אלעזר ואל איתמר בניו

     𝔊   και ειπεν Μωυσης προς Ααρων και Ελεαζαρ και Ιθαμαρ

          τους υιους αυτου τους καταλελειμμενους

Regarding the tidying of the prepositions after the addition of the names, there may be an analogous passage in Exod 10:24ב,א, involving there the addition of Aaron's name (see Chapter II.C.1).

It should be noted that whereas the participle in Lev 10:16 is the same as that in 10:6, the counterpart in 10:12 is καταλειφθεντας; this may suggest that the further expansion in the 𝔊 tradition occurred at the Hebrew stage rather than at the Greek stage, when perhaps a scribe might have copied the word in the nearer context in its exact form.

If the two names in Lev 10:6 are actually a later insertion, then we have evidence that the same sort of expansionism that occurred only in the 𝐐ᵖ𝔚 tradition at Exodus 24 also happened in all three traditions while they were still developing together. A major difference is that in Lev 10 they would have been imported into v 6 from vv 12 and 16, i.e., the immediate context, whereas in Exod 24:1 and 9 they were imported from Exodus 6 or 28, i.e., the much more distant context.

The motivation in Exodus 24 seems to have been the desire to ensure that those who took the place of the first two priests be included in the great theophany on Sinai. The two priests who were killed for sacrilege should not be the only priests besides Aaron who experienced the theophany. They were not expunged from the theophany as they were from life, but they were joined by their two younger brothers who were to supplant them in the memories of the community.

To complete the record: Nadab and Abihu are mentioned by name only 9 times in the Torah, three times in genealogies (Exod 6:23; Lev 26:60; Num 3:2), twice in this theophany (Exod 24:1,9), once in preparation for consecration (Exod 28:1), and three times in the story of the unholy fire, their sudden death, their childlessness, and their being succeeded by Eleazar and Ithamar (Lev 10:1; Num 3:4; 26:61).

In contrast, Eleazar, who according to Deut 10:6 took Aaron's place after Aaron's death, is mentioned by name 42 times, and Ithamar 12 times. But it apparently seemed to an early scribe that they as the true and faithful priests should also be named in Lev 10:6; and another scribe later in the 𝐐ᵖ𝔚 tradition decided that they should have been witnesses to the Sinai theophany. Thus the additions in Exod 24:1 and 9 are taken as major

expansions because they reflect significant exegetical activity on the part
of a scribe who added to the text for the sake of the meaning of the story.

b. Variants Between Q^a and 𝔐 Within the Major Expansions

While Q^a agrees with 𝔐 in preserving these major expansions, there
are nevertheless very small differences between the two witnesses within
the expansions.   In several of these instances it seems possible to
determine the preferable reading.   They were not, however, included in
Chapter II or in any statistics anywhere for preferable readings, since they
occur in passages that are secondary.   Thus there is a three-stage
progression:

(1) 𝔐𝔊 preserve the preferable, shorter reading.

(2) Q^a𝔐 agree in having the major expansion, a secondary reading
symbolized by ++.

(3) In a small bit of text within that secondary reading there is a
discrepancy between Q^a and 𝔐. In six cases, either 𝔐 or Q^a has the more
preferable word or form, and the other has the "tertiary" reading,
symbolized by +, 2v, or X. In two cases, the discrepancy is a synonymous
variant, symbolized by ≅.

(1) Q^a Is Preferable

In three cases Q^a appears to preserve the more preferable reading,
while 𝔐 has the "tertiary" reading.

(a) 𝔐 ++ +

18:25𝔐א   לבדי[ל אוכל]לא ל[ ] לבדי אנכי אוכל לא 𝔐 Q^a ≠ 𝔐 ≠ 𝔐𝔊

This seems to be a routine case of expansion for greater emphasis. In
the source of this expansion, Deut 1:9, 𝔐𝔐𝔊 all agree in the shorter
reading. This expansion, then, must have been "tertiary" in two senses. It
was made by a scribe copying at a later stage than that represented by Q^a,
and by a scribe working on Exodus alone, with no more concern that his text
match that in Deuteronomy. This is one moderate expansion that seems not
to have occurred to scribes in Deuteronomy.   The point here is that Q^a
represents an earlier stage than 𝔐, at least in this one reading.

א9:5^b   **Q**ᵃ   יהוה הדבר הזה   יה[וה

Ш   יהוה את הדבר הזה   **Qᵃ ⊀ Ш ⊀ 𝔪𝔊**

As small as this expansion is, it may be a second indication of the
priority of **Qᵃ** in relationship to **Ш**. Note that in 9:5ᵃ, from which this
sentence of the major expansion was taken, **Ш** has the את, while **𝔪** lacks it
(☐**Qᵃ**). As noted above, except for deliberate changes, **Ш** has exactly the
same text in the command and in the execution in each of the expansions in
the plague narratives -- even in details as small as this. And there is one
variant that suggests that the same was true of **Qᵃ** (see below regarding
7:18^bב). Thus it seems that a series of scribes within the **Qᵃ Ш** tradition
made a habit of maintaining exact agreement between source and expansion
in the particular scroll they were working on at the moment, regardless of
what another scroll might have.

Taking all of these factors into consideration, as well as the fact
that there is a general pattern for **Ш** to have את where **𝔪** lacks it (see
below, Chapter V.B.4), it seems fair to conclude that in this minor reading
Qᵃ is prior to **Ш**, and also that **Qᵃ** lacked the את in 9:5ᵃ in agreement with
𝔪, as well as in 9:5^b.[18]

(b) **Ш** ++ 2V

א7:18^b   **Qᵃ** [ויאמר אליו

Ш   וילך משה ואהרן אל פרעה ויאמרו אליו

As noted above (V.A.3.a.(1)), the regular pattern for the major
expansions within the plague narrative is that whereas the command was
given to Moses alone, Aaron was added in for the execution. The first verb,
referring to their "going to Pharaoh," was left in the singular, but the second
verb, referring to their "speaking," was put in the plural.

Unfortunately the scroll is not extant in this or any of the other
expansions to show whether or not it included Aaron's name. We must leave
open three possibilities, then. In the first stage of the expansion, reflected
in **Qᵃ**, the fulfilment may still have been assigned to Moses alone; Aaron
may have been added and the verb changed in a later stage. Alternatively, in
the first stage Aaron's name may have been inserted, but the verb left

---

[18]The reading of the Cairo MS would also be secondary; see *BHS* 𝔪:
Cairo **T**ᴶ + את.

unchanged. The third possibility, of course, is that this is simply an error in
𝐐ᵐ, and that its *Vorlage* had the plural.

For the sake of this classification, the plural in 𝕸 is taken as the
further stage and that of 𝐐ᵐ as the earlier. This is not purely arbitrary, but
is based on two factors: relatively few errors have been found in 𝐐ᵐ; and
there are a few indications that 𝕸 may reflect a later stage than the scroll.

(2) 𝕸 Is Preferable

Besides the three variants where 𝐐ᵐ seems to have the preferable
reading, there are three others were 𝕸 retains the preferable reading.

(a) 𝐐ᵐ ++ 2ν

7:18ᵇ בת[וך היאר] ‏] ביאר 𝕸   𝐐ᵐ ≠ 𝕸 ≠ 𝔐𝐆

This reading has been discussed in Chapter II.B.2 with its counterpart
in the source of the major expansion:

7:18   היאר[בת]וך ‏] ביאר 𝕸𝔐; εν τω ποταμω 𝐆   𝐐ᵐ ≠ 𝕸𝔐(𝐆?)

The point to be noted here is that 𝐐ᵐ retains the same reading in both
the source and the expansion. Again, whatever the precise relationship
between 𝐐ᵐ and 𝕸, both texts reflect the care of scribes to ensure that the
words of the execution exactly repeated those of the command.

(b) 𝐐ᵐ ++ X

18:25‏בᵐ כוכב [הש]מים ‏] ככוכבי השמים 𝕸   𝐐ᵐ ≠ 𝕸 ≠ 𝔐𝐆

This singular form appears to be an error on the part of 𝐐ᵐ. In Deut
1:10, the source of this expansion, 𝕸𝔐 agree in the reading ככוכבי.

9:19ᵇ א[ל]יך[‏] כל אשר לך 𝕸   𝐐ᵐ ≠ 𝕸 ≠ 𝔐𝐆

Though too little of the leather is preserved to be sure, this appears
to be another error on the part of 𝐐ᵐ. In 9:19ᵃ, the source of this expansion,
𝕸𝔐 agree in the reading כל אשר לך (οσα σοι εστιν 𝐆). It is impossible
to know whether 𝐐ᵐ read כל אשר אליך or כל אליך, i.e., whether it merely
erred in the preposition or, alternatively, lost two letters and ran two
words together.

(3) Q͏ᵇ ≅ ɰ

There are two synonymous variants within these major expansions.

20:19ᵃא   חי [ ] אלהים חיים ɰ   Q͏ᵇ ≅ ɰ ≠ 𝕸𝕲

There is a slight possibility that **Q͏ᵇ** also had the plural adjective. This word appears at the end of a line where the margin is visible. Yet there are a very few instances elsewhere in the scroll where a word seems to have been divided between lines. On the other hand, Skehan noted: "Space requirements within line 27 make it implausible that the ‎-ים were carried over to that line."

This expansion is taken from Deut 5:26[23ɰ], where both ɰ𝕸 have the plural adjective. But there are several parallels to the singular usage with אלהים: see *BHS*ᵖ (ק' חי א' ‎ק) at Deut 5:26 and cf. 𝕸 in Isa 37:4,17 // 2 Kgs 19:4,16.[19] Was the use of the singular to modify אלהים an earlier usage, so that the reading in **Q͏ᵇ** should be considered preferable? Were "corrections" made by later scribes, independently, in both Exodus and Deuteronomy in ɰ and in Deuteronomy in 𝕸? Or, alternatively, were there two equally acceptable usages? Did the first scribe perhaps copy the plural from Deuteronomy, which was retained in ɰ, and a later scribe wrote the singular, which was retained in **Q͏ᵇ**?

In either case, note that the reading here in **Q͏ᵇ** agrees with a reading in at least one Qumran MS of Deuteronomy; and that the reading here in ɰ agrees with that in ɰ -- and 𝕸 -- of Deuteronomy.

9:19ᵇא   למיום] למן היום ɰ   Q͏ᵇ ≅ ɰ ≠ 𝕸𝕲

Both forms are found in 𝕸; למן היום, e.g., in 2 Sam 7:11; 19:25; Jer 7:25; 32:31; and למיום in Jud 19:30; 2 Sam 7:6; and Isa 7:17. In Deut 4:32 and 9:7 both ɰ and 𝕸 agree in למן היום. Thus there seems to be no possibility of establishing which is the preferable reading in the source of this expansion, 9:18, where ɰ has למיום and 𝕸 has למן היום. **Q͏ᵇ** is not extant there; note that here within the expansion it agrees with what 𝕸 has in the source; and that ɰ has the same reading in both places.

Summary: Thus within the major expansions shared by **Q͏ᵇ** and ɰ, those typological readings which put them in the same "text-type," there are

---

[19]I owe the references to Isaiah and 2 Kings to Skehan's notes.

eight minor variations between the two. In three **Qᵐ** seems preferable, in three **𝔐** seems preferable, and two are synonymous variants.

There are at least three issues here. First is the matter of the relationship between the "source" of the expansion, i.e., that text that is in **𝔐G** as well, and the expansion itself. In six of these eight variants the reading of **𝔐** in the expansion agrees with that of **𝔐** in the source; in the other two, the addition (אנכי) or change (ויאמרו) was deliberate. In only one case is **Qᵐ** extant in both places (7:18 and 7:18[b]: בתוך :בתוך). Since it has the same slightly altered preposition in both, it seems fair to infer that more than one scribe was making a conscious effort to maintain strict agreement within each scroll, if not between scrolls. (This would presumably not apply to errors, such as two of the above readings seem to be; there is no indication that the time had yet come when scribes carefully preserved and copied errors -- rather, the reverse seems to be true, that even correct readings could be altered in small ways.)

The second issue is the relationship between the two witnesses. Since there are three variants in which **Qᵐ** appears to be preferable and three in which **𝔐** appears to be preferable, they may seem to cancel each other out. Yet on the other hand there is a qualititative difference in these variants. Two of the three where **𝔐** seems to be preferable involve what appear to be errors in **Qᵐ**; only one (בתוך) seems to reflect a further development in **Qᵐ**. All three of those where **Qᵐ** seems to be preferable, on the other hand, reflect further development on the part of **𝔐**: two are expansions and one is probably a syntactical adjustment to the addition of Aaron's name. Presumably if we were comparing two witnesses that were truly comparable -- i.e., if both were eclectic texts as **𝔐** is, reflecting an editor's choice among twenty or more MSS -- then there would be no actual errors in either witness, and the proportion would be 3:1; whereas **Qᵐ** reflects further development in one reading, **𝔐** reflects further development in three.

A third issue is the relationship of **Qᵐ** and **𝔐**. In the following chart the reading given for **Qᵐ** is that within the major expansion, since except for the one case **Qᵐ** is only extant there. The reading given for **𝔐𝔐**, however, is that within the source of the expansion, whether that is in the same chapter within Exodus, or in Deuteronomy. Note that in all eight cases **Qᵐ** disagrees with **𝔐** within the expansion. The issue in this chart is a comparison with what **𝔐** has in the source.

𝐐ᵃ in Expansion	(𝔪)𝔐 in Source	Type of Variant in Expansion

• 𝐐ᵃ ≠ 𝔪𝔐

18:25ᵇˢᵖ	ככוכב 𝐐ᵃ	ככוכבי 𝔪𝔐 (Deut)	𝐐ᵃ X
9:19ᵇ	אל]יך 𝐐ᵃ	לך 𝔪𝔐 (Exod)	𝐐ᵃ X
7:18ᵇ	בתוך 𝐐ᵃ(also 7:18)	-ב 𝔪𝔐 (Exod)	𝐐ᵃ 2v
20:19ᵃᵃ	חי 𝐐ᵃ	חיים 𝔪𝔐 (Deut)	𝐐ᵃ ≅ 𝔪𝔐

• 𝐐ᵃ - 𝔪𝔐

| 18:25ᵃˢᵖ | אנכי › 𝐐ᵃ | אנכי › 𝔪𝔐 (Deut) | 𝔪 + |
| 7:18ᵇᵃ | singular 𝐐ᵃ | singular 𝔪𝔐 (Exod) | 𝔪 2v |

• 𝐐ᵃ - 𝔐 ≠ 𝔪

| 9:19ᵃᵃ | למן היום 𝐐ᵃ | למן היום 𝔐 (Exod) | 𝐐ᵃ ≅ 𝔪 |
| 9:5ᵇᵃ | את › 𝐐ᵃ | את › 𝔐 (Exod) | 𝔪 + |

As the chart shows, of the eight variants, two are errors in 𝐐ᵃ. We will discount them henceforth; presumably they indicate momentary lapses on the part of one scribe and do not indicate much about the stage that 𝐐ᵃ represents within the tradition. Of the six remaining, then, 𝐐ᵃ presents two readings (בתוך and חי) that agree neither with 𝔪 nor with 𝔐, though they appear to be perfectly acceptable alternatives (one has been judged secondary, one synonymous). Twice 𝐐ᵃ agrees with 𝔐 and 𝔪 in the source, and it is 𝔪 of the expansion that is "tertiary." One of these represents an expansion for the sake of emphasis (אנכי); the other seems to reflect syntactical tidying following the addition of Aaron's name. Finally, in two cases 𝐐ᵃ agrees with 𝔐 against 𝔪, once where 𝔪 has a synonymous variant and once where 𝔪 has made a minor expansion (את).

To summarize the relationship between 𝐐ᵃ and 𝔐:

𝐐ᵃ ≠ 𝔐	3 times	(2 errors, 1 secondary)
𝐐ᵃ ≅ 𝔐	1 time	
𝐐ᵃ - 𝔐	4 times	

To put it another way, while 𝐐ᵃ is typologically different from 𝔐, sharing those typological traits with 𝔪, when it is a matter of a small disagreement with ɰ within a major -- typological -- expansion, half of the time **Q** is unique and half of the time it agrees with 𝔪.

4. ERRORS AND CORRECTIONS IN Q

Six errors have been preserved in **Q**. The first three were listed in Chapter II.B.4, since **Q** alone has the secondary reading, while ɰ𝔪𝔊 have the preferable reading. The next two were discussed in Chapter V.A.3.b, since they occur in major **Q**ɰ expansions which are already secondary. Thus the errors in **Q** are "tertiary." The sixth has not yet been mentioned. It occurs within an entire pericope which is a synonymous variant. Thus while **Q** is clearly in error in this specific word, this reading cannot be counted in statistics for preferable readings.

Only the first three errors show in the chart in Appendix 4, since only those three are clearly secondary. The other three are included in the "4" in parentheses in the "tertiary" column, because they are not counted among the 85 readings where preferability can be established.

28:11א	תפתח] יפתח ɰ𝔪𝔊	(IIB4)	**Q** ≠ ɰ𝔪𝔊
28:41	והלבשת אתם] ו[הלבשתם אתם ɰ𝔪𝔊	(IIB4)	**Q** ≠ ɰ𝔪𝔊
31:4	לעשות בזהב] לעשוב[נהב ɰ𝔪𝔊	(IIB4)	**Q** ≠ ɰ𝔪𝔊
18:25שɰ	ככוכב [הש]מים] ככוכבי השמים ɰ	(VA3b)	**Q** ≠ ɰ ≠ 𝔪𝔊
9:19בɰᵇ	כל אשר לך] [א]ל[ל]יך ɰ	(VA3b)	**Q** ≠ ɰ ≠ 𝔪𝔊
37:13 [38:10𝔊]	על ארבע] לארבע ɰ𝔪𝔊‖; aliter 𝔊		**Q** ≠ ɰ𝔪 ≠ 𝔊

In the first three readings ɰ𝔪𝔊 all disagree with **Q**, the next two occur in major expansions where ɰ is already secondary, and the last occurs within a long synonymous variant.

All six of these are small and easily identifiable errors, each affecting just one word, and one also ignoring a word division. It is especially easy to understand how the scribe made five of the errors, since they are acceptable words in themselves, though not in the context. Several betray the influence of the context on the scribe's fingers. In 28:41 אותם was coming just after והלבשת, and 37:13 has the word "four" twice in very close succession, but with different prepositions: על ארבע...לארבע. Furthermore, four of the six errors occur in the account of the tabernacle, which must have been rather tedious for scribes to copy. Only two occur in narrative passages. Curiously, both of these are within major expansions!

The fact that only six errors are included in this rather well-preserved scroll, consisting of 44 columns, suggests that our scribe was very careful, both in writing and in proofreading.

It is no longer possible to be sure whether these errors were corrected or not, since few margins of the scroll are preserved. Yet one may doubt that these errors which are extant were ever corrected, because we do have two cases of corrections that have been preserved: they are not in the margin, but rather immediately above the line.

Interestingly, both of the corrections which have been preserved are in the same column, and just three lines apart from each other, as if the scribe were having a bad morning. They are on lines 30 and 33 at the bottom of a column; perhaps he was hurrying to finish the column before he would pause from his labors. In the first case he omitted two words, ואת עמו, perhaps because the following word also began with a *waw,* and in the second he omitted one word, יהוה. He inserted the words himself in the space above the line as close as possible to where they belonged (see 17:13ב in Chapter II.C.2.c, where the first case is transcribed). Since the handwriting is the same, either the scribe noticed his own mistake or it was pointed out to him so that he could correct it himself.

We have no case preserved where a letter or word written in error was corrected, so we cannot be sure how such a correction would have been made. But this evidence does make it less likely that the six mistakes that have been preserved were ever corrected.

Besides those six actual errors the four synonymous variants unique to **Qᵐ** which may involve parablepsis should be mentioned once more in this context. The only two corrections that have been preserved were needed because of omission. Should we infer from this that the scribe was prone to parablepsis, and that therefore these four cases should be considered secondary? Or should we, on the other hand, infer that the scribe -- or his supervisor -- was quite scrupulous in his proofreading and that since no correction is visible in the case of these four that his *Vorlage* also had this shorter text? If the latter, would that be an argument in favor of the shorter readings, which lack text that may be imported from other books of the Bible, or merely a criticism of his *Vorlage?*

5. CONCLUSIONS AND SUGGESTIONS

Drawing on the descriptions of the scroll in Chapter I.B and in this section, what can we say about $\mathbf{Q^m}$?

The two dates suggested by palaeographers for the date of this scroll are ca. 225-175 B.C.E. and ca. 100-25 B.C.E. The earlier date would mean that it was copied elsewhere and then brought at a later time to Qumran, according to the standard dating of the origin of the Qumran community around 150-140 B.C.E. In this case we would have no way of knowing where the scroll was copied, but it would seem natural to suppose that someone who visited or joined the Qumran community brought with him a text that was for some reason of importance to him.

Perhaps it originated in northern Palestine, perhaps even in Shechem or its environs. Perhaps it represents a textual tradition that was at home in only a small part of Palestine or by only one geographical or religious community, such as, for example, the community that worshiped on Mount Gerizim. But there is no overriding reason to prefer that area, because $\mathbf{Q^m}$ does not share with the Samaritan Pentateuch that one clearly "Samaritan" characteristic, the expansion regarding the altar on Mount Gerizim. Regardless of its origin, it was, nevertheless, accepted at Qumran at least to the extent of being preserved in that community until, presumably, 68 C.E.

Acceptance of the later date would bring us into even more uncertainty. For then the scroll could have been copied either at Qumran or anywhere else. (There is some likelihood that it was copied at Qumran, judging from the fact that the leather was prepared and the lines and margins were ruled just as other scrolls at Qumran were.) Again it would seem natural to suppose either that its *Vorlage* was in Qumran and was treasured by at least some of that community, so that it was deemed desirable to copy it; or that someone who visited or joined the community brought it with him because it was precious to him for some reason.

According to preliminary reports, fourteen other scrolls of Exodus were found at Qumran, and none of them belong to the $\mathbf{Q^m}$ tradition. Yet that would not necessarily mean that it was the only such scroll that the community owned and treasured, because the remains of their library are so fragmentary and so random. Much has been made of the fact that, for instance, no copy of the book of Esther has been found in the caves, and this may indeed be significant, due to the unusual characteristics of that book. Yet it has also been said that only one fragment from all of Chronicles has been found -- a much longer work, and therefore much more likely still to be represented by fragments. Our knowledge is too incomplete to draw any conclusions as to the place that **Q²** held in the community. It may have been the only one of its kind, or there may have been several others.

On the other hand, there are two other facts that need to be taken into consideration. The first is that a scroll of Numbers has been found at Qumran which, it is claimed, is also similar to the Samaritan Pentateuch in that it contains two interpolations from Deuteronomy.[20] This is evidence that the same sort of expansion which we find in **Q² Ш** in Exodus also characterized other scrolls of other Pentateuchal books. Since both were found at Qumran, that is even more evidence that that community did not find such expansionism distasteful.

Another factor that comes into play here is the patch in col. viii of **Q²**. It appears that the bottom left part of col. viii was somehow damaged and that after it was repaired by sewing a round patch over the damaged part, a second scribe rewrote the words which had been destroyed. The handwriting is quite different, although the script is still the Palaeo-Hebrew, and even the orthography is distinct (this is especially clear in the spelling of Aaron's name, which is spelled in every other instance with a *waw*, whereas only on this patch is the *waw* lacking).

Now col. viii contains part of the plague narrative, which is precisely where the most sustained expansion occurs. It might be fair to suggest that the plague narrative as it appeared in **Q²** was treasured by all or part of the Qumran community, so that they used this part of the scroll to such an extent that it became damaged; and further, that when it was damaged it was still of enough significance to them that they took the trouble to have it patched, by someone other than the original scribe. (Had he long since died?)

What were they using this scroll for? As suggested above, it may be that they used it in their celebrations of the Exodus story, because the series of major expansions made it especially good for dramatic readings, perhaps by different individuals or parts of the congregation. Perhaps one read the threats of Yahweh against Pharaoh as they were spoken to Moses, and another read those same words as they appeared in the expansions as Moses spoke them directly to Pharaoh, as they commemorated the battle between Pharaoh and Yahweh.

---

[20]Cross, *Library*, p. 186 and nn. 35-36.

If there is any merit in the suggestion that the Qumran community liked to use this expanded version of the plague narratives in their liturgical celebrations, it may also be that they shared this preference with the community centered at Mount Gerizim. In any case, they definitely had at least one or two copies of Scripture which shared the most outstanding characteristics of the Scripture that the Gerizim community at some point chose as their own.

As far as we know, Qumran and Gerizim were only two of many communities who treasured expansionist texts like **Q⁴**.   But there is always the possibility that they were the only two who did so. If that were the case, can any reason be suggested for their sharing a respect for this sort of text? If there is any truth in the frequent claim that the Jerusalem Temple was a center for the kind of copying and perhaps even text-critical work which preserved "proto-Massoretic" texts and perhaps even attempted to make them normative in broader circles, then we might expect the most expansionist texts to be preserved in the most anti-Jerusalem circles: Qumran and Gerizim.

B. THE CHARACTER OF 𝕸

1. PREFERABLE, SYNONYMOUS, AND SECONDARY READINGS

Of the 165 readings which have been analyzed so far, 80 have been classified as synonymous variants. Of the remaining 85 readings, 𝕸 preserves the preferable reading 35 times and the secondary reading 50 times.

Based on the total 165 readings, 𝕸 has the preferable reading in 21% of the cases, the secondary reading in 30%, and a synonymous variant in 49% of the cases.

Based on the 85 readings where preferability can be established with some degree of confidence, 𝕸 has the preferable reading in 41% and the secondary reading in 59% of the cases.

The foregoing figures relate to all of the preferable and secondary readings preserved in 𝕸, regardless of whether and which other texts share the same readings.

Of the 29 variants that 𝕸 preserves uniquely, none are preferable, 13 are secondary (45%), and 16 are synonymous (55%). Based on the 13 readings where preferability can be established with some degree of confidence, then, 𝕸 consistently has the secondary reading. This should be compared with the proportion for **Qᵐ**, which has the preferable reading in 33% and the secondary reading in 67% of its 15 unique readings where preferability has been assigned.

2. TYPES OF SECONDARY READINGS AND SYNONYMOUS VARIANTS

Of the 50 secondary readings preserved in 𝕸, 13 are unique to 𝕸:

- 5 expansions unique to 𝕸 (את bis, בם, ארץ-, מן ההר);
- 1 alteration and expansion (סביב ואל העם תאמר);
- 2 variants involving broadening application of a legal pericope;
- 1 case of explicitation (ובאילים);
- 3 uses of more familiar words (שמלת, מכוה, במשפטים);
- 1 altered verbal form (יהיה).

Presumably the three uses of more familiar words were not deliberate, though we cannot be sure; but the five expansions were probably made for the sake of clarification; and four other alterations probably reflect exegetical work on the text of varying kinds.

Thus in contrast to **Qᵐ** (see above, V.A.2), whose 10 unique secondary readings revealed no pattern, but rather the idiosyncrasies of perhaps a single scribe, 9 of those in 𝕸 do seem to suggest a somewhat later stage in the tradition, after one or more scribes had improved the text even more than had been done by the time of **Qᵐ**.

Of the 50 secondary readings preserved in 𝕸, it shares 37 with at least one other witness. The most significant of these are the 12 major expansions of the **Qᵐ𝕸** tradition, which have been discussed in V.A.3, and the 1 major expansion preserved in **Qᵐ𝕸𝕸**, which will be discussed in V.C.3.

The remaining 24 secondary readings shared with at least one other witness include 20 expansions:

- כל עשב הארץ ואת כל פרי;
- 3 second objects (את עבדיו, ולאהרן, למשה);
- 4 verbs or clauses (ויעמדו, לך, ויכם, ועשית להם);
- 1 prepositional phrase (מארעו);
- 1 adjective (הראישונים);
- 1 number (אחד);
- 1 adverb (מאוד);
- 2 designations of time (once each: היום, בבוקר);
- 3 minor words (once each: לו, בני, לאמר);

- 1 accusative suffix;
- 2 conjunctions.

There are also 4 alterations:
  - 1 verb altered to fit the syntax;
  - 1 preposition;
  - 1 prepositional phrase;
  - 1 noun suffix.[21]

Turning to the synonymous variants preserved in ⚏, we find that of the total of 80, ⚏ shares 64 with at least one other witness. These 64 break down as follows:

- ⚏ is longer in 3 involving the length of entire pericopes;
- a series of 6 indicate the existence of one pericope with two different formulations;
- 6 involve difference in order: (1 involves a paragraph of ten verses, 1 a phrase, and 4 one word each);
- 2 affect the representation of the table;
- in 5 ⚏ is shorter (משחים בשמן, 1 locative *he,* 1 definite article, and 2 conjunctions);
- in 11 ⚏ is longer (1 passage of 14 words; 3 clauses, of five, four, and two words; (ו)אולם, אשר, בניכם, 1 locative *he,* 2 definite articles, and 1 conjunction);
- 3 involve כל;
- 13 involve the difference of a word or phrase (ובזרוע נטויה, לפני, עמי, בית, חתן משה, הנה, ששת, וידבר and 5 variations in the designation for God);
- 11 involve different forms of a word (8 in verbs, 1 in a noun, and 2 in pronouns); and
- 4 involve difference in grammatical features (construct state, 3 differences in noun suffixes).

⚏ preserves 16 synonymous variants uniquely. They can be grouped as follows:[22]

- in 5 ⚏ is longer (noun suffix; 3 locative *he*'s; 1 conjunction);
- in 7 ⚏ is shorter (lacking שתי, 1 definite article, 4 conjunctions, 1 את);

---

[21]See Chapter IV for details and affiliation.

[22]The total is greater than 16 because two variants involve more than one minor difference within the word.

- in 3 𝟙𝟙𝟙 has a different word (לכן, אנכי, מדר ודר); and
- in 3 𝟙𝟙𝟙 has minor grammatical differences (noun suffix,
     preposition, accusative suffix instead of prepositional phrase).

None of these synonymous variants unique to 𝟙𝟙𝟙 is interesting. In the case of **Q**, by contrast, three of its unique synonymous variants offer the tantalizing possibility that it preserves significantly shorter readings, both in length and in importance, since the longer text of 𝟙𝟙𝟙𝔐𝔊 may have been brought into Exodus from outside the Pentateuch. With 𝟙𝟙𝟙, on the other hand, the differences are minimal and do not suggest any sort of sustained exegetical work on the text of any of the witnesses, with the possible exception of the locative *he*'s added to the points of the compass.

One negative point should be clear, however: generalizations such as that 𝟙𝟙𝟙 has changed asyndetic constructions to syndetic should not be seen as universal. Just in the passages where **Q** is extant, 𝟙𝟙𝟙 lacks four conjunctions that are in 𝔐.

These cases of secondary and synonymous variants in 𝟙𝟙𝟙 must be viewed along with its preferable readings. Though 𝟙𝟙𝟙 shares 35 preferable readings with other texts (all listed and discussed in Chapter II.A and B), it is important to emphasize once again that 𝟙𝟙𝟙 preserves no unique preferable readings in the extant parts of **Q**.

3. THE RELATIONSHIP OF 𝟙𝟙𝟙 WITH **Q**

The relationship between 𝟙𝟙𝟙 and **Q** has been discussed above, in Chapter V.A.2 and 3. To summarize the major findings: the two texts share some of their most distinctive features with each other -- and not with any other texts of Exodus that have so far been discovered. They both have 12 major expansions, and reconstruction of the scroll suggests that it had at least 4 more as well.[23]

As well as those 12 major expansions, **Q** 𝟙𝟙𝟙 also share the placement of the instructions for the altar of incense (30:1-10: see Chapter III.A.2), a synonymous variant but a distinctive one nevertheless. Those 13 variants are the most weighty for demonstrating the close textual affiliation of 𝟙𝟙𝟙 and **Q**. Beyond those 13, however, there are also 4 other expansions, varying from moderate to minor, plus something as little yet as curious as אחד אל אחד instead of איש אל אחיו, and the lack of a phrase that both 𝔐

---

[23]The unpublished 4QNum[b] apparently shares some similar features; see the discussion of Cross in *Library,* p. 186 and nn. 35-36.

and **G** have (משחים בשמן). In all, they share 18 secondary readings, 12 synonymous variants, and two very minor preferable readings.

Yet there are a number of minor differences between the two. Within the 12 major expansions there are 8 small variants, in 3 of which 𝟭𝟭𝟭 seems to reflect a slightly further stage of development than **Qᵃ**. Elsewhere in Exodus they disagree a total of 60 times; in 29 of those, **Qᵃ** agrees with 𝟙𝟙 against 𝟭𝟭𝟭. In 18 of the disagreements, 𝟭𝟭𝟭 seems clearly to be later than **Qᵃ**; **Qᵃ** seems clearly to be later in 8 and in error in 3; while in 31 the two are merely different, without the possibility of determining chronological relationship. Since 𝟭𝟭𝟭 reflects slightly further development in 18 readings, and **Qᵃ** slightly further development in 8 readings, they seem to represent two very closely related branches of the same family.

4. THE RELATIONSHIP OF 𝟭𝟭𝟭 WITH 𝟙𝟙

Some of these differences between **Qᵃ** and 𝟭𝟭𝟭 may suggest a sustained effort on the part of scribes in the 𝟭𝟭𝟭 branch to attain greater internal consistency. Because of the fragmentary nature of **Qᵃ**, it is helpful to compare 𝟭𝟭𝟭 with 𝟙𝟙, so that the comparison can have a wider base. There remains uncertainty regarding **Qᵃ**, of course, since just because **Qᵃ** agrees with 𝟙𝟙 in a certain feature in one passage does not mean that it necessarily did everywhere else. Yet given the random nature of the remains of **Qᵃ**, a comparison of 𝟭𝟭𝟭 with 𝟙𝟙 seems to be the best that can be done.

Three test comparisons of 𝟭𝟭𝟭 and 𝟙𝟙 follow. Each was occasioned by variants where **Qᵃ** is extant, suggesting a search to see whether a pattern could be found in the entire book of Exodus. The first involves word choice ("to say"); the second, the sign of the accusative; and the third, word order.

a. *Variation in Verbs for Speaking*

There are five variants involving a verb "to say":

8:16[20]	**Qᵃ**	לאמור	𝟭𝟭𝟭𝟙𝟙G	_____		
9:8א	**QᵃG**	לאמור	𝟭𝟭𝟭𝟙𝟙	_____		
32:7א	**Qᵃ𝟭𝟭𝟭G**	לאמור	𝟙𝟙	_____		
10:21א	**Qᵃ**	וידבר	𝟭𝟭𝟭𝟙𝟙	ויאמר	**G**	Ειπεν δε
7:14	**Qᵃ𝟭𝟭𝟭**	וידבר	𝟙𝟙	ויאמר	**G**	Ειπεν δε

Apart from revealing a tendency to add "saying," these also raise the question of whether there might be any pattern of variation between 𝔐 and 𝔪.

The following chart shows all the readings where 𝔐 disagrees with 𝔪 in the use of אמר and דבר.

	𝔐	Q͏	𝔪	G
5:10	וידברו..לאמר	☐	ויאמרו...לאמר	ελεγον...λεγοντες
7:8	וידבר...לאמר	☐	ויאמר...לאמר	ειπεν...λεγων
31:12	וידבר...לאמר	☐	ויאמר...לאמר	και ελαλησεν ...λεγων
36:5	וידברו...לאמר	☐	ויאמרו...לאמר	και ειπαν [ειπεν B] ...‾‾ [λεγοντες A⁺]
32:7א	וידבר...לאמר	לא[מור	‾‾ ...וידבר	και ελαλησεν ...λεγων
33:1	וידבר...לאמר	☐	‾‾ ...וידבר	και ειπεν...‾‾
30:34	וידבר...לאמר	☐	‾‾ ...ויאמר	και ειπεν...‾‾
20:22	וידבר...לאמר דבר	☐	ויאמר...כה תאמר	ειπεν δε...ερεις
7:26²⁴	ויאמר...ודברת...אמר	☐	ויאמר...ואמרת...אמר	ειπεν...και ερεις ...λεγει
9:1	ויאמר...ואמרת...אמר	☐	ויאמר...ודברת...אמר	ειπεν...και ερεις ...λεγει
7:14		וידבר וידבר	ויאמר	ειπεν δε

Is there a pattern here? All but one of these readings (7:14) have two or three verbs for "speaking" in very close succession. In every case but one (9:1) 𝔐 uses both Hebrew verbs rather than just repeating the same verb. These variations may indicate some degree of concern within the 𝔐 tradition to alternate the verbs in such cases for the sake of variety.

---

²⁴7:26 and 9:1 give Yahweh's commands to Moses which are repeated in major expansions in 𝔐. In both cases the first verb, referring to Yahweh, is omitted, while the second and third verbs are retained in slightly altered form. Thus 7:29ᵇ reads וידברו...אמר, and 9:5ᵇ reads ויאמרו...אמר. Q͏ is not extant in either place.

In three of these readings 𝔐 has only one of the verbs. If that one
verb is וידבר in 𝔐, it is also וידבר in 𝔚, which follows it with לאמר.
But if that one verb is ויאמר, it is וידבר in 𝔚, followed by לאמר.   It
seems likely that the 𝔚 tradition reflects first expansionism and then
alteration to create variety.

But in six other readings 𝔐 has two or three verbs (in the case of
לאמר, of course, this may already be the result of expansion) and is content
to repeat the same verb in close succession. Here it may be fair to assume
that some or all of the readings in 𝔚 are secondary, again revealing a desire
on the part of one or more scribes to avoid such close repetition of אמר.

Yet if this was indeed the purpose, 𝔚 was not completely consistent.
If at 7:26 it altered the second verb for variety, at 9:1 it used the same verb
three times while 𝔐, on the other hand, varied the verbs (at 9:1 two 𝔐^MSS
agree with 𝔚 in repeating אמר).

Furthermore there are at least some cases where there is no variation
between 𝔚 and 𝔐, where they both merely repeat the same verb; e.g., 7:19;
8:1,12; and 12:1.

Although unfortunately Q^m is extant in only two of these readings, it
agrees with 𝔚 both times. Yet this is not enough to shed any light on the
question of when such a trend may have begun. At 32:7a Q^m is extant only
enough to show that it did have the expansion לאמור; the earlier verb is
lost. And at 7:14 there is no following verb in either witness; thus
whatever this variant means, it has nothing to do with the trend toward
variety that we suspect elsewhere in 𝔚. And in a third variant Q^m stands
alone, against 𝔚 as well as against 𝔐, in its reading of וידבר.

𝔊 agrees more often with 𝔐, but it is perhaps worth noting that the
Greek verbs present more opportunity for variety, which makes it hard to
tell whether the Greek translator would have had concerns similar to those
in the 𝔚 tradition or not. (5:10 would suggest that he did not). In 31:12 and
32:7a 𝔊 agrees at least formally, if not causally, with 𝔚, since λαλειν
corresponds to דבר in the overwhelming number of cases.   A⁺ have been
revised in 36:5 to agree with the Hebrew in including the second verb.

b. The Sign of the Accusative

The use of the accusative sign את is a very minor feature but one
reflecting concern both for clarity of meaning and for consistency of
neighboring phrases and sentences.   In the extant parts of Q^m there are 5
variants involving את.

- In 2 𝐐ᵃ agrees with 𝔪 in lacking the sign, whereas 𝔐 has it. These seem to be clear additions (**25:29** and **28:39**; see Chapter II.A.3).
- In 1 𝐐ᵃ𝔐 lack it while 𝔪 has it (**34:13**).
- In 1 𝐐ᵃ𝔐 have it while 𝔪 lacks it (**29:22**). Both of these are classified as synonymous variants (see Chapter III.E).
- In 1 𝐐ᵃ lacks it in a major expansion while 𝔐 has it in both the expansion (**9:5ᵇ**) and the source of the expansion (**9:5ᵃ**, where 𝔪 lacks it, as 𝐐ᵃ presumably did as well [see Chapter V.A.3.b]).

To summarize: 𝐐ᵃ lacks את 4 out of 5 times; 𝔪 lacks it 4 out of 5 times; and 𝔐 has it 4 out of 5 times. With these results where 𝐐ᵃ is extant in mind, let us compare the only two complete Hebrew texts we have: 𝔐 and 𝔪.

In the entire book of Exodus 𝔐 has את 34 times (not counting within expansions) when 𝔪 lacks it, whereas 𝔪 has it only 7 times when 𝔐 lacks it. Furthermore, of these 7 where 𝔪 has את, in 2 it also has a definite article lacking in 𝔐: i.e., the two texts are not strictly comparable (27:1 and 36:35). Thus the proportion would be more accurately stated as 34 to 5.

In some of these readings, of course, the case could be made that the shorter text resulted from accidental omission, especially parablepsis. But even in those instances it should be noted that the 𝔪 tradition allowed the shorter reading, which often involves lack of symmetry between phrases and clauses, to stand.

The conclusion from this pattern, taken with all the other differences that are visible where 𝐐ᵃ is extant, might be that each of the three texts represents a different stage in the history of the development of the text:

𝐐ᵃ -- because it is just one scroll that was copied at one time -- froze during a time of relative freedom for scribes, but before any scribe concerned about את happened to make any concerted effort to create consistency in that particular MS.

𝔪 became the authoritative tradition of a religious group that determined not to allow further changes in the text of their Scripture before such consistency was attained in that particular tradition.

𝔐 became the authoritative tradition of a religious group that determined not to allow further changes in the text of their

Scripture <u>after</u> a greater measure of consistency had already
been attained in that particular tradition.[25]

c. Differences in Word Order

Since two variations in word order were found where **Q^a** is extant,
and since **Q^a** agrees with 𝖆 against 𝖒 in both of them -- one involving the
pericope giving instructions for the incense altar and one involving merely
two words -- the question arose about word order in the rest of the book of
Exodus. There follows a list of all differences in word order. In each case
the reading of 𝖆 precedes that of 𝖒.

3:2   וירא אליו מלאך יהוה   בלהבת אש
                        וירא   מלאך יהוה אליו בלבת אש

5:3   נלכה נא המדברה דרך שלשת ימים   ונגבחה ליהוה
             נלכה נא   דרך שלשת ימים במדבר ונגבחה ליהוה

9:34   וירא פרעה כי חדל הברד והמטר   והקולות
                 וירא פרעה כי חדל   המטר והברד והקלת

11:5   אשר אחר הרחים ועד בכור כל   בהמה
                 אשר אחר הרחים   וכל בכור בהמה

19:18   מפני אשר ירד יהוה עליו   באש
                        מפני אשר ירד   עליו יהוה באש

20:18   וכל העם <u>שמע</u> את הקולות ואת קול השופר <u>וראים</u> את הלפדים
         וכל העם <u>ראים</u> את הקלת ואת הלפידם   ואת קול השפר

20:19ª   ++ <u>יאמר יהוה אלהינו</u> ואתה תדבר   אלינו
                 דבר אתה עמנו

---

[25]I am indebted indirectly to James Barr and Patrick W. Skehan for
this line of thinking. In 1955 Skehan pointed out how faithfully the
Samaritan community has transmitted 𝖆 ("Exodus," p. 183), and in 1985
Barr suggested in a seminar in connection with the chronologies in Genesis
that a decisive point in the process of canonization -- the point when no
more changes were to be allowed -- may have arrived in various
communities too soon for certain improvements to be made in their text.

23:12

למען ינוח עבדך ואמתך כמוך   וכל בהמתך   והגר
למען ינוח   שורך וחמרך   וינפש בן אמתך והגר

23:23 והחוי והיבוסי   אל הכנעני והאמרי והחתי והגרגשי והפרזי
אל   האמרי והחתי   והפרזי והכנעני   החוי והיבוסי

23:28

הכנעני ואת האמרי ואת החתי ואת הגרגשי ואת הפרזי ואת החוי
ואת היבוסי
את החוי   את הכנעני ואת החתי

24:7   כל אשר דבר יהוה נשמע ונעשה
כל אשר דבר יהוה   נעשה ונשמע

25:29   ועשית את קערתיו וכפתיו ומנקיתיו וקשתיו
ועשית   קערתיו וכפתיו   וקשותיו ומנקיתיו

26:8   ארך היריעה האחת שלשים באמה   וארבע אמות רחב
ארך היריעה האחת שלשים באמה ורחב   ארבע באמה

26:10   ועשית ללאות חמשים   על שפת היויעה
ועשית   חמשים ללאת על שפת היריעה

30:1-10   10 verses regarding incense altar placed in chapter 26
10 verses regarding incense altar placed in chapter 30

29:18   עלה הוא ליהוה ריח ניחח אשה הוא ליהוה
עלה הוא ליהוה ריח ניחוח אשה   ליהוה הוא

[28]... תרומתם ליהוה [21]ולקחת משמן המשחה ומן הדם אשר על המזבח 29:21
והזית על אהרן ועל בגדיו ועל בניו ועל בגדי בניו אתו
וקדשתו ואת בגדיו ואת בניו ואת בגדי בניו אתו [29]ובגדי הקדש אשר ...

[20]...על המזבח סביב [21]ולקחת מן הדם אשר על המזבח ומשמן המשחה
והזית על אהרן ועל בגדיו ועל בניו ועל בגדי בניו אתו
וקדש הוא ובגדיו ובניו ובגדי בניו אתו [22] ולקחת מן האיל החלב ...

within 29:21

ומן הדם אשר על המזבח והזית			ולקחת משמן המשחה
והזית			ומשמן המשחה			מן הדם אשר על המזבח			ולקחת

30:19

את ידיהם			ורחץ ממנו אהרן ובניו
ורחצו			אהרן ובניו ממנו את ידיהם

34:11			והחתי והגרגשי והפרזי והחוי והיבוסי			את הכנעני והאמרי
והפרזי והחוי והיבוסי			האמרי והכנעני והחתי			את

35:29			לבם להביא			וכל איש ואשה אשר נדב אתם
להביא			לבם אתם			כל איש ואשה אשר נדב

36:1			לדעת			אשר נתן יהוה בהם חכמה ותבונה
חכמה ותבונה בהמה לדעת			אשר נתן יהוה

40:38

ענן יהוה על המשכן יומם ואש תהיה בו לילה			לעיני כל בית ישראל
ענן יהוה על המשכן יומם ואש תהיה			לילה בו לעיני כל בית ישראל

There are a total of 23 differences between 𝔐 and 𝔪 involving order of text. One affects a paragraph (30:1-10), one a verse (29:21), but the other 21 are comparatively insignificant. Some of them involve other minor differences as well (e.g., 11:5). Some reflect exegetical work in smoothing the text for the sake of the meaning (e.g., 20:18, on the part of 𝔐). One is related to a major expansion and may have arisen during the process of importing a major block of text from Deuteronomy (20:19ᵇ). In the case of some it seems quite obvious that a scribal lapse is behind the difference (e.g., 29:21, where two successive verses begin with the same words). Three are the list of seven nations and have already been discussed above (23:23; 23:28; 34:11; see **34:11ב**, Chapter II.A.6).

The question here is not that of preferability, but merely an overview of the degree of difference between these two witnesses to the text of Exodus, 𝔐 and 𝔪. On the whole this appears to be a very short and quite insignificant list of differences in word order. Given a total of forty chapters in Exodus, there is about one difference every two chapters. The sole case of a major difference almost surely reflects the fact that the original text of Exodus completely lacked an incense altar (see Chapter

III.A.1). The one moderate difference, 29:21, is easily explainable as parablepsis later corrected. Scarcely any of the others give evidence of anything other than scribal lapses. Once again we see how close these two traditions are.

5. "SECTARIAN" READINGS

As we have seen,[26] within the book of Exodus there are only two features in 𝔐 which could be called "sectarian." The first is the major expansion, Exod 20:17[b], the new tenth commandment imported from Deut 11:29; 27:2b-7; and 11:30, instructing the Israelites to build an altar on Mount Gerizim.[27] The second is in 20:24, where 𝔐 reads "in the place where I have caused my name to be remembered," as opposed to "in every place where I will cause my name to be remembered," as in 𝔐.

There is no way to know which verbal form 𝐐 had in 20:24. But according to Skehan's reconstruction of this column, there was no room for the major expansion, 20:17[b]. It is on the basis of this reconstruction that the scroll has been classified as "proto-Samaritan" rather than simply as "Samaritan."

The fact that 𝐐 agrees with 𝔐 in all of its major features except for the "sectarian" expansion sheds significant light on the nature of the Samaritan community and of its relation to other Israelites during the last two centuries B.C.E. As has been pointed out by others,[28] if Scriptural texts like theirs were being used elsewhere in Palestine in these centuries, then it is no longer possible to view the Samaritans as a group characterized solely by hostility and isolationism. Rather -- as the development of their beliefs and practices also demonstrates -- regardless of any tensions that may have existed between them and other Israelites, they shared much in common with them.

Furthermore, even if a final break did come about 100 B.C.E., as Purvis and others suggest but which is not proven, that break revealed itself in their Scripture to a very restricted degree. A few verbal forms may have been changed (though we have no contemporary documentation to prove that

---

[26]See Chapter I.B. and D.

[27]𝔐 has "Mount Gerizim" in Exod 20:17[b] and Deut 27:4, whereas 𝔐 has "Mount Ebal" in Deut 27:4. The reading in 𝔐 is probably secondary; see Chapter I.D.

[28]E.g., Purvis and Coggins; see above, Chapter I.D.

the "Samaritan" verbal forms are "sectarian") and a tenth commandment was "created."

But even that "creation" was far from being *ex nihilo.* Every word came from Deuteronomy. The only new aspect was the new position of prominence for this commandment. Investigation of the methods and motives of the scribe or scribes who had already expanded the plague narratives[29] and the narratives of Jethro, the golden calf, and the Sinai theophany[30] enables comparison with the methods and motives of the scribe who made the "sectarian" expansion.

The method was the same. The scribe copied word for word from Deuteronomy, combining two Deuteronomic passages into one and inserting the whole in the narrative of the theophany at Sinai as it is told in Exodus.[31] Another scribe had already combined passages from Deuteronomy 5 and 18 and inserted them after Exod 20:18 and 20:21. This Samaritan scribe combined passages from Deuteronomy 11 and 27 and inserted them after Exod 20:17.

Whereas the effect of the earlier interpolation was the aggrandizement of Moses and the prophet to come, the effect of this interpolation was the aggrandizement of Mount Gerizim. From the viewpoint of the narrative involved, both interpolations were intrusive in the theophany, in the sense that neither Exodus nor Deuteronomy claimed that Yahweh had promised the prophet to come nor commanded the altar on Gerizim during the theophany at Sinai. Both words of Yahweh came from a very different context in Deuteronomy.

Even from the viewpoint of quantity and placement, this scribe was following in the footsteps of his predecessors, for he was inserting a fairly large passage from Deuteronomy in the same context where even larger ones had already been inserted, just a few verses later. Almost all of the major expansions occur in Exodus 7 − 11, 18, 20, and 32, and the longest from Deuteronomy are in chapter 20. The Samaritan scribe merely followed suit.

Furthermore, even the content of the expansion was quite appropriate to the context in Exodus, since the interpolation commanded the building of an altar, while just a few verses later, in Exod 20:24-25, there was already a commandment to build an altar. Thus already following very closely on the

---

[29]See above, V.A.3.a.

[30]See above, V.A.3.a, and Tigay, "Hypothesis."

[31]See Tigay, "Hypothesis," pp. 340-341, for details.

heels of the ten commandments was a commandment to build an altar (made of earth in verse 24; of stones in verse 25).

From every point of view, then, the scribe has done nothing that differed in principle from what his predecessors had done.

Regarding the scribe's motive, it may be only from our perspective today that we understand the expansion about Gerizim to be so much more tendentious than that about Moses and the prophet to come. To borrow a notion from Talmon,[32] perhaps we have been misled by the vicissitudes of history to interpret one expansion as more significant than another. We understand the expansion about Gerizim in light of the Samaritan community, which preserved not only its own identity defined by devotion to Gerizim, but also its peculiar Scripture containing that expansion. What if some other group had preserved its own peculiar identity throughout the centuries as a community defined by devotion to a succession of prophets, as well as its peculiar Scripture containing the expansion about the prophet like Moses? Would we then see them both as tendentious, or "sectarian"?

C. THE CHARACTER OF 𝔐

1. PREFERABLE, SYNONYMOUS, AND SECONDARY READINGS

Of the 165 readings which affect 𝔐,[33] 80 have been classified as synonymous variants. Of the remaining 85 readings, 𝔐 preserves the preferable reading 66 times and the secondary reading 19 times.

Based on the total 165 readings, 𝔐 has the preferable reading in 40% of the cases, the secondary reading in 11.5%, and a synonymous variant in 48.5% of the cases.

Based on the 85 readings where preferability has been assigned, 𝔐 has the preferable reading in 78% and the secondary reading in 22% of the variants, in contrast to $\mathfrak{Q}^{m}$, with 50% preferable, and 𝔪, with 41% preferable.

The foregoing figures relate to all of the preferable and secondary readings preserved in 𝔐, regardless of whether and which other texts share the same readings.

---

[32]See above, Chapter I.C, and Talmon, "Text," pp. 193-199; and "Study," pp. 323-326.

[33]I.e., discounting the "tertiary" readings in $\mathfrak{Q}^{m}$ and 𝔪.

Of the 33 variants that 𝔐 preserves uniquely, 10 are preferable (30%), 7 are secondary (21%), and 16 are synonymous (49%). Based on the 17 unique readings where preferability has been assigned, 𝔐 has the preferable reading 59% of the time, and the secondary reading 41% of the time, in contrast to **Q**ᵐ, with 33%, and 𝔪, with 0% of preferable unique readings.

2. TYPES OF SECONDARY READINGS AND SYNONYMOUS VARIANTS

Of the 19 secondary readings preserved in 𝔐, 7 are unique to 𝔐:

- 𝔐 has 3 unique cases of parablepsis:
  it has lost eight words of a law, one word in the list of seven nations, and one pronoun.
- 𝔐 has only 1 case of expansion: ונשמעה; and
- 𝔐 has 3 actual errors (like **Q**ᵐ but unlike 𝔪𝕲, because it is a diplomatic text), each affecting only one letter.

Thus of the readings which are clearly secondary and are unique to 𝔐, there is no pattern recognizable at all, unless it be precisely the absence of intentional alteration or exegetical expansion.

Of the 19 secondary readings preserved in 𝔐, it shares 12 with at least one other witness. The most significant of these is the one major expansion preserved in **Q**ᵐ𝔪𝔐, which will be discussed in V.C.3.

The remaining 11 secondary readings shared with at least one other witness include:

- 10 expansions:
  a second object (את עבדיו ,למשה);
  a verb or clause (לך ,ועשית להם ,ויעמדו);
  a prepositional phrase (מארעו);
  an adjective (הראשנים);
  a designation of time (once each: היום , בבקר); and
  a minor word (לו).
- 1 alteration: a noun suffix.[34]

Turning to the synonymous variants preserved in 𝔐, we find that of the total of 80, 𝔐 shares 64 with at least one other witness:

- 𝔐 is longer in 3 involving the length of entire pericopes;
- a series of 6 indicate the existence of one pericope with two different formulations;
- 5 involve difference in order (1 involves a paragraph of ten verses,

---

[34]See Chapter IV.A–C for details and affiliation.

1 a phrase, and 3 involve one word each);

- 2 affect the representation of the table;
- in 7 𝕸 is shorter (3 locative *he*'s, 2 definite articles,
  and 2 conjunctions);
- in 14 𝕸 is longer (1 passage of 14 words; 3 clauses, 1 of five,
  1 of four, and 1 of two words; שתי, בניכם, משחים בשמן,
  (ו)אולם), 1 locative *he*, 2 definite articles,
  and 3 conjunctions);
- 3 involve כל;
- 11 involve the difference of one word (חתן משה, לא כן, שבעת,
  בית, עמי, אל, and 5 variations in the designation for God);
- 8 involve different forms of a word (6 in verbs, 1 in a noun,
  and 1 in a pronoun);   and
- 5 involve difference in grammatical features (preposition instead
  of verbal suffix, 3 differences in noun suffixes, and
  (וויהם instead of וי).

The 16 synonymous variants that 𝕸 preserves uniquely include:

- 4 where it is shorter (אשר; את; 2 conjunctions);
- 2 where it is longer (locative *he;* את);
- 1 involving the order of one word;
- 5 involving different words (אל; ויאמר; אני; וביד חזקה;
  מדר דר);   and
- 6 involving different forms of words (2 verbal forms;
  1 absolute state; 2 prepositions; and 1 noun suffix).[35]

None of these synonymous variants unique to 𝕸 is of any particular interest. No pattern has emerged which would suggest any concerted effort of scribes in this tradition to make any special type of alteration or expansion.

For a balanced picture of 𝕸, these 99 cases of secondary and synonymous variants in 𝕸 must be viewed along with its preferable readings. 𝕸 preserves by far the highest number of preferable readings: 66 (compared with 42 in 𝐐ᵃ and 35 in 𝔪). They are listed and discussed in Chapter II.A-C. Once again, there are 10 preferable readings which are unique to 𝕸. They are listed together in Chapter II.C.1.

---

[35]To catalogue each of the synonymous variants gives a total of 18 rather than 16, which indicates the complexities involved in counting such minor variants, where one word or short phrase will involve two variations.

3. A MAJOR EXPANSION SHARED BY Q𝖆𝖒𝖒

As we have seen, a major typological feature of the Q𝖆𝖒 tradition is the expansion of the narrative in Exodus with statements or entire paragraphs from the parallel narrative in Deuteronomy. As Tov has already pointed out, however, even the "recensional traits" of 𝖒 are not unique to that text-type, but are shared by other witnesses as well.[36]

Even as conservative a text as 𝕸 of Exodus shares this feature with Q𝖆𝖒 at least once, in 32:9, we have seen (Chapter II.D). There are four expansions in Exodus 32 which seem to have been inserted under the influence of Deuteronomy (32:7ב G+; 32:9 Q𝖆𝖒𝕸++; 32:10 Q𝖆𝖒++; 32:13א G+), as well as the synonymous variant 32:11ב, where 𝖒G and/or 𝕸 may have been influenced by Deuteronomy. Each tradition, then, has been affected by some expansion within a span of a few verses, but the instances -- and the extent -- of the expansions vary from tradition to tradition. It is, of course, only due to that variation that we can isolate these cases of expansion. Expansion or alteration that occurred early enough to have affected all four witnesses can no longer be detected.

In the case of 32:9, where Q𝖆𝖒𝕸 all share the expansion, it appears that an early scribe wished to make Yahweh's speech in Exod 32:7-10 complete by supplementing it from the parallel speech in Deuteronomy. Thus he added Deut 9:13 into the corresponding position in Exodus, after Exod 32:8. The only alteration he made was the change required by the different context, from אלי to אל משה. Otherwise the texts are identical in all four places, i.e., in Exod 32:9 and Deut 9:13 in 𝖒 and 𝕸, except that both 𝖒 and 𝕸 have לאמור in Deuteronomy. Presumably scribes in both traditions added that minor word in Deuteronomy after this sentence had been inserted in Exodus. Thus it appears that the scribe very deliberately and carefully copied the sentence so that it would be exactly reproduced. Whether he wrote from memory or by opening a scroll of Deuteronomy perhaps depends on the degree to which he relied upon his memory.

He did not, however, bring every expression from the speech in Deuteronomy, nor did he alter the text in Exodus so that it would exactly correspond. Some minor expressions appear in this speech in Deuteronomy but not in Exodus (e.g., ואמחה את שמם מתחת השמים), and there are some minor differences (e.g., העלית מארץ מצרים//הוצאת ממצרים). The possibility must always be considered, of course, that some of these

---

[36]See Tov, *Septuagint,* p. 274 and n. 38, and see above, Chapter I.D.

represent expansions or alterations that occurred later in Deuteronomy, after our scribe took what he wanted (as is most likely the case with the לאמור of 9:13).

Furthermore, the influence does not seem to have gone in the other direction: Deut 9:12-14 has not been supplemented with the extra statements in Exod 32:7-10. This one-directional activity, taken with the partial nature of the expansionism, may suggest that such expansions were very much a personal, perhaps even idiosyncratic phenomenon. It may well be that only one scribe ever made this change, and that from that one moment this major expansion entered the text which later divided into the two traditions we now know as 𝐐ᵃ𝖒 and 𝖒.

Because this one major expansion is shared by 𝐐ᵃ𝖒𝖒, it must have been made late enough so that the tradition behind 𝐆 had already separated but early enough so that 𝐐ᵃ𝖒𝖒 were still together or at least under mutual influence. The major expansion which appears in the very next verse (32:10), and which was taken from just seven verses later in Deuteronomy (9:20), on the other hand, was apparently made later, after 𝐐ᵃ𝖒 and 𝖒 were separated.

4. CONCLUSION

The statistics have shown that for the book of Exodus 𝖒 is by far the best text available to us. This conclusion should not be generalized for the rest of the OT, for each book must be considered separately.

The reason that suggests itself for the high quality of 𝖒 in Exodus, as contrasted with, for instance, its very inferior quality in Samuel and its extreme expansionism in Jeremiah, is that the books of the Torah were treated with an even greater care by some circle of scribes than were the other books. Even if, as Albrektson has suggested,[37] the victory of 𝖒 was due to the historical accident of "what Pharisaic scribes happened to have left after the defeats imposed by the Romans,"[38] it is possible to imagine that in the traumatic circumstances of defeat rabbis were more concerned with which text they salvaged in the case of Exodus than in the case of Samuel or Jeremiah.

As mentioned, 𝖒 does have a few actual errors, due to the fact that it is a diplomatic text and does not reflect modern critical editing and

---

[37]See above, Chapter I.D.
[38]Albrektson, "Reflections," p. 63; quoted above, Chapter I.D.

choosing from among a group of MSS. But apart from a small number of actual errors, and a few other cases of accidental omission of a word or a longer passage, 𝔐 of Exodus reflects the least amount of scribal expansion and alteration of the texts at our disposal.   The other three texts have a much greater number of expansions and alterations, whether deliberately for some exegetical reason such as enhancement of the narrative, harmonization, or internal consistency;   or perhaps with less purpose-fulness, reflecting merely a higher degree of tolerance for variation.

On the other hand, the fact that 𝔐 is the best text available to us for the book of Exodus should not be interpreted to mean that in any particular reading it preserves the best text. As Tov has pointed out,[39] text-critical rules such as the "unequal status of textual sources" and, specifically, preference for 𝔐 are external criteria which relate to the text of a book as a whole, but are not helpful for specific readings:

> Indeed, the readings of MT deserve, on the whole, more respect than readings found in other sources, but this statistical information should not influence decisions in *individual* instances, because the exceptions to this situation are not predictable.   When judgments are involved, statistical information becomes less relevant, although it certainly influences scholars unconsciously.[40]

Thus, for instance, the omission of the Girgashites in 34:11ב, and for that matter in each list of the seven nations in Exodus, probably occurred accidentally after 𝔐 had separated from the other two traditions. Even though Deut 7:1 specifically refers to (and lists) "seven nations," presumably by the time the defective nature of the lists in Exodus in the text of 𝔐 was discovered, the time had come when scribes no longer felt free to add, even from elsewhere in the Torah, or to harmonize in any way. Thus an early mistake of one scribe has been perpetuated.

---

[39]Tov, "Criteria," pp. 435-436.

[40]*Ibid.*, p. 436.   On p. 435 Tov quotes Lagarde on the Septuagint: "...ich glaube...dass keine hds der LXX so gut ist, dass sie nicht oft genug schlechte lesarten, keine so schlecht dass sie nicht mitunter ein gutes körnchen böte" (P. A. de Lagarde, *Anmerkungen zur griechischen Übersetzung der Proverbien* [Leipzig: n.p., 1863] p. 3; spelling as in Tov); and on p. 436 n. 23 he quotes Smith on methodology: "Where G and H show variant readings, both being grammatically intelligible, they have *prima facie* equal claims to attention, and the decision between them must be made on the ground of internal probability" (H. P. Smith, *Samuel*, International Critical Commentary [New York: Scribner, 1899], p. 399).

In conclusion, then, the text of 𝕸 in Exodus is a good one, in general showing less expansion and alteration than the other witnesses.

D. THE CHARACTER OF **G**

1. PREFERABLE, SYNONYMOUS, AND SECONDARY READINGS

While statistics for the three Hebrew texts have been based on 165 readings, those for **G** must be based on 121 readings, i.e., those for which its *Vorlage* can be determined with reasonable confidence. As can be seen in Appendix 2, in 44 formulae **G** appears as one of the following, in descending order of certainty as to *Vorlage* (precise explanations are given at the beginning of the Appendix: **(G)**, **(G?)**, **G?**, /**G**/.

In view of the different base, the percentages given for each of the four witnesses take on a greater significance for the sake of comparison.

Of the 121 readings that affect **G**, 53 have been classified as synonymous variants. Of the remaining 68 readings, **G** preserves the preferable reading 40 times and the secondary reading 28 times.

Based on the total 121 readings, **G** has the preferable reading in 33% of the cases, the secondary reading in 23%, and a synonymous variant in 44% of the cases.

Based on the 68 readings where preferability has been assigned, **G** has the preferable reading in 59% and the secondary reading in 41% of the variants.

The foregoing figures relate to all of the preferable and secondary readings preserved in **G**, regardless of whether and which other texts share the same readings.

Of the 62 variants that **G** preserves uniquely, 8 are preferable (13%), 18 are secondary (29%), and 36 are synonymous (58%). Based on the 26 readings where preferability has been assigned, **G** has the preferable reading 31% of the time, and the secondary reading 69% of the time.

There is a rather striking coincidence in these statistics. Whereas 𝕸 preserves the preferable reading in 41% of the readings where preferability has been assigned and the secondary reading in 59%, the percentages for **G** are exactly reversed: **G** preserves the preferable reading in 59% and the secondary reading in 41% of the readings where both its *Vorlage* and preferability can be determined with some confidence.

2. TYPES OF SECONDARY READINGS AND SYNONYMOUS VARIANTS

Of the 28 secondary readings preserved in **G**, 18 are unique to **G**:

- in 12 **G** is uniquely longer:
    - 1 clause,
    - 3 phrases (on humans and on animals, and before his servants, on the ground),
    - 8 words (signs, holy, in fulness, of stone, onto themselves, the Lord, all bis);
- in 1 **G** has expanded and altered (Go down and warn);
- 3 are alterations of a word (hand, sons, pride); and
- 2 are omissions (1 clause; today).[41]

Thus of the readings which are clearly secondary and are unique to **G**, there is a clear pattern of expansion: 13 out of 18, or 72%, of its unique secondary readings involve expansions.

Of the 28 secondary readings preserved in **G**, it shares 10 of them with at least one other witness. These include:

- 9 expansions:
    - 1 second object (and to Aaron),
    - 1 prepositional phrase (from his land),
    - 4 words (first, sons, saying bis),
    - 1 accusative pronominal object, and
    - 2 conjunctions; and
- 1 alteration of a verbal form.

As has been stated above, there is no necessary relationship between these 10 secondary readings and the same readings in the other texts which share them; they are such minor and such typical expansions that they may all be due to the **G** tradition despite the other texts that preserve the same readings.

Thus it is appropriate to look at the proportions again: of the 28 secondary readings in **G**, 22, or 79%, are expansions.

Turning to the synonymous variants preserved in **G**, we find that of the total of 53, **G** shares 17 with at least one other witness:

- 1 affects the order of the ten-verse pericope regarding the incense altar;
- in 9 **G** is longer (1 14-word passage, 2 clauses, all, smeared with oil, 1 definite article, and 3 conjunctions); and

---

[41]They are listed together in Chapter IV.D.

- 7 are qualitative differences (<u>with outstretched arm, six, behold;</u>
    2 verbal forms, 1 preposition, and 1 noun suffix).

The 36 synonymous variants that **G** preserves uniquely can be grouped as follows:

- 6 where **G** is shorter:
    3 affecting entire pericopes and 1 clause
        (all of these 4 are in the account of the tabernacle);
    <u>your sons</u> and (ו)אולם (both in narrative passages);
- a series of 6 indicating a different form of one pericope;
- 2 affecting the representation of the table;
- 4 affecting word order (1 of a phrase, 3 of a word);
- 9 different words (5 designating God; <u>Jethro, sons, brother, to</u>);
- 7 different forms of words or suffixes (3 verbal forms,
    3 noun suffixes, 1 plural noun); and
- 2 <u>all</u>'s.

Nine of these synonymous variants could be considered significant alone, because they affect the length or formulation of four different pericopes. But probably the most significant point is the quantity of synonymous variants which are unique to **G**. Again **G** is revealed as the one text of the four that is the most distant from the others. The second thing is that in 7 of these 36 **G** is the one text that preserves the shorter reading: and in 4 of those 6 it is substantially shorter. And at the same time only 1 of them involves **G** in a longer reading. Except for that one ambiguous "all," in every case where **G** has uniquely preserved the longer reading (13), it has been pronounced secondary.

3. LONGER AND SHORTER READINGS IN **G**

For a balanced picture of **G**, these cases of secondary and synonymous variants in **G** must be viewed along with its preferable readings. The 40 preferable readings in **G** are all listed and discussed in Chapter II. Only the 8 preferable readings that are unique to **G** are worthy of note again here. Every one of them is a shorter reading: in 1 **Q**ᵃ𝖒𝖒 have a major expansion, in 1 **Q**ᵃ𝖒 have a major expansion while 𝖒 adds one word, and in 6 **Q**ᵃ𝖒𝖒 all add a word or phrase (<u>their slaves, for Moses, in the morning, today, and make for them, and they stood</u>).

Of the total of 121 readings in which **G** is involved, whether preferable, secondary, or synonymous, 35 are longer and 29 are shorter readings. Of the 62 readings unique to **G**, whether preferable, secondary, or synonymous, 14 are longer and 17 are shorter readings.[42] While **G** deserves its reputation of being expansionist in many places, it also deserves to gain a reputation of being shorter in others, sometimes uniquely so.

But if the <u>number</u> of shorter and longer readings which **G** preserves is worthy of note, another aspect of its pattern of readings is also important: the <u>type</u> of expansion which it uniquely preserves. This is best recognized by contrast with the expansions preserved by the **Qᵃ𝔪** tradition. While the unique expansions of **G** are far more numerous than those of **Qᵃ𝔪**, they are also far shorter.

A few examples will illustrate the difference in length. A typical major expansion of **Qᵃ𝔪** has been printed out earlier in this chapter, and its length required seven lines; some of the major expansions are shorter, others are longer. A typical expansion of **G**, on the other hand, is <u>on both humans and animals;</u> again, some are shorter, others are longer.

As another example, let us look again at the four expansions in Exodus 32 which seem to have been inserted under the influence of Deuteronomy (32:7ב **G**+;   32:9 **Qᵃ𝔪𝔐**++;   32:10 **Qᵃ𝔪**++;   32:13א **G**+). Each tradition has been affected by some expansion within a span of a few verses, but the expansions in **G** differ here in a way that is quite characteristic of that tradition in the narrative sections of Exodus in general:[43] they are fairly frequent but usually quite short, in contrast to the **Qᵃ𝔪** tradition, which has relatively few but usually rather long expansions.

This is one of the features of **G** that has removed it further from **Qᵃ𝔪𝔐**. It has substantially more secondary features than **𝔐** or **Qᵃ𝔪**, although most of them are minor. **Qᵃ𝔪**, on the other hand, have numerically far fewer secondary features, but they are usually quite major. This explains why **𝔪** has the reputation of being the most expansionist, whereas **G** has the reputation of being more corrupt. Both are true, depending on whether number or extent of expansions is in view.

Unfortunately, the statistics revealed by this investigation cannot provide an accurate picture of the difference in numbers. They show **Qᵃ𝔪** (taken as one tradition) uniquely exhibiting 18 longer readings (out of a

---

[42]Two of these shorter readings that are unique to **G** have been judged accidental omissions.

[43]The tabernacle account in **G** does not follow this pattern, and must be studied separately.

total of 165 variants), while **G** uniquely exhibits 14 longer readings (out of a total of 121 variants). In **Qᵃ ɯ** the 18 break down as follows: 16 expansions (12 major and 4 moderate to minor) and 2 synonymous variants. In **G** there are 13 expansions and 1 synonymous variant.

But those figures are very misleading. The difficulty is that our statistics are limited to the letters and words where **Qᵃ** is extant, and the nature of the scroll's remains combined with the nature of the expansions in **Qᵃ ɯ** as opposed to those in **G** conspire to deceive. If there is a fragment preserving bits of one word each on three successive lines, that is enough to establish that **Qᵃ** shares a major expansion of ten lines with **ɯ**. But the same sort of fragment will seldom preserve an indisputably shorter reading in the scroll where **G** has an expansion involving only two or three words. I have purposely taken the conservative approach of counting only actual ink on actual leather, rather than the inferences of reconstruction. Hence even when a glance at the plate will show that there was no room for the extra word or phrase present in **G**, if that cannot be documented by ink it has not been counted.

Now that the pattern has been recognized, however, of the scroll's standing with **ɯ ᙏ** against **G** in all extant passages, as well as the pattern of the types of unique expansions in **G**, some of the supplementary material provided especially in Chapter II becomes more meaningful for a general picture of the nature of **G** versus the nature of **Qᵃ ɯ ᙏ**. To take one example, since **Qᵃ** agrees with **ɯ ᙏ** in the shorter reading in 9:8ᴀ, where **G** adds <u>and before his servants</u>, and since this is a very characteristic type of unique expansion for **G**, then presumably **Qᵃ** also agreed with **ɯ ᙏ** in the shorter reading in 7:9,10a;   and 14:8 as well, and our picture of the uniqueness of **G** has been broadened (see Chapter II.A.5).

4. TRANSLATIONAL TECHNIQUE

In general the translator of Exodus seems to have taken pains to render his Hebrew *Vorlage* with a high degree of precision. Yet there are some instances of freedom or paraphrase -- if indeed his *Vorlage* was similar to the Hebrew texts still available to us. A few examples of each type will be given. This is only a random sampling, beginning with a few passages where **Qᵃ** is extant and finding parallels or contrasts elsewhere in Exodus.

a. Different Vorlage or Free Translation?

I will begin with two readings which at first appeared to reflect a different *Vorlage*, but were judged instead to reflect a relative degree of freedom, after study of the translational technique in the rest of the book of Exodus. The results will be given in detail for these two, as examples of the method that has been followed in general in the determination of variants. Because most of Exodus is rendered with a high degree of literalness, readings such as these seemed at first suspect. The first involves the choice of a theologically significant word, and the second investigates the treatment of a clause.

(1) A Theologically Significant Word Choice

In 33:19, when Yahweh promises to reveal to Moses כל טובי, that appears in Greek as τη δοξη μου. A study of the context -- both chapter 33 and the rest of the book of Exodus -- makes it seem likely that the translator was attempting to render the <u>thought</u> of Yahweh's goodness and self-revelation in the best Greek.

To look first at the other occurrences of the Hebrew word: the consonants טוב occur only five times in Exodus. Elsewhere **G** renders with αγαθος (for the land, 3:8; and all the good things Yahweh had done, 18:9), αστειος (to describe the "beautiful" baby Moses, 2:2), and ορθως (for Jethro's negative description of Moses' method of judging, 18:17).

Second, the other occurrences of the Greek word in Exodus: δοξα is used 15 times: 9 times for כבוד; twice for תפארת; once each for גאון (15:7), תהלה (15:11), and טוב (here); and once τας στολας την δοξων υμων translates עדיך (earlier in the same chapter, 33:5, but for the "ornamentation" of the <u>people</u>).

Third, the immediate context: this phrase occurs in a narrative which has many expressions in both languages for God's presence:

33:13	דרכך	σεαυτον
33:14	פני	Αυτος
33:15	פניך	αυτος συ
33:18	כבדך	σεαυτου δοξαν
33:19	כל טובי	τη δοξη μου
33:20	פני	μου το προσωπον

| 33:22 | כבדי | μου η δοξα |
| 33:23 | ופני | το δε προσηπον μου |

It thus appears that the translator was struggling to capture the sense of God's presence and its visible manifestation by various expressions in this extended passage.

In light of the heavy emphasis in Exodus 24 and 40, two of the theological high points of the book, on כבוד = δοξα as the visible manifestation of Yahweh's deity and character (including, of course, goodness) the translator apparently felt that δοξα best captured the meaning here: the self-revelation of Yahweh to Moses. Was he perhaps suggesting that what Moses experienced in chapter 34 all of the people experienced at least from afar in chapters 24 and 40?[44]   Whether or not there was any such theological nuance in his mind, it does appear that he was faithfully producing the same Hebrew that we read in 𝖫𝖬.

(2) Treatment of a Clause

The second extended example is the rendering of a clause:

| 9:7 | וישלח פרעה והנה | ιδων δε Φαραω οτι |

Investigation of all of the occurrences of (ו)(ה)הנ(ה) without suffix in Exodus shows that this reading is most likely not a variant, but is consistent with the method of the translator.

In general, when (ו)הנ(ה) begins a clause and the context is other than one of "seeing," **G** translates 𝖫𝖬 quite literally. Of the 12 occurrences of the pattern (ו)(ה)הנ(ה) followed by pronoun followed by participle or adjective, **G** translates 10 times with ιδου followed by pronoun followed by present or future indicative. (But see Chapter II.A.6., 7:15, for 2 cases where 𝖬 departs from the usual Hebrew pattern.) For example:

| 4:14b | הנה הוא יצא | και ιδου αυτος εξελευσεται |

(Note that **G** translates two different phrases with ιδου in this one verse:

| 4:14a | הלא אהרן | Ουκ ιδου Ααρων ... ;) |

In the other 2 cases out of the 10 **G** paraphrases:

| 4:23 | הנה אנכי הרג | ορα ουν εγω αποκτενω |
| 8:25 | הנה אנכי יוצא | οδε εγω εξελευσομαι |

The freedom of **G** in the rendering of this idiom becomes clearer when 4:23 is seen in its fuller context and then contrasted with another very similar Hebrew passage just four chapters later:

---

[44]Cf. ενδοξασθησομαι for ונפלינו in 33:16.

4:23   ותמאן לשלחו הנה אנכי הרג

ει μεν ουν μη βουλει εξαποστειλαι αυτους,
 ορα ουν εγω αποκτενω

7:27   ואם מאן אתה לשלח הנה אנכי נגף

ει δε μη βουλει συ εξαποστειλαι, ιδου εγω τυπτω

The thirteenth case of הנה with a pronoun is 31:6. Here the Hebrew order and verb are both different from the above pattern, reading instead: pronoun, הנה, perfect tense. **G**, on the other hand, omits הנה, rendering simply: pronoun, aorist or perfect: ואני הנה נתתי

και εγω εδωκα αυτον [δεδωκα A⁺]

In 20 cases (ו)(הנ)ה is followed by a noun or adjective. If the הנה begins a sentence and the context is not explicitly one of "seeing," **G** will tend to render literally, using ιδου. For example:

3:9   ועתה הנה עקת בני ישראל באה אלי

και νυν ιδου κραυγη των υιων Ισραηλ ηκει προς με

16:14   והנה על פני המדבר דק

και ιδου επι προσωπον της ερημου λεπτον

32:34   הנה מלאכי ילך

ιδου ο αγγελος μου προπορευεται

Of these 20 cases, **G** translates literally 11 times. In a 12th occurrence **G** would be literal if we could count its translation in Deuteronomy; the entire verse **32:9**, which appears in **Q^ ш m**, is lacking in **G** (see II.D.1 and V.C.3).

In the remaining 8 cases of הנה followed by a noun, the context involves "looking" or "seeing," explicitly or implicitly, immediately prior to הנה, and **G** paraphrases, omitting the הנה/ιδου. For example:

2:6 (**m** ...ותפתח ותראהו) **ш** ותפתחה ותרא את הילד והנה נער בכה

ανοιξασα δε ορα παιδιον κλαιον

2:13   ויצא ביום השני והנה שני אנשים עברים נצים

εξελθων δε τη ημερα τη δευτερα ορα δυο ανδρας Εβραιους
διαπληκτιζομενους

3:2   וירא והנה הסנה בער באש

και ορα οτι ο βατος καιεται πυρι

In one case **ш** preserves a text in which the Hebrew itself has the verb "to see" before הנה. This should alert us to the ever-present possibility that **G** is precisely translating a longer Hebrew *Vorlage* when it appears to be expansionist and/or paraphrastic:

𝕸 וישאו בני ישראל את עיניהם <u>ויראו</u> והנה מצרים נסעים אחריהם 14:10

𝕸 וישאו בני ישראל את עיניהם _____ והנה מצרים נסע   אחריהם

και αναβλεψαντες οι υιοι Ισραηλ τοις οφθαλμοις ορωσιν,

και _____ οι Αιγυπτιοι εστρατοπεδευσαν οπισω αυτων **G**;

και <u>οιδε</u> οι Αιγυπτιοι ... A⁺

και <u>ιδου</u> οι Αιγυπτιοι ... Syh⁺

In 5 verses, including 9:7, the reading under discussion, הנה is followed by a verb; 3 times the verb is negated. In only 1 of these cases does **G** translate with ιδου:

7:16   והנה לא שמעת   και ιδου ουκ εισηκουσας

In the other 4 cases, **G** paraphrases and omits ιδου:

4:1   והן לא יאמינו לי   Εαν ουν μη πιστευσωσιν μοι

8:22   הן נזבח   εαν γαρ θυσωμεν

9:7   וישלח פרעה והנה לא מת   ιδων δε Φαραω οτι ουκ ετελευτησεν

39:43   וירא משה את כל המלאכה והנה עשו אתה

και ειδεν Μωυσης παντα τα εργα, και ησαν πεποιηκοτες αυτα

On the other hand, it must be noted that not only הנה but also the verb וישלח are rendered paraphrastically in the present verse, 9:7. Two other similar usages of the verb in Exodus may, however, indicate that שלח was sometimes translated literally and sometimes freely. The first is more literal:

9:27   וישלח פרעה ויקרא למשה

αποστειλας δε Φαραω εκαλεσεν Μωυσην

(cf. Gen 31:4; 41:8, 14). The straightforwardness of this translation in contrast to the paraphrase in 9:7 may explain why HR treats 9:7 with hesitation. While HR lists הנה as the Hebrew equivalent of ιδειν 5 times in Genesis through Joshua, only here does the הנה receive a question mark. The other 4 cases are indeed more straightforward:

Gen 24:63   וישא עיניו וירא והנה (ה)גמלים באים

και αναβλεψας τοις οφθαλμοις ειδεν καμηλους ερχομενας

26:8   וירא והנה יצחק מצחק

ειδεν τον Ισαακ παιζοντα

27:6   הנה שמעתי את אביך מדבר

Ἰδε εγω ηκουσα του πατρος σου λαλουντος

Josh 5:13   וישא עיניו וירא והנה איש עמד

και αναβλεψας τοις οφθαλμοις ειδεν ανθρωπον εστηκοτα

(Note that at Josh 5:13 the note in *BHS* states that והנו is lacking in **GSV**, although the examples in Exodus might suggest that this was merely good Greek translational technique.)

In this connection it should be noted that since the verb for 9:7 has not been preserved in **Qᵐ**, the scroll could hypothetically have read: [וירא פר]עה והנה. If the *Vorlage* of the **G** had read thus, then the reading in **G** here should not even raise an eyebrow.

But to return to the two similar usages of שלח in Exodus. While the first, 9:27, was rendered literally, the second was translated more freely:

9:19   ועתה שלח העז את מקנ(י)ך

νυν ουν κατασπευσον συναγαγειν τα κτηνη σου

Conclusion: Although the **G** translation of Exodus is generally quite literal, in the case of הנה, especially when in a context of "looking" or "seeing," the translator was free to paraphrase and to omit ἰδου for the sake of idiomatic Greek. It appears likely that this freedom prevailed in the present instance and indeed even expanded to encompass the preceding verb as well, so that the **G** translation is a legitimate rendering of the Hebrew text preserved in **Ⅲ** and **Ⅲ** and partially in **Qᵐ** in 9:7:

QᵐⅢⅢ   וישלח פר]עה והנה   ἰδων δε Φαραω οτι **G.**

b. Literal Translation versus Free Rendering

Having studied two examples in such detail, we will now look briefly at other readings which illustrate the technique of the translator.

Sometimes his translation is so literal as to have produced wooden "Semitic Greek," whereas in other readings he has rendered into good idiomatic Greek. For instance, in 33:12, he translated idiomatically:

מצאת חן בעיני   χαριν εχεις παρ εμοι.

But in the following verses (13ᵇⁱˢ, 16) we read three variations of this more literal translation (note that "in your eyes" remains idiomatic):

ει ουν ευρηκα χαριν εναντιον σου.

Should we attribute both of these to the same translator?

He consistently translated the idiom for ordination, למלא את ידם,
very literally with τελειουν/πληρουν τας χειρας αυτων (28:41; 29:9,
29,33,35; 32:29).

Often he exercised the freedom to render the Hebrew into good Greek
while maintaining the thought. Compare the following translations in two
successive verses, rendering quite different Hebrew words but interpreted
with a similar meaning:

33:16	ונפלינו אני ועמך מכל העם	και ενδοξασθησομαι εγω τε και ο
		λαος σου παρα παντα τα εθνη
33:17 (cf. 12)	ואדעך בשם	και οιδα σε παρα παντας

The following sampling reveals the translator's freedom in rendering
grammatical and syntactical features:

word order:

25:11	מבית ומחוץ	εξωθεν και εσωθεν

singular/plural:

15:25	חק ומשפט	δικαιωματα και κρισεις
7:4	ב(מ)שפטים	εκδικησις
18:20	הדרך	τας οδους
18:22	כל הדבר...וכל הדבר	το ρημα...τα δε βραχεα[45]
28:3	את בגדי אהרן	την στολην...Ααρων
8:20	ביתה פרעה ובית עבדיו	εις τους οικους Φαραω και εις
		τους οικους των θεραποντων
		αυτου
23:28 et al.	(etc.) את הכנעני	τους Χαναναιους (etc.)
23:29 (referring to nations)	אגרשנו	εκβαλω αυτους

prepositions (freedom not to repeat):

10:9	בנערינו ובזקנינו...בבנינו ובבנותנו בצאננו ובבקרנו
	συν τοις υιοις και θυγατρασιν και προβατοις και βουσιν ημων

(freedom of choice):

10:1	בקרבו	επ αυτους
cf. 17:7	בקרבנו	εν ημιν
6:26	על צבאתם	συν δυναμει
cf. 7:4	את צבאתי	συν δυναμει

---

[45]Note also the absence of "every." Contrast 18:26:

את הדבר...וכל הדבר   παν ρημα...παν ρημα

12:2	לחדשי השנה	εν τοις μησιν του ενιαυτου
28:43 (cf. 29:29)	ולזרעו אחריו	και τω σπερματι αυτου μετ αυτον

prepositional phrases:

18:16	בין איש ובין רעהו	εκαστον

pronouns:

7:9	והשלך לפני פרעה	και ριψον <u>αυτην</u>...εναντιον Φ
15:25	וישלך אל המים	και ενεβαλεν <u>αυτο</u> εις το υδωρ
32:12	הוציאם להרג <u>אתם</u> בהרים	εξηγαγεν αυτους αποκτειναι εν τοις ορεσιν
32:13	אשר נשבעת <u>להם</u>	οις ωμοσας

c. An Error in Translation?

One reading probably represents a misunderstanding on the part of the translator. In 17:15 he translated נסי ("my banner") with μου καταφυγη ("my refuge"). This rendering reflects the struggle of the translator to make sense of the difficult consonantal text before him, which was the same as that preserved in **Qᵐ ⅏ 𝔐**: נסי.

The difficulty is compounded by two facts. First, this reading is found as part of the name of an altar: יהוה נסי or Κυριος μου καταφυγη, which means that there is no clue in the sentence as to the meaning of the word. Second, the etiology in the following verse fails to explain the name. The evidence in verse 16 is confused (see *BHS* ᵃᵖ; since **Qᵐ** is not extant there, this verse is not discussed elsewhere), but all of the preserved readings involve a כ where the name in verse 15 has a נ. Hence none of them explain either נסי or καταφυγη. The confusion in verse 16 was no doubt caused by the lack of agreement between the name and the etiology, which is attributable to the fact that in some Hasmonaean hands the כ and the נ are identical except for a very short horizontal stroke at the top.[46]

There is no way to be certain what meaning is preferable, since the Massoretic pointing, which calls for the meaning "my banner, standard, ensign," arose later. Yet the context of continual war between Yahweh and the Amalekites might point to the idea of a banner as a rallying point

---

[46]See Cross, "Scripts," fig. 1 and 2. For a similar case of confusion between the two letters at 2 Sam 6:6 = 1 Chr 13:9, see Eugene Ulrich, *The Qumran Text of Samuel and Josephus*, HSM 19 (Missoula, MN: Scholars Press, 1978), p. 190.

through the ages rather than to that of Yahweh's being a refuge.   καταφυγη
is used four times in the Torah: twice for מקלט, but once interestingly for
לנוס (Deut 19:3), which is an infinitive construct, and here for נסי.
Although the only noun from this root attested in the OT is מנוס, it seems
clear that the translator was doing his best to make sense of the consonants
before him.

In conclusion, then, it appears that the Hebrew *Vorlage* of **G** agreed
with **Q⁰ⅢⅢ** in reading נסי, which was difficult to interpret because of the
problems in the context, and which he translated as well as he could.

There are three other cases where **Q⁰** is extant, where **G** presents a
different word. They have been dealt with above: see 18:4; 17:6; 18:21א, all
of which have been discussed in Chapter II.A.5, as if they were unique
secondary variants of **G**. Yet it is possible that one or more of them reflect
some confusion on the part of the translator rather than an actual variant.
This seems especially debatable in the case of χειρος for חרב. It was
suggested in the discussion that the auditory similarity combined with the
appropriateness of either word in the context may have given rise to error.

d. Summary

In general, then, **G** in Exodus gives evidence of being a faithful
translation of its Hebrew *Vorlage*. A few readings seem so literal as to
have produced wooden, "Semitic" Greek (e.g., "to fill the hands"), but most
seem relatively literal but without being "translation Greek" (e.g., not
repeating a pronoun when it was required in Hebrew but not in Greek). A
few suggest greater concern for the thought than for the actual words, and
thus greater freedom which still successfully renders the ideas (e.g., "glory"
and "above all").

5. CONCLUSION

In conclusion, **G** is the most significantly different of the four texts
of Exodus studied here. It has by far the greatest number of unique readings,
both secondary and synonymous. It is, of course, impossible to be certain in
any single case whether a variant reading has arisen during the course of
the transmission of the Hebrew *Vorlage,* whether during the translation
itself, or whether during the early transmission of the Greek text. If
scribes copying biblical texts in Hebrew exercised the freedom to expand or
alter as they wrote, then presumably the translator and the copyists in
Greek did as well. Yet when variants which are unique to **G** are nevertheless

similar to variations found among Hebrew texts, it is at least equally possible that they arose during the Hebrew stage as during the Greek stage. Thus they have been treated as variants here.

Any reconstruction of the history of **G** in Exodus must account for the fact that it preserves uniquely preferable shorter readings as well as uniquely secondary longer readings. The concluding section of this chapter attempts to do just that.

E. CONCLUSIONS REGARDING THE HISTORY OF THE TEXT OF EXODUS

As a conclusion to this chapter describing the nature of each of the four texts, the following is suggested as a possible reconstruction of the early history of the text of Exodus. It must be recognized for what it is -- a partial view of that history, since it is based on only four texts that have happened to survive, out of an unknown number of texts that actually existed in the Second Commonwealth. Further, it is based on the new light shed on the question by **Qᵐ**, rather than by all that can be known or inferred about the book of Exodus.

The four texts are so much alike that it appears that there was a period of time in which they belonged somehow together in a group of closely related texts. After all, much of the text of Exodus is preserved without variant among these three (or four) texts. Whether there was an *Urtext* or not, there was at least a limited amount of variation in the early days.

Apparently the tradition behind **G** was the first to become separated from the others in this group. Whether it was taken to Egypt and developed there in Hebrew before being translated, or even whether it was translated in Egypt, is unknown. What it seems possible to say on the basis of the <u>text</u> as revealed in this study is that it must have separated first while it still preserved a number of preferable -- shorter -- readings against all three of the others. It needs to be reiterated that no evidence has surfaced in this study for any kind of special relationship between **G** and **Ш**. Rather, **G** is the most unlike of all four texts, and seems therefore to have been the first to separate.

The *terminus ad quem* for this separation was probably 250 B.C.E., but it may have occurred long before that. This tradition continued developing separately -- i.e., separately from the three in view here -- and through the course of time grew through the successive additions of scribes. It probably was expanded in many readings while it was still in Hebrew. Perhaps the translator himself added more words and phrases as clarifications. And probably even what we call "Old Greek" reflects some additions made following the translation, because it is not possible to reach all the way back to 250 B.C.E. These expansions and other alterations all ranged from minor to moderate. While they were rather numerous, almost every individual one was short or affected only one word or phrase. Thus most pages in **G** reveal a large number of deviations from 𝖒𝖒𝖒, but few are extensive.[47]

It appears that the traditions behind **Qᵐ𝖒** and **𝖒** continued to develop together in a group, probably with many others, during which time they underwent some common expansion and probably some alterations. Most of these expansions were probably only moderate in significance (e.g., "and they stood") or minor (e.g., conjunctions, various grammatical features); but at least one was a major expansion, imported from Deuteronomy.

Next, the tradition behind **Qᵐ𝖒** separated and was copied by at least one scribe, if not several, who wanted to repeat major speeches of Yahweh and to make various parts of Exodus harmonize with each other in order to make more explicit some literary and/or theological parallels; and to harmonize narratives in Exodus with their counterparts in Deuteronomy, probably for similar reasons. He accomplished this by means of a small number of mostly lengthy expansions. Thus certain pages of **Qᵐ𝖒** appear extremely expansionist, whereas the bulk of the text is very close to that of **𝖒**.

Sometime in the second or first centuries B.C.E. **Qᵐ** was copied, perhaps at Qumran. It is the only text of these four that was "frozen" at a certain time and suffered no more corruption. It exhibits a very few scribal errors and lapses, and four ambiguous readings where it either preserves a shorter, preferable reading or else has suffered from parablepsis.

At some point the tradition behind 𝖒𝖒 was taken as the special text of the community that worshiped at Mount Gerizim. I do not say "canonical,"

---

[47]In this reconstruction the matter of the account of the tabernacle is left aside. In very extensive variants in Exodus 25-30 and 35-40 **G** uniquely preserves a shorter reading.

but rather "special," since canonization cannot be dated on the basis of our knowledge. But there is surely evidence that it became "special" to them: the tenth commandment in Exodus 20, imported from Deuteronomy, commanding the building of an altar on Mount Gerizim.

When this happened it is difficult to say on the basis of the text. (On the basis of script and/or orthography, it has been dated by experts in those fields to the Hasmonaean era.) But there is nothing that forces us to put it much, if any, later than the copying of $\mathbf{Q}^{\mathbf{m}}$. In all of its major, typological features it is the same as $\mathbf{Q}^{\mathbf{m}}$ except for the one "sectarian" expansion. And as has been shown above, that one expansion is so much like the other major expansions in method that there is no reason to suppose it could not have been contemporaneous with the others. It is not the method that distinguishes it from the other typological features of the $\mathbf{Q}^{\mathbf{m}}\mathbf{m}$ tradition, but only the motivation. Surely the destruction of their temple and central city could be considered a sufficient motivation, so that from the point of view of text there is no objection to the suggestion of approximately 100 B.C.E. for this expansion. On the other hand, it could have been done somewhat earlier as well. The fact that it is not in $\mathbf{Q}^{\mathbf{m}}$ only suggests that the *Vorlage* of $\mathbf{Q}^{\mathbf{m}}$ did not have it -- perhaps because it was in a collateral line of the family (as some of the minor differences between the two have also suggested) or because it was inserted in ﬡ a short time after $\mathbf{Q}^{\mathbf{m}}$ was copied.

Since ﬡ was not frozen we have no way of knowing when the minor variants arose that indicate that it is later than $\mathbf{Q}^{\mathbf{m}}$. Some of them may predate its becoming "sectarian," while others may have developed through the course of a few centuries. In any case, what Skehan suggested in 1955 has been borne out by this study:

> from the point of view of the text (somewhat less so from the point of view of the orthography) the Samaritan recension as it exists in, for example, A. von Gall's edition, is shown by this scroll to have been preserved with a measure of fidelity, from a time somewhere near the origin of the recension, that compares not unfavorably with the fidelity of transmission of MT itself.[48]

While the other three texts were growing and changing somewhat at the hands of a series of scribes with an exegetical bent, the tradition behind ﬡ was being copied by a rather different breed of scribes. The period of

---

[48]Skehan, "Exodus," p. 183.

relative openness to expansion and alteration had already ended, so that no more interpolations from Deuteronomy found their way into Exodus, and few alterations were still allowed -- except, perhaps, when it was truly necessary for theological and/or political reasons, if indeed "Mount Gerizim" in Deut 27:4 was changed to "Mount Ebal."

Whether these scribes were centered at the temple in Jerusalem or not, it may be the case that their more conservative approach became more and more widely accepted, if it is legitimate to judge from the proportions of expansionist versus shorter scrolls found at Qumran. It may also be the case that if the shorter texts were favored in Jerusalem, then the expansionist texts were for that very reason favored, or at least accepted for some purposes, among communities that had reason to be hostile to Jerusalem, such as those at Qumran and at Shechem.

CHAPTER VI

EDITORIAL AND SCRIBAL PROCESSES
IN THE LATE SECOND TEMPLE PERIOD
AS EXHIBITED IN THE TEXT OF EXODUS

INTRODUCTION

In this chapter we return to the variants already discussed and look at them from a new point of view. Here we are no longer concerned with the character, preferability, or corruption of any textual tradition as it compares with any other. Rather, we will now look at the variant readings as they appear in all of the textual traditions, to determine what kinds of changes scribes of the late Second Temple period made as they copied biblical texts.

Some of these changes were made unintentionally and count either as lapses or as outright errors. These will be brought together and listed, with only brief discussion.

More interesting for the purposes of this study are those changes which appear to have been made with some degree of intentionality. Here of course many questions remain, because we are unable to enter the mind of the scribes. The larger variants, such as major expansions importing passages from Deuteronomy, were clearly done intentionally. Many of the smaller variants, however, may have arisen not because a scribe had determined to alter the text, but rather because he lacked a strong determination that the text should under no circumstances be altered. In other words, he may have felt a certain measure of freedom as he worked, a sense that he would accomplish his task faithfully if he expressed the meaning of his *Vorlage* even if he used a different or a fuller formulation of the thought. Perhaps it simply is not the case that he thought it was so important to prevent all alteration that he had to put forth the effort to try to achieve the results of a photocopying machine, either while he was writing or afterwards while he was proofreading. Was it possible to devote one's life to copying sacred texts while yet having a certain limited degree of freedom in that task?   Did sacredness yet leave room for variation within limits?[1]

Or are we to understand variant readings differently? Perhaps some of them date back to a still earlier time. Perhaps there was no such thing as an *Urtext*, one version of a biblical composition which was *the* book of Exodus. Perhaps as it grew and developed over the centuries at the hands of successive composers, both oral and written, and editors, it developed in several parallel forms that were treasured by various groups. It may be that many of the variants we have found in this study, e.g., those affecting an entire pericope, arose not in the process of textual transmission, but in the process of the compositional development of the text.[2] If that is the case then perhaps more of them should be labeled synonymous variants and there should be no attempt to determine which reading is preferable. At various stages in the process of canonization, there may have been attempts to standardize the text, attempts which met with varying degrees of success. Perhaps the Qumran community has left us some remnants of an earlier age, which for their own reasons they continued to copy and apparently to use, but which Jews in other communities would no longer have found acceptable.

As stated in Chapter I, while we are too far removed in time and we have too little evidence to come to a final answer to this question, I have found nothing in these variants in the book of Exodus which make the notion of an *Urtext* -- or at least a group of texts that did not differ very much from each other -- seem impossible. But it is well to be aware of different possibilities as we think about scribal and editorial practice.

With these questions in mind we will now look at the variants grouped together in categories. The major categories are expansions, omissions, and alterations of the text. In each of these major sections we will begin with those variants which are more striking and proceed to those which are less significant. At each stage we will suggest motivations for

---

[1]Cf. Talmon, "Study," pp. 321-400.

[2]For the distinction between these two stages, see Talmon, "Text," pp. 159-99; Emanuel Tov, "Some Aspects of the Textual and Literary History of the Book of Jeremiah," in *Le Livre de Jérémie: Le prophète et son milieu, les oracles et leur transmission,* ed. P.-M. Bogaert (Leuven: University Press, 1981) pp. 145-167; and Eugene Ulrich, "Horizons of Old Testament Textual Research at the Thirtieth Anniversary of Qumran Cave 4," *CBQ* 46 (1984), pp 613-636.

the variant readings, but it will be obvious that these can only be tentative projections from a later age.

In each sub-category we will first look at those variants for which one reading has been judged preferable, i.e., those discussed in Chapter II. Since the general question of criteria and problems in evaluating readings has been discussed in Chapter I, and the specific question of the preferability of each of these variants in Chapter II, they will be assumed here, and the reading which was judged to be secondary will be classified as the change brought about by a scribe. Since the argumentation and nuancing have all been presented in Chapter II, the data and arguments will not be repeated here. In each case the designation of the variant is given, so that by referring to Appendix 2 the reader can find the discussion of that variant in Chapter II.

The secondary readings will be followed by what have been termed synonymous variants, readings which appear to have a similar claim on preferability. By definition these are variants where it cannot be decided which reading is preferable, if indeed either one is preferable. Hence it cannot be assumed that one of the alternative readings represents the change introduced by a scribe. Thus these discussions will be much more tentative: *if* reading A were preferable, *then* reading B would be the secondary reading, presumably because a scribe wished to achieve the following result or was careless in the following way. Again the designation of each variant is given, so that reference to Appendix 2 will lead the reader to the discussion in Chapter III. As synonymous variants were presented in a separate chapter from preferable-secondary readings, so they will be presented here in separate paragraphs, to show that the discussions of them must all be viewed only as suggestions.

As the preceding chapters have shown, the evidences of scribal activity in this chapter are not to be thought of as pertaining only to the traditions represented by $\mathbf{Q^+ \mathfrak{m}}$ and $\mathbf{G}$. The tradition ultimately represented by $\mathfrak{m}$ has participated in all of these activities of scribes -- to a lesser extent, it is true, but nevertheless in significant ways. Indeed, if we were looking at a book outside of the Pentateuch, we might well find that $\mathfrak{m}$ reflected a greater degree of corruption than other traditions.

Thus in most cases in this chapter the tradition preserving the secondary reading is not mentioned, in an attempt to prevent becoming preoccupied with stereotypes of that tradition. Since all traditions exhibit the results of similar scribal activity, the focus in this chapter is on the type of scribal activity, not the tradition to which any particular reading belongs. For a description of the nature of each of the traditions under investigation, see Chapter V.

Once more it is advisable that the limits of this investigation be defined. In this chapter, as in the others, only "variants" are discussed and are significant for statistics. A "variant" is defined in this analysis as any variation among any of the four texts, $\mathbf{Q^m \mathfrak{m} \mathfrak{M} G}$, in any passage where $\mathbf{Q^m}$ is extant. Each of these variants has a constant reference consisting of chapter-verse-(Hebrew letter) in boldface characters. This special reference is consistently used and may be found in the complete list in Appendix 2. Thus, for example, "**22:24א**" or "**22:25**" refers to a variant, which by definition is a place where $\mathbf{Q^m}$ is extant. On the other hand, "22:25" refers to a verse in Exodus which exhibits some phenomenon under discussion. In this latter case there is no variant as defined here: either $\mathbf{Q^m}$ is not extant, or, if it is extant for the word under discussion, there is no variation among the four witnesses, $\mathbf{Q^m \mathfrak{m} \mathfrak{M} G}$.

All statistics are based on variants only. From time to time, however, a broader pattern may be mentioned which involves passages where $\mathbf{Q^m}$ is not extant. Such passages are introduced only to supplement the picture of the text of Exodus; they are not counted for statistical purposes.

A. CATEGORIES OF SECONDARY READINGS

1. MAJOR EXPANSIONS

a. *Major Expansions From Outside the Pentateuch*

There are no indisputable cases of major expansions from outside the Pentateuch.

There are, however, two synonymous variants which should be mentioned very tentatively here.

First, if the shorter reading in **10:21ב** were to be judged preferable, then it would appear that a scribe inserted the words "that one may feel [grope in] the darkness" for the purpose of heightening the drama of the plague narrative. This clause is found in almost exactly the same form in Jb 12:25, and the rare word for "feel" or "grope" is also found in Deut 28:29, a passage threatening Israel with judgments similar to the plagues. It is possible that the presence of the expression in Job and of the word in Deuteronomy influenced a scribe to add these words here. Incidentally, this possibility is mentioned here with major expansions not because of its length, but because of the greater degree of license that would be exhibited here if it were an expansion: an entire clause would have been added which came neither from the context nor from anywhere in the Pentateuch.

Second, if the shorter reading in **31:13-14** were to be judged preferable, then it would appear that a scribe inserted a long passage of fourteen words: "for it is a sign <u>between me and you throughout your generations, that you may know that I am Yahweh who sanctifies you. And you shall keep the sabbath, for it is holy</u> to you." If this is not a case of parablepsis, then a scribe has inserted expressions from Ezek 20:12, 20.

<u>Summary</u>: While there are no indisputable cases of major expansions from outside the Pentateuch, there are two possible cases: one from Job, and one from Ezekiel. A clear answer would have been most desirable here, for it might have suggested how the scribes involved in our texts viewed the relationship between the books of the Torah and other books in Scripture. Could they import passages from the Prophets or from the Writings into Exodus? Was there any distinction in their minds between the various parts of the Bible, as far as holiness was concerned?

Perhaps the use of Palaeo-Hebrew script provides an analogy here. If, apart from patriotic contexts, that old script was used only for the names and titles of God and for books in the Pentateuch, is that tangible evidence that a special degree of sacredness attached to the Pentateuch that did not attach to other biblical books? If that sacredness sometimes influenced the style of script that scribes used, did it also limit the opportunities for expansion that scribes allowed themselves? On the other hand, one scroll outside of the Torah has been found in Palaeo-Hebrew script: Job, that one book in the Writings which seemed to emanate from patriarchal times. Would that indicate a special status for Job, so that even if expansions could not be brought in from other books, Job was considered an exception? And in the other case, that of Ezekiel, it could be that because that book shared so much of concepts and terminology with large parts of the Torah, it constituted another exception.

We are left with questions for which the data give no answer.

b. Major Expansions Not From Parallel Passages

In one sense 24:1 and 24:9 are the most striking of the clear cases of major expansions, for these are the additions of the names of Aaron's two younger sons, Eleazar and Ithamar, which are found not in a parallel version of the narrative, but rather in genealogical passages, such as 6:23, and in the Priestly instructions for ordaining priests, 28:1. The only narrative that mentions them is in Lev 10:1-7, the story of the death of the two older sons, Nadab and Abihu, and of their being succeeded by Eleazar and Ithmar. Of course this may be a rather academic matter, since any scribe of the Pentateuch would have known these genealogies and narratives so well that he could easily have determined to supply these names from his own memory, without resort to another passage.

Whatever the source of these expansions, the motivation is significant, since it seems to have been the desire to ensure that the two brothers who did ultimately attain preeminence be credited with having experienced the great theophany on Mount Sinai along with the two older brothers who lost their positions and their lives as a result of their sin.

It would be interesting to know whether this motivation was more theological, political, or merely literary in nature. Theologically, it could have reflected a desire that the wicked not excel the righteous in receiving a revelation of God. Politically, it could have related somehow to conflicting claims of different priestly groups. Literarily, it could have arisen from a desire that the narrative spanning the entire Torah -- not just Exodus -- cohere.

c. Major Expansions From Deuteronomy

There are four major expansions which appear to have been inserted into Exodus from parallel passages in Deuteronomy for various purposes.

Two of these expansions occur in chapter 32 and were apparently imported from Deuteronomy 9 for the purpose of filling out the story. Both highlight the negative aspects of the story, which was already very negative indeed. The expansion in 32:9 quotes Yahweh's complaint in Deut 9:13 about the stubbornness of the people, and the expansion in 32:10 quotes Deut 9:20 about Yahweh's anger against Aaron individually, so that Moses had to pray for his life.

Each of these expansions agrees word for word with the corresponding sentence in Deuteronomy, except that changes have been made as required by the different context in Exodus, such as the change from

"Yahweh said to me" to "Yahweh said to Moses." (In 𝕸𝕿 Deut 9:13 has the word "saying," which is lacking in 𝕸𝕿 in Exod 32:9 [□𝐐ᵐ]. This, however, is almost surely an addition made in Deuteronomy after the text of Exodus was expanded.)

Incidentally, there is a third expansion influenced by Deuteronomy 9 in this chapter, 32:7ב. Because of its brevity it is counted with moderate expansions; see below.

If we were to look only at the expansion in 32:10 concerning Aaron, we might be tempted to suppose that this is due to a scribe with strong sentiments against Aaron or against the priesthood in general. But taken in conjunction with the other two expansions from the same narrative in Deuteronomy, as well as the major expansions in the plague narratives, this possibility seems less likely. (See the discussion of Aaron in the Excursus.) On the other hand, taken in conjunction with the two expansions in chapter 20 (see below) we may detect a desire to heighten the prestige of Moses. In other words, if there was no specifically anti-Aaron/priesthood sentiment, there may nevertheless have been a specifically pro-Moses/prophet sentiment. A possible theological motive of both 32:9 and 10 was the desire to heighten the contrast between the wickedness of the Israelites, including Aaron specifically, and the righteousness -- and the righteous anger -- of Yahweh (see also the discussion of motivation in Chapter V.A.3).

The major expansion in 18:25𝕸 is from the parallel narrative in Deut 1:9-18. The text and the motivation of the scribe have been discussed by Tigay[3] and above, in Chapter V.A.3. It seems clear that the motivation was not merely a desire for greater fullness, but primarily that of harmonizing the two accounts of the choosing of judges, by placing the roles of Jethro and of Moses in chronological succession rather than allowing them to seem mutually exclusive.

This appears to betray a concern that every parallel passage in the Torah be clearly and immediately harmonious, so that a scribe felt obligated to create such clear harmony even if it required a rather wooden approach to the narrative. Does this mean, then, that the same scribe who expanded the narrative in Exodus to create harmony, or a colleague, similarly expanded Deuteronomy with the passage in Exodus so that Jethro's role would be clear there? Or does it mean that, since the version in Deuteronomy is put in

---

[3]Jeffrey H. Tigay, "An Empirical Basis for the Documentary Hypothesis," *JBL* 94 (1975), pp. 333-335.

Moses' mouth, so that he is narrating his own experiences, that version was considered even more authoritative than Exodus, and was allowed to stand? If this latter was the case, then there was a hierarchy of authority even within the Torah.

The limited evidence available to us suggests that all of the expansion and harmonization went in one direction, in other words, that Deuteronomy was in fact considered more authoritative. Of the witnesses that have been preserved for us, we have no evidence that Deuteronomy was expanded so that it harmonized with Exodus. In the Samaritan Pentateuch Jethro has not been brought from Exodus 18 into Deut 1:9-18, and Deut 9:12-14 has not been supplemented with statements from Exod 32: 7-10 (see above, Chapter V.C.3). (Deut 5 has been supplemented with the commandment to build the altar on Gerizim, but that comes from elsewhere within Deuteronomy.)

Of course, as we recognize that 𝔐 is not a homogeneous text-type, but displays different characteristics in different books, we must be open to the same possibility in the case of 𝔐. Just because Deuteronomy as it has been preserved in 𝔐 has not been expanded from Exodus does not mean that no scribes were expanding Deuteronomy. Thus we must look at other scrolls from Qumran. The only other similar example that I know of in Qumran scrolls is the expansion of Num 27:23 with Deut 3:21, and of Num 20:13 with Deut 3: 23-24.[4] In both cases the narrative of Moses' experiences has been expanded with his own first-person report. It could be that Moses' own words were given precedence in a case of apparent conflict, or it could be merely that the fragmentary remains preserved for us misrepresent the actual situation, and that Deuteronomy was also subjected to similar treatment as Exodus and Numbers.

The major expansion in **20:19ᵃ** was taken from Deut 5:24-27, and that in 20:21ᵇ (☐𝐐ᵃ) from Deut 5:28-29; 18:18-22; and 5:30-31. The text and the scribal motivation have been discussed by Tigay[5] and above, in Chapter V.A.3. The point to be reiterated here is that by bringing in text from Deuteronomy 5 about the prophet like Moses, the scribe dealt somewhat more freely with the narrative of Sinai than we have seen elsewhere, since that promise is not related in Deuteronomy to the theophany at Sinai.

---

[4] See Cross, *Library,* p. 186 n. 35, re 4QNumᵇ.
[5] *Ibid.,* pp. 335-340.

Similar free handling of the narrative is one of the more striking features of the "Samaritan sectarian" expansion in 20:17[b], where the command to build the altar on Gerizim is also added to the decalogue, and thus to the narrative of Sinai. Thus an especially significant feature of 20:21[b], a major expansion belonging to the 𝐐ᵐ𝔪 tradition and not considered "sectarian," is that it shares this free handling of the narrative with the "sectarian" expansion, showing that the "Samaritan" scribe was only following in his predecessors' footsteps.

In each case the text in Exodus corresponds exactly to that in Deuteronomy except for deliberate changes related to the new context of the text. This precise agreement would suggest one of three alternatives. Either the scribe who made the expansion knew the passage in Deuteronomy by heart, or else he took the trouble to look up the passage and copy from it, or else one scribe inserted something resembling the passage in Deuteronomy and a later scribe took the trouble to make it agree exactly. In any one of the three alternatives, the text in Exodus and/or Deuteronomy must have been held inviolable in some sense. Either the text in Exodus could only be expanded if it were done with other precise words from Scripture, and/or the text in Deuteronomy could only be interpolated if it were copied precisely.

It is curious to realize that when interpolations were brought into Exodus from Deuteronomy they were letter perfect, whereas when the simple text of Exodus was copied from an old to a new scroll of Exodus, there was latitude for small differences. If one were going to take the somewhat audacious step of interpolating text from a scroll other than Exodus, did one hesitate to allow oneself any extra liberties?

Or is this difference due merely to the individual habits of the one or two or three scribes who made the major expansions? Or is it perhaps more likely that the different types of developments arose in different periods? In other words, did the small expansions and alterations, such as the addition of <u>and he defeated them</u> or the alteration from איש אל אחיו to אחד אל אחד, occur during a period of tolerance for minor variations, whereas the major expansions were made when there was no such tolerance?

If this is so, then it would seem that the major expansions were made later than the smaller expansions and alterations, since the trend would probably move from greater to lesser tolerance. In a very few cases, then, after the scribes had lost their tolerance for variation, an overriding reason for a major expansion must have made itself manifest, such as the need for harmonization or the theological point. In these cases the text was allowed to increase in size, but only with the exact words which were already found in Scripture elsewhere.

An alternative chronology could be suggested: perhaps major interpolations from Deuteronomy were first brought in without too much regard for precision in copying, and then in a later period of greater strictness other scribes proofread the text in Exodus against that in Deuteronomy to achieve exact agreement. This suggestion could work more easily for the long expansions in Exodus 20, where a scribe could still know what text "belonged" to Exodus and what had come from Deuteronomy, than for the much shorter expansions in Exodus 32, where the two versions still look rather different despite the importations in Exodus. Even in chapter 32, if a scribe were comparing three scrolls at once: an unexpanded scroll of Exodus, an expanded scroll of Exodus, and an unexpanded scroll of Deuteronomy, he could have accomplished his purpose. But this would show a remarkable degree of laxity regarding differences between two scrolls of Exodus in the same scribe who was remarkably concerned that there be no difference in two sentences between a scroll of Exodus and one of Deuteronomy. It seems unlikely that these two approaches would be combined in one person.

Summary: These four major expansions from Deuteronomy were added with great care on the part of a scribe who apparently opened a scroll to the parallel passages and copied word for word, only changing as the changed context required. It appears that various motives were involved. There were the literary motives: a desire that the narrative in Exodus 32 be more complete and that the narrative in Exodus 18 agree with the parallel narrative in Deuteronomy. There may well have been theological motives as well, such as a desire to emphasize the righteousness of Yahweh's anger against the sin of the Israelites (chapter 32) and the great glory of Yahweh such that the Israelites could only communicate with God through a mediator, Moses or a follower (chapter 20), and that even the great high priest Aaron needed Moses' intercession (chapter 32). This last point may suggest political motivation as well: to bolster the prestige of "the prophet like Moses," whether a figure recognized in a certain community or one awaited in the future.

In any event, regardless of the type or the strength of the motivation, the solution in the four texts under investigation reached no further than to quote words already in the Torah. No new words were written. Whatever newness was created arose from the new combination of existing but separate passages. As we have seen, major expansions from Deuteronomy were treated very carefully indeed. The scribe who sensed a lack or a discrepancy in his text of Exodus was free to make up that lack or to smooth away that discrepancy if he were scrupulous in doing so only with other parts of Scripture. If revelation were in one place deficient, it could be improved, but only by revelation that already existed elsewhere in written form. The scribe was not free to add to revelation by creating his own words.

It seems, then, that the words of revelation were treated with more care than the form and structure of revelation. Words from Deuteronomy could be brought into Exodus even if they were thus out of their revealed position. Apparently the scribes attributed greater revelatory significance to exactness of wording than to the structure of a pericope or of a scroll. This freedom extended even to a certain disregard for time and place in narratives. If Yahweh had ever at any time in Moses' life promised a prophet to come (or commanded the building of an altar on Gerizim!), then those words could be placed during the theophany at Sinai.

As we have indicated, however, and as will become clearer in the rest of this chapter, if such an insistence on exactness of wording did character-ize the scribe or scribes who made the major expansions, it was not typical of many scribes, who seem not to have been disturbed by variety of wording.

d. Major Expansions From Parallel Passages in Exodus

The only major expansion from a parallel passage in Exodus occurs in the tabernacle account, at 27:19^b, where an introductory sentence to a new subsection of the instructions was composed out of phrases from the parallel passage in the account of the fulfilment of the instructions (39:1).

Unfortunately this sentence is misplaced by two or three verses in the extant witnesses! This may suggest that the expansion was originally meant to serve as a rubric rather than as part of the text proper. Perhaps it was first written in the margin as an aid for finding the pericope, was later inserted in the text itself, but accidentally placed too early; later still, scribes must no longer have felt the freedom to tamper with the text that they were copying. This variant may not belong with the other major expansions, because it may have entered the text proper by error rather than purposefully.

In any event, even this expansion, which may have originally been a marginal rubric, is made up exclusively of words that already appeared elsewhere in the text of Exodus. Whatever creativity was involved consisted in putting together in a new combination words and phrases that were already in the parallel passage, to form a new sentence. Thus even a rubric, if it was that, was treated very conservatively: only words appearing already in the revealed text were used.

There is one other possible major expansion from a parallel passage: **36:21-24**, which involves the presence or absence of a pericope of twenty-five verses describing the making of the various coverings, frames, and bars of the tabernacle and representing the counterpart of 26:3-30. If it was originally lacking, then it must have been added by a scribe who wanted the second section of the tabernacle account, that describing its construction, to correspond more closely with the first section, that describing the instructions. Once again, the need for harmony, and in this case symmetry, could be supplied with text from elsewhere in the scroll.

e. Major Expansions From the Context in Exodus

In the plague narratives the major expansions generally repeat an entire paragraph from the immediate context, in which Yahweh tells Moses what to say to Pharaoh in the conflict for the liberation of the Hebrews. Those extant in **Qᵐ** are 7:18ᵇ;   7:29ᵇ;   8:19ᵇ;   9:5ᵇ;   9:19ᵇ;   and 10:2ᵇ. Yahweh's message to Pharaoh was repeated word for word, but Yahweh's instructions to Moses as to when and where he was to give the messsage were greatly summarized.

These expansions have been discussed in detail in Chapter V.A.3. Here it is enough to point out again that while the motivation is usually assumed to have been the desire to make it explicit that Yahweh's instructions were fulfilled to the letter, closer observation of which features were exactly repeated and which were omitted or summarized makes it seem much more likely that the purpose was theological, liturgical, and/or didactic instead. From a theological point of view, the theme of the entire narrative is the warfare between the two gods, Yahweh and Pharaoh. There may well have been a desire to highlight that conflict by showing that Yahweh's warlike challenges were delivered exactly to the enemy. From a liturgical or didactic point of view, it seems appropriate to suggest that such a text would have been especially suited to liturgical celebrations of the exodus and of the kingship of Yahweh. The expansions may have been used for some sort of audience participation, with antiphonal recitation.[6]

Finally, a brief reminder of two major expansions (not extant in $\mathbf{Q}^{n}$, but see Chapter V.A.3.a[1]) from a greater distance but still within the plague and exodus narrative: the complaint of the Hebrews to Moses and Yahweh's threat to Pharaoh about his first-born son. These are remarkable because they indicate a broader sweep of concern, a desire to harmonize the narratives of the plagues and exodus as a whole and to make explicit two parallels that, because they were so far removed from each other, were not completely obvious.

f. Summary

Thus we have seen major expansions in the text of Exodus from four sources, and possibly a fifth: from passages that were not parallel (Eleazar and Ithamar); from passages in Deuteronomy, both parallel (narratives of Sinai, the choosing of the judges, and the golden calf) and otherwise (promise of a prophet like Moses, and in the "sectarian" expansion the commandment about Gerizim); from parallel passages in Exodus (the two parts of the tabernacle account); and from the context in Exodus, both immediate (Yahweh's speeches to Pharah) and farther removed (the Hebrews' complaint to Moses and Yahweh's threat against Pharaoh's first-born son); and finally, possibly from outside the Torah, specifically from Job and Ezekiel.

While it is always hazardous to impute motives to someone from this distance, speculations have included the following. Some motivations might have been chiefly literary, such as filling out one version of the story with elements from another, harmonizing seeming conflicts, drawing explicit parallels, creating better symmetry, heightening the dramatic, for instance, by adding a description of the plague of darkness.

Some motivations might have been chiefly or partially theological, such as harmonizing if that were done in order to protect Scripture (as opposed to any literary text) from the appearance of conflict, importing theological motifs such as a description of the sabbath, highlighting the

---

[6]The use of the plagues in Psalms 78 and 105, and the -- tediously -- repeated writing out of antiphonal refrains such as in Ps 136 show that other biblical scrolls included liturgical compositions of similar nature. The book of Exodus itself calls for antiphonal response: see Exodus 15.

warlike nature of Yahweh's victory over Pharaoh, emphasizing God's judgment against sin and the need for intercession by a third party, or emphasizing God's glory and the need for mediation by a prophet.

One motivation of a liturgical nature was suggested, in the case of the repetition of Yahweh's challenges to Pharaoh, perhaps for the sake of antiphonal recitation in worship and celebration.

Several of these theological motives may have involved a political aspect as well, especially those that related to Moses' position vis-à-vis the people as a whole or vis-à-vis Aaron. Certainly the "Samaritan sectarian" expansion would fit into both categories: theological and political.

Several of the motivations suggested would imply that the community had either requested or at least appreciated the expansions. It would be most interesting to have more light on the relationship of the scribe with his colleagues and with his community. Did he make the kinds of expansions in the narratives that he knew a certain group of people would find desirable, or had actually commissioned him to make?

To summarize the limitation involved: even in the case of the most significant expansions discovered in **Q⁰ⅲⅲⅢG**, the words and sentences involved appeared already in the text of Exodus, or at least in that of Deuteronomy or another book considered canonical today by both Jews and Christians. The scribe of Exodus remained a copyist even when he was copying Deuteronomy. At most he made new combinations of words, phrases, and paragraphs, changed the person or tense of a verb or pronoun, and omitted words or phrases inappropriate or deemed unnecessary in the new context.

Thus the scribe or scribes involved exercised freedom in their work, but a strictly limited freedom. The freedom other writers felt to add from their own imaginations to the text, as exhibited, for example, in the *Genesis Apocryphon*, was certainly not exercised by the scribes involved in the traditions represented in **Q⁰ⅲⅢG**. Or perhaps it would be more accurate to say: that freedom was not exercised by the scribes as they were engaged in producing a new scroll of Exodus. Perhaps when all of the Qumran scrolls have been published it will become clear that some individuals were responsible for copying and/or composing very different sorts of texts in their lifetimes. Is it impossible to imagine that one person could copy a very conservative text of a biblical book, similar to 1QIsᵇ, as well as copy -- and add to? -- somewhat more expansionist scrolls such as **Q⁰**, and also to copy or even compose more paraphrastic or even "rewritten Bible"[7] scrolls? Were these differences in texts matters of the personality of scribes, or were they matters of the tasks taken on at particular times? Could one scribe devote a painstaking springtime to carefully reproducing a "proto-Massoretic" text because his colleagues wanted another text like the one that was wearing out, a more ingenious summer to copying and expanding a text of Exodus because his community wanted a text that had been harmonized and supplemented, and a creative autumn composing a "rewritten Bible" for more lighthearted moments in community life?

It is hard to believe that a scribe would not have been aware of the differences among the various texts that he copied and used during his lifetime. Or did each scribe copy only one sort of text? Did each scribe have his own specialty? Was there a specific word for each kind of text? Were there different verbs for the activities involved in copying the different kinds of texts? Did a scribe think of different texts as belonging to different genres, as intended for different people or at least different purposes? Were they equally valid if used for the intended purpose? Was it equally worth his time to copy them?

Again, we only have the Qumran library to guide us. But certainly in that very tightknit community that was so hostile to all outsiders, some strikingly different texts have been found. Were they tolerated by the same people? Were they copied by some of the same people? Were they used by the same people?

But if the scribes involved in the major expansions in the text of Exodus did not exercise the degree of freedom that others did in the composition of paraphrastic texts of the "rewritten Bible" sort, it is nevertheless true that they could make additions of remarkable length to the text, as long as they found the words elsewhere in Scripture. The compulsion to reproduce exactly the text of their *Vorlage*, as exhibited, for example, in the work of the Massoretes, was certainly not characteristic of scribes during some early stages of these four texts, **Qⁿ ⅲ𝔪G**.

That approach was to make any further such expansions impossible, but it became prevalent at different times for different groups. Already in the days of the Qumran community many texts were being treated very

---

[7]Vermes' term for works such as the *Genesis Apocryphon*; see, e.g., *Perspective*, p. 66: "From the literary point of view, it is the Bible rewritten, i.e. made colourful by supplementary stories and interpretations."

conservatively, while others were still undergoing expansion and alteration. If that stricter approach is one of the steps in the gradual process of canonization, then different texts give evidence of having reached that stage at different times.

Perhaps it is worth repeating that all or most of these expansions may well have been the work of one scribe, or of just a very small circle of scribes. These motives and methods should not be attributed to scribes generally in the Second Temple period. They are for the most part represented only in one tradition, and may all -- or almost all -- have been perpetrated in a very short span of time, if not by one scribe, then perhaps in one scribal center.

g. Excursus Regarding the Treatment of Aaron's Name in the Textual Transmission of Exodus

At first sight one might expect frequent disagreement among the textual traditions in the mention of Aaron's name, considering the general proclivity in Exodus for expansion, greater fullness, and concern for harmonizing narratives, as well as the specific interest in the Second Temple period in priestly functions and genealogies. Yet surprisingly this is not the case.

For a discussion of the treatment of Aaron in the major expansions in the plague narratives preserved in the 𝐐ᵃ 𝖑𝖚 tradition, see Chapter V.A.3.

Comparison of the complete text of Exodus in 𝖑𝖚 and 𝖒 shows that apart from those major expansions, there is only one place in all of Exodus where 𝖑𝖚 (or 𝐐ᵃ) has Aaron when 𝖒 does not: 10:24ב; (see Chapter II.C.1).

Comparison of the (highly unsatisfactory) list in HR with that in Mandelkern[8] shows likewise a very high level of agreement between the occurrences of Aaron's name in 𝖒 and 𝐆.

Taking Rᵉᵈ as the standard in all cases (8) where HR shows intra-Greek MS variation, the two lists match almost exactly. 𝖒 has the name 115 times. 𝐆 has the name in all of those cases[9] except two. In 29:9 𝖒 has the name twice, 𝐆 only once; and in 12:28 Rᵉᵈ agrees with 𝖒 in having the name, though it is lacking in BA⁺.[10]   Whereas in 29:9 the entire

---

[8]There are at least two printing errors in Mandelkern's list: 28,19 should read 28,29; and 24,2.4 should read 28,2.4.

[9]Including both verses that apparently correspond to Hebrew 39:1: 39:1 and 13.

[10]Hence this verse is not listed in HR.

pericope concerns the consecration of Aaron and his sons, in 12:28 the variation affects the standing of Aaron alongside of Moses. Thus only the second passage is analogous to 10:24ב, because the question of Aaron's prestige is involved. Did the Israelites do as Yahweh commanded Moses alone, or as Yahweh commanded both Moses and Aaron (12:28)? Did Pharaoh call Moses alone, or both Moses and Aaron, to tell them to leave Egypt (10:24ב)?

On the other hand, **G** has Aaron's name only twice where it is lacking in **M**. In both cases Aaron is already named in the same verse, but subsequently **M** refers to him with a pronominal suffix whereas **G** names him again (28:38; 35:19).

Thus, contrary to expectations of a wholesale adding in of Aaron's name in the various textual traditions, either for the sake of priestly prestige or of narrative harmonization, there are only two cases of disagreement where Aaron's presence and/or prestige could conceivably be at stake, and only in 10:24ב is there relative unanimity within the tradition that omits Aaron's name (as opposed to 12:28, where R[od] rejects the reading of BA[+]). The study of **Q[a]** has brought to light one other variant involving the relationship of Moses and Aaron; for a discussion of 6:27ג, see chapter III.A.5.

Thus none of the textual traditions reflects any concerted effort of its own to make Aaron's explicit presence and action consistent in the plague narratives, with the result that he receives only haphazard mention. Nevertheless, a look at the context of our sole variant regarding the addition of the name, 10:24ב, shows that throughout the eighth plague (locusts) in chapter 10, Aaron's name does appear regularly (10:3,8,16), although many of the verb forms remain singular. Thus it appears that whatever drive did exist to include Aaron's name, while it antedated the division of the text into the various extant traditions, it occurred late enough in the literary history to disturb syntactical relationships.

Summary: It appears that if -- and to the extent that -- Aaron's name was added in the text of Exodus, this occurred at two discrete stages: earlier, during the compositional stage, while the book was still developing, and where we have no documentation in the form of textual variants, though some syntactical phenomena probably reflect the expansions; and much later, during the stage of the transmission of the tradition of **Q[a]M**, where we have textual variants as documentation. Apart from the **Q[a]M** tradition, there is no evidence of any effort to maximize either Moses or Aaron at the expense of the other.

2. MODERATE EXPANSIONS

a. *Moderate Expansions Influenced by Deuteronomy*

There is one case of a moderate expansion influenced by Deuteronomy. It is **32:7ב**, which has already been mentioned in section 1.c., with the major expansions from Deuteronomy. The shortest form of the command to Moses, and that which has been judged preferable, is "Go down." While one tradition has added a merely routine expansion, "Go," another has added not only "Go" but also "quickly from here," which appears in Deuteronomy 9:12. (See the chart in Chapter II.A1, showing all the versions in both Exod **32:7ב** and Deut 9:12).

It should be noted that this moderate expansion seems to be of a somewhat different nature than the major expansions from Deuteronomy which are discussed above. Those are entire sentences or paragraphs which agree word for word with the text in Deuteronomy and have been carefully copied. In this case, on the other hand, the expanded version in Exodus, as short as it is, is not exactly the same as the text in Deuteronomy. The scribe does not appear to have looked up the parallel passage in Deuteronomy, but merely to have made an expansion under the influence of his memory of that passage.

If he was making this expansion with the same sort of care that the scribes of the major expansions put into their work, then he seems to have felt the freedom to bring in a phrase or two from Deuteronomy as well as a verb from a similar context elsewhere in Exodus (e.g., 19:24) to create a slightly different sentence. On the other hand, he may not have thought all that much about what he was doing. Perhaps as he added the phrases in Deuteronomy that had occurred to him, he also added another word as well, since it was a "natural," creating a combination that was typical of narrative style, including that of Exodus. We will see other examples later of "natural" additions, where a little word or phrase was added to another word with which it often was paired (e.g., "sons of Israel"). Again, regardless of how much thought he gave to this, he was using only words that occurred elsewhere in similar contexts in Exodus and Deuteronomy.

b. Moderate Expansions from Parallel Passages in Exodus

No certain case of a moderate expansion from a parallel passage in Exodus has been discovered in this study.

There is, however, one possible case: **31:5**. It cannot be considered certain because the reading in **Q** is fragmentary. It may be a case of expanding the first section of the tabernacle account, that giving the instructions, to match the parallel sentence in the second section, that giving the construction of the tabernacle. Only one word is involved: the text may have been expanded from "every craft" to "every skilled craft," as in 35:33.

c. Moderate Expansions to Broaden the Application of Case Laws

Although **Q** is only extant for two variants, **21:29** and **21:31**, the entire legal pericope 21:28-36 has been consistently expanded and altered to make case laws originally applying to injuries caused by oxen apply now to similar injuries caused by any animal. The pericope was expanded four times: the words "or any animal" were added after "ox." The alterations, which will also be listed below (see VI.A.7.c), are as follows: nine times "animal" was substituted for "ox," and five times the more general verb "kill" was substituted for the more specific "gore." Thus the laws have been made applicable to many more situations.

Again, these words were already in the broader context in connection with other laws. The scribe was merely carrying out more consistently what had presumably already been done occasionally in the context in his *Vorlage*.

The question arises again of the relationship between the scribe and his community. As we cannot be certain whether a scribe made major expansions at the request of a group of people, so we cannot be certain in an instance of expanding the applicability of a legal pericope. Did the scribe's action here accurately reflect the custom and the concerns of his community, or was it merely a piece of academic manipulation of the text, unrelated to his daily life?

d. Moderate Expansions for the Purpose of Harmonization

The one instance of a moderate expansion for the purpose of harmonization within one narrative occurs in the account of the seventh plague. Whereas 9:19, 22, and 25 threaten and then describe the coming of the hail on both animals and humans who are left in the fields, according to verses 20-21 the Egyptians responded to the threat by bringing only their animals in from the fields. A scribe with a tidy mind seems to have wanted to make this response adequate to the threat, and thus **9:20** and 21 insert the phrase "his slaves and" before "his animals."

Note that although the precise word, "slaves," was not in the immediate context, the thought was there in the recurring word "humans." The scribe added a specific word that was not in the text but that was implicit.

The foregoing is the only clear instance of a moderate expansion for the purpose of harmonization. There is, however, another possible case, which has been classified as a synonymous variant because it is not possible to be certain about preferability. If the shorter reading were preferable in **29:2**, then a scribe must have added the words "spread with oil" under the influence of the requirements for peace offerings in Lev 7:12.

e. Moderate Expansions for Emphasis in a Narrative

There are six cases where a relatively significant individual word or phrase has been added to a narrative for the sake of emphasis.

Two of these additions heighten the drama in the narrative of the contest between Moses and Aaron and Pharaoh's magicians. In one tradition in 7:9, 10a, and **9:8**, after reference to Moses and Aaron standing "before Pharaoh" the words "and before his servants" have been inserted. This has the effect of keeping the magicians more explicitly in view as taking a continuing adversarial role in the action. Since they were already explicitly mentioned after Pharaoh in all the traditions represented in this study in 7:10b, the scribe was not creating *ex nihilo* when he added them in three other verses. But by means of the addition the reader is reminded to watch to see what the fate of the magicians will be.

Another tradition has emphasized this contest by making a different addition. In the narrative of the sixth plague the verb "and they stood" has been inserted into the sentence about Moses and Aaron's throwing ashes into the sky to bring boils. As has been argued in the discussion of **9:10**, this seems to be a word play to further dramatize the contest between Moses and Aaron on the one hand, who are able to stand even before Pharaoh, and the Egyptian magicians on the other, who despite all the points they have won until this plague are now unable to stand before Moses, because of the pain they are suffering from the boils (9:11). Thus their defeat is further accentuated by the contrast between them and the Hebrew leaders.

Two other additions also heighten the narrative of the plagues. In **10:5** the expanded reading has: "all <u>the plants of the ground and all the fruit of</u> the trees of yours which grow in the field." The effect is to dramatize the destruction wrought by the locusts and to make the prediction of the plague correspond more closely to the description of its results in 10:15. Note that this is not a "clean" addition. It is not that the text originally read "all the fruit of the trees" and a scribe added "all the plants of the ground." Instead, the scribe has not only added one entire member but has also expanded the first member. If it be agreed that this is indeed a secondary expansion, then it may shed light on the probability of the secondary nature of other readings that are similarly "not clean" (cf., e.g., **31:13–14**).

The fourth moderate expansion for emphasis in the plague narrative is less striking. In 8:12[16] and **9:9ג** the phrase "<u>on humans and on animals</u>" is added to emphasize the totality of the damage done by the plagues of gnats and boils. This phrase already occurs four times in chapters 8 and 9, so it was a very natural addition.

Besides those four moderate expansions in the plague narrative, there are two others in succeeding narratives. In **17:13ב** a second verb has been added to the sentence, "and Joshua defeated Amalek and his people <u>and he struck/destroyed them</u> with the edge of the sword." Thus the degree of the victory of Israel over Amalek, according to 17:16 the Israelites' perpetual enemy, is intensified.

This expansion, though it consists of only one word, and indeed a very common word for battles, is nonetheless noteworthy because the word does not occur in the context, nor is there a parallel in Exodus or in Deuteronomy. Yet this verb, נכה, is used outside the Pentateuch for the action of other Israelites against the Amalekites. Perhaps the declaration here in Exodus 17 of "war with Amalek from generation to generation" brought to the scribe's mind one or more of those other passages: e.g., 1 Sam 14:48; 15:7; 2 Sam 1:1; 1 Chron 4:43 (cf. also Num 14:45, where the Amalekites defeated Israel, and Gen 14:7, where Chedorlaomer's alliance defeated the Amalekites).

If there was in the scribe's mind anything more than a desire to intensify the miraculous aspect of the narrative, there may possibly have been a desire to draw an explicit contrast as a reminder that when Moses was in charge the Israelites defeated the Amalekites, whereas when they defied Moses, as in Numbers 14, they were defeated by the Amalekites; or that Joshua (under Moses' leadership) was obedient in battling the

Amalekites where Saul was not. In 1 Sam 15:3 Samuel conveyed Yahweh's command to Saul: לך והכיתה את עמלק והחרמתם את כל אשר לו.   An argument against the latter possibility is the fact that the contrast would have been more clearly brought out by using the second verb in 1 Sam 15:3, חרם; note the exact correspondence of the entire clause in 1 Sam 15:8 with Exod 17:13ב: ואת כל העם החרים לפי חרב.   The problem, of course, is stated in the following verse: Saul spared the king Agag and the best of the spoils.

In this one expansion, then, either the scribe added a word out of his own thoughts because it belonged "naturally" with the phrase "by the mouth of the sword," not caring that it was not in the context; or else he deliberately chose a word that occurred in significant passages elsewhere in the Torah but especially in the Former Prophets.   Either would be remarkable. Either he took the liberty of adding a foreign word, or else he brought in a word from a non-parallel passage outside the Torah or at least outside Exodus-Deuteronomy, and with the intention of making a theological point.

In 18:1ב, after an expansion, Moses' father-in-law Jethro hears "all that God had done <u>for Moses and</u> for Israel his people."   Thus the personal aspect of Jethro's interest is emphasized, in keeping with the fact that this sentence introduces the account of Jethro's visiting Moses and bringing Moses' wife and sons with him.

<u>Summary</u>: Five of the six additions for the purpose of emphasizing the miraculous or otherwise enhancing the narrative already occur in the context in Exodus ("and before his servants," "stood," "the plants of the ground and all the fruit of," "on humans and on animals," and "Moses").

Only the verb "struck, destroyed" is not in the immediate context and required an extra step on the part of the scribe who inserted it. This last addition stands out as very unusual among the variants revealed in the present investigation. It may reflect the greater degree of license taken by one individual. Certainly it is not typical of the other variants here. Most additions can be shown to have come at least from the broader context, including parallel passages in Deuteronomy or Leviticus.

f. Other Moderate Expansions From the Context

There are eight instances of moderate expansion from the context which seem to have been added more out of a desire for greater fullness or completeness of the narrative or for fuller description of objects or for more exact correspondence between different references to the same thing, than for either emphasis or clarification. Since these additions already appeared elsewhere in the immediate context, it is difficult to know how aware a scribe was of the fact that he was expanding the text. One scribe may have intentionally added a word or two to make different references agree, while another scribe may have merely written what he was accustomed to from another passage, without giving much thought to the fact that the fuller formulation did not occur in his *Vorlage* in this present verse.

One expansion that seems to have taken some thought, because it also involved changes, is in **19:10**, where the command "Go to the people (לך אל העם)" became "Go down and warn the people (רד העד בעם)," as in 19:21. At least this first instance seems to have been done deliberately, because of the change involved. Perhaps the scribe wanted greater correspondence between Yahweh's two commands to Moses, especially since the idea of "warning" was already implicit in **19:10**. As in the case of **9:20** (see above, 2.d), where a scribe added "his slaves" in a context mentioning human beings, perhaps some scribes took to themselves the freedom to make explicit what was implicit. In **19:10** the words already appeared in the pericope, whereas in **9:20** the precise word was not in the context.

An expansion that may have been occasioned by a desire for consistency in the story is in **10:24ב**, where Aaron's name is added to that of Moses. Since both men were explicitly mentioned in 10:3,8, and 16, and since the situation in 10:8 was so similar to that in **10:24**, it may have been deemed appropriate to add his name here as well. Yet the other occurrences of his name in the preceding verses may point rather in the direction of unintentional repetition.

Additions that may well have been made with very little thought, because the words "naturally" belong together, are:
"Cast it down on the ground before Pharaoh" (**7:9**; this fuller
    expression occurs in 4:3aα,β)
"Moses went down from the mountain" (**19:25**; as in 19:14)
"Aaron's holy garments" (**28:3**, as in 28:2 and 28:4)
"stone tablets" (**32:15**, as five of the thirteen times these tablets are
    mentioned)
"and make for them" (**28:40**; similar to two other verbs in the
    sentence)

A puzzling expansion is in **15:27**, where three witnesses have: "Then they came to Elim, and *there* there were twelve springs." One, however, reads: "Then they came to Elim, and <u>at Elim</u> there were twelve springs." In Hebrew the three texts read ...אילמה ושם..., whereas the fourth reads ...אילים ובאילים... It is difficult to understand why any scribe felt that that change was necessary!

<u>Summary</u>: In all of these cases of moderate expansion, as we have seen, the words added and/or substituted have been taken from the context in Exodus. The scribe took a very small degree of liberty with the text, since the expansions were relatively short, quite natural, and also very handy.

The preceding eight readings were all moderate expansions from the context. In other words, it has been determined that the shorter reading in each case is preferable.

There is also one synonymous variant involving a longer vs. a shorter reading that should be mentioned in this category. If the shorter reading in **28:11ב** were to be established as preferable, it would mean that a scribe has inserted the instructions to make settings for the two stones in the ephod in this verse, apparently copying the words "<u>and make gold filigree</u>" from two verses later, 28:13, and adding the word "<u>settings</u>" to explain the purpose. Since the phrase "settings of gold filigree" occurs in the account of the construction of the tabernacle eleven chapters later, at 39:6, that passage may also have influenced the expansion here -- if indeed it is an expansion.

g. Moderate Expansions for Clarification

Fourteen instances of expansion for clarification were found, which is a relatively small number. It must be said that few of these seem truly to contribute to the reader's understanding. Most are included here because clarification seems more likely to have been the motivation than any other.

To begin with one that does seem helpful: the word "<u>each</u>" (אחד) has been added to clarify the restitution required by a law (**22:3[4]**).

A second expansion for which the purpose can easily be seen was apparently made to clarify a text that had been altered. In **19:12** "set bounds for the *people* round about, saying..." became "set bounds round about the *mountain,* <u>and to the people</u> you shall say...." The change from "people" to "mountain" was apparently made for the purpose of harmonizing within the Sinai narrative; see below. The aspect to be considered here is that after that alteration was made, it was then deemed helpful to add to the text in order to clarify the audience to whom Moses was to speak.

Only one subject has been added: "the Lord" in 19:24, which not only clarifies who it is who will do the action, but also makes this sentence match another one two verses earlier. And only one object has been added, and that not a separate noun, but merely an accusative suffix (32:13בּ). Twice the sign of the accusative object, את, has been added (25:29; 28:39).

Two indications of time have been added, both of which are also in the immediate context: "today" (32:29בּ) and "in the morning" (34:2).

Other modifiers include:

"to let the people of Israel go out of his land" (7:2);

"the first tablets" (34:1);

"like the stars of heaven in number" (32:13א, as three times in
Deuteronomy);

"bring guilt upon themselves" (28:43בּ, as, e.g., in Leviticus).

Two expansions are difficult to give proper due in English. In 18:27 the idiomatic Hebrew prepositional phrase לוֹ, "for himself," was added to the report of Jethro's leaving, and in 29:33 the phrase "by them," בם, was repeated two words after it occurred already.

Summary: Almost all of these clarifying expansions occur, if not in the immediate context ("the Lord," "today," "in the morning"), then in the same expression elsewhere in Exodus ("out of his land," "first") or in the Torah ("in number," "upon themselves"). Other additions such as the accusative sign or the idiom לוֹ are so minor that the scribe may not even have been aware that he was adding anything. Only the addition of "each" in the law about restitution, and perhaps the addition of "and to the people" to clarify the instructions to Moses, seem to have involved much in the way of exegetical deliberation from the scribe.

There are two possible cases of expansion for clarification, both synonymous variants:

אשר	(18:20)
את	(34:13)

3. MINOR EXPANSIONS

a. *Minor Expansions for Emphasis in a Narrative*

There are three cases where a very minor word was added for emphasis. First, in **8:20[24]** the adverb "very" may have been added to strengthen the adjective "heavy" which already describes the severity of the plague of flies.

Then there are two cases of expansion with the word "all" for emphasis. In **17:13א** one tradition emphasized the completeness of Israel's victory over the Amalekites: "Joshua defeated Amalek and all his people"; contrast the addition of the verb "destroy" by another tradition (**17:13ב**; see above). In **18:13א** the addition "all the people stood about Moses from morning to evening" heightened the problem of which this narrative gives the resolution.

Although these words which have been added are very insignificant in themselves, they take on somewhat greater importance when viewed as part of the pattern which emerged in section VI.A.2.e. of expanding to heighten the effect of narratives.

b. *Minor Expansions to Fill Out Standard Expressions*

The following "natural" expansions probably occurred because the expression often appeared in its fuller form:

"from the land of Egypt"	(6:27ב)
"signs and wonders"	(11:9)
"sons of Israel"	(9:7ב)

These expressions occurred so commonly in the Bible that the scribe may well have written the fuller form almost out of habit, without any conscious thought on his part.

c. *Other Minor Expansions*

Other minor additions are the following:

"saying"	(8:16[20]; 9:8א; 32:7א)
"and"	(7:15א; 17:2ב; 26:24א; 32:27)

It seems most likely that such additions were so routine that they were made almost without thinking.

d. *Summary*

All of these minor expansions could have occurred more out of habit than deliberation.   Possible exceptions are those which lend greater emphasis to a narrative, since there is a pattern of both major and moderate expansions for that purpose.

But if the scribe first wrote these additions more out of habit than deliberation, the fact remains that they were allowed to stay in the text. This means either that during the period when such minor expansions could be made proofreading was done rather carelessly, or else that the proof-reader, whether he was the same scribe or another, noticed them but took a liberal attitude toward such minor expansions.   Was it more important to have a neat scroll than a precise, "pristine" scroll?   Or were such minor expansions perceived as quite proper, perhaps appreciated because of their contribution toward clarification, emphasis, and fulness?

e. Possible Minor Expansions
The following are synonymous variants, where there is a difference in length but no preferability can be established.   It is possible that these represent expansions:

your sons	(32:2)
two 2°	(28:23)
אולם	(9:16)

Next, there are three synonymous variants involving the word "all." First, it may have been added in **9:9א**. And finally, in **10:6א, ב** the word "all" occurs in two different places in the traditions: should it be "the houses of all your servants" or "and all the houses in all the land"?   Or would the preferable reading lack both all's?   Or would it have both all's?

f. Grammatical and Syntactical Expansions
No clear cases of expansion for grammatical or syntactical reasons have been found.

There are, however, fifteen synonymous variants involving the presence or absence of grammatical and syntactical features.   These will be briefly listed here since they do involve shorter vs. longer readings, although it cannot be considered certain that they represent expansions.

There are six cases of variation in the conjunction *waw:* **13:5; 17:16; 18:16א;   18:21ב, ג;   28:4**.

Four synonymous variants involve the presence or absence of the definite article: **18:13ב; 22:24ב; 26:8; 29:22ב**.

There are five cases of variation in the locative *he:*   9:8בַ;   21:13;
27:9;   27:11בַ;   36:23.

4. MAJOR OMISSIONS

No indisputable cases of major omissions have been found in this
study.

There is, however, one synonymous variant (36:21-24), involving the
presence or absence of twenty-five verses in the second section of the
tabernacle account. Since they concern only the curtains, coverings, frames,
and bars, and especially since they repeat in slightly different form the
instructions in 26:3-30, might a scribe have omitted them purposely? This
possibility seems slight because in almost all other cases of omission in
this study, as will become clear in this and the following sections, a cause
of accidental omission can be detected in the text. Hence this variant has
already been discussed in VI.A.1.d., with major expansions, specifically for
the purpose of symmetry between the two parallel accounts of the
tabernacle.

Another synonymous variant which may involve parablepsis is
31:13-14. If it were indeed an omission, the scribe would have skipped
fourteen words between two occurrences of היא.

5. MODERATE OMISSIONS

Only two clear cases of moderate omissions have been found in this
study. The first is **22:4[3]**, where eight words are lacking in one tradition.
This lack is significant for the meaning of the case law, for one statement
of restitution is omitted although its corresponding case is included, and
one statement of a case is omitted, although its corresponding restitution
is included. The explanation of this omission is simple, however: it is
almost certainly a case of homoioteleuton. Thus this omission is the result
of carelessness and even though it creates a fairly significant discrepancy
in the text it arose harmlessly enough.

The other omission of moderate length occurs in **25:33**, where the
same seven-word phrase occurs twice in the Hebrew, quite properly for
Hebrew syntax, to indicate duplication. It occurs only once in one tradition,
again due almost certainly to homoioteleuton.

Summary: In both of these cases, then, there has been a clear omission on the part of one tradition, but it is the result of a very understandable lapse on the part of the scribe. Both of these omissions do, however, raise the question of proofreading. It is quite possible -- and, if true, would be understandable -- that the proofreader's eye skipped from one place in the *Vorlage* in the same way that had happened during the copying. But that would indicate somewhat lower standards of proofreading than were to come into vogue with the Massoretes. For such omissions to stand shows that no one was counting the words, let alone the letters.

There are several synonymous variants where one reading is substantially shorter, but where it has not been possible to determine that these are necessarily omissions. It is also possible that the shorter reading is preferable, and that some scribe or scribes have added to the text.

If the longer reading were preferable in 28:11ב, then a scribe must have inadvertently omitted the clause "and make for them settings of gold filigree." There is no obvious reason for parablepsis here.

If the longer reading were preferable in 29:2, then a scribe must have inadvertently omitted the phrase "spread with oil." This would not be a clear case of homoioteleuton or homoiarchton, but there is a good deal of repetition of words in the verse which could have given rise to the omission.

If the variant in 10:21ב were a case of omission, it would be a case of homoiarchton where two words were lost: "that one may feel [grope in] the darkness."

6. MINOR OMISSIONS

Only three clear cases of minor omissions have surfaced in this study. In this case the underlined words are those which have been omitted.

"Observe what I command you today."   (34:11א)

"...the Girgashites..."   (34:11ב)

The third omission is best reproduced in Hebrew, since it involves only the explicit use of a personal pronoun which is otherwise implied:

הנה הוא יוצא   (7:15ב).

Each of these three omissions is the result of simple parablepsis on the part of a scribe.

Summary: Thus no case of intentional omission has been found. In almost every case a glance at the Hebrew letters involved indicates how easily a scribe's eye would have skipped over the word or group of words involved. But these unintentional omissions indicate that proofreading left something to be desired in the periods when these occurred. Perhaps the proofreader only read the copy, and did not compare it with the _Vorlage_. If the copy made sense, then it was allowed to stand. Or perhaps he did compare both, but not quite carefully enough. A greater degree of control was needed.

For possible cases of minor omissions, see the synonymous variants listed in VI.A.3.e. and f., as possible minor expansions.

7. ALTERATIONS

These are secondary readings which do not involve length of text, but rather a different order, word, or form.

a. Different Form of a Pericope
There are no clear instances of a secondarily altered pericope.

There are, however, four instances where there appear to be two different forms of a pericope, neither of which can be established as preferable. The first is 18:9-11, which involves six variants. Does this mean that there were from the beginning two forms of this narrative, or that through the course of transmission so many developments -- expansions and alterations -- occurred that the entire paragraph now seems quite different?

The second is 37:1-24 [38:1-17 **G**], which occurs in a longer and a shorter form, describing the construction of the ark, table, and lampstand; **Q**ᵐ is extant in **37:9-16**.

The third such synonymous variant is **28:23-29**, involving both order and amount of detail in instructions concerning the breastpiece of judgment.

There are two other variants which together involve at least part of a pericope: **25:23** and **25:24**, which give two different representations of the table in the holy place of the tabernacle. Was the table to be made of pure gold, or was it to be made of acacia wood overlaid with gold?

b. Different Order of Pericope or Words

No instances of different order have arisen where it can be clearly recognized that one order is preferable and another secondary.

There are, however, six synonymous variants involving different order.

In two instances $\mathbf{Q^a}$ $\mathbf{\mathfrak{m}}$ differ in word order from $\mathbf{\mathfrak{m}}$ but no preferability can be established. 30:1-10 involves an entire pericope, while 26:10 involves only the difference between "fifty loops" and "loops fifty."

These two instances where $\mathbf{Q^a}$ $\mathbf{\mathfrak{m}}$ differ from $\mathbf{\mathfrak{m}}$ in word order point to a broader pattern of varying word order between $\mathbf{\mathfrak{m}}$ and $\mathbf{\mathfrak{m}}$ where $\mathbf{Q^a}$ is not extant. Such variations in Hebrew witnesses are significant, since they show the frequency and the nature of transpositions that arose within the Hebrew transmission, and thus remind us not to attribute all variations in word order that occur in $\mathbf{G}$ to the process of translation. There are a total of 23 such cases. Only one involves an entire pericope, and it is one of the two where $\mathbf{Q^a}$ is extant: 30:1-10. There is one of moderate length, 29:21, which involves one verse; and there are 21 more instances involving only a word or phrase (including 26:10, one of the most minor of all). See Chapter V.B.4.c.

Many of the small variations involving only a word or phrase are probably to be explained by a variety of minor lapses, such as the following three-step process: inadvertent omission of a word or phrase, subsequent addition in the margin, and ultimate insertion in a different place. Others, however, may point to a degree of indifference in minor matters which was, however, not to last, since both the Massoretes and the Samaritans were later to institute a much stricter approach (see section B of this chapter).

The variation in the position of 30:1-10 belongs in a class by itself and may well be one of several indications that the original account of the tabernacle did not include a golden altar of incense; see the discussion in Chapter III.A.2. If this pericope was a later addition, it may be that it was inserted in two different places by two individual scribes who tried to place it in a logical position. If so, it can only be said that both scribes failed to find the one place where it fits best according to the spatial organization of the entire pericope -- chapter 25 -- and that neither seems to have sensed the discrepancy created by its lack in chapter 25.

The preceding discussion pertained to varying order among extant Hebrew witnesses. There are also four synonymous variants where only $\mathbf{G}$ differs. They are treated separately because of the possibilities that, first, the Greek order is secondary, and second, the variant reading arose during the course of the translation. It should be emphasized, however, that these are two separate issues. Even if the issue of preferability were to be decided, as has been deemed impossible in this study, it would be a second matter to claim that the translator was responsible for the variant. The 23 variations in order mentioned above between 𝕃𝕃𝕃 and 𝕄 warn us not to lay all such variants at the door of the translator.

One of these four variants involves the order of two short phrases (19:11), and the other three each affect the position of one word in a phrase: "sacrifices and burnt offerings" (10:25); "boils breaking out into blisters" (9:9ב); and "Moses and Aaron" (6:27א).

Summary: One of these six synonymous variations in order may be quite significant, suggesting a major expansion in the tabernacle account: that of the incense altar. A second may indicate a desire on the part of a scribe (or translator) to alter the order of the names of Aaron and Moses for literary reasons. Depending on which reading were earlier, a scribe may have put Moses first in order to make the transition from chronological priority to priority of role. Alternatively, a scribe may have put Aaron first, whether to improve on the inclusio or to emphasize the priority of Aaron as spokesman to Pharaoh.

The other four, however, are of little significance in themselves. Because they are part of a larger pattern they may suggest a lesser degree of concern for exactitude in the reproduction of biblical scrolls in this early period than in the Massoretic and later Samaritan period.

c. Alteration of Words for the Purpose of Broadening the Application of Case Laws

There is one case where individual words have been consistently altered within a pericope in order to make a law more generally applicable. This has been discussed above, in VI.A.2.c, since moderate expansion was also involved. Nine times the word "animal" is substituted for "ox," and five times the more general verb "kill" has been substituted for the more specific "gore." There is a clear exegetical motive in this alteration.

d. *Alteration of Words for the Purpose of Harmonization Within Exodus*

There are two instances where a word has been altered, apparently for the purpose of creating greater harmony. One occurs within the tabernacle account as a whole, and one within a single narrative.

The first instance appears to be another case similar to several that we have already seen, where the second section of the tabernacle account has influenced the first section. In 25:20 the Hebrew idiom "one to another" has been altered from איש אל אחיו to אחד אל אחד, so that it will appear in chapters 25 and 26 (and also in 37) as it appears consistently in chapter 36.

The second instance of substitution seems to have been motivated by a desire for harmonization within one narrative. In 19:12 the command to "set bounds for the people" has probably been changed to "set bounds for the mountain," which is the way it appears in 19:23. Then in order to clarify the command, another alteration was needed: "saying" was changed to "and say." Finally a clarifying expansion was added: "to the people." Both of these changes were felt necessary since reference to the people had been removed so that the verb would apply to the mountain both times it appears.

These are the only two instances of alteration for harmonization where preferability can be established. There is, however, a third case (13:6) where it appears that a scribe or scribes "corrected" a word to make it agree with the context. Unfortunately we cannot know which word represents the original and which the "corrected" version: "six days" or "seven days"?

e. *Other Alteration of Words*

There are five instances of substitution of one word occurring in narrative passages where no motivation is discernible. Three can be expressed in English:

"delivered me from the sword of Pharaoh"	»	hand	(18:4)
"in the sight of the elders of Israel"	»	children	(17:6)
"who hate unjust gain (or a bribe)"	»	pride	(18:21א).

Since no motive can be discerned for these three substitutions, they are considered to be quite unintentional. It should be pointed out that in all three cases the secondary reading occurs in **G**. Thus the possibility that the alteration occurred during the process of translation must be kept in mind. (See the discussions of each variant in Chapter II, and Chapter V.D.4.c.)

The other two alterations in words are clearer in Hebrew:

(בג7:18, 7:18)   בתוך היאר   »   ביאר

(א10:21)   וידבר   »   ויאמר

(Note that there is another case involving variation between אמר and דבר, at 7:14; since this is a synonymous variant, it is kept separate.)

Since none of these changes is substantial, we cannot be sure that the scribe was necessarily even aware of the change he was making. Each may have occurred when the scribe was preoccupied with the meaning of the text rather than the exact words of his *Vorlage*.

Nor can we be sure that the proofreader -- whether he was the same scribe or another -- noticed the difference. If he merely read the copy on its own terms, he would have approved it because it made good sense. If he compared the copy with the *Vorlage*, he may not have done so carefully enough to notice such slight differences. If he did notice, either he was not at all disturbed by such variations, or else, if he was somewhat concerned about exactness of reproduction, he was even more concerned to have a neat scroll.

One qualification must be mentioned, however. If, as seems quite likely, in either 7:18 or 7:18בג it was merely through a lapse, rather than deliberately, that a scribe wrote the longer form of the preposition, yet at some point in the history behind Q^n a scribe must have purposely changed the preposition in the other verse to agree. Note that one witness (**lll**) has the shorter preposition in both places, i.e. in the original text as well as in the major expansion; whereas one witness (Q^n) has the longer preposition in both places.

This suggests that at some time after the idea for the major expansion was conceived and carried through, another scribe concerned for complete correspondence between the original text, in which Yahweh speaks to Moses, and the major expansions, in which Moses repeats those words to Pharaoh, changed one shorter preposition to the longer, so that both would be identical. The only other possibility, it seems, is that one scribe wrote the longer form in both places. If so, he must have done so with some degree of deliberation. Thus, while at some stage there could be disagreement between two different scrolls, there could not be ultimately any disagreement within each scroll, when Yahweh's words were being repeated by the prophet to Pharaoh.

The preceding five are the instances of alteration of words where preferability can with some confidence be established. There are, however, fifteen synonymous variants involving different words. The first seven are variations in extant Hebrew witnesses:

strong arm//outstretched arm//strong hand		(32:11ב)
הנה	אני	(18:6)
לא כן	לכן	(10:11)
אני	אנכי	(22:26ב)
אל משה	למשה	(18:6א)
לפני פרעה	אל פרעה	(7:10)
עד דור	מדר	(17:16)

Of the eight where only **G** differs, six involve the designation of a person, and two relate to Israelites more generally:

יהוה	θεος	(16:33; 19:8; 32:30)
אלהים	κυριος	(18:1א; 20:1)
Jethro	Moses' father-in-law	(18:14)
house of Israel	sons of Israel	(16:31)
my people	your brother	(22:24א)

f. More Familiar Words

There are four instances where a scribe substituted a more familiar word for a less familiar word. Again, the differences are so minor that they are expressed better in Hebrew:

שפטים	»	משפטים	(7:4)
כויה	»	מכוה	(21:25)
שלמה	»	שמלה	(22:25)
ושתי	»	ושמתי	(23:31א)

Since each change involved only one letter, it is quite possible that a scribe made the change through habit or carelessness rather than deliberately. Yet each case must be treated separately, since if it could be shown that a witness always had the more familiar and never the less familiar word, it might mean that there had been a concerted effort to make the substitution.

Since שפט occurs elsewhere in **M**, which reads the more familiar משפט here, this reading appears to be more the result of oversight than of a

deliberate attempt at consistency. מכוה/כויה is such a rare word in the
Pentateuch that no conclusions can be drawn. The evidence in von Gall's
edition for שמלה/שלמה is questionable, but it may be that a scribe or
scribes in the **ɯ** tradition (after **Qᵃ**) created consistency by always writing
the more familiar form.

    Qᵃ is too fragmentary for us to know whether it ever had the less
common word שית.

    Summary: In general it seems likely that in these cases where a more
familiar word has been substituted for a less familiar word with the same
meaning and involving a change of only one letter, this may have been due
more to oversight and carelessness than to a deliberate effort by the scribe.

g. Grammatical and Syntactical Alterations

    There are four cases where it appears that a scribe has made
grammatical or syntactical alterations. Two seem to have been done
deliberately in order to improve the text. In **21:6** a *yod* was apparently
added to bring conformity with the convention that "master" be plural. In
17:12 a singular verb was changed to the plural because the subject is plural.

    Two variants seem to represent scribal lapses. In **12:6** an accusative
object in the singular was written as plural, presumably under the influence
of the context. A jussive became a normal imperfect in **10:10**.

    In the preceding four variants one reading has been judged to be
preferable. There are also nineteen cases of synonymous variants involving
differences of a grammatical or syntactical nature. These will be listed
briefly here, although it is impossible to know whether the difference dates
back to a stage in the literary development of the book or whether it is truly
a scribal matter, having arisen during the transmission of the text.

    There are eight cases of variation in the forms of verbs:

Nif'al vs. *Pu'al*	(22:6)
Nif'al third singular vs. *Hip'il* first plural	(10:26)
Hop'al third singular vs. middle second plural	(10:24ג)
Hip'il first singular plus accusative	
vs. transitive second plural	(16:32)
infinitive vs. indicative	(6:27א)
jussive vs. imperfect	(32:11א)

singular vs. plural		(18:16ב)
masculine singular vs. feminine singular		(8:14[18])

Once there is variation in the expression of an object:

ישמע אלי	ישמעני	(6:30)

The suffixes of four nouns vary:

her sons with her	your sons with him	(18:6ג)
your generations	their generations	(30:10)
its pillars	their pillars	(27:10)
its Asherim	their Asherim	(34:13)

There is one case of variation between the absolute and construct forms of a noun (26:26), and one between the construct form (with a noun following) and the noun with its own suffix (27:11ג).

The number of one noun varies: (18:12).

There are three cases of variation in the *mater lectionis* in the personal pronoun (22:26א *bis;* 31:13).

Summary: We have seen four cases where it has been determined that a scribe altered the text for reasons of syntax, twice deliberately and twice probably inadvertently. There are also nineteen cases of synonymous variants involving grammatical and syntactical differences. Again, these show a degree of tolerance for minor differences on the part of the scribe and/or the proofreader.

8. ERRORS

In this study errors have been defined as those scribal mistakes which have created readings that are grammatically or syntactically incorrect. This definition excludes simple lapses, such as omissions and substitution of more familiar words, that result in readings which still make sense. Only nine errors defined as such have appeared. The first three are in 𝔐, and the last six are in Q̅. They are so minor that they can best be shown in Hebrew:

את	»	אל	(16:34)
תנה	»	תנו	(17:2א)
אל	»	על	(18:23)

(בⁿ9:19)	א[ל]יך	»	לך
(בש18:25)	ככוכב [הש]מים	»	ככוכבי השמים
(א28:11)	יפתח	»	תפתח
(28:41)	ו[הלבשתם אותם	»	והלבשת אתם
(31:4)	לעשוב]נהב	»	לעשות בנהב
(37:13)	על ארבע	»	לארבע

All nine of these errors are minor, involving only one letter each. In one error the scribe also ran two words together. The low number of errors suggests a high degree of care on the part of scribes to prevent actual grammatical mistakes. This degree of effort should be kept in mind in contrasting the somewhat more relaxed attitude toward variant readings which still made sense. For instance, if the proofreader read only the copy and did not compare it with the *Vorlage*, then he would only notice actual errors rather than mere variations or omissions as long as they still made sense. Or if he did compare both texts and did notice the variations, but was more concerned for neatness that for exactness, apparently when it was a matter of an actual error he tended to insist on correction.

It is important to note that these errors are found only in **Qⁿ** and **𝔐**, the two diplomatic texts involved in this study. It is quite natural that there should be no actual errors, as opposed to other variants, in the eclectic texts **𝔐** and **𝔊**, since the editors have been able to choose the correct reading from many manuscripts.

The fact that there are only six actual errors in **Qⁿ** shows the relatively high degree of accuracy of this scribe. The fact that there are only three errors in the same portions of **𝔐**, even though it was copied approximately one thousand years later, suggests two discrete stages in the development behind **𝔐**. Other errors besides these three must have arisen over the centuries, which were apparently smoothed out along the way, suggesting that the Massoretes did at some periods take the liberty to correct the text when error was involved. Yet the fact that **𝔐** itself, i.e., the Leningrad codex, does have three errors in the portions of text under investigation (and presumably a comparable number in other portions) suggests that it retains very faithfully the characteristics of a single text.

B. SCRIBAL ATTITUDES AND PRACTICES

In this chapter we have seen secondary readings that involve expansion, omission, and alteration of various lengths of text, most of them leaving the text still understandable, but a few of them, the errors, resulting in actual grammatical or syntactical mistakes. The largest category of secondary readings consists of expansions, and the smallest category, other than errors, consists of omissions.

The synonymous variants discussed in Chapter III have also been acounted for in this chapter, tentatively assigned to categories but always discussed as suggestions rather than as conclusions.

1. MAJOR EXPANSIONS

The major expansions show that some scribes in this period felt the freedom to add liberally to the biblical text for literary purposes, such as filling out the narrative or creating greater harmony with a parallel in another part of Exodus or in Deuteronomy, or for theological and perhaps political purposes, such as magnifying the glory of Yahweh, either in opposition to the sinfulness of the people or in support of the mediatorship of Moses or a prophet like him.

However -- and this is a crucial qualification -- the major expansions found in these four witnesses were severely restricted to passages that were already in the Torah (and possibly from Job and Ezekiel). None of the major expansions which have been discovered involved freedom to compose text. No new text was added. Instead, whatever new effect was achieved resulted from repetition of passages already in Exodus, or from importation of passages already in Deuteronomy, or from new combinations of passages already in Exodus and/or Deuteronomy.

Coupled with this lack of freedom to compose text was the rigid precision with which these major expansions were copied. The scribe who made a major interpolation of text did so with an exactness that contrasted fairly sharply with the relative laxity of scribes who merely copied their *Vorlage* and made no major expansions.

This has led to the conclusion that the scribes of the major expansions were not free to add <u>words</u> to revelation or to change those words, except as clearly required by the change in context. The words of revelation had already been fixed. Yet at the same time they did feel free to tamper with the _form_ or _structure_ of revelation, both on the literary and the narrative level.

Literarily, for instance, they could import a text into a quite new position, whether to make a parallel more explicit, or to harmonize, or to make a theological point. The aspect of revelation that they could not change seems to have been the words themselves, rather than the position of those words or the structure of the work.

A factor complicating our understanding of what was in their minds is that all of the clear cases of major expansions involve actual speeches, whether of Yahweh (e.g., regarding the prophet like Moses), of Moses (e.g., regarding the Gerizim altar), or the Israelites (the complaint about dying in the wilderness). It may be just possible that the reason for the precision in copying is the belief that these were the _ipsissima verba_ of the persons involved and as such could not be altered in any way. There is no way to know how these particular scribes would have treated third-person text by the narrator.

Regarding the narrative, they could import into the narrative of Sinai speeches that were attributed to Yahweh or to Moses at later times in the story of the wilderness wanderings. As authors and editors before them had retrojected laws and speeches back to Sinai, so this scribe or these few scribes retrojected a later promise of Yahweh and a commandment of Moses back to Sinai. Whether an author, an editor, or a scribe did it, the motive and result were the same: to raise these texts to the highest level of importance.[11]

Thus if we have found a much greater degree of freedom to expand the biblical text than anything to which we are accustomed from the Massoretes, on the other hand it is important to emphasize that this is a strictly limited freedom. Whatever sense of "canon" these scribes may have had, they at least seem not to have been free to expand the text with any words other than those that were already in their Torah.

It is very clear, then, that these scribes saw themselves as making comparatively minor improvements on a text that already existed in

---

[11]If we may judge from Deuteronomy in 𝕸, the speeches were retained in their original position as well as being retrojected into the Sinai narrative. Thus 𝕸 has the commandment to build the altar on Gerizim in four places: its two components are still in their original places in Deuteronomy 11 and 27, and the combined passage is in Deuteronomy 5 and Exodus 20.

practically its permanent form. Even as they were refocusing the thrust of the text, in order, for example, to make it relevant to a new situation (e.g., the need to legitimate the shrine on Gerizim) or to emphasize theological points (e.g., the mediatorship of Moses and of the prophet to come), they did it in the manner of one improving a text that was already set in all of its major features.

Is it possible to fix the period when these major expansions occurred? The evidence of $\mathbf{Q}^{\mathbf{n}}$, which clearly preserves eleven, and may well have had all but one, of the major expansions previously known only in 𝕬, shows that most -- and presumably all but that one -- of these had been made at least prior to the date of its copying, which, as we have seen, has been estimated as either ca. 225–175 or ca. 100–25 B.C.E.

The one exception is the eleventh commandment in Exodus 20 to build the altar on Mount Gerizim. Yet as we have seen in Chapter V.B.5, even this "sectarian" expansion followed a pattern identical to that of other expansions. The method was exactly the same as that involved in some of the other expansions; only the motivation was different. It has been very plausibly suggested that the motivation for this expansion was the destruction of the Samaritans' temple and central city just before 100 B.C.E. There is nothing in the text that would preclude this date. Nor, on the other hand, does the text preclude a somewhat earlier date. Perhaps the expansion of the decalogue actually pre-dated the destruction of the temple.

Thus the *terminus ad quem* for these eleven major expansions is the period 200–50 B.C., and it is likely that the "sectarian" expansion also occurred during these early centuries, but in a sub-tradition separate from $\mathbf{Q}^{\mathbf{n}}$. Furthermore, since 𝕸 shares one major expansion with $\mathbf{Q}^{\mathbf{n}}$𝕬, that expansion must be dated even earlier, to the time before the tradition behind $\mathbf{Q}^{\mathbf{n}}$𝕬 separated from that behind 𝕸.

2. MODERATE AND MINOR EXPANSIONS AND ALTERATIONS

We have also found many expansions or alterations of moderate length, for purposes such as making a legal pericope more generally applicable, filling out the story, harmonizing minor features of the text, emphasizing aspects of a narrative, usually the miraculous, and for clarification. Varying degrees of deliberation seem to have been involved on the part of the various scribes.

In general, these additions were found to come from the immediate context (e.g., "or any animal", "Go down and warn the people"), or from a parallel passage elsewhere in Exodus (e.g., "skilled") or in Deuteronomy (e.g., "quickly from here") or perhaps in Leviticus (e.g., possibly, "spread with oil"), or from standard Pentateuchal expressions that naturally belonged together (e.g., "signs and wonders").

Two additions were found which reflect somewhat greater liberty on the part of the scribe. The addition of "his slaves and his animals" seems to have been legitimated by the reference to "human beings" in the context. Thus the idea was present but the word -- a common one -- was not explicitly present. The addition of "and he struck/destroyed them with the edge of the sword" -- again a common word in conjunction with swords -- either originated in the mind of the scribe or else in other passages (especially in 1-2 Samuel but possibly also in Numbers) about the Amalekites.

There are many expansions or alterations of a minor character, such as varying order of words and phrases, substitution of more familiar for less familiar words, addition or omission of minor words and morphemes, unconscious harmonization to the immediate context or to stock expressions in one's mind. Some minor additions, such as מאוד, אולם, and morphemes such as an accusative suffix or the sign of the accusative, may have come from the logic of the context as much as from the explicit text. Some were no doubt made for the sake of greater clarification and some for greater emphasis.

Other minor additions and minor alterations may have arisen through habit, carelessness, preoccupation, and the like. There may be other reasons for the large number of these minor variants. The first relates to one method which may have been used for copying; another relates to the attitude of the scribe, and therefore of his community.

The first reason may be that much of the copying was done by scribes who listened to the text read aloud and then wrote from their memory of what they had just heard.[12]   Alternatively, even if the scribe were reading a text that lay in front of him, he may have read a rather large chunk of text

---

[12]James R. Royse, "Scribal Habits in the Transmission of New Testament Texts," in *The Critical Study of Sacred Texts,* edited by Wendy Doniger O'Flaherty (Berkeley: Graduate Theological Union, 1979), page 152, reporting the suggestion of Ernest C. Colwell, in *Studies in Methodology in Textual Criticism of the New Testament* (Grand Rapids: Eerdmans, 1969), p. 117.

at one time and then kept his eyes on his own scroll rather than on the
Vorlage. Such scribes may have

> ...copied not syllable by syllable or word by word, but rather by
> grasping the "idea-content" of the text, and then reproducing
> that content without the strict attention to reproduction of the
> actual words in their given order which textual critics would
> prefer.[13]

The method of the scribes is closely related to a second factor which
seems likely. As has been suggested above, it seems probable that the
attitude of the scribes of this period was rather different from that of the
Massoretes. Their task of copying sacred texts does not seem to have
created in them a compulsion to reproduce their *Vorlage* exactly, to the
letter. They seem to have been somewhat relaxed about the work, aiming to
reproduce the intent of the text if not in every case its exact words and
letters. If one speaks of a "relaxed" attitude, however, one must again
recognize that it was quite limited. The majority of the text of Exodus
exhibits no variation among the four texts investigated. Obviously the
scribes permitted themselves only a small amount of freedom.

There may have been more to it than a "relaxed" attitude which
allowed for unintentional changes. There may also have been a sense of the
legitimacy of a scribe's occasionally deliberately altering the text to suit
his own style. As the composers and editors who had gone before, some
scribes may have had the sense that they were legitimately participating --
to a much more limited degree -- in the creative process. As Talmon has
said:

> ... no hard and fast lines can be drawn between authors'
> conventions of style and tradents' and copyists' rules of
> reproduction and transmission. It may be said that in ancient
> Israel ... the professional scribe seldom if ever was merely a
> slavish copyist of the material which he handled. He rather
> should be considered a minor partner in the creative literary
> process. To a degree, he applied on the reproductive level
> norms and techniques which had informed his predecessors, the
> ancient authors, and which had become his literary legacy. The
> right to introduce variations into the biblical text, within
> limits, had come to the Bible-oriented copyists...together with
> the transmitted writings.[14]

---

[13] *Ibid.*
[14] Talmon, "Study," page 381.

The evidence of the variants revealed in this study confirm what both Colwell and Talmon have said. Minor differences such as between ישמע אלי and ישמעני or between ב- and בתוך or minor additions such as "sons of Israel" would appear to relate to Colwell's suggestions and to stem from a scribe's own individual preference or habit of speaking. In the first case he may have made the change deliberately because it seemed more pleasing to him, while in the second case he may not even have been aware that he was making a change. Expansions such as "and they stood before Pharaoh" and "and he destroyed them with the edge of the sword" would appear to relate to Talmon's suggestions and to stem from a scribe's setting out purposefully to improve the text, sensing his role as that of a junior partner. If Talmon is right, and the authority to make such variations had come to the scribes "together with the transmitted writings," then some of the scribes at least considered themselves to be involved in a continuing process of revelation. There is no question that they were junior or minor partners. But they may have taken great satisfaction in the fact that they shared with Moses and Ezra in their work.

The equanimity about variations and expansions must have existed at several different stages for evidence of it to have reached us. First, the scribe himself, while he was copying, at times took the liberty of making deliberate expansions and alterations (Talmon) and at times allowed himself that degree of indifference which prevented exact reproduction of his *Vorlage* (Colwell). Second, the proofreader, whether he was the same scribe or a colleague, at times must have noticed the new features of the copy and appreciated them, and at times perhaps allowed himself that degree of indifference which prevented his noticing them. Third, a community either overlooked or tolerated such new features, so that the copy was preserved and presumably used. Fourth, a later scribe either was unaware of or else appreciated the features of the scroll enough to make a new copy from it. And so the cycle continued.

Finally, however, the day came when the cycle of equanimity stopped. James Barr[15] has described the process of canonization as taking place in four stages. In the first stage there was still freedom to make major additions and alterations. In the second stage there was freedom for minor expansions and alterations. In the third stage only what were perceived as

---

[15]In a seminar at the University of Notre Dame in April 1985.

mistakes in the *Vorlage* could be corrected. And finally in the fourth stage not even obvious mistakes could be corrected.

How would the variants of this study fit into Barr's four-fold process? In the first stage would fall the major expansions. Many of the moderate and minor features would have arisen in the second stage. Such phenomena as the insertion of the sign of the accusative, the change from הוא to היא or vice versa, and altering verbal forms to make them fit the subject may perhaps stem from the third stage. Finally in the fourth stage would fall the errors and some of the omissions in 𝔐, on the theory that they were recognized as at least peculiar (Deuteronomy referred to seven nations, but Exodus has not a single list of seven nations) if not wrong (a plural verb with a singular subject), but that it was too late to change them.

The two traditions 𝔐 and 𝔐 entered this fourth stage rather early. The Massoretes made their approach explicit. The Samaritans' strictness of approach can be inferred from two phenomena. First, the similarity of 𝔐 to Q^a shows that even in the early days no major differences were allowed. Once the "sectarian" expansion was made, no further growth occurred. It is quite possible that the minor variations between Q^a and 𝔐 had already arisen by the time Q^a was copied, if it did indeed belong to a collateral line of the family. If not, they could all easily have arisen within a few years. Second, the fact that almost all of the variants in von Gall's apparatus relate to matters of *plene* versus defective orthography shows that in the intervening centuries only very minor variants indeed were allowed. In both the Jewish and the Samaritan communities, then, the final stage of canonization had been reached, and no further changes or additions, even for the sake of clarity or harmony, could be made.

3. CONCLUSION

In conclusion, then, a few scribes felt free to make major expansions in order to improve on the text; yet even these major expansions came straight out of the biblical text. Some if not many scribes felt free to make moderate expansions and alterations to improve their *Vorlage*; these again almost always came from a biblical text. Perhaps most scribes in this early period felt both a certain relaxation, an indifference to exactness of reproduction, and also a right deliberately to introduce small changes; both of these atittudes, then, allowed minor variations in expressions to arise even as the scribes were very faithfully reproducing the intent of the text.

Another way to put it is to say that all of the variants in this study are small. Within the general category of "small variants," some have been classified as major, some as moderate, and some as minor. In comparison to developments in other scrolls such as the *Genesis Aprocryphon,* all of the changes are minor. The scribes whose work is represented in these four texts had indeed a very limited degree of freedom in their work.

CHAPTER VII

CONCLUSIONS

A. CONCLUSIONS REGARDING THE FOUR TEXTS ANALYZED

1. $\mathbf{Q}^\pi$: 4QpaleoExod^m

4QpaleoExod^m was copied sometime between 225 and 25 B.C.E. If it was not copied at Qumran, then it was brought and preserved there. The fact that it was patched and that lost text was rewritten by a scribe other than the first scribe shows that it was treasured and used by some individual or group. This is significant, since it is the only scroll found at Qumran that combines all three distinctive characteristics: Palaeo-Hebrew script, full orthography, and Samaritanlike text. It is a carefully copied scroll with only six errors in the portions of 44 columns that have been preserved, as well as four other unique cases of shorter text that may either reflect parablepsis or the preferable, unexpanded text.

The text of $\mathbf{Q}^\pi$ belongs to the text-type or tradition which previously was known to us only in its later representative, the Samaritan Pentateuch. The scroll shares all major, typological features with $\mathbf{m}$, including all the major expansions of that tradition where it is extant (twelve), with the single exception of the new tenth commandment inserted in Exodus 20 from Deuteronomy 11 and 27 regarding the altar on Mount Gerizim. Altogether $\mathbf{Q}^\pi$ and $\mathbf{m}$ share 18 secondary readings, 12 synonymous variants, and 2 preferable readings, for a total of 32 agreements.

Yet in smaller variants the scroll disagrees 69 times with $\mathbf{m}$. It preserves 36 unique readings,[1] it agrees with $\mathbf{m}$ against $\mathbf{m}$ in 29 readings, and with $\mathbf{G}$ against $\mathbf{m}$ in 4 readings. Counting in this way alone is quite misleading, since it treats a major expansion of eight lines taken from Deuteronomy shared by $\mathbf{Q}^\pi \mathbf{m}$ on the same level with a *waw* shared by $\mathbf{Q}^\pi \mathbf{G}$.

---

[1] Including the eight variants between $\mathbf{Q}^\pi$ and $\mathbf{m}$ within the major expansions (see Chapter V.A.3.b) and the one variant within a larger synonymous variant (see Chapter V.A.4). The number 36 is obtained by adding the 27 readings which show as unique in Appendix 3 (where only secondary, preferable, and synonymous readings are included) and the 9 readings which show in the "tertiary" column in Appendix 4.

Hence the many lists in the preceding chapters, to keep the necessary distinctions constantly in view. To put it a different way, the variants that reflect the most license, the most purposefully exegetical work on the part of a scribe or scribes are shared by $\mathbf{Q^a}$Ⅲ, while variants that probably reflect independent exegesis or even independent scribal lapses rather than any relationship are shared by $\mathbf{Q^a}$**G**.

$\mathbf{Q^a}$ represents a textual tradition that is very close to that known to us in the Massoretic text. Working from a base very much like what has come down to us as Ⅲ, one or several scribes expanded certain specific sections of the text, with the result that many columns of the scroll look quite similar to Ⅲ, while other columns -- even in their present fragmentary state -- have six or seven lines not found in Ⅲ.

Despite its expansionism in a total of 13 major passages, however, $\mathbf{Q^a}$ also preserves 42 preferable readings, 5 of which are shorter readings which it preserves uniquely.

2. Ⅲ: THE SAMARITAN PENTATEUCH

The discovery of 4QpaleoExod[m] made it possible for the first time to view the Scriptures of the Samaritan community in the context of some of the other texts that existed in the last one or two centuries before the Common Era. Because $\mathbf{Q^a}$ shares so many of the more significant features of Ⅲ it is now clear that the community centered around Gerizim use a biblical text that is a very natural descendant of texts that other groups also used at that time. All but one of the major expansions and even the different placement of the instructions concerning the incense altar were features that already existed in other non-"sectarian" texts. And perhaps even more important, all of the characteristics of that "sectarian" expansion about Gerizim had their precedent in those shared expansions.

Ⅲ appears to represent a very close collateral line of the $\mathbf{Q^a}$Ⅲ textual family and/or a slightly later representative than $\mathbf{Q^a}$. Whereas $\mathbf{Q^a}$ has 42 preferable readings, 5 of them unique, Ⅲ has only 35 preferable readings, none of them unique. Some of its unique secondary readings suggest deliberate exegetical work beyond that reflected in $\mathbf{Q^a}$, such as the broadened application of a legal pericope and the more consistent addition of the sign of the accusative.

Yet it would appear that rather soon after the "sectarian" expansion was added Ⅲ began to be treated somewhat as the Massoretes were ultimately to treat their text, prohibiting further expansion and alteration. The text did not develop very much further than the stage represented by $\mathbf{Q}^{\mathbf{n}}$.

3. $\mathbf{m}$: THE MASSORETIC TEXT

Of the four texts of Exodus, the Massoretic is clearly the best preserved. Of the variants isolated in this study, i.e., where the scroll is extant, $\mathbf{m}$ presents 66 preferable readings (10 of them unique), as opposed to totals of 42 and 35 for $\mathbf{Q}^{\mathbf{n}}$ and $\mathbf{m}$.

On the other hand $\mathbf{m}$ does preserve one major expansion from Deuteronomy of the same type as those peculiar to the $\mathbf{Q}^{\mathbf{n}}\mathbf{m}$ tradition, as well as 18 other secondary readings, 7 of them unique. Of the 7 unique secondary readings, 3 are accidental omissions, 1 is an expansion, and 3 are actual grammatical or syntactical errors.

In general, however, the Massoretic text is a good one in Exodus, showing significantly less expansion and alteration than the other three witnesses.

4. $\mathbf{G}$: THE OLD GREEK

Accurate statistics for $\mathbf{G}$ are very difficult to obtain, because of all the uncertainties about the *Vorlage* of the Greek translation, due to the fact that so far no Hebrew text has been published that very closely or consistently resembles $\mathbf{G}$ in Exodus.[2] First of all, how many of the apparent variations where only $\mathbf{G}$ is different from the other three are due to an actual difference in the Hebrew text from which it was translated, and how many are due to an intentional or unintentional change introduced by the translator or by early copyists of the Greek version? Second, in many variants where the Hebrew witnesses differ among themselves, it is completely impossible to judge what the Hebrew behind $\mathbf{G}$ would have had, because something like a sign of the accusative cannot be expressed in good Greek, and something like a locative *he* would be expressed in good Greek whether it was actually in the Hebrew or not. Third, even when the Greek appears to agree with one Hebrew text against another, is that agreement due to a relationship between the two or merely to exegetical work of

_____

[2]See, however, the preliminary publication of 4QExod[a] in Cross, *Library,* pp. 184-186 and nn. 31-32. As Cross put it in then (in 1961), this scroll "belongs systematically to the Egyptian textual tradition reflected in the Septuagint; though at points it appears to offer a more consistent form of that tradition than the Septuagint itself."

scribes working independently? Fourth, the results in this study pertain to the narrative -- and to a lesser extent the legal -- portions of the book of Exodus. The complicated questions involved in the tabernacle account have not been illuminated by the discovery of the scroll, because it is scarcely extant in the second half of that account, and whenever it is extant in the first or second parts, it agrees consistently with 𝔐𝔐 against 𝕲.

In spite of all those difficulties, however, it remains true that 𝕲 is by far the most different of the four witnesses. Out of a total of 121 variants where the *Vorlage* of 𝕲 can be determined with relative confidence, 62 of them are unique to 𝕲. In other words, in half of the cases where 𝕲 is clearly different from one Hebrew text, it is different from all three of them. Once again we have indirect evidence of the closeness of the 𝐐ᵐ𝔐 tradition and the 𝔐 tradition.

A special word is in order about the relationship of 𝕲 and (𝐐ᵐ)𝔐, since they are so often considered to be closely affiliated. Of the 121 variants, 𝕲 shares 21 with 𝐐ᵐ and/or 𝔐: 4 are preferable readings and therefore are of little significance for determining affiliation; 9 are synonymous variants and are thus hard to judge; 8 are secondary and thus possibly to be considered significant for affiliation. Yet only 1 of the 21 variants is important enough in itself to suggest a causal relationship: the difference between "six" and "seven" days. The admittedly random sampling involved in this study gives no reason at all to suspect a relationship between the two traditions.

Apart from the statistics, 𝐐ᵐ𝔐 and 𝕲 are very different in the <u>type</u> of secondary reading that they preserve. While 𝐐ᵐ𝔐 exhibit much longer expansions, 𝕲 exhibits far more numerous expansions. One column of 𝐐ᵐ𝔐 might have only one expansion, but it might be eight lines in length. The same passage in 𝕲 would be likely to have one or two expansions in every sentence, but each would be only three or four words in length.

But to return to 𝕲 viewed on its own terms, not all of its 62 unique readings are secondary; 18 do seem clearly secondary, but 36 have been classified as synonymous variants, and 8 are actually preferable (all of them the shorter reading).

In the narrative and legal sections of Exodus the Greek translation is a good and faithful rendering of its *Vorlage*, sometimes tending more toward wooden, "Semitic" Greek, and sometimes slightly more toward the idiomatic. In general it is quite literal.

The final word about **G** should be that while it deserves its reputation of being expansionist, it nevertheless preserves some preferable shorter readings as well.

B. CONCLUSIONS REGARDING THE HISTORY OF THE TEXT OF EXODUS

The nature of each of the four witnesses suggests the following reconstruction of the early history of the text of Exodus. It should be clearly kept in view, however, that this can only be a partial reconstruction, for two reasons. First, we have only some of the texts that were used then; and second, even the most extensively preserved text of Exodus from Qumran, 4QpaleoExod^m, is very fragmentary, and it is upon these fragments alone that this study is based. One result of the fragmentary nature of this reconstruction is that it applies only to the narrative and legal portions of the text, not to the tabernacle account.

Whether or not there was ever an *Urtext* of Exodus, there does at least seem to have been a time when these four texts were very close to each other. The tradition behind **G** seems to have separated off first, because it still preserves some unique preferable readings. It quickly developed an expansionist tendency, however, so that it is now the most different of the four.

The traditions behind **Qᵃ ɯ ɱ** apparently developed for a time together, since they share some secondary readings against **G**. These are all longer readings, the most notable of them being a major expansion from Deuteronomy.

The tradition behind **Qᵃ ɯ** then separated and underwent some major expansions, perhaps at the hand of one scribe. Because these typological features shared by **Qᵃ ɯ** are so few, it is possible that they arose shortly before **Qᵃ** was copied in the first or second century.

Some time in the same general period when **Qᵃ** was copied or afterward, a text very much like it received one more major expansion from Deuteronomy, this one "sectarian" in the sense that it represented an attempt to legitimate worship on Gerizim, as opposed to Jerusalem, on the basis of Scripture. This was adopted as a special text of the community at Gerizim and has been preserved by them ever since. A comparison of the MSS used by von Gall for his critical edition with each other and with **Qᵃ** shows how faithfully it has been preserved.   Presumably the many minor differences between ⅢⅢ and **Qᵐ** arose in the early days of their separate existence, and fairly soon that final stage of canonization took effect so that no more changes were allowed. Thus, for instance, ⅢⅢ exhibits signs of scribes' having achieved a somewhat greater degree of internal consistency, but that process had certainly not reached its end when the time of tolerance came to its end.

Meanwhile the tradition behind Ⅲ was being preserved by scribes of a new and more conservative approach who eschewed deliberate expansion and alteration. Probably expansions and alterations that had already been made were no longer recognized as such, so that they have been preserved. But because the "proto-Massoretic" text entered that stage of the prohibition of change earlier than the "proto-Samaritan" text, it still preserves an earlier stage of the text. Also, a small number of accidental omissions and of actual errors continued to be made, before methods of proofreading reached their ultimate degree of sophistication.

C. CONCLUSIONS REGARDING EDITORIAL AND SCRIBAL PRACTICE

The variants in this study have been found to reflect five different kinds of scribal change. Major expansions were accomplished by a distinct minority of scribes who, probably for a variety of literary, theological, and political motives, took the liberty of altering the structure of the work of Exodus (and of Deuteronomy) but not that of altering the words.[3]   It was suggested that somehow revelatory significance attached to the specific words in a way that did not affect the form of the work as a whole or the order of the narrative.   Or the focus may have been slightly different. Because all of these expansions involved the speech of Yahweh, Moses, and the Israelites, the refusal to change the words may have risen from the belief that these were the *ipsissima verba* of the persons involved.

The moderate and minor expansions and alterations seem to have been accomplished by a different breed of scribes, since they reveal a different

---

[3]This is deliberately somewhat oversimplified. For instance, the words of Yahweh instructing Moses where and when to confront Pharaoh could be drastically summarized, but the words of Yahweh to Pharaoh were not changed except for one suffix. For details, see Chapter V.A.3.

attitude toward the words of Scripture. If the first type of scribes could participate in the continuing process of work on Scripture by rearranging major blocks of text, these scribes could participate by <u>deliberately adding words into sentences or altering words or phrases</u>. Of course almost all of the words were already there in the context or elsewhere in Exodus or Deuteronomy. Many additions and changes seem to have been made for the purpose of enhancing the narrative in various ways, of emphasizing the miraculous, of harmonizing expressions and ideas, of filling out common expressions.

Another type of moderate and minor expansion and alteration was quite likely attributable to the same scribes who created the deliberate variants, but was due to another aspect of their approach to their task. Not only could they deliberately make small improvements in the text, they were not disturbed if they <u>inadvertently caused slight accretions and variations</u> in the text. At the level of the initial copying, the proofreading, community acceptance, and the recopying of the scrolls, there seems to have been an attitude of indifference toward some minor variations.

These varying attitudes produced some interesting combinations of treatment of parts of the text. If the reading בתוך could arise instead of ב– either because the scribe actively preferred the longer form or merely because he did not take the trouble to prevent its happening, that was accepted. But at some point some scribe did take the trouble to ensure that the scroll(s) that read בתוך in one instance of Yahweh's challenge to Pharaoh should also read בתוך in the second instance of that same speech. The scroll did not have to agree with other scrolls that read ב– in both places, but it did have to agree within itself. The words of Yahweh had to be exactly the same when they were first spoken to Moses and when Moses and Aaron relayed them to Pharaoh. Was this because they were the *ipsissima verba* of Yahweh, or because a prophet would be scrupulously careful to repeat a message exactly? Or were both reasons inseparable in the mind of the scribe? Perhaps he did not analyze his motives so carefully.

No cases of deliberate omission have been found. Again it appears that the respect due to words of revelation prevented the scribes from ever deleting any text except by accident. Some cases of <u>accidental omission</u> -- even the loss of eight words -- were not caught by the scribe or by the proofreader. This means either that proofreading was not done by comparing the copy with the *Vorlage*, but only by reading the copy itself on its own merits; or else that the proofreader was not careful enough to prevent his own eye from skipping in the same way that the copyist's eye had. In either case it may be that the proofreader was the same scribe who had done the copying, which means that he was less likely to discover his oversight.

These inferences about the method of proofreading receive some support from the low incidence of errors in the scroll. Whereas some copyists and proofreaders had a relatively high degree of tolerance for variations and expansions, they did manage to prevent very many actual grammatical and syntactical mistakes that impaired the sense of the sentence. Even a proofreader reading only the copy, and only a copy he had made himself, would tend to notice actual errors.

D. CONCLUSIONS REGARDING TEXT-TYPES IN THE SECOND TEMPLE PERIOD

This study has confirmed that **Qⁿ III** together represent one text-type because they fulfill the two requirements.[4] First, they share typological characteristics, including the four kinds of major expansions and the one distinctive difference in placement of text. Second, they are two witnesses which deserve to be grouped together. Yet it has also been pointed out that all of these typological characteristics may be traceable to one or possibly two scribes. While one individual may be responsible for the creation of the typological characteristics that establish the existence of this text-type, perhaps a series of scribes are responsible for the introduction of the many minor differences between the two members of this text-type.

The results of this study have shown that in the narrative and legal portions of the book of Exodus **G** is the most different of the four witnesses. It preserves uniquely shorter preferable readings but also a greater number of uniquely longer secondary readings. While -- among the four witnesses investigated -- there is not another text that could be grouped with **G**, it is worth asking whether there are typological characteristics that can be recognized in **G**.

The type of longer readings discovered in **G** is quite different from the type discovered in **Qⁿ III**. They are much shorter, limited to words and phrases usually from elsewhere in the context, occasionally from parallel expressions in Deuteronomy, and they are much more numerous. Now of

---

[4]See above, Chapter I.C, and Tov, "Outlook," p. 23.

course it is true that each of the other witnesses, including 𝕸, shares a few of this type of short, clarifying or harmonizing or emphasizing expansion. Thus these are not unique to 𝕲. On the other hand, neither are the major expansions unique to 𝐐ᵃ𝖒. Cross has announced the existence of a scroll of Numbers which has major interpolations from Deuteronomy similar to but not identical with those in 𝖒,[5] and this study has revealed that even 𝕸 has one interpolation from Deuteronomy. Thus it appears that the definition of a text-type relates to characteristics that are found frequently and according to a pattern rather than uniquely. According to this definition 𝕲 -- in the narrative and legal portions of Exodus -- may well deserve to be said to be especially characterized by typological secondary readings, as if it underwent the treatment of one or several scribes who were especially prone to brief expansions.

If this is granted, then the other fourteen scrolls of Exodus at Qumran should be investigated to see if any of them can be grouped with 𝕲. In such an investigation, of course, there would have to be latitude for many small differences between the scroll and 𝕲. Each scroll would exhibit unique readings, and each would agree with 𝕸 (and possibly even with 𝐐ᵃ𝖒) against 𝕲 some of the time, as has been the case with 𝐐ᵃ𝖒.[6] Of course, the lack of any such scrolls could not be interpreted to mean that there never was such a group, since our remains are so fragmentary.

If 𝕲 does in fact represent a text-type, then it might be legitimate to suggest that 𝕸 -- in the narrative and legal portions of the book of Exodus -- represents a text-type in a negative way. Its readings also follow a pattern, but a negative one: they are characterized by the lack of expansion, modernization, and harmonization. This pattern is not universally consistent even within the portions of Exodus studied, of course, because the tradition behind 𝕸 first went through a period of common development, expansion, and alteration with 𝐐ᵃ𝖒. But because the tradition was subjected earlier to the third and fourth stages of canonization, where fewer and fewer secondary readings were allowed, it has a much higher and

---

[5]Cross, *Library,* p. 186 and nn. 35-36.

[6]To return to Cross's description of 4QExodᵃ: out of six variants (four preserved in one fragment and two more based on its reconstruction), "four readings are in agreement with the Septuagint; one is unique, but probably points to an Egyptian text form superior to that used by the translators of the Septuagint; one probably agrees with the Masoretic text against the Septuagint" (pp. 184-186).

more consistent number of preferable readings. And its unique secondary readings also belong to this pattern, for they are with only one exception accidental omissions or actual errors, rather than additions or deliberate alterations.

But as Tov has suggested, it is perhaps more useful to address the issue with different questions. To use the categories suggested by Tov,[7] the results of this study would suggest that each of the four witnesses can be characterized according to the scribal approach reflected.

All four of them reflect a period during which that free approach prevailed which allowed for the variety of changes discussed in Chapter VI. But the tradition behind 𝔐 rather quickly[8] began to be treated differently, and the more conservative approach very soon prevailed which attempted to prevent the introduction of secondary readings.

Q𝔪 continued to be handled freely, especially in terms of the insertion of large blocks of material. After Q was copied (or perhaps before, in a parallel sub-tradition) 𝔪 continued to be treated freely in that one more large block of text was inserted, but otherwise that freedom shifted its focus to smaller bits of text, harmonizing, modernizing, creating greater consistency. Relatively soon, however, 𝔪 as well entered its conservative period, so that few more changes were allowed.

𝔊 continued to be handled freely but in a different way. Its scribes were free especially to make a large number of brief expansions from the context. The results of this study, then, place 𝔊 of the narrative and legal portions of Exodus in the free rather than in the conservative category.[9]

---

[7]See above, Chapter I.E. and Tov, "Outlook," p. 26.

[8]The word "quickly" is used not to refer so much to chronological time, as if we could determine the number of months or years involved, but to refer to the time it took for the other witnesses to develop their secondary readings. As pointed out, these could be attributable to one or a few scribes.

[9]Contrast Tov, "Outlook," p. 26, referring to 𝔊 in general terms, rather than in one specific book or section.

E. CONCLUSIONS REGARDING THE ORIGINS AND NATURE OF SAMARITANISM

The results of this study demonstrate more clearly that the worshipers at Gerizim shared their Scriptures with others in Palestine during the last centuries before the Common Era. There is no way to be sure how many groups and individuals were using such texts, but it is possible to speculate.

Perhaps expansionist texts were especially favored by groups hostile to Jerusalem, because circles in leadership positions in Jerusalem were -- again, perhaps -- attempting, possibly with a good degree of success, to establish a more conservative text -- at least as far as the Torah is concerned -- as authoritative. As some refused to worship in Jerusalem, so some may also have preferred to use biblical texts that were frowned on in Jerusalem. This would of course not be true of the Qumran community as a whole, since many biblical scrolls found there do belong to the more conservative type. Yet there may have been a contingent at Qumran who delighted in the use of expansionist texts, whether for their own intrinsic value or because they were not "official," or for both reasons.

The major expansions in Exodus may have been made by one individual at Shechem or at Qumran or at some third place; or several scribes of a similar bent, if not necessarily working in the same place, may have been involved. Presumably texts with these major expansions were, if not created, at least popular, at Shechem for some time before the "sectarian" expansion was made, since that last expansion reveals the same approach to Scripture. For such an expansion to be conceived in the first place and to be accepted as both legitimate and powerful in the second place, the community must already have been accustomed to and must have valued the text as we know it from Qumran.

This last expansion was different in that it used Scripture as the instrument to legitimate the community's place of worship against the place of worship of a rival community. It took two commands recorded in Deuteronomy and attributed to Moses but not related to the theophany at Sinai, combined them, and created a new tenth commandment out of them, thus raising them from the status of the Pentateuch as a whole to the status of the Ten Words.

Yet if the motivation of this expansion was specific and tendentious, its method was the same as that which had already been used in creating some of the other major expansions. Already a major expansion had been inserted in Exodus 20 which was composed of two separate passages in Deuteronomy and which was attributed to a different time and place during the wilderness wanderings, not to the experience at Sinai.

That earlier expansion in Exodus 20 had seemed appropriate because the motif of the fear of the people and their pleading with Moses to mediate between them and Yahweh was already present in the passage. The expansion merely served to emphasize it and to bring out its ramifications, especially concerning the prophet like Moses who was to come.

And so it was with this expansion. The specific motif of building an altar, along with other liturgical matters, was already present immediately after the giving of the ten commandments, in Exod 20:22-26, and the first commandment (20:4-6) already dealt with worship. This expansion merely served to emphasize what was already in the text and to give one more specific liturgical command, the location of the altar. Yet even the location of worship had already been referred to in 20:24, which probably read "in every place where I will cause my name to be remembered...." Probably at the same time as the major expansion the much smaller change was made to "in the place where I have caused my name to be remembered..." Was this not merely a minor alteration designed to create better harmony within Scripture?

This major expansion, then, could have been composed by an individual scribe -- possibly even by the same scribe who had made all or some of the others, earlier in his life -- or by a group of scribes and/or religious leaders. He or they would not necessarily have thought that they were doing anything audacious, or taking liberties with revelation. It had all been done before.

And it would probably be done again in the future, in another tradition, when the commandment in its original place in Deut 27:4 and its fulfilment in Josh 8:30 would be altered to read "Mount Ebal" instead of "Mount Gerizim." When the motivation was strong enough, continuing participation in the work of revelation could be viewed as legitimate.

Once one or both of those changes had been made, however, the two communities involved were in a fundamentally different relationship with each other. It had long been the case that more than one temple had been used by different groups of Israelites. Whether or not that was "tolerated" by all concerned, it was in fact the case. Now, however, Scripture was being used, apparently by both sides, as a weapon against the other community.   The weapon was not, be it noted, the interpretation of Scripture, but the actual text of Scripture.[10]

Unfortunately we cannot know whether the Gerizimites' use of Scripture as a weapon preceded or followed the Hasmonaeans' use of military weapons against them. Did the destruction of their temple and of their central city, Shechem, cause the traumatic situation that both suggested and legitimated the use of Scripture in this way? Or had their Scripture first been altered, and was that perhaps one last argument for John Hyrcanus to wipe out their temple?

On the basis of the text, either chronology could be correct.   Or perhaps the "sectarian" expansion actually came fifty or so years later. But if it is true that different instances of a similar treatment of Scripture belong within one period of time, then it may be that the evidence of Q^m suggests that the "sectarian" expansion should not be dated too much later. Here again one wishes that Q^m could be more precisely dated.

As far as the chronology is concerned, we are clearly in the realm of speculation. But it is the nature of the community that is more important. The conclusions of this study lend very specific support to the findings of Coggins, Purvis, Pummer, and others[11] about the nature of the Samaritan religion. In one more way their group has been shown to be quite at home in

---

[10]And soon the script of Scripture was likewise to become a weapon, as the Samaritans insisted on their gradually-evolving Palaeo-Hebrew script and the rabbis insisted on the square script. McLean ("Palaeo-Hebrew," p. 23) says after a review of rabbinic evidence: "Palaeo-Hebrew survives in the Samaritan script until this day because of its official sanction and role in legitimizing the claims of the Samaritan sect. Palaeo-Hebrew was lost to the 'normative' community for much the same reason as it was retained by the Samaritan, the need to define the community and its tradition so as to prevent its dissolution. It was not a lack of knowledge of the Palaeo-Hebrew script and its use that caused it to disappear; rather it was its official condemnation by the rulers and teachers of the 'normative' community." Even if that description may be somewhat oversimplified, it is at least true that the polemic continues today on the Samaritan side. Their own tourist booklet says: "All the Samaritans ... use the old Hebrew language in their prayers and religious masses. The best clue is given by the acknowledgment of the Jews who use the new Hebrew writing that differs from the old one" (Hasanein Wasef Kahen, "The Samaritans: Their History, Religion, Customs" [Nablus, 1974], p. 8).

[11]See above, Chapter I.D.

the "rich complex of Judaism."[12] They were not the only ones to treat their Scriptures as they did. Or, at the very least, even if they were the creators of all of the major expansions, a scroll with all but the Gerizim expansion was accepted and used in a different and very isolationist and hostile group. Even the most tendentious aspect of their Scripture followed a pattern also found at Qumran and, we may suppose, elsewhere as well.

---

[12]Coggins, *Samaritans and Jews,* p. 163.

APPENDIX 1

PASSAGES EXTANT IN 4QpaleoExodᵐ

This Appendix lists each column that has been preserved in the scroll, 4QpaleoExodᵐ, with the chapters and verses of Exodus that are extant. The verse is listed if any portion of it, even one letter or several letters, appear on the leather. Verse numbering follows that of von Gall's edition of the Samaritan Pentateuch, which agrees with that of *BHS* with one extra feature. A small raised **a** or **b** is used as in von Gall's edition to refer to the major expansions that occur in the textual tradition to which **Qᵐ** and **𝔐** belong. In this Appendix verse numbers in brackets indicate placement of reconstructed verses.

COLUMN   PASSAGE

i   6:25 – 7:16

ii   7:16-19

iii   7:29ᵇ – 8:1 ... 8:12-18

iv   8:19ᵇ-22

v   9:5ᵇ-16 ... 9:19ᵇ-21

vi   9:35 – 10:1 ... 10:2ᵇ-5

vii   10:5-12 ... 10:19-24

viii   10:25-28 ... 11:8 – 12:2

ix   12:6-8 ... 12:13-15 ... 12:17-22

x   12:31-32 ... 12:34-39

xi   13:3-7 ... 13:12-13

xii   14:3-5 ... 14:8-9

xiii   14:25-26

[xiv   lacking]

xv	15:23 - 16:1 ... 16:4-5 ... 16:7-8
xvi	16:31-32
xvii	16:32 - 17:16
xviii	17:16 - 18:18 ... 18:20-21
xix	18:21 - 19:1
xx	19:7-17 ... 19:23 - 20:1
xxi	20:18-19[b]
xxii	[20:21[b] - 21:4] 21:5-6
xxiii	21:13-14 ... 21:22-32
xxiv	22:3-4 ... 22:6-7 ... 22:11-13 ... 22:16-18
xxv	22:20-30 ... 23:15-16
xxvi	23:29-31 ... 24:1-4 ... 24:6-11
xxvii	25:11-12 ... 25:20-22
xxviii	25:22-29 ... 25:31-34
xxix	26:8-15 ... 26:21-30
xxx	[26:35; 30:1-9] 30:10; [26:36-37]; 27:1-2 ... 27:9-14
xxxi	27:18-19; 28:3-4; 28:8-11
xxxii	28:22-24 ... 28:26-28 ... 28:30-39
xxxiii	28:39 - 29:5
xxxiv	29:20, 22-25 ... 29:31-34
xxxv	29:34-41; [29:42-46; 30:11] 30:12-18
xxxvi	30:29-31 ... 30:34-38; 31:1-7
xxxvii	31:7-8 ... 31:13-15 ... 32:2-9
xxxviii	32:10-19 ... 32:25-30
xxxix	33:12-15
xl	33:16 - 34:3 ... 34:10-13
xli	34:15-18 ... 34:20-24 ... 34:27-28

APPENDIX 2

COMPLETE LIST OF VARIANTS

This Appendix lists every variant among **Qᵃ ɯ𝔪G** in chapter-verse order. Verse numbering follows that of von Gall's edition of the Samaritan Pentateuch, which agrees with that of *BHS* with one extra feature. A small raised ᵃ or ᵇ is used as in von Gall's edition to refer to the major expansions that occur in the textual tradition to which **Qᵃ** and **ɯ** belong. If the verse numbering in a Greek edition and/or the *RSV* differ, that number is provided in brackets. A Hebrew letter following the verse number indicates the number of the variant within that verse. Thus, for example, **9:19ᵇ** refers to a major expansion, while **9:19ᵇא** indicates the first variant within that expansion between the two texts that preserve it. This chapter-verse-(Hebrew letter) designation in boldface type is used consistently throughout the dissertation to identify each variant.

A variant is defined in this work as any disagreement among the four texts **Qᵃ ɯ𝔪G** of Exodus in every passage where **Qᵃ** is extant. The determination of variants is not based simply on disagreement with **𝔪**, but rather on any disagreement on the part of any of the four texts. Purely orthographical differences are not considered as variants. The evidence of **Qᵃ** is treated with caution. Only those variants are considered which are actually still preserved in ink. The evidence of space requirements and reconstruction is not used for determining variants or other statistics, though it is occasionally referred to as supplementary to what is actually extant.

Following the designation of each variant, the reading of **Qᵃ** is listed, followed by those of the other three texts.

In the right margin is indicated the chapter(s) and section(s) where each variant is discussed. Parentheses indicate inclusion in a list only briefly discussed.

Below the listing of the reading there is a formula showing the agreements and disagreements among the four texts. The underlined characters indicate which text or texts are considered to preserve the preferable reading. The degree of certainty as to the Hebrew *Vorlage* of the Greek reading is indicated as follows:

G   full agreement

(G)   probably favors, but not certain

(G?)   possibly favors

; **G?** the Hebrew *Vorlage* of this Greek reading cannot be determined

/**G**/   material agreement but meaningless; i.e., the Greek does on the
surface appear to agree with one Hebrew text, but there is no
necessary dependence

To the right of the formula, a symbol indicates the nature of the
variant as well as which text is judged to preserve the secondary reading.
The following symbols are used:

+   Expansion, defined as a minor or moderate addition to the original.

++   Major Expansion, defined as a more extensive and deliberate expansion
to the original text. All but one occur only in the textual
tradition to which **Qᵐ** and 𝖜 belong.

−   Omission, defined as an unintentional omission from the original text.

2V   Secondary variant, defined as a qualitatively different reading which
is considered to be secondary.

~   Transposition.

X   Error, defined as a reading which is not only secondary but actually
grammatically or contextually wrong.

≅   Synonymous variant, defined as two or more readings, either or all of
which could have been original, which are parallel, and which
have similar claim on originality. They are two or more good
ways of expressing the same thing.

A fuller list of witnesses including Targum, Peshitta, Old Latin, and
Vulgate, will soon be available in the *DJD* edition of 4QpaleoExodᵐ.

6:27א   להוציא 𝖜𝖬] κα ε̇ξηγαγον **G**   IIIA5
         Qᵐ = 𝖜𝖬 ≠ **G**   **Qᵐ**𝖜𝖬 ≅ **G**   (IVA5)

6:27ב   ממצרים 𝖬**G**] מארץ מצרים 𝖜   IIA7
         Qᵐ = 𝖬**G** ≠ 𝖜   𝖜 +   (IVB1a)

6:27ג   משה ואהר(ו)ן 𝖜𝖬]   IIIA5
         Ααρων και Μωυσης **G**   (IVA5b)
         Qᵐ = 𝖜𝖬 ≠ **G**   **Qᵐ**𝖜𝖬 ≅ **G**

6:30   ישמע אלי 𝔐] ישמעני ש;   IIIA3
       εισακουσεται μου 𝔊   (IVA3b)
       Q^a = 𝔐 ≠ ש; 𝔊?   Q^{a}𝔐 ≅ ש

7:2^{fin} ישר[אל] ³ · [   ] [ו]אני ³   IIA1
       ש𝔐𝔊 ישראל מארעו ³ואני   (IVB4a)
       Q^a ≠ ש𝔐𝔊   ש𝔐𝔊 +

7:4   במשפטים 𝔐] בשפטי[ם] ש;   IIA3
       συν εκδικησει 𝔊   (IVB1a)
       Q^a = 𝔐(𝔊) ≠ ש   ש 2v

7:9   והשלך ש𝔐] + εζι οντι 𝔊 עחץ עחז   IIA5
       Q^a = ש𝔐 ≠ 𝔊   𝔊 +   (IVDa)

7:10   לפני פרעה 4QExod^{b}ש𝔊] 1°   IIIA6
       אל פרעה 𝔐   (IVA6b)
       Q^a = ש𝔊 ≠ 𝔐   Q^{a}ש𝔊 ≅ 𝔐

7:14   וידבר\[†] ש] ויאמר 𝔐; Ειπεν δε 𝔊   IIIA2
       Q^a = ש ≠ 𝔐(𝔊)   Q^{a}ש ≅ 𝔐(𝔊)   (IVA2)

7:15א   והנה] הנה ש𝔐𝔊   IIB4
       Q^a ≠ ש𝔐𝔊   Q^a +   (IVA1a)

7:15ב   יצא 𝔐] הוא ש𝔊 [יצא   IIA6
       Q^a = ש𝔊 ≠ 𝔐   𝔐 -   (IVC1a)

7:18   היאר] בת[וך] ביאר ש𝔐;   IIB2
       εν τω ποταμω 𝔊   (IVA1a)
       Q^a ≠ ש𝔐(𝔊?)   Q^a 2v

7:18^b hab ש] > 4QExod^{b}𝔐𝔊   (IIC2,IVA2a)
       Q^a = ש ≠ 𝔐𝔊   Q^{a}ש ++   VA3a

7:18^{b}א   ויאמרו] ויאמר ש   VA3b
       Q^a ≠ ש ≠ 𝔐𝔊   ש ++ 2v

7:18^ב   בת[וך היאר]] ביאר 𝔐   (IIB2)

Q^a ≠ 𝔐 ≠ 𝔐𝔊   Q^a ++ 2v   VA3b

7:29^b   hab 𝔐] > 4QExod^c𝔐𝔊   (IIC2,IVA2a)

Q^a = 𝔐 ≠ 𝔐𝔊   Q^a𝔐 ++   VA3b

8:14[18]   ויהי ה[כ]נים] ותהי הכנ(י)ם 𝔐𝔐;   IIIB2

και εγενοντο οι σκνιφες 𝔊   (IVB2b)

Q^a ≠ 𝔐𝔐; 𝔊?   Q^a ≅ 𝔐𝔐

8:16[20]   לאמור] אל משה] אל משה 𝔐𝔐𝔊   IIB4

Q^a ≠ 𝔐𝔐𝔊   Q^a +   (IVA1a)

8:19^b   hab 𝔐] > 𝔐𝔊   (IIC2,IVA2a)

Q^a = 𝔐 ≠ 𝔐𝔊   Q^a𝔐 ++   VA3a

8:20[24]   [𝔐 כבד] מאד   IIC2

כבד 4QpaleoExod^l(vid)𝔐𝔊   (IVA2a)

Q^a = 𝔐 ≠ 𝔐𝔊   Q^a𝔐 +

9:5^b   hab 𝔐] > 𝔐𝔊   (IIC2,IVA2a)

Q^a = 𝔐 ≠ 𝔐𝔊   Q^a𝔐 ++   VA3a

9:5^bא   הדבר] את 𝔐 pr   VA3b

Q^a ≠ 𝔐 ≠ 𝔐𝔊   𝔐 ++ +

9:7   בני ישראל 𝔐𝔊] ישראל 𝔐   IIC1

Q^a = 𝔐𝔊 ≠ 𝔐   Q^a𝔐𝔊 +   (IVA6a)

9:8א   לאמור 𝔊] > 𝔐𝔐   IIB2

Q^a = 𝔊 ≠ 𝔐𝔐   Q^a𝔊 +   (IVA4a)

9:8ב   הש[מ]ים 𝔐] השמימה 𝔐;   IIIA2

εις τον ουρανον 𝔊   (IVA2b)

Q^a = 𝔐 ≠ 𝔐; 𝔊?   Q^a𝔐 ≅ 𝔐

9:8ג   𝔐] לעיני פרעה + και εναντιον   IIA5
       των θεραποντων αυτου **G**   (IVDa)
       Q = 𝔐 ≠ **G**   **G** +

9:9א   𝔐G על כל ארץ [על ארץ   IIIB4
       Q ≠ 𝔐G   **Q** ≅ 𝔐G   (IVB4b)

9:9ב   𝔐] ל[ש]חין פ(ו)(ר)ח אבעבע(ו)ת   IIIA5
       ελκη φλυκτιδες αναζεουσαι **G**   (IVA5b)
       Q = 𝔐 ≠ **G**   **Q**𝔐 ≅ **G**

9:9ג   𝔐] בכל pr εν τε τοις ανθρωποις   IIA5
       και εν τοις τετραποσιν και **G**   (IVDa)
       Q = 𝔐 ≠ **G**   **G** +

9:10   𝔐] ויעמדו > **G**   IID
       Q = 𝔐 ≠ **G**   **Q**𝔐 +   (IVA5a)

9:16   𝔐] ו[אולם και **G**   IIIA5
       Q = 𝔐 ≠ **G**   **Q**𝔐 ≅ **G**   (IVA5b)

9:19ᵇ   𝔐] hab > 4QExodᶜ𝔐G   (IIC2,IVA2a)
       Q = 𝔐 ≠ 𝔐G   **Q**𝔐 ++   VA3a

9:19ᵃᵇ   𝔐 למיום [למן היום   VA3b
       Q ≠ 𝔐 ≠ 𝔐G   ++ **Q** ≅ 𝔐

9:19ᵇᵇ   𝔐 לך [א[ל]יך   VA3b
       Q ≠ 𝔐 ≠ 𝔐G   **Q** ++ X

9:20   𝔐] את עבדיו [ואת מקנה(ו)]   IID
       τα κτηνη αυτου **G**   (IVA5)
       Q = 𝔐 ≠ **G**   **Q**𝔐 +

10:2ᵇ   𝔐] hab > 𝔐G   (IIC2,IVA2a)
       Q = 𝔐 ≠ 𝔐G   **Q**𝔐 ++   VA3a

10:5   ‫ш] כל עשב הארץ ואת כל[פרי‬   IIC2
          ‫כל 𝕸𝕲‬   (IVA2a)
          Q^a = ш ≠ 𝕸𝕲 Q^a ш +

10:6א,ב   ‫𝕸ш] ובתי כל עבדיך וב[תי‬   IIIA5
          και αι οικιαι των θεραποντων   (IVA5b)
          σου και πασαι αι οικιαι 𝕲
          Q^a = ш𝕸 ≠ 𝕲 Q^aш𝕸 ≅ 𝕲

10:10   ‫יה[י] 𝕸𝕲] ш יהיה‬   IIA7
          Q^a = 𝕸𝕲 ≠ ш   ш 2v   (IVB1a)

10:11   ‫לא כן [𝕸] לכן ;ш חμ ουτως 𝕲‬   IIIA3
          Q^a = 𝕸/𝕲/ ≠ ш Q^a𝕸/𝕲/ ≅ ш   (IVA3b)

10:21א   ‫וידבר/[✝] шм ויאמר; Ειπεν δε 𝕲‬   IIB2
          Q^a ≠ шм(𝕲) Q^a 2v   (IVA1a)

10:21ב   ‫[מער]\ים ויט‬   IIIB4
          ‫שмℭ מערים וימש (ה)חשך ויט‬   (IVB4b)
          Q^a ≠ шмℭ Q^a ≅ шмℭ

10:24א   ‫אל משה [ш] אל משה 𝕸; Μωυσην 𝕲‬   IIC1
          Q^a = ш ≠ 𝕸; 𝕲? Q^a ш 2v   (IVA2a)

10:24ב   ‫ולאהר(ו)[ן ш𝕲] > 𝕸‬   IIC1,VIA1g
          Q^a = ш𝕲 ≠ 𝕸 Q^aш𝕲 +   (IVA6)

10:24ג   ‫יצג [шм] υπολειπεσθε 𝕲‬   IIIA5
          Q^a = шм ≠ 𝕲 Q^aшм ≅ 𝕲   (IVA5b)

10:25   ‫ו[עלות ש𝕸] ~ 𝕲 גב[ח]ים‬   IIIA5
          Q^a = шм ≠ 𝕲 Q^aшм ≅ 𝕲   (IVA5b)

10:26   ‫נשאר [𝕲 תשאר шм‬   IIIA4
          Q^a = 𝕲 ≠ шм Q^a𝕲 ≅ шм   (IVA4b)

11:9   מופתי 𝔖𝔐] pr τα σημεια και G   IIA5
       Q^m = 𝔖𝔐 ≠ G   G +   (IVDa)

12:6   אותם [אתו 𝔖𝔐G   IIB4
       Q^m ≠ 𝔖𝔐G   Q^m 2v   (IVA1a)

13:5   וה]חתי 𝔐G] 𝔖 החתי   IIIA3
       Q^m = 𝔐/G/ ≠ 𝔖   Q^m𝔐/G/ ≅ 𝔖   (IVa3b)

13:6   בעת[ש 𝔐] ששת 𝔖G   IIIA3,B3
       Q^m = 𝔐 ≠ 𝔖G   Q^m𝔐 ≅ 𝔖G (IVA3b,B3b)

15:27 ו]𝔐G] 𝔖 ובאילים שם   IIA7
       Q^m = 𝔐G ≠ 𝔖   𝔖 2v   (IVB1a)

16:31 בית 𝔖𝔐] οι υιοι G   IIIA5
       Q^m = 𝔖𝔐 ≠ G   Q^m𝔖𝔐 ≅ G   (IVA5b)

16:32 האכ]לתי אתכם 𝔖𝔐]   IIIA5
       εφαγετε υμεις G   (IVA5b)
       Q^m = 𝔖𝔐 ≠ G   Q^m𝔖𝔐 ≅ G

16:33 יה]וה 𝔖𝔐] του θεου G   IIIA5
       Q^m = 𝔖𝔐 ≠ G   Q^m𝔖𝔐 ≅ G   (IVA5b)

16:34 אל משה 𝔖] א[ת מ]שה 𝔐;   IIA2
       τω Μωυση G   (IVC1a)
       Q^m = 𝔖 ≠ 𝔐; G?   𝔐 X

17:2א תנו 𝔖G] תנה 𝔐   IIA6
       Q^m = 𝔖G ≠ 𝔐   𝔐 X   (IVC1a)

17:2ב מה 𝔖G] מה ומה 𝔐   IIC1
       Q^m = 𝔖G ≠ 𝔐   Q^m𝔖G +   (IVA6)

17:6   נקני 𝔖𝔐] των υιων G   IIA5
       Q^m = 𝔖𝔐 ≠ G   G 2v   (IVDa)

17:12   ויהיו ‬G‬שׁ‬ [ויהי ‬𝕸‬   IIC1

             Qᵃ = ‬שׁ /G/ ≠ 𝕸   Qᵃ‬שׁ‬/G/ 2v   (IVA2a)

17:13א   ‬שׁ𝕸‬] ואת עמו

             και παντα τον λαον αυτου G   (IIA5)

             Qᵃ = ‬שׁ𝕸‬ ≠ G   G +

17:13ב   לפי 𝕸G‬ [ויכם לפי ‬שׁ‬   IIC2

             Qᵃ = ‬שׁ ≠ 𝕸G‬   Qᵃ‬שׁ‬ +   (IVA2a)

17:16   מדר דר :‬שׁ‬ מדר ודר [עד דור ודו]ר‬ 𝕸: IIIE

             απο γενεων εις γενεας G   (IVE)

             Qᵃ ≠ ‬שׁ ≠ 𝕸 ≠ G   Qᵃ ≅ ‬שׁ ≅ 𝕸 ≅ G

18:1א   ‬שׁ𝕸‬] אלה]ים κυριος G   IIIA5

             Qᵃ = ‬שׁ𝕸‬ ≠ G   Qᵃ‬שׁ𝕸‬ ≅ G   (IVA5b)

18:1ב   Ισραηλ ‬שׁ𝕸‬] למשה [ולישראל‬   IID

             Qᵃ = ‬שׁ𝕸‬ ≠ G   Qᵃ‬שׁ𝕸‬ +   (IVA5a)

18:4   ‬שׁ𝕸‬] εκ χειρος G מח]ר[ב‬   IIA5

             Qᵃ = ‬שׁ𝕸‬ ≠ G   G 2v   (IVDa)

18:6א   𝕸] אל משה ‬שׁ‬; Μωυση G למשה‬   IIIA3

             Qᵃ = 𝕸 ≠ ‬שׁ‬; G?   Qᵃ𝕸 ≅ ‬שׁ‬   (IVA3b)

18:6ב   אני 𝕸 [הנה ‬שׁ‬G‬   IIIA6

             Qᵃ = ‬שׁ‬G‬ ≠ 𝕸   Qᵃ‬שׁ‬G‬ ≅ 𝕸   (IVA6b)

18:6ג   ‬שׁ𝕸‬] עמה בנ[יה]‬   IIIA5

             υιοι σου μετ αυτου G   (IVA5b)

             Qᵃ = ‬שׁ𝕸‬ ≠ G   Qᵃ‬שׁ𝕸‬ ≅ G

18:9א   ‬שׁ𝕸‬] ו]יחד εξεστη δε G‬   IIIA5

             Qᵃ = ‬שׁ𝕸‬ ≠ G   Qᵃ‬שׁ𝕸‬ ≅ G   (IVA5b)

18:9ב   [𝔐𝔪 לישר[אל ... העילו   IIIA5
          αυτοις ... εξειλατο αυτους G   (IVA5b)
          Qᵃ = 𝔪𝔐 ≠ G   Qᵃ𝔪𝔐 ≅ G

18:9ג   [𝔪𝔐 מצרים]   IIIA5
          + και εκ χειρος Φαραω G   (IVA5b)
          Qᵃ = 𝔪𝔐 ≠ G   Qᵃ𝔪𝔐 ≅ G

18:10א   [𝔪𝔐 אתכם] τον λαον αυτου G   IIIA5
          Qᵃ = 𝔪𝔐 ≠ G   Qᵃ𝔪𝔐 ≅ G   (IVA5b)

18:10ב   פרעה אשר העיל א[ת העם מתחת   IIIA5
          ם](י)ד מערי [𝔪𝔐 Φαραω G   (IVA5b)
          Qᵃ = 𝔪𝔐 ≠ G   Qᵃ𝔪𝔐 ≅ G

18:11   [𝔪𝔐 כי בדבר] ενεκεν τουτου G   IIIA5
          Qᵃ = 𝔪𝔐 ≠ G   Qᵃ𝔪𝔐 ≅ G   (IVA5b)

18:12   [𝔪𝔐 ע(ו)לה] ολοκαυτωματα G   IIIA5
          Qᵃ = 𝔪𝔐 ≠ G   Qᵃ𝔪𝔐 ≅ G   (IVA5b)

18:13א   [𝔪𝔐 ה]עם] pr πας G   (IIA5)
          Qᵃ = 𝔪𝔐 ≠ G   G +   (IVDa)

18:13ב   [ערב]   [בוקר] הבקר ... הערב ;𝔪𝔐   IIIB2
          πρωιθεν ... εσπερας G   (IVB2b)
          Qᵃ ≠ 𝔪𝔐; G?   Qᵃ ≅ 𝔪𝔐

18:14   [𝔪𝔐 משה] חתן Ιοθορ G   IIIA5
          Qᵃ = 𝔪𝔐 ≠ G   Qᵃ𝔪𝔐 ≅ G   (IVA5b)

18:16א,ב   ו[ב]א 𝔪 ; בא 𝔰𝔪] באו ו[ב]א 𝔪; και ελθωσιν G
          א: Qᵃ = G ≠ 𝔪𝔐 (ו-)   Qᵃ G ≅ 𝔪𝔐   IIIB2,A4
                                                   (IVB2b,A4b)
          ב: Qᵃ = 𝔐 ≠ 𝔪G (-ו)   Qᵃ𝔐 ≅ 𝔪G   IIIA3,B3
                                                   (IVA3b,B3b)

18:20   הדרך אש]ר ⅏] הדרך 𝕸;   IIIA2
      τας οδους, εν αις **G**   (IVA2b)
        Q^a = ⅏/**G**/ ≠ 𝕸   **Q^a**⅏/**G**/ ≅ 𝕸

18:21א   בע]ע ⅏𝕸] υπερηφανιαν **G**   IIA5
        Q^a = ⅏𝕸 ≠ **G**   **G** 2v   (IVDa)

18:21ב   שרי מאות ⅏**G**] ושרי מאות 𝕸   IIIA2
        Q^a = ⅏ /**G**/ ≠ 𝕸   **Q^a**⅏/**G**/ ≅ 𝕸   (IVA2b)

18:21ג   שרי חמשים ⅏𝕸] ש]רי חמשים **G**] ושׁ   IIIA4,B2
        Q^a ‒ **G** ≠ ⅏𝕸   **Q^{a}G** ≅ ⅏𝕸   (IVA4b,B2b)

18:23   אל ⅏] על 𝕸; εις **G**   IIA2
        Q^a = ⅏(**G**) ≠ 𝕸   𝕸 X   (IVC1a)

18:25⅏   // Deut 1:9-18 ⅏]   (IIC2,IVA2a)
      aliter et brevius 𝕸**G**   VA3a
        Q^a = ⅏ ≠ 𝕸**G**   **Q^a**⅏ ++

18:25א⅏   אוכל] + אנכי ⅏   VA3b
        Q^a ≠ ⅏ ≠ 𝕸**G**   ⅏ ++ +

18:25ב⅏   ככוכב] ככוכבי ⅏   VA3b
        Q^a ≠ ⅏ ≠ 𝕸**G**   **Q^a** ++ X

18:27   וילך] + לו ⅏𝕸; και απηλθεν **G**   IIA1
        Q^a/**G**/ ≠ ⅏𝕸   ⅏𝕸 +   (IVB2a)

19:8   יהו]ה ⅏𝕸] τον θεον **G**   IIIA5
        Q^a = ⅏𝕸 ≠ **G**   **Q^a**⅏𝕸 ≅ **G**   (IVA5b)

19:10   לך ⅏𝕸] Καταβας διαμαρτυραι **G**   IIA5
        Q^a = ⅏𝕸 ≠ **G**   **G** 2v +   (IVDa)

19:11   𝔐𝔪[העם על הר ס[י]ני לעיני כל]העם על הר ס[י]ני   IIIA5

        επι το ορος το Σινα   (IVA5b)

        εναντιον παντος του λαου **G**

        Qᵃ = 𝔪𝔐 ≠ **G**   **Qᵃ𝔪𝔐 ≅ G**

19:12   𝔪**G**[סבי[ב לאמ(ו)ר   IIA7

        𝔐 סביב ואל העם תאמר   (IVB1a)

        Qᵃ = 𝔪**G** ≠ 𝔐   𝔐 2v +

19:24   𝔪𝔐[ב[ם + κυριος **G**   IIA5

        Qᵃ = 𝔪𝔐 ≠ **G**   **G** +   (IVDa)

19:25   𝔪**G**[+ מן ההר משה   𝔐   IIA7

        Qᵃ = 𝔪**G** ≠ 𝔐   𝔐 +   (IVB1a)

20:1   𝔪𝔐[אל[הים κυριος **G**   IIIA5

        Qᵃ = 𝔪𝔐 ≠ **G**   **Qᵃ𝔪𝔐 ≅ G**   (IVA5b)

20:19ᵃ   𝔐[דבר אתה עמנו ונשמעה ;hab 𝔐[(IID;IVA2a,C1a)

        Λαλησον συ 𝔪עמנו **G**   VA3a

        Qᵃ = 𝔪 ≠ 𝔐 ≠ **G**   **Qᵃ**𝔪 ++ 𝔐 +

20:19ᵃᵃ   חי] 𝔐 חיים   VA3b

        Qᵃ ≠ 𝔐 ≠ 𝔪**G**   ++ **Qᵃ** ≅ 𝔐

21:6   𝔪𝔐[אדניו];   IIA1

        ο κυριος αυτου **G**   (IVB2a)

        Qᵃ ≠ 𝔪𝔐; **G**?   𝔪𝔐 2v

21:13   שמה 𝔪𝔐; εκει **G** [שם   IIIB2

        Qᵃ ≠ 𝔪𝔐; **G**?   **Qᵃ** ≅ 𝔪𝔐   (IVB2b)

21:25   𝔐[מכוה 𝔪; κατακαυματος **G** כויה   IIA3

        Qᵃ = 𝔐 ≠ 𝔪; **G**?   𝔐 2v   (IVB1a)

21:29   𝔪**G**[הבהמה תסקל הש[ור יסקל]ל   𝔐   IIA7

        Qᵃ = 𝔪**G** ≠ 𝔐   𝔐 2v   (IVB1a)

21:31   𝔖; יכה או בת] א[ו בת י[גח   IIA7
     𝔐; יגח או בת יגח   (IVB1a)
     κερατιση η θυγατερα 𝔊
     Q^a = 𝔐𝔊 ≠ 𝔖   𝔖 2v

22:3[4]   שנים 𝔐; שנים]אחד 𝔖[IIC1
     διπλα αυτα 𝔊   (IVA2a)
     Q^a = 𝔖 ≠ 𝔐; 𝔊? Q^a𝔖 +

22:4[5] Q^a [כל]ן]
אחר שלם ישלם משדהו כתבואתה ואם כל השדה יבעה 𝔖
𝔐   אחר
𝔊 ετερον, αποτεισει εκ του αγρου αυτου κατα το γενημα
αυτου· εαν δε παντα τον αγρον καταβοσκηση
     Q^a = 𝔖𝔊 ≠ 𝔐   𝔐 -   IIA6
                                 (IVC1a)

22:6   וגנב]𝔖 ו[נגנב 𝔐; και κλαπη 𝔊   IIIA2
     Q^a = 𝔖 ≠ 𝔐; 𝔊? Q^a𝔖 ≅ 𝔐   (IVA2b)

22:24א   את ע]𝔖𝔐[מי τω αδελφω 𝔊   IIIA5
     Q^a = 𝔖𝔐 ≠ 𝔊 Q^a𝔖𝔐 ≅ 𝔊   (IVA5b)

22:24ב   עני]𝔐 העני[𝔖; τω πενιχρω 𝔊   IIIA3
     Q^a = 𝔐 /𝔊/ ≠ 𝔖 Q^a𝔐/𝔊/ ≅ 𝔖   (IVA3b)

22:25   שלמת 𝔐] שמלת 𝔖; ιματιον 𝔊   IIA3
     Q^a = 𝔐 ≠ 𝔖; 𝔊?   𝔖 2v   (IVB1a)

22:26א   הוא ... הוא 𝔐] הי]𝔖 א[... הי[א   IIIA2
     τουτο ... τουτο 𝔊   (IVA2b)
     Q^a = 𝔖 ≠ 𝔐; 𝔊? Q^a𝔖 ≅ 𝔐

22:26ב   אני 𝔐] אנכי 𝔖; ειμι 𝔊   IIIA3
     Q^a = 𝔐 ≠ 𝔖; 𝔊? Q^a𝔐 ≅ 𝔖   (IVA3b)

23:31   וש[מתי (vid)] ושתי 𝕊𝔐; και θησω 𝕲   IIB2
              𝑸ᵃ ≠ 𝕊𝔐; 𝕲?   𝑸ᵃ 2v   (IVA1a)

24:1   [𝕊 ואביהוא אלעזר ו[איתמ]ר   (IIC2,IVA2a)
              ואביהוא 𝔐𝕲   VA3a
              𝑸ᵃ = 𝕊 ≠ 𝔐𝕲   𝑸ᵃ𝕊 ++

24:9   [𝕊 ואביהוא אלעזר וא[יתמר   (IIC2,IVA2a)
              ואביהוא 𝔐𝕲   VA3a
              𝑸ᵃ = 𝕊 ≠ 𝔐𝕲   𝑸ᵃ𝕊 ++

25:20   איש אל אחיו [𝕊 אחד א[ל אחד 𝔐;   IIC1
              εις αλληλα 𝕲   (IVA2a)
              𝑸ᵃ = 𝕊 ≠ 𝔐; 𝕲?   𝑸ᵃ𝕊 2v

25:23   עצי שטים [𝕊𝔐] χρυσιου καθαρου 𝕲   IIIA5
              𝑸ᵃ= 𝕊𝔐 ≠ 𝕲   𝑸ᵃ𝕊𝔐 ≅ 𝕲   (IVA5b)

25:24   וצפית [𝕊𝔐] > 𝕲 א(ו)תו זהב טהור   IIIA5
              𝑸ᵃ = 𝕊𝔐 ≠ 𝕲   𝑸ᵃ𝕊𝔐 ≅ 𝕲   (IVA5b)

25:29   קע[ר]ת[י]ו 𝔐] pr את 𝕊;   (IIA3)
              τα τρυβλια αυτης 𝕲   (IVB1a)
              𝑸ᵃ = 𝔐 ≠ 𝕊; 𝕲?   𝕊 +

25:33   ושלשה גבעים משקדים   IIA5
              בקנ]ה האחד] כפתר ופרח [𝕊𝔐] > 𝕲   (IVDa)
              𝑸ᵃ = 𝕊𝔐 ≠ 𝕲   𝕲 –

26:8   היריעות [𝔐 יריע(ו)ת 𝕊;   IIIA3
              ταις...δερρεσι 𝕲   (IVA3b)
              𝑸ᵃ = 𝔐 ≠ 𝕊 /𝕲/   𝑸ᵃ𝔐 ≅ 𝕊/𝕲/

26:10   חמשים ללאת [𝕊 1° ללא[ות חמשים 𝔐;   IIIA2
              αγκυλας πεντηκοντα 𝕲   (IVA2b)
              𝑸ᵃ = 𝕊 /𝕲/ ≠ 𝔐   𝑸ᵃ𝕊/𝕲/ ≅ 𝔐

26:24　ויחד(י)ו 𝕸] יחדו 𝔚;　　　　　　　　　　　　　IIIA7

και κατα το αυτο 𝔊　　　　　　　　　　　　(IVA7b,B1b)

Qᵃ = 𝕸𝔊 ≠ 𝔚　　　　　　　　　Qᵃ𝕸𝔊 ≅ 𝔚

26:26　בריחי 𝔚] בריחם 𝕸; μοχλους 𝔊　　　　　　　　IIIA2

Qᵃ = 𝔚 ≠ 𝕸; 𝔊?　　　　　　　Qᵃ𝔚 ≅ 𝕸　(IVA2b)

30:1-10　post 26:35 𝔚] post 29:46 𝕸𝔊　　　　　　　IIIA2,C2

Qᵃ = 𝔚 ≠ 𝕸𝔊　　　　　　　Qᵃ𝔚 ≅ 𝕸𝔊 (IVA2b,C2b)

30:10　ל[ד(ו)]רתיכם 𝔚𝕸]　　　　　　　　　　　　IIIA5

εις τας γενεας αυτων 𝔊　　　　　　　　　(IVA5b)

Qᵃ = 𝔚𝕸 ≠ 𝔊　　　　　　　Qᵃ𝔚𝕸 ≅ 𝔊

27:9　נג[ב] תימנה 𝕸] נגבה תימנה 𝔚;　　　　　　　IIIA3

το προς λιβα 𝔊　　　　　　　　　　　　(IVA3b)

Qᵃ = 𝕸 ≠ 𝔚; 𝔊?　　　　　　　Qᵃ𝕸 ≅ 𝔚

27:10　ועמד[יו 𝔚𝕸]　　　　　　　　　　　　　IIIA5

και οι στυλοι αυτων 𝔊　　　　　　　　　(IVA5b)

Qᵃ = 𝔚𝕸 ≠ 𝔊　　　　　　　Qᵃ𝔚𝕸 ≅ 𝔊

27:11א　צפון 𝕸] צפונה 𝔚;　　　　　　　　　　　IIIA3

τω προς απηλιωτην 𝔊　　　　　　　　　(IVA3b)

Qᵃ = 𝕸 ≠ 𝔚; 𝔊?　　　　　　　Qᵃ𝕸 ≅ 𝔚

27:11ב　ווי 𝕸𝔊] וויהם 𝔚　　　　　　　　　　　IIIA7

Qᵃ = 𝕸𝔊 ≠ 𝔚　　　　　　　Qᵃ𝕸𝔊 ≅ 𝔚　(IVA7b)

27:19ᵇ　נחשת] ועש[ית בגדי תכלת וארגמן ותולעת　(IIC2,IVA2a)

𝔚] שני לשרת (לשדת mend ᵉᵈ 𝔚) בהם בקדש　VA3a

נחשת 𝕸𝔊

Qᵃ = 𝔚 ≠ 𝕸𝔊　　　　　　　Qᵃ𝔚 ++

28:3 א[ת בגדי א]הר(ו)ן ‏ 𝔐ᵕ‎] IIA5

τ𝛼ς στολας τας αγιαν Ααρων **G** (IVDa)

𝗤ᵃ = 𝔐ᵕ ≠ **G** **G** +

28:4 וכתנת 𝔐] ‏ᵕ‎ כיתנת; και χιτωνα **G** IIIA3

𝗤ᵃ = 𝔐 /**G**/ ≠ ᵕ 𝗤ᵃ𝔐/**G**/ ≅ ᵕ (IVA3b)

28:11א]יפתח תפתח ᵕ𝔐**G** (IIB4)

𝗤ᵃ ≠ ᵕ𝔐**G** 𝗤ᵃ X (IVA1a)

28:11ב]מ(ו)ס[בת [משב]צות נ]הב תעשה אתם 𝔐ᵕ IIIA5

＞ **G** (IVA5b)

𝗤ᵃ = ᵕ𝔐 ≠ **G** 𝗤ᵃᵕ𝔐 ≅ **G**

28:23-29 hab ᵕ𝔐] hab vv 29, 29a (ex 23-28) **G** IIIA5

𝗤ᵃ = ᵕ𝔐 ≠ **G** 𝗤ᵃᵕ𝔐 ≅ **G** (IVA5b)

28:23 שתי 2° 𝔐] ＞ ᵕ; clause lacking **G** IIIA3

𝗤ᵃ = 𝔐 ≠ ᵕ ≠ **G** 𝗤ᵃ𝔐 ≅ ᵕ ≠ **G** (IVA3b)

28:39 הכתנת 𝔐] pr את ᵕ; (IIA3)

των χιτωνων **G** (IVB1a)

𝗤ᵃ = 𝔐 ≠ ᵕ; **G**? ᵕ +

28:40 ועשית[להם ᵕ𝔐] και **G** IID

𝗤ᵃ = ᵕ𝔐 ≠ **G** 𝗤ᵃᵕ𝔐 + (IVA5a)

28:41]ו[הלבשת והלבשתם ᵕ𝔐**G** (IIB4)

𝗤ᵃ ≠ ᵕ𝔐**G** 𝗤ᵃ X (IVA1a)

28:43 ישאו ᵕ𝔐] + προς εαυτους **G** IIA5

𝗤ᵃ = ᵕ𝔐 ≠ **G** **G** + (IVDa)

29:2 סלת ᵕ] משחים בשמן pr 𝔐**G** IIIA2,C2

𝗤ᵃ = ᵕ ≠ 𝔐**G** 𝗤ᵃᵕ ≅ 𝔐**G** (IVA2b,C2b)

29:22 א   ;𝔐 והאליה ;𝔖 את האליה [ואת[...   IIIE
           > G (vid.)   (IVE)
           Q^a ≠ 𝔖 ≠ 𝔐; G?   Q^a ≅ 𝔖 ≅ 𝔐

29:22 ב   ;היותרת[תרת(ו)י 𝔖𝔐; τον λοβον G   IIIB2
           Q^a ≠ 𝔖𝔐; G?   Q^a ≅ 𝔖𝔐   (IVB2b)

29:33   למל[א 𝔐G] בם + 𝔖   IIA7
           Q^a = 𝔐/G/ ≠ 𝔖   𝔖 +   (IVB1a)

31:4   ;לעשות בזהב [לעשוב[נהב 𝔖𝔐   (IIB4)
           εργαζεσθαι το χρυσιον G   (IVA1a)
           Q^a ≠ 𝔖𝔐G   Q^a X

31:5   מלאכת [מלאכה 𝔖𝔐; τα εργα G   IIB2
           Q^a ≠ 𝔖𝔐; G?   Q^a 2v   (IVA1a)

31:13   הי[א 𝔖] הוא 𝔐; εστιν G   IIIA2
           Q^a = 𝔖 ≠ 𝔐; G?   Q^a𝔖 ≅ 𝔐   (IVA2b)

31:13-14   Q^a   כי]אות הי[א ל]כם מחלל[יה
           כי אות הי\וא ביני וביניכם לדרתיכם לדעת
           כי אני יהוה מקדשכם ¹⁴ושמרתם את השבת   IIIB4
           כי קדש הי\וא לכם מחלליה   𝔖𝔐G   (IVA1a,B4b)
           Q^a ≠ 𝔖𝔐G   Q^a ≅ 𝔖𝔐G

32:2   בניכם [𝔖𝔐] > G   IIIA5
           Q^a = 𝔖𝔐 ≠ G   Q^a𝔖𝔐 ≅ G   (IVA5b)

32:7 א   לא[מור 𝔖G] > 𝔐   IIC1
           Q^a = 𝔖G ≠ 𝔐   Q^a𝔖G +   (IVA6a)

32:7 ב   רד [לך רד 𝔖𝔐; Βαδιζε καταβηθι   IIA1
           το ταχος εντευθεν G   (IVB2a,Da)
           Q^a ≠ 𝔖𝔐 ≠ G   𝔖𝔐 + G +

32:9	ויאמר יהוה]אל מש[ה ראיתי את העם	IID,VC3
	‭[‬𝕸ш הזה והנה עם קשה ערף הוא	(IVA5a)
	‭>‬ **G**	
	Q = ш𝕸 ≠ **G**	Q‍ш𝕸 ++

32:10	ובאהר(ו)ן התאנף יה[ו]ה מאד להשמידו	(IIC2,IVA2a)
	ш[ו[י]תפלל משה בעד א[הר](ו)ן	VA3a
	‭>‬ 𝕸**G**	
	Q = ш ≠ 𝕸**G**	Qш ++

32:11א	יחר ш[יחרה 𝕸; θυμοι **G**	IIIA2
	Q = ш ≠ 𝕸; **G**?	Qш ≅ 𝕸 (IVA2b,C1b)

32:11ב	ш**G**; ו[בגרוע נטויה] ובגרוע חזק[ה	IIIB3
	וביד חזקה 𝕸	(IVA1,B3b,
	Q ≠ ш**G** ≠ 𝕸	Q ≅ ш**G** ≅ 𝕸 C1b)

32:13א	ш𝕸] ככו[כבי[ה[שמים	IIA5
	τω πλαθει **G** +	(IVDa)
	Q = ш𝕸 ≠ **G**	**G** +

32:13ב	ונחלו 𝕸 [ш**G**] ונחל[וה	IIC1
	Q = ш**G** ≠ 𝕸	Q‍ш**G** + (IVA6a)

32:15	ш𝕸] + λιθιναι **G** ל(ו)חת	IIA5
	Q = ш𝕸 ≠ **G**	**G** + (IVDa)

32:27	עברו 𝕸 [ш**G**] ועב[רו	IIC1
	Q = ш**G** ≠ 𝕸	Q‍ш**G** + (IVA6a)

32:29	היום ш𝕸] ‭>‬ **G**	IID
	Q = ш𝕸 ≠ **G**	Qш𝕸 + (IVA5a)

32:30	ш𝕸] י[הוה τον θεον **G**	IIIA5
	Q = ш𝕸 ≠ **G**	Qш𝕸 ≅ **G** (IVA5b)

34:1   הלוח]ות [+ ני(ו)ם + הרא(י)ש(י)נים 𝔪𝔐𝔊   IIA1
           Qᵃ ≠ 𝔪𝔐   𝔪𝔐 +   (IVB4)

34:2   קר(ו)ב בב[𝔪𝔐] > 𝔊   IID
           Qᵃ = 𝔪𝔐 ≠ 𝔊   Qᵃ𝔪𝔐 +   (IVA5a)

34:11א   היום [𝔪𝔐] > 𝔊   IIA5
           Qᵃ = 𝔪𝔐 ≠ 𝔊   𝔊 -   (IVDa)

34:11ב   Qᵃ   [והגרגשי   IIA6
         והחתי והגרגשי והפרזי והחוי 𝔪   (IVC1a)
         והחתי _____ והפרזי והחוי 𝔐
         𝔊 και Χετταιον και Φερεζαιον
            και Ευαιον και Γεργεσαιον
           Qᵃ = 𝔪𝔊 ≠ 𝔐   𝔐 -

34:13   ואשריהם [ואשריו 𝔪; ואת אשריו 𝔐;   IIIE
         και τα αλση αυτων 𝔊   (IVE)
           Qᵃ ≠ 𝔪 ≠ 𝔐; 𝔊?   Qᵃ ≅ 𝔪 ≅ 𝔐

34:16א   לב[ניך [𝔪𝔐] + και των θυγατερων   IIA5
         σου δως τοις υιοις αυτων 𝔊   (IVDa)
           Qᵃ = 𝔪𝔐 ≠ 𝔊   𝔊 +

34:16ב   והזנו [pr אחרי אלהיהן בנתיו וזנו 𝔪𝔐;   IIIB4
         pr και εκπορνευσωσιν αι θυγατερες   (IVB4b)
         σου οπισω των θεων αυτων 𝔊
           Qᵃ ≠ 𝔪𝔐𝔊   Qᵃ ≅ 𝔪𝔐𝔊

36:21-24 hab 𝔪𝔐] > 36:10-34 𝔊   IIIA5
           Qᵃ = 𝔪𝔐 ≠ 𝔊   Qᵃ𝔪𝔐 ≅ 𝔊   (IVA5b)

36:23   נגב תימ]נה [𝔐 נגבה תימנה 𝔪;   IIIA3
         36:10-34 lacking 𝔊   (IVA3b,B1b)
          Qᵃ = 𝔐 ≠ 𝔪 ≠ 𝔊   Qᵃ𝔐 ≅ 𝔪

37:9-16   hab 𝔐] aliter **G** (cf. *BHS* note 36:8b)   IIIA5
  [38:8-12**G**]   **Qᵃ** = 𝔐 ≠ **G**   **Qᵃ**𝔐 ≅ **G**   (IVA5b)

37:13   על ארבע [לארבע 𝔐**G**ᴵᴵ; aliter **G**   VA5
  [38:10**G**]   **Qᵃ** ≠ 𝔐 ≠ **G**   **Qᵃ** X

APPENDIX 3

CHART SHOWING TEXTUAL AFFILIATION

	TEXT SEC RDGS	SYN VARS	PREF RDGS	UNIQUE RDGS	Q^aM	Q^am	Q^aG	Mm	MG	mGQ^aMm	Q^amG	Q^aMG	MmG
Q^a	43				10	18	0	1			7	7	0
		80			12	12	14	3			35	2	2
			42		5	2	5	0			18	4	8
TOTAL	43/165	80/165	42/165		27	32	19	4			60	13	10
M	50				13	18		3	0		7	7	2
		80			16	12		7	4		35	2	4
			35		0	2		5	0		18	4	6
TOTAL	50/165	80/165	35/165		29	32		15	4		60	13	12
m	19				7		0		3	0	7	0	2
		80			16		14		7	2	35	2	4
			66		10		5		5	14	18	8	6
TOTAL	19/165	80/165	66/165		33		19		15	16	60	10	12
G	28				18		1		0	0	7	0	2
		53			36		3		4	2	2	2	4
			40		8		0		0	14	4	8	6
TOTAL	28/121	53/121	40/121		62		4		4	16	13	10	12

CHART SHOWING NATURE OF TEXTS

TEXT SEC RDGS	SYN VARS	PREF RDGS	LONGER Maj	Mod	Min	SHORTER Maj	Mod	Min	QUALITATIVE Maj	Mod	Min	Err	TERTIARY
Q^a 43			13	10	9	0	0	0	0	0	8	3	(4)
	80		1	3	15	2	2	9	1	10	38	--	(2)
		42	0	0	5	0	16	9	0	6	8	--	(3)
TOTAL 43 / 165	80 / 165	42 / 165	14	13	29	2	18	18	1	16	54	3	(9)
Ш 50			13	15	13	0	0	0	0	2	8	0	(3)
	80		3	4	14	0	1	12	1	10	37	--	(2)
		35	0	0	5	0	13	3	0	4	11	--	(3)
TOTAL 50 / 165	80 / 165	35 / 165	16	19	32	0	14	15	1	16	56	0	(8)
m 19			1	8	3	0	0	3	0	0	1	3	
	80		3	5	14	0	0	12	1	10	38	--	
		66	0	0	2	11	20	13	0	6	15	--	
TOTAL 19 / 165	80 / 165	66 / 165	4	13	19	11	20	28	1	16	54	3	
G 28			0	13	9	0	0	2	0	4	1	0	
	53		2	2	6	1	3	3	1	26	9	--	
		40	0	0	3	13	12	4	0	2	6	--	
TOTAL 28 / 121	53 / 121	40 / 121	2	15	18	14	15	9	1	32	16	0	

Note: To catalogue each of the variants according to type sometimes gives a total greater than that in the left margin, because of the complexities involved in counting according to the nature of the variant. Thus, for example, 19:10 counts as only 1 variant in the total of secondary readings in **B**, but as 2 variants when the types of variants are counted, since it involves not only alteration but also expansion.

BIBLIOGRAPHY

TEXTS

Biblia Hebraica Stuttgartensia. Edited by K. Elliger and W. Rudolph. Stuttgart: Deutsche Bibelstiftung, 1967–77.

Der Hebräische Pentateuch der Samaritaner. Edited by August Freiherr von Gall. Giessen: Alfred Töpelmann, 1918.

The Old Testament in Greek According to the Text of Codex Vaticanus, Supplemented from Other Uncial Manuscripts, with a Critical Apparatus Containing the Variants of the Chief Ancient Authorities for the Text of the Septuagint. Vol. I: *The Octateuch.* Edited by Alan England Brooke and Norman McLean. Cambridge: Cambridge University Press, 1906.

Septuaginta, Id est Vetus Testamentum graece iuxta LXX interpretes. 2 vols. Edited by Alfred Rahlfs. 9th ed. Stuttgart: Württembergische Bibelanstalt, 1971.

Skehan, Patrick W. "Edition of 4QpaleoExod^m with Textual Notes and Variants." Completed in 1975. Unpublished.

Wevers, John Wm. *Exodus.* To be published in the series Septuaginta: Vetus Testamentum Graecum Auctoritate Academiae Scientiarum Gottingensis. Göttingen: Vandenhoeck & Ruprecht.

REFERENCE WORKS

Arndt, William F. and Gingrich, F. Wilbur. *A Greek-English Lexicon of the New Testament and Other Early Christian Literature: A Translation and Adaptation of Walter Bauer's Griechisch-Deutsches Wörterbuch zu den Schriften des Neuen Testaments und der übrigen urchristlichen Literatur, 4th rev. ed., 1952.* Chicago: University of Chicago Press, 1957.

Blass, F. and Debrunner, A. *A Greek Grammar of the New Testament and Other Early Christian Literature.* Translated and revised by Robert W. Funk. Chicago and London: University of Chicago Press, 1961.

Brown, Francis; Driver, S. R.; and Briggs, Charles A. *A Hebrew and English Lexicon of the Old Testament ... Based on the Lexicon of William Gesenius as Translated by Edward Robinson.* Boston and New York: Houghton Mifflin Company, 1907.

Davidson, A. B. *Hebrew Syntax.* 3d ed. Edinburgh: T. & T. Clark, 1901.

Gesenius' Hebrew Grammar, as edited and enlarged by E. Kautzsch. 2d English ed. rev. by A. E. Cowley. Oxford: Clarendon Press, 1910.

Hatch, Edwin, and Redpath, Henry A. *A Concordance to the Septuagint and the Other Greek Versions of the Old Testament.* 3 volumes. Oxford: Clarendon Press, 1897.

Liddell, Henry George, and Scott, Robert, eds. *A Greek-English Lexicon.* 9th ed. rev. and augm. throughout by Henry Stuart Jones. Oxford: Clarendon Press, 1940.

Mandelkern, Solomon. *Veteris Testamenti Concordantiae Hebraicae atque Chaldaicae.* Lepzig: Veit, 1906.

Williams, Ronald J. *Hebrew Syntax: An Outline.* 2d ed. Toronto: University of Toronto Press, 1976.

STUDIES

Ackroyd, Peter R. "Archaeology, Politics and Religion: The Persian Period." The Inaugural Lecture of the Walter G. Williams Lectureship in Old Testament. Denver: Iliff School of Theology, 1983.

_____. "The History of Israel in the Exilic and Post-Exilic Periods." *Tradition and Interpretation: Essays by Members of the Society for Old Testament Study.* Edited by G. W. Anderson. Oxford: Clarendon Press, 1979. pp. 320-325.

_____. *Israel under Babylon and Persia.* New Clarendon Bible. Vol. 4. Oxford: Oxford University Press, 1970.

Albrektson, B. "Reflections on the Emergence of a Standard Text of the Hebrew Bible." VTSup 29 (1978), 49-65.

Albright, W. F. "A Biblical Fragment from the Maccabaean Age: The Nash Papyrus." *JBL* 56 (1937), 145-76.

_____. "New Light on Early Recensions of the Hebrew Bible." *BASOR* 140 (1955), 27-33.

Allegro, J. M. "Further Messianic References in Qumran Literature." *JBL* 75 (1956), 174-87.

_____, ed. *Qumran Cave 4:1.* Discoveries in the Judaean Desert of Jordan, 5. Oxford: Clarendon Press, 1968.

Baillet, Maurice. "Le texte samaritain de l'Exode dans les manuscrits de Qumran." *Hommages à André Dupont-Sommer.* Edited by A. Caquot and M. Philonenko. Paris: Librairie d'Amerique et d'Orient Adrien-Maisonneuve, 1971. pp. 363-381.

Barthélemy, Dominique. *Les devanciers d'Aquila.* VTSup 10 (1963).

_____. "Text, Hebrew, History of." *IDBS* (1976), 878-884.

Ben-Hayyim, Z. Book Review of *The Samaritan Pentateuch and the Origin of the Samaritan Sect* by James D. Purvis (Cambridge, MA: Harvard University Press, 1968), *Biblica* 52 (1971), 253-255.

Benoit, P. "Le travail d'édition des fragments manuscrits de Qumran." *RB* 63 (1956), 49-67.

Bergmeier, R. "Zur Frühdatierung samaritanischer Theologumena." *JSJ* 5 (1974), 121-153.

Birnbaum, S. A. *Hebrew Scripts.* Leiden: E. J. Brill, 1971.

Blenkinsopp, Joseph. "Fragments of Ancient Exegesis in an Isaian Poem (Jes 2:6-22)." *ZAW* 93 (1981), 51-62.

_____. "Interpretation and the Tendency to Sectarianism: An Aspect of Second Temple History." *Jewish and Christian Self-Definition.* Vol. 2: *Aspects of Judaism in the Graeco-Roman Period.* Edited by E. P. Sanders with A. T. Baumgarten and Alan Mendelson. Philadelphia: Fortress Press, 1981. pp. 1-26, 299-309.

_____. "Tanakh and the New Testament: A Christian Perspective." *Biblical Studies: Meeting Ground of Jews and Christians.* Edited by Lawrence Boadt, Helga Croner, and Leon Klenicki. New York: Paulist Press, 1980. pp. 96-119.

Bloch, Renée. "Methodological Note for the Study of Rabbinic Literature." Translated by William Scott Green and William J. Sullivan. *Approaches to Ancient Judaism: Theory and Practice.* Edited by William Scott Green. Brown University Judaica Studies 1. Missoula, MT: Scholars Press, 1978. pp. 51-75.

_____ "Midrash." Translated by Mary Howard Callaway. *Approaches to Ancient Judaism: Theory and Practice.* Edited by William Scott Green. Brown University Judaica Studies 1. Missoula, MT: Scholars Press, 1978. pp. 29-50.

Bowman, John. "Contact between Samaritan Sects and Qumran?" *VT* 7 (1957), 184-189.

_____ *The Samaritan Problem: Studies in the Relationships of Samaritanism, Judaism, and Early Christianity.* Translated by Alfred M. Johnson Jr. Pittsburgh Theological Monograph Series, 4. Pittsburgh: Pickwick, 1975.

_____ "The Samaritans and the Book of Deuteronomy." *Transactions of the Glasgow University Oriental Society* 17 (1957-58), 9-18.

Campbell, Edward F. and Ross, James F. "The Excavation of Shechem and the Biblical Tradition." *BA* 26 (1963), 1-27.

Childs, Brevard S. *The Book of Exodus: A Critical, Theological Commentary.* The Old Testament Library. Philadelphia: Westminster Press, 1974.

Clarke, Ernest G. Book Review of *The Samaritan Pentateuch and the Origin of the Samaritan Sect* by James D. Purvis (Cambridge, MA: Harvard University Press, 1968), *JNES* 30 (1971), 144-146.

Coggins, R. J. Book Review of *The Samaritan Pentateuch and the Origin of the Samaritan Sect* by James D. Purvis (Cambridge, MA: Harvard University Press, 1968), *JSS* 14 (1969), 273-275.

_____ "The Samaritans and Acts." *NTS* 28 (1982), 423-434.

_____ *Samaritans and Jews: The Origins of Samaritanism Reconsidered.* Atlanta: John Knox, 1975.

Cross, Frank Moore, Jr. *The Ancient Library of Qumran and Modern Biblical Studies.* Rev. ed. Garden City, NY: Doubleday, 1961.

_____ "The Contribution of the Qumran Discoveries to the Study of the Biblical Text." *IEJ* 16 (1966), 81-95.

_____ "The Development of the Jewish Scripts." *The Bible and the Ancient Near East: Essays in Honor of William Foxwell Albright.* Edited by G. Ernest Wright. Garden City, NY: Doubleday, 1961. pp. 170-264.

_____ "The Evolution of a Theory of Local Texts." *Qumran and the History of the Biblical Text.* Edited by Frank Moore Cross and Shemaryahu Talmon. Cambridge, MA: Harvard University Press, 1975. pp. 306-20.

_____ "The History of the Biblical Text in the Light of Discoveries in the Judaean Desert." *HTR* 57 (1964), 281-299.

_____ "A New Qumran Biblical Fragment Related to the Original Hebrew Underlying the Septuagint." *BASOR* 132 (1953), 15-26.

_____ "The Papyri and their Historical Implications." *Discoveries in the Wadi ed-Daliyeh.* Edited by Paul W. Lapp and Nancy L. Lapp. *Annual of the American Schools of Oriental Research* 41 (1974), 17-29.

_____ "Problems of Method in the Textual Criticism of the Hebrew Bible." *The Critical Study of Sacred Texts.* Edited by Wendy Doniger O'Flaherty. Berkeley Religious Studies Series. Berkeley: Graduate Theological Union, 1979. pp. 31-54.

Dexinger, Ferdinand. "Das Garizimgebot im Dekalog der Samaritaner." *Studien zum Pentateuch: Walter Kornfeld zum 60. Geburtstag.* Edited by Georg Braulik. Vienna: Herder, 1977. pp. 111-33.

_____ "Limits of Tolerance in Judaism: The Samaritan Example." *Jewish and Christian Self-Definition.* Vol. II: *Aspects of Judaism in the Graeco-Roman Period.* Edited by E. P. Sanders with A. I. Baumgarten and Alan Mendelson. Philadelphia: Fortress Press, 1981. pp. 88-114, 327-38.

Driver, S. R. *The Book of Exodus.* Cambridge: University Press, 1953.

_____ *Notes on the Hebrew Text and the Topography of the Books of Samuel.* 2d rev. ed. Oxford: Clarendon Press, 1913.

Fee, Gordon D. "Modern Text Criticism and the Synoptic Problem." *J. J. Griesbach: Synoptic and Text-Critical Studies 1776-1976.* Edited by

Bernard Orchard and Thomas R. W. Longstaff. SNTSMS, 34. Cambridge: Cambridge University Press, 1978.

Ford, Josephine M. "Can We Exclude Samaritan Influence from Qumran?" *RQ* 6 (1967), 109-129.

Gaster, Moses. *The Samaritans: Their History, Doctrines and Literature.* The Schweich Lectures, 1923. London: British Academy, 1925.

Gaster, T. H. "Samaritans." *IDB,* IV (1962), 190-197.

Gooding, D. W. *The Account of the Tabernacle: Translation and Textual Problems of the Greek Exodus.* Texts and Studies, N.S. VI. Edited by C. H. Dodd. Cambridge: Cambridge University, 1959.

_____. "An Appeal for a Stricter Terminology in the Textual Criticism of the Old Testament." *JSS* 21 (1976), 15-25.

Goshen-Gottstein, M. H. "The Textual Criticism of the Old Testament: Rise, Decline, Rebirth." *JBL* 102 (1983), 365-399.

Greenberg, Moshe. "The Stabilization of the Text of the Hebrew Bible, Reviewed in the Light of the Biblical Materials from the Judean Desert." *JAOS* 76 (1956), 157-167.

Hanhart, Robert. "Zu den ältesten Traditionen über das Samaritanische Schisma." *Eretz-Israel: Archaeological, Historical and Geographical Studies.* Vol. 16. H. M. Orlinsky Volume. Jerusalem: Israel Exploration Society, 1982.

Hanson, Richard. "Paleo-Hebrew Scripts in the Hasmonean Age." *BASOR* 175 (1964), 26-42.

Jellicoe, Sidney. *The Septuagint and Modern Study.* Oxford: Clarendon Press, 1968.

_____. *Studies in the Septuagint: Origins, Recensions, and Interpretations.* New York: Ktav, 1974.

Klein, Ralph W. *Textual Criticism of the Old Testament: The Septuagint after Qumran.* Philadelphia: Fortress Press, 1974.

Macdonald, John. Book Review of *The Samaritan Pentateuch and the Origin of the Samaritan Sect* by James D. Purvis (Cambridge, MA: Harvard University Press, 1968), *JJS* 21 (1970), 69-72.

_____ *The Theology of the Samaritans.* London: SCM, 1964.

McLean, Mark David. *The Use and Development of Palaeo-Hebrew in the Hellenistic and Roman Periods.* Harvard University dissertation, 1982.

Montgomery, James A. *A Critical and Exegetical Commentary on the Book of Daniel.* The International Critical Commentary. Edinburgh: T. & T. Clark, 1927.

_____ *The Samaritans, The Earliest Jewish Sect: Their History, Theology and Literature.* Philadelphia: J. C. Winston, 1907.

Noth, Martin. *Exodus: A Commentary.* The Old Testament Library. Philadelphia: Westminster Press, 1962.

O'Connell, Kevin G. "Greek Versions (Minor)." *IDBS* 377-381.

_____ "The List of Seven Peoples in Canaan: A Fresh Analysis." *The Answers Lie Below. Essays in Honor of Lawrence Edmund Toombs.* Edited by Henry O. Thompson. Lanham, MD: University Press of America, 1984. pp. 221-241.

_____ *The Theodotionic Revision of the Book of Exodus.* HSM, 3. Cambridge, MA: Harvard University Press, 1972.

Pietersma, Albert. "Kyrios or Tetragram: A Renewed Quest for the Original Septuagint." *De Septuaginta: Studies in Honour of John William Wevers on His Sixty-fifth Birthday.* Edited by Albert Pietersma and Claude Cox. Mississauga, Ontario: Benben Publications, 1984. pp. 85-101.

Porton, Gary G. "Defining Midrash." *The Study of Ancient Judaism.* Vol. I: *Mishnah, Midrash, Siddur.* Edited by Jacob Neusner. New York: Ktav, 1981. pp. 55-92.

Pummer, Reinhard. "The Present State of Samaritan Studies." *JSS* 21 (1976), 39-61; and 22 (1977), 24-47.

_____ "The Samaritan Pentateuch and the New Testament." *NTS* 22 (1976), 441-443.

Purvis, James D. "The Fourth Gospel and the Samaritans." *NT* 17 (1975), 161-198.

_____ Book Review of *Samaritans and Jews: The Origins of Samaritanism Reconsidered* by R. J. Coggins (Atlanta: John Knox, 1975), *JTS* 27 (1976), 163-165.

_____ "Samaritan Pentateuch." *IDBS* (1976), 772-776.

_____ *The Samaritan Pentateuch and the Origin of the Samaritan Sect.* HSM, 2. Cambridge, MA: Harvard University Press, 1968.

_____ "The Samaritan Problem: A Case Study in Jewish Sectarianism in the Roman Era." *Traditions in Transformation: Turning Points in Biblical Faith.* Ed. Baruch Halpern and Jon D. Levenson. Winona Lake, IN: Eisenbrauns, 1981. pp. 323-350.

_____ "Samaritans." *IDBS* (1976), 776-777.

Roberts, Bleddyn J. *The Old Testament Text and Versions: The Hebrew Text in Transmission and the History of the Ancient Versions.* Cardiff: University of Wales, 1951.

_____ Book Review of *The Samaritan Pentateuch and the Origin of the Samaritan Sect* by James D. Purvis (Cambridge, MA: Harvard University Press, 1968), *JTS* 20 (1969), 569-571.

_____ "Samaritan Pentateuch." *IDB,* IV (1962), 190.

_____. "Text, OT." *IDB,* IV (1962), 580-594.

Rowley, H. H. "The Samaritan Schism in Legend and History." *Israel's Prophetic Heritage. Essays in Honor of James Muilenberg.* Edited by Bernhard W. Anderson and Walter Harrelson. New York: Harper, 1962. pp. 208-222.

_____ "Sanballat and the Samaritan Temple." *Bulletin of the John Rylands Library* 38 (1955-56), 166-198.

Royse, James R. "Scribal Habits in the Transmission of New Testament Texts." *The Critical Study of Sacred Texts.* Edited by Wendy Doniger O'Flaherty. Berkeley Religious Studies Series. Berkeley: Graduate Theological Union, 1979.

Sanders, James A. "Text and Canon: Concepts and Method." *JBL* 98 (1979), 5-29.

_____ "Text and Canon: Old Testament and New." *Mélanges Dominique Barthélemy. Études bibliques offertes à l'occasion de son 60e anniversaire.* Edited by P. Casetti, O. Keel, and A. Schenker. Fribourg: Éditions Universitaires, 1981.

Scrolls from the Wilderness of the Dead Sea: A Guide to the Exhibition, The Dead Sea Scrolls of Jordan, Arranged by the Smithsonian Institution in Cooperation with the Government of the Hashemite Kingdom of Jordan and the Palestine Archaeological Museum. London: Trustees of the British Museum, 1965.

Skehan, Patrick W. "The Biblical Scrolls from Qumran and the Text of the Old Testament." *BA* 28 (1965), 87-100.

_____ "The Divine Name at Qumran, in the Masada Scroll, and in the Septuagint." *BIOSCS* 13 (1980), 14-44.

_____ "Exodus in the Samaritan Recension from Qumran." *JBL* 74 (1955), 182-187.

_____ "The Period of the Biblical Texts from Khirbet Qumran." *CBQ* 19 (1957), 435-440.

_____ "Qumran and the Present State of Old Testament Text Studies: The Massoretic Text." *JBL* 78 (1959), 21-25.

_____ "The Qumran Manuscripts and Textual Criticism." *VTS* 4 (1957), 148-160.

_____ "The Scrolls and the Old Testament Text." *New Directions in Biblical Archaeology.* Edited by David Noel Freedman and Jonas C. Greenfield. Garden City, NY: Doubleday, 1971. pp. 99-112.

Smick, Elmer B. "A Lesson in Textual Criticism as Learned from a Comparison of Akkadian and Hebrew Textual Variants." *Bulletin of the Evangelical Theological Society* 23 (1967), 127-133.

Smith, Morton. *Palestinian Parties and Politics that Shaped the Old Testament.* New York: Columbia University, 1971.

_____ Book Review of *The Samaritan Pentateuch and the Origin of the Samaritan Sect* by James D. Purvis (Cambridge, MA: Harvard University Press, 1968), *Anglican Theological Review* 53 (1971), 127-129.

Strugnell, John. "Notes en marge du volume V des 'Discoveries in the Judaean Desert of Jordan.'" *RevQ* 7 (1970).

Talmon, Shemaryahu. "Aspects of the Textual Transmission of the Bible in the Light of Qumran Manuscripts." *Textus* 4 (1964), 95-132.

_____ "Conflate Readings (OT)." *IDBS* (1976), 170-173.

_____ "DSIa as a Witness to Ancient Exegesis of the Book of Isaiah." *Annual of the Swedish Theological Institute* 1 (1962), 62-72.

_____ "The Old Testament Text." *The Cambridge History of the Bible.* Vol. I. *From the Beginnnings to Jerome.* Edited by P. R. Ackroyd and C. F. Evans. Cambridge: Cambridge University Press, 1970. pp. 159-199.

_____ "The Samaritan Pentateuch." *JJS* 2 (1951), 146-150.

_____ "The Textual Study of the Bible--A New Outlook." *Qumran and the History of the Biblical Text.* Edited by Frank Moore Cross and Shemaryahu Talmon. Cambridge, MA: Harvard University Press, 1975. pp. 321-400.

_____ "The Three Scrolls of the Law That Were Found in the Temple Court." *Textus* 2 (1962), 14-27.

Thompson, J. A. "Textual Criticism, OT." *IDBS* (1976), 886-891.

Tigay, J. "An Empirical Basis for the Documentary Hypothesis." *JBL* 94 (1975), 329-342.

Tov, Emanuel. "Criteria for Evaluating Textual Readings: The Limitations of Textual Rules." *HTR* 75 (1982), 429-448.

_____ "Determining the Relationship between the Qumran Scrolls and the LXX: Some Methodological Issues." *The Hebrew and Greek Texts of Samuel.* Edited by Emanuel Tov. Jerusalem: Academon, 1980. pp. 45-67.

_____ "A Modern Textual Outlook Based on the Qumran Scrolls." *HUCA* 53 (1982), 11-27.

_____ Some Aspects of the Textual and Literary History of the Book of Jeremiah." *Le Livre de Jérémie: Le prophète et son milieu, les oracles et leur transmission.* Edited by P.-M. Bogaert. Leuven: University Press, 1981. pp. 145-167.

_____ *The Text-Critical Use of the Septuagint in Biblical Research.* Jerusalem Biblical Studies. Edited by Ora Lipschitz and Alexander Rofé. Jerusalem: Simor, 1981.

_____ "The Textual Affiliations of 4QSam^a." *JSOT* 14 (1979), 37-53.

_____, and Kraft, Robert A. "Septuagint." *IDBS* (1976), 807-815.

Ulrich, Eugene C. "Horizons of Old Testament Textual Research at the Thirtieth Anniversary of Qumran Cave 4." *CBQ* 46 (1984), 613-636.

_____ "4QSam^c: A Fragmentary Manuscript of 2 Samuel 14-15 from the Scribe of the *Serek Hay-yahad* (1QS)." *BASOR* 235 (1979), 1-25.

_____ *The Qumran Text of Samuel and Josephus.* HSM, 19. Missoula, MT: Scholars Press, 1978.

VanderKam, James C. Book Review of *The Qumran Text of Samuel and Josephus* by Eugene C. Ulrich (Missoula, MT: Scholars Press, 1978), *JBL* 98 (1979), 599-601.

Vermes, Geza. "Bible and Midrash: Early Old Testament Exegesis." *The Cambridge History of the Bible.* Vol. I. *From the Beginnings to Jerome.* Edited by P. R. Ackroyd and C. F. Evans. Cambridge: Cambridge University Press, 1970. pp. 199-231.

_____ "Dead Sea Scrolls." *IDBS* (1976), 210-219.

_____ *The Dead Sea Scrolls: Qumran in Perspective.* Rev. ed. Philadelphia: Fortress, 1981.

_____ "Manuscripts from the Judean Desert." *IDBS* (1976), 563-566.

_____ *Scripture and Tradition in Judaism: Haggadic Studies.* 2d, rev. ed. *Studia Post-Biblica.* Vol. IV. Leiden: E. J. Brill, 1973.

Waltke, Bruce K. "The Samaritan Pentateuch and the Text of the Old Testament." *New Perspectives on the Old Testament.* Edited by J. Barton Payne. Waco, TX: Word, 1970. pp. 212-239.

Wevers, J. W. "Septuagint." *IDB,* IV (1962), 273-278.

Widengren, Geo. "The Persian Period." *Israelite and Judaean History.* Edited by John H. Hayes and J. Maxwell Miller. Philadelphia: Westminster Press, 1977.

Wright, Addison J. *The Literary Genre Midrash.* Staten Island: Alba House, Society of St. Paul, 1967.

Wright, G. Ernest. *Shechem: The Biography of a Biblical City.* New York: McGraw-Hill Book Company, 1965.